FRENCH

CINEMA

FRENCH CINEMA

COLIN CRISP

A CRITICAL FILMOGRAPHY
VOLUME 1, 1929–1939

INDIANA UNIVERSITY PRESS
Bloomington and Indianapolis

This book is a publication of

INDIANA UNIVERSITY PRESS
Office of Scholarly Publishing
Herman B Wells Library 350
1320 East 10th Street
Bloomington, Indiana 47405 USA

iupress.indiana.edu

The paper used in this publication meets the minimum requirements of the American
National Standard for Information Sciences—Permanence of Paper for Printed Library
Materials, ANSI Z39.48-1992.

Manufactured in the United States of America

Library of Congress Cataloging-in-Publication Data

Crisp, C. G.
 French cinema : a critical filmography / Colin Crisp.
     volume cm
 Includes bibliographical references and index.
 Contents: Volume 1. 1929–1939.
 ISBN 978-0-253-01696-6 (vol 1 pbk. : alk. paper) — ISBN 978-0-253-01703-1 (vol 1 ebook)
 — ISBN 978-0-253-01695-9 (vol 2 pbk. : alk. paper) — ISBN 978-0-253-01702-4 (vol 2 ebook)
 — ISBN 978-0-253-01795-6 (vol 3 pbk. : alk. paper) — ISBN 978-0-253-01796-3 (vol 3 ebook)
 1. Motion pictures—France—Catalogs. I. Title.
 PN1993.5.F7C783 2015
 016.79143'750944—dc23
                              2015008318
1 2 3 4 5 20 19 18 17 16 15

Talkies and sonorised films are something entirely new. They're interesting inventions but I can't see them remaining fashionable very long.
—Louis Lumière

Sound cinema, as it is currently practised, neglects 15 years of progress towards cinematic independence. . . . It is re-living, with juvenile inanity, all those errors that the silent cinema overcame.
—Jean Epstein, *Cinéa-Ciné*, November 1930

Let's not pretend like certain moralists that the cinema depraves us. It doesn't deprave us any more than life itself, founded as it is on profit, greed, the oppression of the weak, selfishness and injustice.
—Georges Altman, *Ça, c'est du cinema*, 1931

It's almost true to say that a blind man faced with a genuine theatrical work or a deaf man faced with a genuine cinematic work, though they may both lose something of the work presented to them, should not lose the essence of it.
—René Clair, *Le Temps*, 18 July 1932

Let's identify some principles that will serve as the basis of our theory of sound film:

- ✧ The silent film was the art of "printing"—of recording and disseminating—pantomime.
- ✧ Just as printing had a great influence on literature, the silent film [through people like] Chaplin, Gance, Griffith and René Clair, served to re-invent pantomime.
- ✧ Sound film is the art of "printing"—of recording and disseminating—theatrical works.
- ✧ Sound film . . . must [therefore] re-invent the theatre.

—Marcel Pagnol, *Les Cahiers du film*, 15 December 1933

Here we have a machine capable of devouring the known universe,
and all we're allowed to feed it is scraps and leftovers.
—Jacques Feyder, 1946, somewhat condensed by Chavance

Carné? Just one of Prévert's quainter inventions.
—Henri Jeanson

Although the avant-garde in its most extreme and typical form has
disappeared, it doesn't follow that the spirit of research and adventure
is dead. If those who represent it no longer make "marginal" films
it's because for the most part the cinema industry has absorbed
them, but has not by any means completely tamed them.
—Jacques B. Brunius, *En marge du cinéma français*, 1954

It is impossible for a government that aspires to create a new social order
to allow a means of propaganda as powerful as the cinema to remain in
the hands of groups who may well have interests opposed to its own.
—Paul Faure, confidant of Léon Blum, April 1936

Charlotte Lysès (Guitry's wife, at the time): "I know of only two geniuses—
Sacha and Hitler."
St. Exupéry (Later when she has left): "The coming war will be far worse than
previous wars, because it will be a civil war that dare not speak its name."
—Carlo Rim, *Mémoires d'une vieille vague*, regarding April 1938

Those [Jews] that settled in Paris were essentially the worst sort
of scum, the lowest grade of con-men, money-grubbing parasites
cold-shouldered even by their fellow Jews of any standing.
—Lucien Rebatet, *Les Tribus du cinéma et du théâtre*, 1941

CONTENTS

ACKNOWLEDGMENTS

I would like to thank the Australian Research Council, for funding the purchase of the many videotapes of films without which this series of books could not have been written; Griffith University, for providing the time and the funding to visit the crucial archives in France; and Timothy Barnard, of Caboose Books, for providing the motivation to begin work on the series, and for suggesting the general format for the books and for the individual entries.

FRENCH CINEMA

The French Cinema in the 1930s

The decade covered by this filmography was, of course, one of the most turbulent in the history of Europe, and particularly in the history of France. The Great Depression, which affected most of the Western world from 1929, did not strike France until somewhat later—it reached its apogee in 1932—but persisted somewhat longer. Coinciding as it did with the needs of the film industry to invest millions of francs in the conversion to sound, it caused a radical transformation of the industry. Politically, the implosion of capitalism that the Depression seemed to signal forced many to look elsewhere for an acceptable economic system or alternative ideology. The rise of fascism in Italy, then in Germany and Spain, together with the increased adhesion of left-leaning citizens to socialist or communist parties in the wake of the Russian Revolution, intensified debates around the government of France. The left-wing Popular Front under Léon Blum came to power in the crisis year of 1936, but the progressive disaffection that accompanied its three years in power, even among those who initially supported it, together with the fact that Blum himself was of Jewish extraction, ensured that political controversy would persist right through to the declaration of war in 1939. Then after six months of "phony" war, the disastrous collapse of the French Army in 1940 and the ensuing occupation would make for further national self-questioning, and impose additional constraints on the film industry as on every other area of society.

Despite this extreme turbulence, during the ten years from 1929 to 1939, France managed to produce some 1,300 films. The films in this filmography have been selected from among those. Their selection was based on two or more of the following criteria:

> ✋ The film has survived in a viewable form (a large percentage have not, especially from the early 1930s—only two such, #5 and 29, are included despite that).

> ✋ The film is widely recognized as significant to the development of French cinema, because it was innovative, because of the personnel involved, or because of the popularity of the genre that it represents.

- ↩ The film can be seen as representative of certain typical themes, techniques, or procedures common to many other films of the period, or that distinguish it from other films of the period.
- ↩ The film has been the subject of debate and contention within the nation or the critical community.

Within these parameters, every effort has been made to include all the films of high quality that have survived. In particular, those directed by filmmakers acclaimed as "auteurs"—René Clair, Jacques Feyder, Jean Vigo, Jean Grémillon, Marcel Carné, and Jean Renoir—have been accorded due space. But an attempt has also been made to do justice to lesser-known directors such as Marc Allégret, Pierre Chenal, and Edmond T. Gréville, as well as to the prevailing genres of the age, and to promote a number of lesser-known films that deserve attention, including several of the most amusing comedies ever made in France: Sacha Guitry's marvelous *Le Roman d'un tricheur* (#53); Fernandel's neatest comedy, *Tricoche et Cacolet* (#80); two entertaining films with Michel Simon and Arletty, namely *Fric-Frac* and *Circonstances atténuantes* (#96); and little-known gems such as *Les 5 Gentlemen maudits* (#14), *Monsieur Coccinelle* (#83), and *Quelle drôle de gosse* (#40). There are others that could within the given criteria have been included, but I have resisted the temptation to continue further.

The basic aim of the filmography is twofold: first, to relate all of these films to their social, political, and institutional origins, taking into account the filmmaking personnel and techniques that they used in the production of the films, in such a way as to build up a coherent overview of the French cinema of the decade and of its place and function in French society; and second, to provide sufficient information for contemporary film enthusiasts to know which of the relevant films would be of interest and of use to them. To ensure a wide coverage of the period, a limit of one thousand words per film has been imposed. This has the disadvantage of preventing full justice being done to films that have been the subject of extensive critical debate, such as Vigo's *L'Atalante* and many Carné and Renoir films, where whole books have already been written on or around a given film.

It would be wrong to treat this decade as a coherent and unified whole. Despite its relative mildness in France, the Great Depression ("la Crise") had reduced economic productivity to 72 percent of its 1929 level by 1932 and had caused a series of bankruptcies (including that of Citroën and several banks), which reached a peak in 1934. These often involved scandal and corruption, as in the Stavisky, Hanau, and Ostrovsky affairs, the first of which, occurring in January 1934, brought down Camille Chautemps's government. The sense of crisis was exacerbated by groups of right-wing demonstrators who on 6 February 1934 massed outside the Chambre des Députés and demanded a strong government along the lines of that of Mussolini and of the recently elected Hitler. In reaction, left-wing groups (socialists, communists, radicals) began to seek an alliance where they had until recently competed, forming a united front (the "Popular Front"), and on 14 July 1935, half a million demonstrators marched through Paris demanding that democracy and the republic be protected. Elections were due on 26 April and 3 May 1936; from January, the Communist and Socialist Party leaders Maurice Thorez and Léon Blum campaigned in a concerted and effective fashion, winning 378 of the 578 seats. In the month before they could take power, however, there were widespread strikes from impatient workers (2.4 million on strike), many of whom occupied their workplaces and staged meetings—but also dances, communal songfests, and theatrical performances—in a spirit of exhilaration and expectation. On taking power, the new government introduced what became known as the Matignon Accords between employers and employees ensuring for everyone, and for the first time, paid holidays (fifteen days per year), a forty-hour work week ("the Tyranny of Idiocy," according to the film industry), and worker representation on collective agreements for each category of work.

These economic and sociopolitical events inevitably had a significant effect on the cinema of the decade, given the ideological character of film and the costly nature of cinematic production. Alongside the other industrial collapses, the four largest French production firms of the period 1930–1933—Gaumont, Pathé-Natan, Haïk, and Osso—collapsed, and statistics confirm a serious downturn in production in 1934 (see table 1). In all, this period of sociopolitical crisis lasted for two and a half years, from January 1934 to June 1936, so rather than as a coherent decade, we should see the 1930s as divided into three periods—1930–1933, 1934–1936, and 1937–1939. In the last of these periods, of course, frustrations encountered by the Popular Front led to the limitation then reversal of some social gains, while the possibility of war was never far from anyone's mind. The Munich agreements, which seemed for a moment to avert that possibility, were signed on 29 September 1938, but war broke out just under a year later, on 3 September 1939.

The first of the three periods was itself far from problem-free for the French cinema. Sound films had been made in the United States since 1926. When it became possible to make them in France in late 1928, the French cinema was not in a healthy position. Having invented the medium in 1895 and exploited it with unparalleled efficiency for twenty years, the French had seen their market dominance eroded by the disruptions of World War I, much of which was fought on French soil. Since that time, it had been the American cinema that had dominated the global market, while the French cinema had been reduced to little

TABLE 1. KEY STATISTICS FOR THE 1930S

	1929	1930	1931	1932	1933	1934	1935	1936	1937	1938	1939
Approximate number of sound films usually categorized as French[a]	8 (52)	108	146	155	151	117	129	144	125	120	100
U.S. films on the French market	211	237	220	208	230	220	248	231	230	239	
Total films on the French market	437	478	453	496	577	436	466	448	424	426	
Percentage of French sound films on the French market	2	23	32	31	26	27	28	32	30	28	
Spectator numbers, in millions, for all of France	150	200	234	233	219	208	231	225	225	220	180
Approximate receipts, for all of France, in millions of francs[b]	280	320	370	420	430	440	480	520	470	470	330
Actual receipts, in millions of francs[c]	598	801	938	933	879	832	750				

Notes:

[a] Numbers vary with definition and dating; also, many are French versions of English or German films. Total production for 1929 in parentheses includes silent films.

[b] Corrected to 1938 francs (for interest, the 1925 figure would be about 190 million and the 1940 figure about the same).

[c] According to *Ciné France*, 11 June 1937.

more than a rump, providing only 10 percent of the films for its own market while America provided over 80 percent. The field of technical and aesthetic experimentation, the stylistic exploration of the expressive power of the image track, was the single aspect of film production of which the French could still feel proud in the period 1915 to 1929. The works that Abel Gance, Germaine Dulac, Louis Delluc, Marcel L'Herbier, Jean Epstein, René Clair, and others directed during these years can still be viewed with interest and admiration; but this was no longer a mass cinema, and the number of feature films produced each year was usually fewer than seventy.

Sound changed all that by erecting semi-rigid barriers between the cinemas of different linguistic communities. The American cinema no longer had automatic access to countries such as France, and dubbed films proved less popular than native language productions. Consequently, the number of French films produced each year abruptly doubled to 150, their share of the national market tripled to 30 percent, and their percentage of box office takings soared to approach 50 percent—equal to that of the American cinema. From taking in 30 percent of receipts from all forms of entertainment in the 1920s, the French cinema leapt to 65 percent in the 1930s. In Paris in particular, which was always to contribute about a third of total French receipts (despite being only from 6–7% of the population), film receipts rose 280 percent between 1925 and 1935. Investors were intoxicated by the possibility of quick profits, and masses of small production companies were set up, often making no more than one or two films, as cheaply as possible. The demand for skilled personnel was intense in all fields, most notably those central to sound cinema—script-writing and dialogue, sound recording, and directing. This demand could not always be met, so it is not surprising that many of the resultant films are clumsy, and that the sound is often of inadequate quality. What is astonishing is that so many of them are, on the contrary, unforgettably brilliant.

A large number of films were in production at the time of the introduction of sound. Foreseeing the commercial value of the new process, many producers opted to upgrade their silent films by the addition of greater or lesser degrees of sonorization. Many of the films of this period, therefore, while not silent, are not 100 percent sound films either. Early sound patents were held by American and German companies. Permission to use these patented processes largely offset the profits they attracted, reputedly resulting in a drain toward the patent-holders of 40–50 percent of the box office receipts. Moreover, in a bid to overcome the newly erected language barrier, these foreign firms set up companies to produce their films in France. For this they needed studios, because the introduction of sound had made control of the production environment even more essential than in the 1920s. Most studios were in or near Paris. The Pathé studios at Joinville-le-

Pont, southeast of Paris, built in 1923 by the immigrant Polish entrepreneur Lewinsky and leased to Pathé, were bought by Natan in 1927 and equipped with RCA sound. Hundreds of films were made there during the 1930s by directors such as Julien Duvivier, Marcel Carné, Jacques Feyder, Marcel Pagnol, and Maurice Tourneur—some estimate 50 percent of all of French production between 1925 and 1950. Indeed, until 1934 it seemed possible that Pathé-Natan would develop into a vertically integrated company on the Hollywood model, since it owned three studio complexes and 15 percent of all French cinemas, and had an impressive array of actors on contract—Jean Gabin, Charles Vanel, Gaby Morlay, Victor Francen, Renée Saint-Cyr, and Gabriel Gabrio. Still hailed in December 1934 as the hero of French cinema, worthy of the Légion d'Honneur, Natan was however brought low by a trial for embezzlement at which rumors surfaced that he had been subject to bribery over pornographic activities. He was imprisoned in 1938, and when the Germans arrived, he was deported because of his Jewish ancestry, dying in Auschwitz.

In April 1930, Paramount leased a Gaumont site at St. Maurice near the Pathé-Natan studio at Joinville. There they built a modern studio consisting of five or six stages, thirty production offices, forty-one actors' lodges, and ten editing suites, with associated workshops and laboratories, where they proposed to centralize all of their European production. Equipped with RCA Photophone sound, St. Maurice was within two years producing 20 percent of all French films, sometimes using the general shots of an American original and interspersing these with close-ups retaken with a French cast. This technique allowed for cut-price production of films in any language desired, so Paramount was soon producing up to 150 "versions" of its films each year in France, in as many as fourteen different languages, for distribution throughout Europe. In 1934, however, Paramount decided that dubbing provided a more economical alternative. Until that point, St. Maurice was notorious as "Babel-sur-Seine," where teams of actors succeeded one another on the same set to shoot the same scene, each team in its own language, thus "nationalizing" them. "The bosses are American, the administration Hungarian, the writers French, the directors Russian, the technicians German, the assistants Italian, the labourers from the Balkans. They film while eating, while sleeping, while swimming, while arguing. The great river of dollars flows endlessly. . . . It's Babel."[1] Christian-Jaque directed twelve films there in two years. The Hungarian director Alexander Korda was hired to film Pagnol's *Marius* there, with the French actors from the theatrical production playing their accustomed roles, but also in German and Swedish versions.

Other American majors did the same, but based in Hollywood rather than in France. Britain was soon producing French and German versions of many of its films in England; the German firm UFA produced some 11 percent of the 1,300 "French" films of the 1930s, both at its Neubabelsburg studio in Berlin and at its Épinay studio just north of Paris, which it had bought in 1929 and equipped with Tobis Klangfilm sound in order to produce French films locally. UFA focused on quality rather than quantity (it was there that Clair made his first four sound films), which was, if anything, more disconcerting to the French than Paramount's mass-market potboilers, since it challenged them in what they had hitherto held dearest. In Berlin, where the Neubabelsburg facilities were the envy of all visiting filmmakers, Raoul Ploquin was in charge of French production and had under contract Arletty, Annabella, Florelle, Jules Berry, Charles Boyer, Marie Bell, Pierre Brasseur, Fernandel, Fernand Gravey, Jean Murat, Albert Préjean, and Pierre-Richard Willm.

Within a few years of the introduction of sound, over a third of the films officially labeled "French" had actually been produced in the United States, Britain, or Germany, or in France from modified American or German films. Despite serious apprehensions about this foreign "takeover," the French cinema flourished during that decade. When the worst of the Depression finally hit France in 1932, the French cinema resisted its effects markedly better than most other areas of the economy, and remained a relatively promising target for investors throughout the decade.[2] Consequently, the number of studios expanded: Pathé-Natan owned the other studios at Épernay, alongside those of Tobis, together with the Francœur studio inside Paris, built by Natan in 1927 and sonorized with Tobis sound in 1929. The largest studio in Paris was the Gaumont "cité LG" at Buttes-Chaumont, with nine stages. In the environs, there were studios at Courbevoie (two stages) and Billancourt, the latter of which burned down in 1933 but was rebuilt with three, then six stages. Outside of the Paris region, the most significant production facilities were on the Riviera, at Nice (La Victorine, between five and seven stages; Nicaea, two, then three), and in Marseilles, where Pagnol, flush with funds, had in 1934 cobbled together three stages and supplemented them with a property at La Treille near Aubagne for exteriors, complete with fake Provençal village. In total, there were some fifty stages available at the beginning of the decade and sixty at the end, so the production of some 150 films a year suggests a low rate of production (about 2.5–3 films per stage per year), mainly because the Riviera studios were little used.

French production differed from that of other countries in these early sound years, even before the collapse of the majors, in that it consisted of several hundred small production firms, almost all of which produced no more than one or two films per year, or even in total. Moreover, very few of them owned production facilities, which had to be hired, preferably for as short a time as possible. Again, few producers had any guarantee of access either to distribution or exhibition, which remained in separate hands throughout the rest of the decade. After 1932, therefore, there was nothing remotely resembling the array of American majors, with their vertical integration of production, distribution, and exhibition, or the single dominant firms—Rank and UFA, respectively—in Britain and Germany. Both Pathé and Gaumont could have assumed such a role within French cinema, early on absorbing a number of smaller companies that could no longer compete, but before they could begin to monopolize the market, the succession of scandals relating to financial mismanagement and banking collapses brought them both down.

This "incoherence" of the French industry was exacerbated when more effective forms of dubbing influenced the foreign majors to renounce their multiple language productions and reduce the number of films made in France. Consequently, the 150 films produced in any given year were funded by as many as sixty separate small companies, which then depended on independent distribution and exhibition firms to market and screen them. These small production companies were in a constant state of crisis. One source of their problems was the diminishing returns for their product, as exhibitors sought to gain an advantage over rivals by offering a double program, or even live acts and food with their films. In extreme cases, six or ten films were offered for a single entry price. The resulting returns per film were correspondingly lower. Moreover, competition resulted in a price squeeze that made cinema a cheap form of popular entertainment: the average entry price was 6 francs, as against 25 francs for a boxing match and 35–45 francs to go to the theater or music hall. In these circumstances, despite the fact that the French cinema was probably globally profitable, the French language market was too small to guarantee adequate returns to the majority of producers, and the language barrier that had permitted the national cinema's renaissance was threatening to stifle it. One solution to the limited national market would have been the development of an export market, yet the industry proved unable or unwilling to develop and exploit foreign markets. More systematic attempts to do so in the late 1930s, based on success in high-profile events such as the Venice Biennale, came to an end with the outbreak of World War II.

As a result of these financial limitations, studio owners were reluctant or unable to invest in upgrading their facilities, and the deteriorating standard of these locations was a constant source of complaint. Furthermore, every film was a crucial financial investment for these small producers, and any miscalculation meant that the firm could go bankrupt. Since up to a third of each year's films failed to cover costs, the 1930s saw hundreds of fly-by-night firms appear then crash, only to reappear under another name to make another (equally risky) film. The government was well aware of this chaotic situation and commissioned two reports in the course of the decade (by Maurice Petsche in 1934 and Guy de Carmoy in 1936) with a view to resolving it. These produced admirable recommendations, which, if followed, might well have consolidated the French cinema, but the government was never in a position to implement them. Consequently, the film industry settled into the form that it retained throughout the decade and indeed in many respects beyond: a patchwork of production, distribution, and exhibition firms, lacking any coherent legislative framework within which to operate, lacking any large-scale organizations capable of dominating and driving the industry, lacking any continuity of personnel, and lacking any assured funding for production, let alone for the modernization of facilities.

French film personnel viewed 1930 as a feverish year of high hopes in their industry, while the following three years saw an enormous number of mostly incompetent productions—often remakes of theatrical works—that caused anguish among reviewers and decreasing returns to the producers. Only in the 1934–1935 season did the industry's confidence begin to return, as a series of well-made films received both critical acclaim and encouraging box-office returns. Headlines from that season announced "Quantity diminishes, but quality seems to be improving" and "Astounding Recovery of the French Cinema."[3] As Raymond Borde said in his typically aggressive way, after the tyranny of all those bad plays,

> The fog lifts towards 1934: With *Le Grand Jeu, L'Atalante, Toni, La Bandera* and *La Kermesse héroïque*, French production has hit its straps, and it proceeds right through till the war to experience an astounding period. These are the years of total success, of creation in every sense of the word, and it is obvious that any national film industry capable of producing one after the other *La Belle Équipe, Le Crime de Monsieur Lange, L'Homme de nulle part, Pépé le Moko, Quai des brumes, Mollenard, La Bête humaine, Regain, Le Jour se lève, Derrière la façade* and *La Règle du jeu* is an art that has overcome its contradictions. . . . Against the films of the right (*Trois de Saint-Cyr, L'Appel du silence, Un de la légion*) there will now be films from the left: the Groupe Octobre, Prévert, Carné, Renoir fairly often, and sometimes Duvivier. Our screens will now reflect what they had hitherto the task of concealing—the division of France into two factions.[4]

The number of films included in this filmography from the final three years of the decade is sufficient indication of the degree of exhilaration and even euphoria that prevailed during that final prewar period, as festival successes and prizes recognized the French industry's production as second only to that of America, and as international releases began at last to supplement local box-office returns.

It may be difficult to understand how, within the fragmented and chaotic system that still prevailed, so many high-quality films could have been produced, but there is no doubt that many filmmakers preferred, and even flourished in, this anarchic environment. In subsequent decades, when governmental regulation, financial stability, technical professionalism, and union regulation came to be accepted as normal and even inevitable, many looked back nostalgically to the 1930s as a heroic age—a moment when everything depended on personal contacts, and when what counted was improvisation, imagination, and the ability to get the best out of inadequate funds and technology.

The procedures that the filmmakers adopted in these trying circumstances allow the resultant sound films to be grouped under three general headings:

- One option was to record preexisting theatrical successes. A large number of boulevard comedies were transcribed more or less directly to film, as were vaudevilles, farces, musical comedies, and operettas, as well as more serious dramas. This strategy was favored because of its cheapness, since it required little extra work or expense; it was strongly defended, at least initially, by playwrights such as Marcel Pagnol and Sacha Guitry. One effect was to import theatrical structures and acting styles into the cinema, where they proved less appropriate.

- A second option was "realism" of the sort generally seen as originating in the nineteenth-century novel, which involved the use of sound simply as a support to the image and to reinforce its credibility. An extreme form of this strategy was used in particular for the representation of working-class environments and the underworld, resulting at times in a raw documentary or social realist style, often termed "naturalism."

- The third option, which was favored by avant-garde directors who had worked in the 1920s cinema, was a more ambitious form of sound-image relationship, often described by the musical term "counterpoint," and requiring strenuous interpretative strategies on the part of the spectators.

The films best remembered from 1930–1933 are those made by this latter category of avant-garde directors—Luis Buñuel, Jean Cocteau, Carl Dreyer,

Georg-Wilhelm Pabst, and René Clair. Relatively few of the films from that category attracted large audiences. Moreover, most of these directors found it impossible to continue the avant-garde techniques of the 1920s beyond 1933 because of the markedly higher cost of production of sound films. Rich patrons were few and far between, and faced with the Depression, commercial producers were less and less willing to risk funds on films that had no chance of reaching mass audiences. Furthermore, initially the cumbrous nature of sound technology increased the difficulty in realizing fluid or adventurous sequences. Both Abel Gance and Marcel L'Herbier suffered from this set of problems, the latter (and even the former on occasion) resigning himself to commercial projects in order to fund the occasional more ambitious film. Already by 1931, therefore, it had become apparent that French cinema was to be dominated by theatrical translations and by more or less realistic fiction films with a coherent narrative and with conventional social and psychological characterization based on that developed in the novel during the eighteenth and nineteenth centuries. Also, despite desperate attempts by the industry's spokespeople to distinguish French from American cinema, which was seen as disastrously dependent on generic patterns bearing little relationship to "real life," it is not too hard to see a number of genres emerging in France in the course of the decade. In some cases, this was because the genres already existed in the literary and theatrical worlds on which the cinema was so heavily dependent for its scripts; in others because (as in America itself) one year's successes tended to be replicated in slightly variant forms in the following year. After 1933, however, since neither cast nor crew were on the long-term contracts available to American producers, a French producer could not call on the same writers, actors, or technicians from one year to another as they could in America. Consequently, this generic replication was less "efficient" and less formulaic in France than it was in Hollywood films.

The film entries for the 1930s are organized chronologically according to the date on which they were first commercially released, except where they were not released (or not released commercially) until much later (e.g., *La Vie est à nous*, #49, and *Une partie de campagne*, # 55) or where films substantially completed in 1939 were delayed by the outbreak of war. These latter are included at the end in order of release. About 70 percent of the production of the early sound years has been lost, or is not readily viewable, including the great majority of sound feature films from 1929 and 1930, but the annual count of films lost or unavailable reduces to about 10 percent by the end of the decade. In all, about 500 of the 1,300 films are readily available for study, and a somewhat smaller number for public screening. All the films mentioned have been viewed except for the two noted as probably not surviving—#5 and 29. Most of the others can be obtained (without subtitles) from René Chateau. The rest are viewable at the BiFi in Paris or the Cinémathèque de Toulouse. In each entry, where no English title is in common use, the French title has been literally translated and shown in parentheses on the line beneath the French title. Cross-references between entries are signalled by #, so #19 means "see entry number 19."

In conclusion, the decade of the 1930s was an exhilarating one for the French cinema. As a result of the introduction of sound, French films rediscovered their national audience. Because of France's status as a refuge for those displaced by the Russian Revolution and the rise of fascism, the cinema was able to profit from the expertise of numerous foreign technicians. Finally, toward the end of the decade, the French cinema's successes in international competitions and festivals brought to the attention of the world one of the great stylistic and thematic movements of all time, Poetic Realism. The theory behind that movement was best expressed by the set designers who developed it—Lazare Meerson and his three great disciples, Alexandre Trauner, Léon Barsacq, and Georges Wahkévitch, all of whom worked with him as assistants at one time or another, and assimilated his notion of stylization through simplification. As Barsacq put it,

> You should choose *the most typical elements* [of the proposed locale]. *A transposition is necessary* to obtain on the screen the equivalent of reality . . . ; and that transposition is only possible if one designs *a decor which recreates what is most essential in a particular locale.* . . . To obtain the "equivalent" reality it is necessary to bring out the rich or the sordid, the cluttered or the bare, the light or the heavy aspect of a setting, *by exaggerating the dominant character of the elements that go to make it up while suppressing the useless details.*[5]

The heightened reality that resulted would be more real than the real, more credible than the documentary. In asserting this, he was drawing on the work and pronouncements of Alexandre Trauner, who designed most of the sets for Marcel Carné and who said, "The important thing is *to isolate in whatever locale one is representing the principal characteristic details,* and to bring them out at the expense of those which don't contribute to the atmosphere. . . . Sometimes it is the shape of a window, of a door, of a roof which the spectators will register immediately as a Parisian house, or a Northern house, or a Provençal house; or it may be the paving of a street, the trolley of a tramway. *We seek to awaken memories inscribed in the spectator's subconscious.*"[6]

Notes

1. Nino Frank, "Babel-sur-Seine," in Frank, *Petit Cinéma sentimental*, 65–73.

2. For more details on industrial matters, see Crisp, *Classic French Cinema*, chs. 1 and 2.

3. See, for instance, *La Cinématographie française*, 3 November 1934.

4. Raymond Borde, "Introduction," in Courtade, *Les Malédictions du cinéma français*, 10.

5. Barsacq, *Le Décor de film*, 102–103, emphasis added.

6. Quoted in Leprohon, *Les 1001 métiers du cinéma*, 138, emphasis added. See also Crisp, *Classic French Cinema*, 367–376.

PART I

The Introduction of Sound

1. *Prix de beauté*

Miss Europe
France-Germany-Italy, 1930, 92 min, b&w

Dir Augusto Genina; *Asst dir* Edmond Gréville, André d'Ollivier, and Fernand Lefebvre; *Prod* SOFAR (Société des Films Artistiques); *Scr* Augusto Genina, René Clair, Bernard Zimmer, and Alessandro de Stefani, from an idea of Georg-Wilhelm Pabst; *Cinematog* Rudolph Maté; *Music* Wolfgang Zeller, René Sylviano, and H. Shephard; *Art dir* Robert Gys; *Edit* Edmond Gréville; *Act* Louise Brooks (Lucienne Garnier), Jean Bradin (Prince Grabovsky), Georges Charlia (André), H. Bandini (Antonin), André Nicolle (secretary), Yves Glad (Maharaja), Gaston Jacquet (Duc de la Tour Chalgrin), Alex Bernard (photographer), and Marc Ziboulsky (manager).

The bewildering list of credits for direction and script above give some idea of the complicated origins of this film, but the reality is even more astonishing. The film was begun in 1929 as a silent film. Most sources say the scenario was primarily René Clair's, from an idea by Georg-Wilhelm Pabst, and that Clair intended to direct it himself, but the final scenario departed significantly from the original proposal and was rejected by the producer. Meanwhile, Clair had seen the first talkies and had revised the script to include sound. It was still rejected, however, perhaps for financial reasons, and was finally allocated to the experienced Italian director Augusto Genina. SOFAR was an Italian-German-French production company, so it decided for tactical reasons to shoot the film silent, then post-synch it in four languages, dubbing with different actors. Louise Brooks's voice, for example, was dubbed in the French version by Hélène Regelly. It is astounding that such a multi-sourced film should be so coherent and so powerful, and no less astounding in that sound seems integral to the design of the film as it now stands. The climactic final scene, which had been central to Clair's scenario, must nevertheless have been conceived in its present form *after* the decision to sonorize.

The story is simple: Lucienne becomes a star, and it proves fatal to her. At first she and André are a humble working-class couple; she works as a typist in a pressroom but dreams of a more glamorous life. Thanks to a beauty contest, she is able to achieve it; we follow her from office girl to Miss France and finally to her crowning in Spain as Miss Europe. She is courted by a prince, a duke, and a maharajah, and invited to do a screen test. The high life turns her head, and André issues an ultimatum: return to Paris and marry him, or it is all over. She is torn but accepts, and we see her trying to reconcile herself to a meager living in a sordid apartment with André. Finally, unable to endure it, she slips away to do the screen test. While she is watching the rushes with the producer, André sneaks into the projection room and shoots her dead.

The film is, then, clearly reflexive: its focus is on the making of a film, and more generally on the corrupting effect of the media. It constitutes a critique of the myth of the star, which was clearly, along with the beauty contest, the "idea" suggested to Clair by Pabst. This makes the presence of Louise Brooks in the central role particularly appropriate, since her abrupt rise to fame in the preceding three years had made of her just such a star, notably in two Pabst films (*Pandora's Box* and *The Diary of a Lost Girl*). *Prix de beauté* picks up on several of her previous roles as a basically good-hearted girl whose intense sexuality almost accidentally entrains fatal consequences. From our first meeting with the couple, André is intensely jealous of the admiring glances she attracts, and she attempts to defuse the situation by putting on a record of the song "Ne sois pas jaloux" ("Don't be jealous this evening, I only have one love, and it's you. . . . You must forgive me," etc.). It becomes their theme song, and what outrages André in the final scene is that, in the rushes of the film, she is singing "their" song. As she collapses dead, her giant recorded image continues above the scene of the murder, singing gaily on. Here already in the form "reality versus representation" we find the contrast of recorded versus real, and public gaiety versus private grief, which were to become regular motifs of 1930s films. The final images are of the flickering light of the screen illuminating fitfully their two faces—André somber, her dead.

Although this critique of the star is central to the film, what is no less fascinating is the exploration of sonorization techniques used in what had begun as a silent film. The sound-track is omnipresent, but only rarely are there moments of diegetic conversation or diegetically sourced sound and music (that is, sound for which the source is either visible on the screen or implied by the actions on the screen). The early beach and street scenes are accompanied by a babble of bathers and of traffic, out of which occasional identifiable voices arise. The pressroom scene that follows celebrates the futurist dynamism of the machines with bustling music, a player piano, the typewriters joining in a quasi-symphonic sound-mix, and a loud-speaker announcing the beauty competition.

All of this is accompanied by a montage of images, including documentary-style "hidden camera" images of the street scene. Lucienne's fashion magazines inspire her with apparently unrealizable yearnings, and these dreams are forcefully contrasted with her actual existence, both when we see André returning from work with grubby hands and broken fingernails, and again when she and friends visit a fairground. There, grotesque images of "the people" aggress her until she wonders what she is doing amid this crush of unlovely individuals.

Throughout her ascent to Miss Europe, this montage of sounds and images accompanies and comments on her aspirations and fears, but also (once she has decided to marry André) on his jealousy and frustrations. In the bleaker central section, in their unhappy flat, her moment of fame cannot be forgotten: her image intrudes in newspapers used as wrapping, and fans inundate her with mail and photos to sign. André rips them all up and wanders disconsolate through the streets, finally spying on her encounter with the prince/producer of her film. Technically, then, this is an enormously ambitious film, including location shooting, a series of rapid camera movements, and several long tracking shots, all of which were shot with a silent camera and the likes of which were to become well-nigh impossible for the next few years, as the heavily blimped camera (that is, enclosed in soundproof casing) lumbered around the confined spaces of the studio.

Genina was to direct another five films in France in the next few years, one of which, interestingly, was called *Ne sois pas jalouse,* while another, *Paris béguin* (Paris Infatuation), with Jean Gabin, likewise dealt with the preparation of a performance and ended with his murder beneath a giant poster of the star who loves him, and who has to perform smiling through her tears. Pabst was also to make five more films in French versions, two of which are included here (#7 and 16), while even as this film came out, René Clair was putting the finishing touches to his first sound film, *Sous les toits de Paris,* which we examine next.

2. *Sous les toits de Paris*

Under the Rooftops of Paris
France-Germany, 1930, 96 min (but most current
copies are approximately 80 min), b&w

Dir and Scr René Clair; *Asst dir* Georges Lacombe, Marcel Carné, and Jacques Houssin; *Prod* Tobis; *Cinematog* Georges Périnal; *Music* René Clair, in conjunction with the conductor Armand Bernard; *Songs* Raoul Moretti, René Nazelles, and André Gailhard; *Art dir* Lazare Meerson; *Sound* Hermann Storr and W. Morhenn; *Edit* René Le Hénaff; *Act* Pola Illéry (Pola), Albert Préjean (Albert), Gaston Modot (Fred), Edmond Gréville (Louis), Bill Bocket (Émile the thief), Aimos (a crook), Paul Olivier (drunken café client), and Jane Pierson.

René Clair has become by far the best-known of early sound directors, which is a little surprising given that more than any other, he spoke out against the introduction of sound. He had been a journalist, writer, and film actor before making his name as a director, notably with two art films (*Paris qui dort*, 1923, and *Entr'acte*, 1924) and two adaptations of popular comedies by Eugène Labiche (*Un chapeau de paille d'Italie*, 1927, and *Les Deux timides*, 1928). Clair was responsible for both the script and direction of his first five sound films, all made in France, of which this was the first. Both here and later in *Le Million* (1931, #9) and *Quatorze juillet* (1933, #22), he appealed to a particular mythic view of Paris and of "the little people" who are seen as essential to its vitality—not professionals or the rich, who are consistently mocked and ridiculed, but working-class people whose hardships are never dwelt on and whose *joie de vivre* is irrepressible. Clair's art director, Lazare Meerson, produced an unforgettable representation of the poorer quarters of Paris, featuring narrow streets and tall apartment buildings with steep stairwells and austere but well-lit rooms, aesthetically worn and stained, looking out over endless tiled rooftops. The male characters tend toward the artistic (street singers, accordionists, sculptors) or the mechanical (taxi drivers), while the females are usually associated with flowers or with laundering—purity or nature. *Sous les toits de Paris* and its "sequels" follow the entanglements of such characters from bedrooms to bars to dance halls. There is always one exotic, capricious girl (often Eastern European) who plays male friends off against each other, and this behavior invariably leads the narrative toward the margins of the law, where amiable crooks and colorful fences, casually accepted as mates, confuse the borderline between the poor and the underworld. No stigma attaches to criminality, only to wealth, and no stigma attaches to sexuality or inconstancy: the characters' entanglements are presented as moves in an elaborate game, with momentary winners and losers, where moralizing is irrelevant.

In *Sous les toits de Paris*, Albert is a street-singer who sees Pepe the pickpocket at work on the rich among his circle of listeners and gets paid off for holding his tongue.[1] Fred is a beggar who pretends blindness to con the wealthy. Albert introduces himself to the flirtatious Pola by "finding" her purse, and from then on, she gives the narrative such direction as it has by being the object of desire of Albert, of Fred, and of Albert's mate Louis. In Albert's absence, Louis wins her; when they break up, however, she goes off with Fred. Consolation is never far

---

1. This opening sequence had originally been written for *Prix de beauté* and been conceived while Clair was shooting *Le Fantôme du Moulin Rouge* in 1924. Billard, *L'Âge classique du cinéma français*, 153; Dale, *The Films of René Clair*, 1:137.

away for the "losers." Toward the end, she attempts to play them all off against each other, but in a Clair film, the women can never be taken too seriously: their main function is to clarify and ratify the relationships among the men. Friendship will always triumph over desire. Here the men finally throw dice for Pola, and Albert cheats to allow her to go off with Fred. This foregrounding of the game-like patterning of relationships is confirmed in the final circular sequence in which Albert is back singing in the street and flirting with someone else: another day, another girl, and so it goes.

If the film is, then, sentimental about the settings and atmosphere, it is far from sentimental about the characters and their relationships. No real attempt is made to exploit identification mechanisms that might invite the viewer to take seriously the characters' losses, confusions, and infidelities. For Clair at this time, individuals were clearly less important than atmosphere and milieu. This disavowal of drama in favor of a sort of ballet-like set of advances and retreats is only heightened by the foregrounding of sound-image relationships. Much of the action is patterned on the verses of the songs or a record-player or the dance-hall orchestra. Elsewhere, non-diegetic music comments comically on the action, with a death march for instance, or with raindrops or with "cat-like tread." Conversations that risk turning dramatic are totally drowned in orchestral sound, leaving nothing but frenetic gestures, and any threatening intimacy is distanced by being unheard—witnessed, for instance, through a glass door. There is, in fact, little synchronized dialogue. The first example is well into the film. Partly this is because sound mixing was not yet available, and the soundtrack had to be recorded integrally. But also Clair professed nostalgia (already!) for the silent film, and such was his dislike of the constant chatter that had resulted from the introduction of sound that he strove here to produce essentially a silent film with just a little supporting dialogue to avoid cumbersome subtitles. "People use dialogue," Clair said, "when they can't figure out how to carry off a scene visually."[2] "The sonorized film is the last hope for partisans of the silent film."[3] Indeed, in all of these early sound films, he considered dialogue so secondary that he merely gave his actors general indications, allowing them to improvise the precise phrases "as in commedia dell'arte."[4]

Critically acclaimed for its exploratory use of sound, Sous les toits de Paris experienced, perhaps because of its somewhat sardonic tone, at best a desultory general release in Paris, only gradually over the following years acquiring the audi-

2. Ibid., 1:141.
3. Clair, Cinéma d'hier, cinéma d'aujourd'hui, 197.
4. Charensol and Régent, Un maître de cinéma, 97–98.

ence that it deserved.[5] Outside of France, however, and particularly in Germany, where it was lauded as the most beautiful film ever made, it was immensely popular. Arguably this was due to the fact that this poeticized version of Paris was more recognizable to foreigners than to the French themselves, constructed as it was, or was to be, by foreigners such as Meerson, Kertesz, and George Brassaï.[6]

The studio boss of the French arm of Tobis, Henckel, was so delighted with the film's triumph in his homeland that he renewed Clair's contract on very favorable terms, giving him a free hand to make his next three films with them. The two other Parisian films were likewise largely devoid of dramatic plot, employing analogous formal patterns. Each of the three is a musical of a sort, expressing Clair's affection for popular ballads and his apparent conviction that their musicality was a manifestation of the working class's vitality, sincerity, and integrity. It is one of the more interesting aspects of Clair's films that high culture and wealthy businessmen should be so mocked by an author wedded to that very culture and born into a wealthy business family.

3. L'Âge d'or

(*The Golden Age*)
France, 1930, 65 min; b&w

Dir Luis Buñuel; *Asst dir* Jacques-Bernard Brunius and Claude Heymann; *Prod* Vicomte de Noailles; *Scr* Luis Buñuel and Salvador Dalí;[7] *Cinematog* Albert Duverger; *Music* Georges van Parys and works of Mendelssohn, Mozart, Beethoven, Debussy, and Wagner, as well as a paso doble; *Art dir* Pierre Schildknecht; *Sound* Peter-Paul Brauer; *Edit* Luis Buñuel; *Act* Gaston Modot (the lover), Lya Lys (the Marquise's daughter), Max Ernst (bandit chief), Pierre Prévert (a bandit); also Germaine Noizet, Lionel Salem, Duchange, Caridad de Lamberdesque, Llorens Artigas, Brunius, Valentine Hugo, and Paul Éluard.

The release of *L'Âge d'or* was accompanied by the notorious Surrealist Manifesto, which was designed in part to promote Luis Buñuel as the only authentic surrealist filmmaker. Film had been a central focus from the beginning of the surrealist movement, both because of the analogy of screen and mirror and because of the dreamlike conditions in viewing films, which should favor the communication of the unconscious. Arising out of the Dadaist movement and deriving its

---

5. See Icart, *La Révolution du parlant*, 385–390.
6. See the argument in Bergfelder et al., *Film Architecture*, 174–178.
7. The two had parted company by this time, and little of Dalí subsists in the film.

theory from a surprisingly ebullient version of Freudian dream theory, surrealism saw society as inherently repressive and the surrealist's task as the liberation of the spectator's repressed self. Since this neatly complemented the contemporary communist proposition that capitalist society repressed the working classes and that a revolutionary, class-based liberation was required, there was from early on a close relationship between communism and surrealism, between social and psychic revolutions, and between the two main cultural proponents of these movements in 1930s France, Louis Aragon and André Breton. Both signed the manifesto that accompanied *L'Âge d'or,* which foreshadowed the imminent annihilation of capitalist society and which noted that the film was being released at a moment when the rotting hulk of capitalist society was at its most enfeebled, struggling to survive through the agency of priests and of the police. The manifesto praised the film's violent attacks on religion and its assertion of the need for a transfigurative and redemptive "Love" (i.e., uninhibited sexuality)—"that principle of Evil in the bourgeoisie's demonology"—to achieve these twin forms of liberation.

Buñuel had of course produced an earlier film based on surrealist principles —the short *Un chien andalou* (1928).[8] No one who has seen the film will ever forget it, if only because of the prostrate priests and the dead mule carcasses draped over a grand piano that are dragged on stage (symbolizing, according to Raymond Durgnat, "the dead weight of education"[9]), not to mention the girl's eye sliced open with a cut-throat razor. Sound film was to severely restrict the production of such avant-garde films as this, because of the high cost of sound production and the relatively limited audience. A private patron was one possible solution, and fortunately there were still several available at this time. René Clair (for *Entr'acte*) and his brother, Henri Chomette, had already received such support. Carl Dreyer was about to benefit from another patron. In 1929, the Vicomte de Noailles decided to commission a series of experimental films as a gift to his wife.[10] Jean Cocteau (*Le Sang d'un poète,* #13) and Man Ray both benefited from his generosity, as did Buñuel for *L'Âge d'or.* Initially shot silent, it was subsequently sonorized. Several early accounts suggest that a silent version also circulated.

L'Âge d'or has been accused of being obsessed with sacrilege. Certainly it goes out of its way to provoke and offend as many right-minded people as possible. A blind man is knocked down, a dog kicked, a son casually slaughtered by his father, the female lead's old mother brutally slapped, and so on. But it is clearly the religious who are the main target: a Christ figure is seen emerging from one of

8. *L'Âge d'or* was initially to be entitled *La Bête andalouse* and was conceived as a sequel.

9. Durgnat, *Luis Buñuel,* 30. A fuller description of the film is to be found here.

10. See Abel, *French Cinema,* 269–270.

the Marquis de Sade's orgies (in the scenario, representatives of all the major religions were to participate); archbishops are discovered celebrating mass on a deserted rock, and when next seen, have rotted away to skeletons (still in full regalia); later, two of them are hurled out a window by the "hero" together with a burning Christmas tree and a giraffe. The film ends with a cross decked out in grotesque ornaments, notably pubic hair. Clearly Buñuel's religious upbringing has something to do with the satisfaction he takes in ridiculing the church and the dignitaries who revere it (here, politicians, nuns, the military, curates, etc.) and who proceed to build their church on this desolate rock. Unlike the effete esthetics of Cocteau's films, this no less inventive film passionately attacks the bases of contemporary society. Right-minded people were justified in their desire to demolish it.

Against these forces of convention and oppression, the leading male and female figures, first discovered writhing in the mud in a violently sexual embrace and ululating mating cries, struggle futilely throughout the film. Brutally separated by the outraged citizens, they strive repeatedly and angrily to be reunited but are thwarted. Arguably by the end of the film, the male lead has managed to liberate himself from the moral repressions of his social upbringing; though critic Peter Harcourt sees actor Gaston Modot's character, on the contrary, as being at that point definitively defeated by the conventions of the society he is in rebellion against.[11] It would be inappropriate, then, to give the impression that the film is structured around any readily recognizable narrative.[12] What matters is the alliance of sexuality and revolt. Images succeed one another according to patterns of association rather than of temporal or logical causality, and reference to psychoanalytical theory is often necessary to interpret them. Implicitly, the film mimics the way the unconscious works. And when sound was added to the film, any tentative realist interpretation was further distanced by the lack of synchronicity. At one point, the soundtrack provides a subjective voice off; at another, the lovers, dressed and in public, are nevertheless accompanied by a bedroom dialogue. For the most part, however, the music is used to characterize or comment on silent scenes, the final blasphemous images being accompanied by a jocular dance tune.[13]

11. Harcourt, *Six European Directors*, 112–114.

12. For a notional narrative, see Kyrou, *Luis Buñuel*, 22, and Pornon, *Le Rêve et le fantastique*, 101–111.

13. By contrast, see Kyrou, *Le Surréalisme au cinéma*, 212–214, who makes more ambitious claims for the soundtrack, and further remarks on it in Fescourt, *La Foi et les montagnes*, 351–352.

Approved for release in the normal fashion, *L'Âge d'or* was first screened in Studio 28, an art cinema catering to the Ciné-Club movement. This movement, begun in 1921 by a group of directors, critics, actors, and painters meeting at Canudo's Club des Amis du Septième Art, had been effective in creating for film an aesthetically informed audience, and a number of specialist cinemas had been established to cater to their taste.[14] Founded in 1928, Studio 28 was the third of these (preceded by the Vieux Colombier and the Ursulines). On 3 December 1930, two months after *L'Âge d'or* opened in it, a cabal of right-wing critics (reputedly from the League of Patriots and the Anti-Jew League) disrupted the screening with shouts, smoke-bombs, and ink bombs. Cinema seats were broken, and paintings by Salvador Dalí, Max Ernst, Man Ray, Joan Miró, and Yves Tanguy were slashed. A week of agitation by the right-wing press, which denounced the film as satanic and as obscene surrealist garbage ("Âge d'or, âge d'ordure"—Golden Age, garbage age), calling it "Bolshevik propaganda dragging through the mud all that we French hold most sacred," saw first the excision by the censors of the archbishop scenes, then on 11 December, the total prohibition of the film and temporary closure of the cinema. Officially the film remained banned until 1981—a remarkable achievement for the forces of repression given that censorship has never been particularly aggressive in France and was at its least effective in the chaotic 1930s.[15]

4. *Le Chemin du paradis*

(*The Road to Paradise*)
Germany-France, 1930, 99 min (now runs 89 min), b&w

Dir Wilhelm Thiele (Max de Vaucorbeil for the French version); *Prod* UFA/ACE; *Scr* Franz Schulz and Paul Franck (French dialogue Louis Verneuil); *Cinematog* Franz Planer; *Music* Werner Heymann; *Art dir* Otto Hunte; *Sound* Hermann Fritzsching; *Act (French version)* Henri Garat (Willy), René Lefebvre (Jean), Lilian Harvey (Liliane Bourcart), Olga Tchekowa (Édith de Tourkoff), Jacques Maury (Guy), Gaston Jacquet (Monsieur Bourcart), Hubert Daix (Maître Dupont-Belleville), and Jean Boyer (bailiff).

Le Chemin du paradis was one of the first musical successes of the sound cinema in France, and made of Henri Garat and Lilian Harvey the leading roman-

14. See Crisp, *Classic French Cinema*, 226–233, for a fuller account.
15. See Kyrou, *Luis Buñuel*, 30–33, and Altman, "Censorship in France," in *Ça c'est du cinéma*, 217–226. See also Crisp, *Classic French Cinema*, 250–263, and Prédal, *La Société française à travers le cinéma*, 195–204.

tic couple of the day. A 1931 poll of the French public seeking to identify the stars they thought most photogenic placed Henri Garat second (after Suzy Vernon) and Lilian Harvey third. Yet the film that established them can now seem clumsily put together and sung without much talent or panache. In 1930, sound itself was a sufficient attraction for the viewing public, regardless of story or style, and when combined with a few rousing songs, sound films rapidly came to seem to production companies a route to effortless profitability. In *Le Chemin du paradis*, the hit song "Avoir un bon copain" (When you have a good mate) served to promote the film on the streets and in the drawing rooms, and survived through the decade as a celebration of mateship. The film's theme song, "Tout est permis quand on rêve" (Everything is possible in a dream), usefully defines the feel-good fantasy world in which these musicals customarily took place.

Garat, like many of the stars who were to feature prominently in the musicals (and indeed the mainstream films) of the 1930s, had already made his name in the world of popular music. Several, such as Georges Milton, Maurice Chevalier, Florelle, Yvonne Printemps, Gaby Morlay, Viviane Romance, Fernandel, and Jean Gabin, had come from the music hall and caf'conc (café concert) scene. Gabin's first film, *Chacun sa chance* (Steinhoff and Pujol, 1930), was the transcription to film of a musical, and in view of his later roles, it is amusing to see a slim, sleek Gabin playing the romantic lead in that film. Garat himself was making another musical for UFA at the same time—*Flagrant délit*—partnering Blanche Montel, where Lilian Harvey and Willy Fritsch sang in the original German version, but it was not so successful as *Le Chemin du paradis* so UFA continued thereafter to record the French versions of its musicals with the Garat/ Harvey (French/British-born German) couple—successively *Princesse, à vos ordres* (Schwarz and de Vaucorbeil, 1931), *La Fille et le garçon* (Thiele and le Bon, 1931), *Le Congrès s'amuse* (Charell and Boyer, 1931), and *Un rêve blond* (Martin, 1932), not to mention *Moi et l'impératrice* (Hollaender and Martin, 1932), where Charles Boyer replaced Henri Garat.

Such was the demand for these musicals that, in parallel with these films for UFA, Henri Garat was starring in a series of them for Paramount at its Saint Maurice studios with Meg Lemonnier as his partner—*Rive gauche* (Korda, 1931), *Il est charmant* (Mercanton, 1931), *Une petite femme dans le train* (Anton, 1932), *Simone est comme ça* (Anton, 1932), and finally *Un soir de réveillon* (Anton, 1933). This list constitutes a relatively small selection of the musicals produced in France in these three years. Certain ones among them were very popular, especially *Le Congrès s'amuse,* which was more efficiently narrated than its predecessor and where the music was largely integrated into the diegesis. Like *Le Chemin du paradis*, it has a theme song foregrounding its dreamlike nature—"Serait-ce un rêve, un joli rêve" (Could it all be a beautiful dream?)—though when the tsar is called away from his romantic dalliance to deal with Napoleon, it turns into "It was only a beautiful dream."

The storyline of *Le Chemin du paradis* itself is rudimentary. Three friends down on their luck—Willy, Jean, and Guy—establish a service station; one of their first customers is Liliane, daughter of a wealthy businessman. All three meet her separately and fall in love; a mild rivalry ensues until she invites them all to a restaurant where it becomes apparent she has chosen Willy (Garat, played in the German original by Willy Fritsch). Her father buys the service station and appoints the three to sinecures, where they are bored out of their minds in a gentle mockery of capitalism analogous to *À nous la liberté* (#12). The business is called sade—la Société Anonyme des Dépots d'Essence, "à responsabilité extrêmement limitée" (an extremely limited company). Willy resigns in disgust, only to find he has accidentally signed a marriage contract.

That one or the other of the protagonists should be wealthy or aristocratic was a prerequisite of these fantasy musicals. As their titles imply, aristocratic flirtations lie behind *Le Congrès s'amuse*, *Moi et l'impératrice*, and *Princesse, à vos ordres*, while Gabin in *Chacun sa chance* is a salesman who finds himself mistaken for a baron, courting a theater chocolate-girl under the impression she is a wealthy businesswoman. Indeed, impersonation and mistaken identity are standard narrative ploys in these frivolous musicals. Tsar Alexander I in *Le Congrès s'amuse* has a body double to stand in at boring or dangerous events while he circulates incognito, so the humble glove salesgirl does not realize that her beau is the great tsar. For much of the time, the spectator also is uncertain which is which, given that both are played by Garat. Along with wealth and a title, the stellar glamor of theaters, nightclubs, and balls is a common element—each film includes a visit to a glamorous nightclub or restaurant, where tap-dancers dance to a piano (or in one case *on* the piano), or to the Folies, where girls dance in spangled g-strings. Later in the decade, it became more common to aim for a greater degree of realism in musicals, by totally integrating the performance element into the narrative (Tino Rossi as a singer with a problem, or Mistinguett rehearsing and staging a revue, for example), but at this point, the artifice of performance was usually enjoyed for its own sake. Extra-diegetic orchestras swell up whenever the characters turn to the camera to sing, and barmen or tradesmen put down tools to sing and dance as a chorus. Indeed, tentative forms of special effects were considered appropriate to the artifice of such films: in *Le Chemin du paradis*, the furniture flies out the door of its own accord (which presumably was what impressed Clair when he saw it), while in *Le Congrès s'amuse*, the chairs sway in time to the orchestra. In *Il est charmant*, the law student tempted by love and the Folies Bergère daydreams a miniaturized performance on his desktop, while in *Chacun sa chance*, a presenter says, "Since this is a talkie, let's talk," and proceeds to introduce the cast and (otherwise extra-diegetic) orchestra in the pit in front of the stage curtain. Likewise, in *Le Chemin du paradis*, when the curtain closes at the end of the film, Willy and Liliane embrace, then "notice" that their audience is waiting for the obligatory finale, so they reprise the big song and dance number. Nevertheless, *Le Chemin du paradis* is exceptional for its time in rejecting the fantastic, the glamorous, and the aristocratic, mobilizing "ordinary human beings" in relatively realistic surroundings.[16]

Incidentally, René Lefebvre who here plays Willy's gormless, bespectacled assistant, was to play the lead in Clair's *Le Million* (#9), partly inspired by the success of *Le Chemin du paradis*, and later in Renoir's *Le Crime de Monsieur Lange* (#46). During the war, he became a resistance leader in the south of France.[17]

5. *Le Roi des resquilleurs*

(*The King of Conmen*)
France, 1930, unknown length, b&w

Dir Pière Colombier; *Asst dir* Harold Earle; *Prod* Pathé-Natan; *Scr* Colombier and René Pujol; *Cinematog* Fédote Bourgassoff; *Music* Ralph Erwin and Casimir Oberfeld; *Art dir* Jacques Colombier; *Sound* Carl Livermann; *Act* Georges Milton (Bouboule), Pierre Nay (René Francis), Hélène Perdrière (Lulu), Hélène Robert (Arlette), Mady Berry (Madame Francis), Jean Garat (Sycleton), Henri Kerny, Bérétrot, Jim Prat, Léon Bernstein, and Bob Desmarets.

This film seems to have disappeared, which is unfortunate since it was the most popular film of the whole decade in Paris, rivaled only by *La Grande Illusion* (#60), and in the next decade, *Les Enfants du paradis*. Released about 15 November 1930 in a two-thousand-seat cinema, it was still in exclusive release at the end of the following year (for a total of eighteen months), at which point it was released generally into some forty-one suburban cinemas, earning in all 30 million francs. It would have been fascinating to see just what made it so successful. Aside from contemporary accounts, however, we also have a remake from 1945 that has survived, with Rellys (as Mimile) in the lead role rather than Georges Milton (as Bouboule), and since it works with roughly the same scenario as the 1930 film (but was far less successful), we can assume a reasonable similarity.

16. See reviews and comments in Icart, *La Révolution du parlant*, 332–336, and O'Brien, *Cinema's Conversion to Sound*, 74–77.
17. See his memoirs, *Le Film de ma vie*.

Bouboule is a trickster figure straight out of vaudeville. Like so many popular characters in the early 1930s, he is a street singer, strolling through Montmartre with his mate and a small band, singing and selling their songs. Again like many contemporary popular figures, he is a master of disguise, passing himself off first as a baron, in order to impress a pretty girl. The consequent need to squire her to various elegant events while avoiding the outlay of nonexistent cash constitutes a central, ongoing joke. He bets on the wrong horse by mistake, but it wins; he bets on a boxing match but loses when his discarded apple-core rings the bell; he avoids paying for a lavish meal by anonymously telephoning the chef with the news that he and his party are government food inspectors who must on no account see the cost of the meal; he gets chucked out of one venue by the administrator who is forever hounding him, then impersonates a higher official and has that administrator chucked out in turn. His trickster characteristics are further in demand when he needs to get into the beauty parlor where his girl works. He pretends to be a plumber, bursting in on various women in states of undress, then to get out has to disguise himself in discarded female clothes, at the risk of being subjected to breast-enhancement and depilatory treatments. His final rendezvous with her is at a rugby match, which he cons his way into by dressing in the team colors. Taken for the new team member, he rather lets the side down until an accidental injection of horse-dope triggers fantastic feats of physical prowess, and he is carried off in triumph by his teammates, having been instrumental in his side winning the game. Multiple transformations of persona have allowed him to cross both class and gender barriers, finally winning the day and, if not the girl, at least her stepmother. Working-class affection for sporting events ensures that four of the six episodes which constitute the narrative line of the film take place in sporting arenas—the races, a boxing match, a bicycle race, and a horserace track.

Physical, raucous, boisterous, slightly risqué, at their best headlong and unstoppable, these popular vaudevilles embody a belief in working-class vitality. The scenario of this one was primarily due to René Pujol. Author of revues and vaudevilles for the Bordeaux theater since early in the century, Pujol moved to film with the advent of the talkie, and participated in no less than seventy-six films in the course of the 1930s. "He produces one of his Pujoleries every two months," complained an exasperated *Cinémonde* reviewer in 1938.[18] He wrote lyrics for the songs, and was involved in scripting thirty-nine films and directing twenty others, often to his own scripts. Nearly all were lighthearted romps— vaudevilles, military vaudevilles, and farces—often with well-known comedians such as Milton, Bach, Alibert, or his Bordelais compatriot Tichadel in the lead

18. Peyrusse, *Le Cinéma méridional*, 72.

roles. Pujol participated in several films figuring later in this book, notably *Théodore et Cie* (#24) and the Fernandel vehicle *Tricoche et Cacolet* (#80), both directed, as was this film, by Colombier, as well as *Si j'étais le patron* (#33) and the Tino Rossi vehicle *Marinella*. Milton, for whom he wrote this script, was short, plump, balding, bouncy, a clown, singer, and acrobat who came to the cinema from cabaret and music halls. A "resquilleur" is an uninvited guest, a gate-crasher, and he made that role his own in a number of films. He was so popular as Bouboule in this film that a sequel was inevitable—indeed four sequels: he returned as Bouboule in *Le Roi du cirage* (1931, also directed by Colombier); *La Bande à Bouboule* (1931) and *Bouboule 1er, roi nègre* (1933), both directed by Léon Mathot; and finally *Prince Bouboule* (1938). The first two of these figured in the top ten of the 1931–1932 season, but the latter two were progressively less successful, as the early taste for vaudeville faded during the decade.

We can get some idea of Milton and his persona from the surviving film *Le Comte Obligado* (1934) in which he plays Antoine, an elevator operator who inherits a fortune. This provides the film an opportunity to explore various populist themes—the taxmen and lawyers, who steal most of the money; hangers-on who try to sting him but of course get stung instead; his faked elegance as the imaginary Count Obligado, which allows him to hobnob with rich snobs who are all too ready to offer him their (largely naked) wives in return for investment in their firms. Antoine rapidly gets tired of their slimy, upper-class ways and chases them from his apartment. He ends up winning the lottery and buying the fashion house where he had worked the elevator to give to his girl. Again, the essence of the plot is a lower-class character full of *joie de vivre* who, through ingenuity and luck, outwits his "betters" and promotes the values of the heart over the crass preference for money—but gets the money, too.

6. *La Petite Lise*

(*Young Lisa*)
France, 1930, 84 min, b&w

Dir Jean Grémillon; *Prod* Pathé-Natan; *Scr* Charles Spaak; *Cinematog* Jean Bachelet and René Colas; *Music* Roland-Manuel; *Art dir* Guy de Gastyne; *Sound* Antoine Archaimbaud; *Act* Nadia Sibirskaïa (Lise), Pierre Alcover (Berthier), Julien Bertheau (André), Alexandre Mihalesco (pawnbroker), Alex Bernard (customer), and Raymond Cordy.

Jean Grémillon had a documentary background and had made two feature films during the silent period. He was better prepared than most for the advent of sound, since he had studied at the Conservatorium under Vincent d'Indy, had been a violinist in film orchestras, and was to compose some of the music for his own films. Like René Clair, he was a proponent of the ambitious use of ambient sound, music, and dialogue to integrate sound and image tracks in a kind of operatic continuum, but unlike Clair, saw sound film as a totally new art form in which all the techniques learned during the silent period would need to be rethought.[19] His initial sound film, *La Petite Lise,* was one of the first to be made by Pathé-Natan when Natan took it over on Pathé's retirement in March 1929, and it was scripted by that great Belgian scriptwriter Charles Spaak (thirty-four films in the decade, including *La Grande Illusion* and most of his compatriot Jacques Feyder's films). In it Grémillon exploited the newly introduced RCA photophone process to develop a number of ambitious sonorization procedures.

The whole first "act" of the film is set in a French Guiana jail, where Berthier has been granted a reprieve for his bravery in recent events, so opts out of an escape planned by his fellow prisoners. The soundtrack begins before the titles, with a bass chord and a ticking sound that evolve as the images open into an African-themed chant. The prisoners are being herded back into prison. The babble of unsourced voices and snatches of phrase that follow accompanies their talk of Paris and of women (graffiti), their cooking an evening meal (smoky haze of light), their amusements (tracking camera from cards to dice to "coconut shy" at a man in a barrel), then finally erupts into an extremely moving chorus that covers the escape of the other prisoners. This is one of the masterpieces of early sound cinema, and an early foreshadowing of the poetic realism of the late 1930s. It was put to music by the composer Roland-Manuel, who was to write the music for several of the more ambitious 1930s films, notably *La Bandera* (#42) and *L'Étrange Monsieur Victor* (#77). He worked with the benefit of a meticulously timed score developed by Grémillon, which integrated all visual and aural elements of the film.

The rest of the narrative is less innovative, more melodramatic, but never less than interesting: Berthier returns to Paris and gradually discovers that his daughter, Lise, has in his absence been forced into prostitution but is in love with André, an unemployed man who does not know of her dubious activities. In a desperate attempt to escape from poverty, she and André try to extort money from a (parodic) Jewish pawnbroker, in the course of which Lise accidentally kills him. At a dance hall, André resolves to confess to the crime to save Lise. Berthier realizes where events are leading him: it is he who must confess to the murder of the Jew, to save his daughter and her lover. At this point, a subjective "memory"

19. See Sellier, *Jean Grémillon,* 69.

sequence of the Cayenne prison is accompanied by the voice of the governor, ironically telling Berthier that he is now a free man. He thrusts his way through the dancing crowds and enters a police station. Through its window, soundlessly, we see him confessing to the crime, while the soundtrack is still filled with the hectic celebrations of the raucous dancing crowd. This is another early instance of a trope, already mentioned in connection with *Prix de beauté*, that became extremely popular with the more ambitious French scriptwriters and directors— the ironic contrast between public celebration and private despair. One thinks immediately of *Hôtel du Nord* (#89), *Au Bonheur des dames, Lumière d'été,* and *Sortilèges,* but a dozen other noteworthy examples could be cited from the period 1930–1945, not least Baptiste's desperate attempt to pursue Garance through the celebratory throng at the end of *Les Enfants du paradis.* As noted elsewhere, this trope often (though not always) serves to represent the people as a communal source of vitality—the only true source—but at the same time as individually doomed to a joyless destiny.[20]

Moreover, the dislocation of sound and image, as we see but do not hear Berthier's false confession, reverses an earlier occasion when we hear but do not see, because of a half-closed door, Lise returning from an assignation to find her father installed in her flat (and momentarily mistaking him for a "client"). The details of this awkward encounter are left visually to our imagination. Earlier, during the escape scene, the camera had abandoned the central dramatic elements related to the escape in order to linger on prisoners lost in lonely thought. An analogous incident later in the film has the camera linger endlessly on Lise's blank face, obliging us to reconstruct her bitter reflections on the accidental murder of the pawnbroker, with its inevitable consequences. Jean Robin was right to emphasize the power of the silences in this film.[21]

Grémillon conceived the musical sequences of his film in a symphonic way, contrapuntally, with the various sonorous elements interwoven and developed as in a fugue. But quite aside from these inventive technical strategies, *La Petite Lise* presents us in Berthier, as played by Pierre Alcover, with the first of those stolid, bulky working-class protagonists whose unbecoming if not downright ugly exterior belies his emotional integrity, and who is trapped by a seemingly inescapable social fatality into becoming or being treated as a criminal. The best-known of the actors to play this type was of course to be Jean Gabin, whose trajectory can be followed in later entries in this filmography, but it is worth recog-

20. Crisp, *Genre Myth and Convention,* 19.

21. *Cinémonde,* 12 November 1930, quoted in Icart, *La Révolution du parlant,* 392–394. See also Porcile, *La musique à l'écran,* 106–108.

nizing that the persona preexisted Gabin's more famous roles, and that Gabin himself grew into it only slowly. Its social origin was, of course, the impoverishment of a large segment of the working class in the late 1920s and early 1930s: the stress of a life on the edge, where those one loves are forced into desperate measures to stay alive, make of working-class existence a trap for which the Cayenne prison stands as a metaphor. The trap is only underlined by the circularity of the narrative, which dooms Berthier to return to the jail where we first found him. As he confesses to the crime he has not committed, the camera tracks back from the window, and a bell tolls and reverberates, uncomfortably loudly. This film takes very seriously the link between poverty and criminality that had already been sketched in lightly in René Clair's films.

Two final senses in which this film foreshadows crucial themes of the next fifteen years are first, the almost incestuous obsession of a father with his daughter, which will be taken up later, and second, the willingness of a parent to sacrifice him- or herself for a child. The Depression and later the defeat by Germany produced in different ways a sense of guilt in the older generation: without actually having done anything wrong—indeed often because they have done precisely nothing—parents feel responsible for their offspring's having to endure an unreasonably hard existence, and they sacrifice themselves in an attempt to mitigate that suffering.

The film was totally unsuccessful with the public, which (combined no doubt with the fact that it had been approved behind his back, and involved the murder of a sordid Jew) so enraged Natan, himself of course a Jew, that he swore that Grémillon, notionally contracted long-term to his company, would never again work for him.[22]

7. L'Opéra de quat'sous

The Threepenny Opera
United States–Germany–France, 1931, 113 min (German version), 104 min
(or 93 min, French version), b&w

French version: Dir Georg-Wilhelm Pabst; *Asst dir* Solange Bussi; *Prod* Warner Brothers–First National and Tobis–Nero Film; *Scr* Leo Lania, Ladislaus Vajda, and Bela Balazs, from the 1928 opera by Bertolt Brecht and Kurt Weill, based

22. See Sellier, *Jean Grémillon*, 70–90, for an account of Natan's "sabotage" of the premiere.

on *The Beggar's Opera* by John Gay (1728); *French adapt* André Mauprey, Solange Bussi, and Ninon Steinhoff; *Cinematog* Fritz Arno Wagner; *Art dir* Andrej Andrejew; *Music* Kurt Weill, arranged by Theo Mackeben; *Edit (German)* Hans Oser, *(French)* Henri Rust; *Act (French version)* Albert Préjean (Mackie), Florelle (Polly Peachum), Jane Marken (Mrs. Peachum), Gaston Modot (Peachum), Jacques Henley (Tiger Brown), Antonin Artaud (a beggar), Margo Lion (Jenny), and Bill Bockett (hand organ).

L'Opéra de quat'sous was filmed in Germany in two versions, with the French cast featuring Florelle, Albert Préjean, and Gaston Modot. The practice of importing French actors to Germany, England, or America to make "French" films had been normal when French studios were not yet equipped for sound, but continued throughout the early 1930s for French versions of local films (see *L'Étrange Monsieur Victor,* #77). *L'Opéra de quat'sous* was the first of Georg-Wilhelm Pabst's films to be so made. It was the second in what is sometimes called his pacifist, or more accurately "social," trilogy, coming between *Westfront 18* (*Quatre de l'infanterie*) and *Kameradschaft* (*La Tragédie de la mine*). The first of the trilogy was a war film calculated to incite a detestation of all wars, while the last was set in a mine deep below the Franco-German frontier, where during a disaster, German miners come to the help of their French colleagues. Class sympathies are stronger than national rivalries, but after a brief period of fraternization, the grills come down once again and national differences are officially reasserted.

Pabst's principal preoccupations of the time have been summarized by Lee Atwell as "the transcendent value of love and friendship, a distrust of capitalism, of bourgeois values and of the establishment in general, and a strong moral obligation to oppose . . . armed conflict."[23] A quite different style of criticism of capitalism operates in *L'Opéra de quat'sous,* as does a quite different set of techniques from the relatively traditional narrative and critical practices operating in Pabst's framing films. This is undoubtedly due to the fact that it was based on the work of Bertolt Brecht, whose fundamental principle was to intervene in all forms of bourgeois culture with a view to deconstructing them, and in doing so, to ensure that the spectators' rational independence should be respected. They should not be emotionally manipulated by being invited to identify with characters in a psychodrama, but should be distanced from the material and allowed to consider it more objectively. To achieve this, Brecht used a number of techniques, some of which are apparent in this film:

23. See Atwell, *G-W Pabst.*

- A presenter intervenes from time to time to address the audience openly, as do the characters.

- Any dramatic tension is undercut and dispersed by songs that comment on the state of play. Thus, initially a street-singer sings of Mackie the murderer, while Mackie himself listens, eyeing Polly Peachum. Eight further songs ensue, set to Kurt Weill's astringent and unromantic music.

- The reality of the characters is undercut by foregrounding from time to time dummies, mechanical humans, and mannequins.

- The acting style aims not to construct "real" characters by way of interior development but rather to present "typical" characters in tableaux.

What results is somewhat closer to a medieval morality play than to a popular entertainment.

The story dates back to John Gay's *Beggar's Opera* of 1728. Mackie is a gang boss, fence, and womanizer who wins the heart of Polly, daughter of the beggars' leader, Peachum. Mackie is in cahoots with the police chief, who drops in to congratulate him on his forthcoming marriage, but Peachum is outraged and tries to get Mackie arrested, threatening otherwise to turn his army of the poor, the blind, and the maimed on society. Mackie prudently disappears, leaving Polly in charge of his criminal empire; she proves remarkably adept. Her mother, Mrs. Peachum, is a brothel madam. One of her girls thinks of betraying Mackie, but eventually decides to warn him, and he escapes. Nevertheless, betrayed by his former lover, he is captured, and Mrs. Peachum has to arrange his escape. Polly's "managerial staff" organize the beggars into a massive and irresistible throng that surges through the city streets, coming into confrontation with the crowds cheering a royal procession. Mackie and Peachum will henceforth collaborate; they offer the police chief, now discredited, a job in their business empire; they will use the newly recognized power of the poor to increase their own wealth.

Basically the story involves a cynical view of capitalism as a form of thuggery, just as Gay's original involved a cynical view of the court, likening it to a criminal conspiracy: the police chief is happily corrupt and readily manipulated by the crooks; everyone worships money, however criminal the source; and the poor are dupes, manipulated by their leaders for selfish purposes. Where normally in this decade it is the poor who move easily back and forth across the frontier between legality and illegality, it is here the rich who do so. At the wedding of

Mackie and Polly, the thugs wear frockcoats, making them very clearly a parody of capitalists, and Polly's entrepreneurial ability extends to founding a bank. As she says, "Why risk suffering the rigor of the law when we can exercise our profession under its protection?" During the march of the beggars, the poor carry banners saying, "We too were made by God in his image," but the final shots see them dispersing desultorily, having achieved nothing. Nevertheless, those who have seen the original German film suggest that the much shorter French version softened its incisive, satirical edge, producing something more mellow, even lackluster. This is usually attributed to the different personae and acting style of the French cast.[24]

The film is often visually interesting, its nocturnal scenes and baroque clutter combining elements of expressionism and surrealism, but it is painfully slow-moving and all too successful in its aspirations toward coldness. Consequently it is hard to like, or more importantly, to admire. To some extent, this may be due to disagreements between Pabst and Brecht as to how the work should be adapted to the cinema.[25] Brecht and Weill took legal proceedings against Nero Films because Pabst's film betrayed their original, though they ultimately lost and had to pay costs. Still, in a detailed analysis, film critic Thomas Elsaesser convincingly argues that their main aim in suing was to demonstrate the contradiction between an auteurist cinema and commercial ownership (in neither of which, incidentally, Brecht believed). It was, therefore, primarily an opportunity for deconstructive grandstanding.[26]

Clearly the film was not expected to do well, since it opened in the Ursulines, a small art theater. Banned by the censors after its corporate presentation, supposedly because of the representation of the police (or, according to Georges Altman, because it was offensive to the British crown!), the film was re-released seven months later with the excision of a minute's running time, long after the German version's release and even the French version's overseas release. To everyone's surprise, it proved sufficiently attractive to draw audiences to the Ursulines and later the Pagode for about two years. Admittedly one of the large theaters would have accumulated the same number of spectators in just four weeks, screening throughout the day, yet the film's continuous presence month after month in Parisian cinema programs made it an inescapable element of the cultural scene during 1932 and 1933. Incidentally, the German version was also

24. See Icart, *La Révolution du parlant*, 407–408, quoting contemporary reviews.

25. Some of these problems may also be due to the fact that surviving prints are somewhat degraded.

26. Rentschler, *The Films of G. W. Pabst*, 103–115.

(after several ineffectual attacks) finally banned—in August 1933, by the Film-prufstelle (the German censorship authority). Barthélémy Amengual in his account of Pabst's films implies that this was unnecessary: "So what if Hitler comes on the scene; the old queen will happily make him Chancellor. Mackie and his gang will provide the muscle. Peachum will organize concentration camps and furnaces for him. As the hand-organ player's song says *Revolt has retreated to the wings; it will remain hidden there a long time.*"[27]

8. *David Golder*

(*David Golder*)
France, 1931, 86 min, b&w

Dir and Scr Julien Duvivier, from the novel by Irène Nemirovsky; *Prod* Vandal et Delac; *Cinematog* Georges Périnal; *Music* Walter Goehr; *Art dir* Lazare Meerson; *Sound* Hermann Storr; *Edit* Jean Feyte; *Act* Harry Baur (David Golder), Jackie Monnier (Joyce Golder), Paule Andral (Gloria Golder), Jean Coquelin (Fischi), Gaston Jacquet (Hoyos), Jacques Grétillac (Marcus), Jean Bradin (Alec), Camille Bert (Tubingen), and Paul Franceschi (Soifer).

It is customary for critics to speak of Julien Duvivier as an honest crafts-man, an artisan with a profound understanding of his "métier." That he was always more than that is sufficiently attested by his first sound film, *David Golder,* which both dramatically and technically provides evidence of a mastery far exceeding this assessment. Moreover, contrary to received opinion, he was from the first a director fascinated by ideas, and his output reveals a consistently bleak view of humanity. This film lends itself to a reading as a bitter critique of his fellow citizens, seen as cynical and ruthless, and of Western capitalism as the source of their greed and egotism. His dark view is particularly apparent here with regard to women, seen as frivolous and selfish when they are not simply malevolent. Misogynist and misanthropist, he also lays himself open here to an accusation of anti-Semitism.

Golder is a wealthy Jewish businessman married to a hard, grasping woman. Their beautiful daughter, Joyce, is a self-indulgent, spoiled brat whose eager caresses of her father, designed to maintain the flow of his money, can easily be read as quasi-incestuous, especially when he manifests an impatient jealousy of her boyfriend, Alec. All critics of the time remarked on the relentlessly negative

27. Amengual, *Georg-Wilhelm Pabst,* 54.

depiction of the female characters, seeing Golder as the victim of their greed, but their parasitic relationship to him is typical of nearly everyone in the film. All depend on the apparently effortless ease with which he earns or wins his wealth. Speculation and gambling, card deals and business deals, are assimilated in the film's representation of his endless profits, with which he literally showers his daughter. Money is the center and motivation of everyone's lives in the film, though Golder himself is "saved" from this otherwise universal materialism by his love for his (supposed) daughter. Ultimately, however, it is this love that brings about his death. In this world, affection is a weakness that can kill. It was this that led many critics to see the film as a critique of capitalism, though communists such as Léon Moussinac also saw it as an attack on the workers' republic, outraged that Golder should extort every cent he can from the Soviet oil deal to indulge his spendthrift daughter.

Anti-Semitism has a long and unpleasant history in France, and it would be hard to defend this film against the accusation of playing to those prejudices. Golder's associate, Soifer, a minor and late figure in the novel, holds center stage in the early sequences of the film version, and is one of the vilest anti-Semitic parodies to appear in the decade's output. A sly, skinny, weasely figure with a wispy beard, he slurps his food greedily and, though wealthy, walks on tiptoe to preserve the soles of his shoes. For Noël Burch and Geneviève Sellier, who discuss this film at length, this unproductive "bad Jew" is foregrounded by the film in order to set off Golder, the "good Jew," assimilated to French society, industrious, and productive.[28] Indeed, for those critics, industry and capitalism itself are benignly represented in the film, and David Golder becomes their first instance of a "sacrificial father" who here dies nobly to fund a daughter who is not actually his and who certainly does not deserve it.

This interpretation seems too black and white. One of the great virtues of the film is to construct a complex and nuanced portrait of Golder the capitalist. Certainly the montage of modernity and industry behind the titles is exhilarating, and we tend to feel for Golder because filmic techniques invite us to identify with him in his triumphs and his defeats. Not surprisingly in the context of the Depression, however, industrialists, and Golder in particular, are early shown to be ruthless and rapacious. Golder refuses to help a former associate in need who has, in Golder's view, defrauded him, resulting in the man's suicide. "Je m'en fous," says Golder, of this and various other misfortunes suffered by others. "Not caring" is his motto, and he has become rich by being more ruthless than others. He is far from the simple "good Jew," and Soifer is there as friend and

28. Burch and Sellier, *La Drôle de Guerre des sexes*, 33–36.

companion to remind us of this rather than simply to contrast with it. The positives that Burch and Sellier see in Golder were not apparent to contemporaries. "What, not a single sympathetic character, not a single smile, not a single break in the gloom?" asked the *Pour vous* reviewer, noting that Golder dies pitiably but gets no more than he deserves.[29]

Like other early sound films, *David Golder* provides a fascinating study in the transition to sound. As Charles O'Brien has pointed out, Duvivier's previous (silent) film, *Au Bonheur des dames,* had been edited into over 1,000 shots (with an average shot length [ASL] of 5 seconds), whereas *David Golder* consists of 318 shots (ASL: 15 sec).[30] The introduction of speech commonly had this effect; yet in the context of that year's production, this film was seen as edited with an impressive vigor, perhaps even a residue of Soviet montage, using speech with relative discretion while retaining from the silent era a surprising degree of camera mobility. The soundtrack is interestingly complex—the rasping of Golder's breathing in the silence of the sickroom is effective, and many critics remarked on the ambition of the final sequence in which Golder dies on the ship returning him to France, his deathbed punctuated by the ship's mournful foghorn and accompanied by the plangent Hebrew chanting of the immigrant Jewish passengers. Among contemporary films, only the opening quasi-operatic sequence of Grémillon's *La Petite Lise* and some sequences in Duvivier's next film (*Les 5 Gentlemen maudits,* #14) can compare with this symphonic passage.

A further residue of the transition to sound is provided by the variations in acting styles. That of Harry Baur, sober and weighty, was to stand him in good stead throughout the decade, while the highly gestural, over-the-top sensuality of the acting of Jackie Monnier playing the daughter is a residue of silent days when gesture had to stand in for words. Add to all this those moments when expressionist lighting contorts faces and the astonishing vertical shot of the Stock Exchange floor, reminiscent of Marcel L'Herbier at his best, and this film rapidly comes to seem a major—perhaps *the* major—dramatic film of the French transition to sound. Irène Nemirovsky had approved a stage version, which appeared some weeks before the film's release, also with Harry Baur. This caused bitter recriminations and threats of litigation, which faded when the play bombed and the film succeeded.[31]

29. See Icart, *La Révolution du parlant,* 396–398.

30. Charles O'Brien, *"Sous les toits de Paris* and Transnational Film Style," *Studies in French Cinema* 9, no. 2 (2009): 117.

31. For this debate, see the 29 November and 13 December 1930 issues of *La Cinématographie française.*

9. *Le Million*

(*The Million Franc Note*)
Germany-France, 1931, 91 min, b&w

Dir and Scr René Clair, from the play by Georges Berr and Marcel Guillemaud; *Asst dir* Georges Lacombe; *Prod* Tobis; *Cinematog* Georges Périnal; *Music* Georges van Parys, Armand Bernard, and Philippe Parès; *Art dir* Lazare Meerson; *Sound* Hermann Storr; *Edit* René le Hénaff; *Act* René Lefebvre (Michel), Annabella (Béatrice), Wanda Gréville (Wanda), Odette Talazac (Madame Ravallini, the opera singer), Paul Olivier (Crochard, le Père la Tulipe), Louis Allibert (Prosper), Constantin Stroesko (Sopranelli), Raymond Cordy (taxi driver), André Michaud (butcher), Pitouto (theater director), Eugène Stuber and Pierre Alcover (policemen), Armand Bernard (orchestra director), and Jane Pierson (in grocery store).

Of the five early sound films that René Clair directed in France, *Le Million* was the only one based on another author's work—a prewar vaudeville by Georges Berr and Marcel Guillemaud. It resembles Clair's silent film *Un chapeau de paille d'Italie* (1927), also based on a vaudeville and organized primarily around a chase—in that case, for the eponymous straw hat, in this for a jacket containing that mythic 1930s object, a winning lottery ticket. Clair urged Tobis to acquire the rights, only to realize that the play was too dependent on dialogue. Since Tobis had paid for the rights, he was committed, so he settled on the idea of replacing much of the dialogue with songs and music, including a totally new opera sequence. The scenario thus evolved toward an operetta, in which everyone sang except the main actors.[32]

The risk Clair ran by transforming it into a musical was that the songs might interrupt the frenetic pace of the chase, so he made sure that the visual action continued alongside the singing. The classic instance, much admired by critics and audiences alike at the time, was the opera sequence, where the chase continues behind the fat tenor's grotesquely romantic declamations, the "real-life" lovers mime their "sincere" love behind the singer's totally insincere performance, and the jacket is passed from hand to hand to the accompaniment of a rugby match crowd's cheering their team's ball-passing skills. This disjunction of sound

---

32. Charensol and Régent, *Un maître de cinéma*, 120–121, but see also Billard, *L'Âge classique du cinéma français*, 168.

and image—a sort of counterpoint—was one of Clair's more interesting developments here and in later films. What is seen is not necessarily what is heard, and vice versa.

This inventiveness applied to the soundtrack generated several recording problems, notably when successive verses of the same theme song are sung by the chorus of creditors and various other characters, passing from street to stairway, stairway to corridor, and corridor to bedroom, each time with a different decor and separated from the preceding verse in both space and time. Clair and Georges van Parys used a metronome to impose strict regularity on the different performers, then imposed this rigorously regular soundtrack on the fragmented image track. A similar rigor elsewhere allowed dialogue, image, music, and song to be recorded directly. While usually more relaxed about dialogue, Clair was always meticulous about the preparation of the decoupage. He would normally spend several months elaborating the scenario and a few weeks shooting it. As he said, "If you have something to say, why wait to work out the best way to say it till you are in the studio, which costs millions to hire, when you can do it just as easily beforehand with a pencil and paper."[33]

Some elements of the scenario are recognizably related to his surrounding films, *Sous les toits de Paris* (#2) and *Quatorze juillet* (#22). The focus of the action is a pair of unremarkable young people, far from heroic but connected to the arts. Michel is a hard-up painter who has to flog his jacket (with the winning ticket in the pocket). René Lefebvre was to make this sort of uncharismatic character peculiarly his own in the course of the decade, most notably in *Le Crime de Monsieur Lange* (#46). The second-hand shop where the jacket turns up is run by Le Père la Tulipe, an amiable fence and head of a gang of thieves, who sells it on to the operatic tenor. As is typical for a Clair film, the thieves' hearts are in the right place—always ready to rob the rich, they are equally ready to help the needy—and equally typically, opera itself is mocked, as is all bourgeois culture. So while the painter chases the jacket, the chorus of creditors chases him, and the cops chase the thieves—and all of these chases culminate on stage at the theater, where the tenor tries desperately to continue his performance as chaos breaks out around him.

Clair liked to work with a small group of compatible collaborators. Annabella, Paul Olivier, Raymond Cordy, and Pola Illéry recur in these early sound films, and his technical team of Lazare Meerson and Georges Périnal was particularly important to Clair. He left a moving account of the close collaboration

---

33. Charensol and Régent, *Un maître de cinéma*, 124.

with these two men: while preparing the scenario, they practically lived together, tossing ideas back and forth such that it was difficult to say who was individually responsible for which idea. Here, Meerson's schematic "poetic" decors, theatrical to the point of incorporating elements such as shelves and a bicycle painted on the backdrop, certainly contribute to the atmosphere of fantasy at which Clair was aiming, as does the veil of gauze between actors and sets. On the soundtrack, the voices of conscience, of duty, and of remorse playfully elaborate this atmosphere. For some critics, this foregrounded fantasy was reprehensible, an excess of artifice, but others praised it as "a little masterpiece of wit, charm and poetry."[34] Certainly the public took to it enthusiastically. It was the only one of Clair's prewar films to gain widespread and immediate approval, both in France and overseas. Twenty years later, a *Cahiers du cinéma* survey of film personnel (1952) was still placing it the sixth best film of all time, while a 1960 survey of filmgoers from forty different countries also placed it among the ten greatest films.

Nevertheless, no one (least of all Clair himself) saw it as a profound film. For a director who was at the time moving steadily leftward, it was singularly insubstantial, which serves to explain why his next film would be the far more ideological *À nous la liberté*. Indeed, Clair's daughter Bronia asserts that making *Le Million* was a deliberately populist strategy to ensure that her father had the funding to make *À nous*, this time to his own script.[35] But rather than see these two films as opposed, one can see both as forms of mythic fantasy—this film, the lottery win, as a fantasy of sudden wealth; the next, the open road, as a fantasy of reckless freedom.

10. *Marius*

Marius; remade as *Port of Seven Seas* (1938)
United States–France, 1931, 119 min, b&w

Dir Alexander Korda and Marcel Pagnol; *Prod* Paramount; *Scr* Pagnol, from his play of the same name; *Cinematog* Ted Pahle; *Music* Francis Gromon; *Art dir* Alfred Junge and Zoltan Korda; *Edit* Roger Spiri-Mercanton; *Act* Raimu (César), Pierre Fresnay (Marius), Fernand Charpin (Panisse), Orane Demazis (Fanny), Alida Rouffe (Honorine), Valentine Ribe (a customer), Milly Mathis (Claudine), Quéret (Félicité), Alexandre Mihalesco (Piquoiseau), Paul Dullac (Escartefigue), Robert

---

34. Nino Frank in *Pour vous*, 26 May 1931. See Icart, *La Révolution du parlant*, 354–358, for this and other comments, including Clair's own.

35. Toulet, *René Clair*, 171.

Vattier (Monsieur Brun), Édouard Delmont (Le Goelac), Maupi (Innocent Mangiapan, the chauffeur), and Lucien Callamand (ferryman).

When sound cinema arrived, Marcel Pagnol had only recently erupted onto the theatrical scene with a series of successful plays, notably *Marius,* which played in Paris for over five hundred performances (1929–1930), and rapidly became available on disk. He refused all requests to film it until Paramount offered him supervisory control (and reputedly the role of Marius if he wanted), whereupon it was filmed at their Joinville studio outside Paris, with Alexander Korda as nominal director.[36] The film was no less a success than the play, attracting more spectators than any other film that season. Its success was the greater for Pagnol's skillful and provocative promotion. In an interview with Roger Régent, Pagnol asserted there had been three great inventions: printing (recording words), the phonograph (recording music), and the cinema (recording plays).[37] This bald statement —a proposition supported by another prominent playwright of the decade, Sacha Guitry—was to be the subject of heated debate throughout the decade. Film was supposedly not itself a creative art but merely a means of recording and disseminating such an art, so the scriptwriter was always more important than the director. René Clair, who regarded the script as secondary and occasionally left it to the actors to invent in context, replied in a particularly sardonic article:

> [Marcel Pagnol,] surprised to learn that the box-office receipts of a film were greater in two months than those of his plays in a year, suddenly became attracted to the screen and proclaimed that henceforth the cinema would be the property of playwrights or would not exist at all. [But in fact] this new form of expression needs new men. We will not find such men, except by chance, among those who have devoted their lives to the theatre or to fiction. They are already deformed, lost to the cinema, from which they no doubt derive some material profit, but to which they cannot contribute any spiritual profit.[38]

Certainly the theatrical origins of *Marius* are still glaringly apparent: interior stage sets predominate, the dialogue is extremely wordy (the impression is

36. For the prehistory of the film, see Blanc, *Marcel Pagnol inconnu,* 87–92. German and Swedish versions were filmed as well as the French version.

37. See *La Cinématographie française,* 28 October 1933.

38. "Les Auteurs de films n'ont pas besoin de vous," in Abel, *French Film Theory and Criticism,* 57–58. See also Lapierre, ed., *Anthologie du cinéma,* 2:284–294.

of never a moment's silence), and the actors (the same cast as for the play) overact in a grossly self-indulgent manner, as if playing to the back row of a playhouse. Pagnol's claim to have "opened out" the play by introducing Marseilles street scenes and shots of the Vieux Port are hard to defend—such scenes amount to a few perfunctory establishing shots or intercut scenes of sailors preparing to set sail. As a critic of the time said, "The play is perfectly recorded. It's a triumph of canned theatre—one possible formula for the talkie, which has few supporters in the business but which the public seems to love."[39] Critics often quote Pagnol's subsequent manifesto, published in his own film journal, succinctly stating that "Sound cinema is printed—recorded and disseminated—theatre," but this scarcely does justice to his comments which already in 1931 were markedly more sophisticated.[40] The quoted statement is only one portion, and in context, there is no mistaking the overall message of the manifesto: sound cinema must *reinvent* theater, generating a totally new dramatic form. This makes Pagnol's later nontheatrical work more comprehensible within the development of his thought.

The sketchy narrative framework around which *Marius* is constructed consists of a tension within the protagonist (Marius himself—the proprietor's son in a Vieux Port bar, where he is also waiter) between his love for Fanny and an unquenchable craving to set sail for exotic, faraway lands. This latter dream was of course to become one of the recurrent tropes of 1930s French cinema: constrained, stultified, unfulfilled, trapped as Marius feels himself to be trapped, all day every day, behind his bar, the decade's male protagonists (often later figured as criminals *needing* to escape) dream of a richer, fuller life "out there" or "over there," where they might start new lives free from the strictures of the unjust society that has condemned them. For Marius, it is Madagascar, Brazil, the Windward Isles, but for others it was to be North Africa, the Orient, Quebec, even Arizona or Australia. What mattered, as Marius mutters, is "Partir . . ." (Heading off/Setting sail). In the film, this craving materializes aurally in the form of the foghorn of departing ships and visually in the eccentric old salt, fateful messenger of the gods, who repeatedly tempts Marius with news of positions available on the crews of departing ships. Such ships, and the docks from which they were to sail, likewise became a familiar trope of the 1930s, culminating in the well-known final images of *Pépé le Moko* (#56).

39. Géo Saacke in *Ciné-Journal*, 27 November 1931, quoted in Icart, *La Révolution du parlant*, 264. See also his interesting comments in *Le Courrier cinématographique*, 10 October 1931, 166–168.
40. Icart, *La Révolution du parlant*, 166.

But this central narrative core does not constitute the principal appeal of the film. For that we must look to the representation of the Provençal character as it is constructed here and elsewhere by Pagnol. Amiable, emotional, vociferous, volatile, indolent, histrionic, these Provençal personalities (especially as played by Raimu as César, Marius's father) are irresistibly charming, and despite their abruptly flaring antagonisms (equally abruptly forgotten), form a close-knit community with a distinctive accent and atmosphere—except, that is, for Pierre Fresnay, whose engagement to play Marius enraged the Provençal cast ("un *alzatien*"), and who felt it necessary to immerse himself in Provençal life before accepting the role.[41]

Even before *Marius* had finished its theatrical run, Pagnol had prepared a sequel, *Fanny* (filmed in 1932, nominal director Marc Allégret, released 28 October 1932), in which Fanny gives birth to an illegitimate son from her night with Marius, but Panisse is still happy to marry her. Three years later, Marius returns from his voyaging to find that Fanny still loves him but is determined (with César's timely help!) to be loyal to Panisse. The resolution comes in *César* (1936, #54, directed by Pagnol himself): young Césariot learns he is not the son of Panisse, who has just died. The boy meets Marius, and after much awkwardness and antagonism, the biological family finally forms.[42] *Fanny* and *César* were, if anything, even more successful with the public than *Marius*. All three of them figure among the twenty-five top box-office films of the decade in Paris, and were no doubt even more successful in Provence.

11. *La Chienne*

(*The Bitch*); remade as *Scarlet Street* (1945)
France, 1931, 109 min, b&w

Dir Jean Renoir; *Asst dir* Pierre Prévert, Claude Heymann, Pierre Schwab, and Yves Allégret; *Prod* Braunberger-Richebé; *Scr* Renoir and André Girard, from the novel by Georges de la Fouchardière; *Cinematog* Théodore Sparkhul and Roger Hubert; *Art dir* Gabriel Scognamillo; *Sound* Marcel Courmes, Joseph de la Bretagne, and Denise Batcheff; *Edit* Marguerite Houllé-Renoir, Renoir, and Paul Fejos; *Act* Janie Marèse (Lulu), Michel Simon (Maurice Legrand), Georges Flamant (Dédé), Magdeleine Bérubet (Adèle Legrand), Colette Borelli, Doryane, Jane Pierson, Romain Bouquet, Max Dalban, Jean Dasté, Jean Gehret, and Jacques Becker.

---

41. Ford, *Pierre Fresnay*, 27–31.

42. Pagnol seems to have borrowed elements of *Maurin des Maures* when elaborating these sequels

The conception and production of this film are seriously contested. According to the authorial version, Renoir had since 1929 wanted to make this as his first sound film, because it accorded with his personal vision (as in *Nana*, 1927) and because he could see a perfect role in it for Michel Simon.[43] The producers required Renoir to prove his commercial credentials, which he did by casually tossing off *On purge bébé* in under three weeks—a film that was profitable by week four. Having received approval to film, he cunningly concealed the script and the rushes from the producers to give himself a free hand; the latter were horrified when they finally saw the post-production screening, because they had expected a frivolous comedy. They banned him from the studio and had it reedited, but finally had to eat humble pie and invite him back. After the usual period of misunderstanding that any true work of art must experience, and which could have seen it disappear forever but for the courage of an eccentric entrepreneur, it proved a triumph.

According to the producers' version, Roger Richebé read the novel and bought the rights, then bravely invited Renoir to direct it ("bravely" because Renoir had just directed two disastrously over-budget silent flops and was ostracized by the whole profession).[44] Richebé and Georges de la Fouchardière both saw and approved the script, and both producers monitored every day's rushes, so they were all the more horrified by the incompetence of the final edited version. When advised of their dissatisfaction, Renoir stormed out. Richebé had the film reedited by Paul Fejos, restoring a comprehensible story order and rhythm, and it is this version that proved a wild success.

Needless to say, despite its inherent improbability, it is the authorial version that is widely credited, though the editing of Renoir's next film suggests there might be some truth in the producers' account. Neither Renoir nor Fejos, however, are usually credited with the editing, but Marguerite Houllé, who in later years became Houllé-Renoir or simply Marguerite Renoir, thus bridging the gap between Renoir's first wife, the actress Catherine Hessling, from whom he had separated in 1930, and the translator/secretary Dido Freire with whom he traveled to America in 1940 and whom he married in 1946.

The narrative of *La Chienne* is well-known: Legrand, a humble cashier with a shrewish wife, saves a prostitute from being beaten by her pimp, and establishes an apartment for her, only to discover she still loves and is sleeping with the pimp. Enraged, Legrand kills her and allows the pimp to be executed for the crime. As Noël Burch and Geneviève Sellier have rightly pointed out, there is

43. See, for instance, Renoir, *Écrits*, 56–57, and Loubier, *Michel Simon*, 86–93.
44. Richebé, *Au-delà de l'écran*, 74–88; Braunberger, *Cinémamémoires*.

nothing particularly estimable about what Renoir called his "pet topic"—the representation of women as either harridans or prostitutes.[45] Moreover, the prostitute is devious and treacherous, so stabbing her to death is understandable, and he apparently deserves to get off scot free. His wife is a loud-mouthed shrew from whom he attempts to escape into the realm of art (he is an amateur painter). Her first husband, it turns out, has also escaped her, in his case by exploiting a wartime absence, and, when he turns up unexpectedly as a tramp, Legrand is able to use his presence as a pretext to himself disappear. Exchanging the French equivalent of high-fives, the two ex-husbands depart happily for the open road.

Based on a naturalist "slice of life" novel, which sought the truth of society in its grimmest and ugliest aspects, *La Chienne* is a central film in Renoir's move from avant-garde experimentation toward a form of realism. One aspect of this realism is his growing respect for great actors, and his belief that they should be allowed room to develop the relevant character role, for only thus could the director hope to capture some authentic glimpse of social or psychological reality.[46] The long take was one aspect of this practice of respecting the actor's work (the average shot length of *La Chienne* is 21.2 seconds, whereas that of Clair's 1931 films is 8.2 and 8.6 seconds, respectively; Duvivier's is 5.9).[47] Renoir's long takes combine with great depth of field to establish that form of realism, involving several levels of action, for which André Bazin so praised Renoir.[48] Moreover, the decision to shoot much of the film on location, in real streets and apartments, was a significant move at a time when sound recording still rendered that practice rare. Indeed, a principal claim to realist status is the film's ambitious striving for an authentic complexity on the soundtrack. Dense Altmanesque layers of sound, both in the street scenes and the interiors, from which crucial fragments of conversation momentarily detach themselves, provide a sort of "aural depth of field," while counterpointed songs and music support or comment ironically on the images. A sentimental street-singer intones, "O toi ma belle inconnue," as Legrand kills Lulu; and as he steals his wife's money, the little girl endlessly practicing the piano across the street sings a folksong, which returns later as a comment on the first husband. Clearly, despite his forcefully expressed distaste for sound as an inessential addition to the filmic medium, Renoir already intended to use it in as constructive a way as possible.

45. Burch and Sellier, *La Drôle de guerre des sexes*, 86.

46. A view he often expressed, notably in Renoir, *Renoir on Renoir*, 73–77.

47. For the average shot length of early 1930s films, see O'Brien, *Cinema's Conversion to Sound*, 191–196.

48. In various essays, collected as Bazin, *Jean Renoir*.

Critics on the whole admired the pitiless authenticity of the far from admirable central trio: "Jean Renoir has managed with an austere realism—immediate, even raw—to evoke the unforgettable characters of this infernal triangle—the petty bourgeois, rancorous yet sentimental; the 'bitch', a sensual woman without morals; and the third, her pimp, brutal, lazy and sardonic."[49] A final aspect of this aspiration toward realism was the use of Georges Flamant, reputedly a real-life pimp, in the latter role. During filming, in parallel with the plot, a rivalry developed between Flamant and Michel Simon for Janie Marèse's favors, which Flamant won. As in the film, he bought a new car to court her but crashed it, killing Marèse. Simon's biographer records his distress and anger.

La Chienne was Renoir's great dramatic and financial success of the early 1930s, attracting the admiration of several influential critics, such as Jean-Georges Auriol, who nevertheless regretted the incoherence of the editing and the poor integration of the various narrative lines.[50] The Catholic film weekly *Choisir,* on the other hand, approved town mayors who banned the screening of such obscene films as *La Chienne.*[51] Fortunately for Renoir, audiences paid no attention but flocked to see it—over 400,000 in Paris alone—which helped tide Renoir over during a very difficult period in his career.

12. À nous la liberté

(Freedom, Now!)
France-Germany, 1931, 97 min, b&w

Dir and Scr René Clair; *Asst dir* Albert Valentin and Ary Sadoul; *Prod* Films Tobis; *Cinematog* Georges Périnal and Georges Raulet; *Music* Georges Auric; *Art dir* Lazare Meerson; *Cost* René Hubert; *Sound* Hermann Storr; *Edit* René le Hénaff; *Act* Raymond Cordy (Louis), Henri Marchand (Émile), Rolla France (Jeanne), Germaine Aussey (Maud, Louis's mistress), Paul Olivier (Jeanne's tutor/uncle), André Michaud (foreman), Alex Darcy (the gigolo), Jacques Shelly (Paul), William Burke (gangster chief), Léon Lorin (a deaf official), Marguerite de Morlay, Maximilienne, Ritou Lancyle, Vincent Hyspa, Léo Courtois, Albert Broquin, Eugène Stuber, and Robert Charlet.

---

49. J. Sorel, quoted in Icart, *La Révolution du parlant,* 394.

50. See the translation of Auriol's article in Abel, *French Film Theory and Criticism,* 2:86–89.

51. See Crisp, *Classic French Cinema,* 255–263, for excerpts from *Choisir.*

Sous les toits de Paris (#2) demonstrates how central to all René Clair's early sound films was his somewhat sardonic championing of the poor against the pomposity and pretentiousness of the rich and the powerful. He subsequently acknowledged that never was he so sympathetic to the ideals of the political left as in these Depression years, and this political preference came to the fore in the best-known of his early sound films, *À nous la liberté*, where he wanted "to combat the machine wherever it becomes a source of servitude instead of contributing as it should to human happiness."[52] The result is more of a morality play than political propaganda, and its moral points are made in relatively autonomous segments:

- Louis and Émile are prisoners, toiling in a workhouse. They plan an escape, but Émile sacrifices his chance so that Louis can succeed (mateship is the most solemn of bonds: mates look after one another and will do anything for one another).

- Louis gets a job as a gramophone salesman and rapidly works (or cons) his way up to owning a giant assembly-line factory (formerly a thief, he can now afford to return a dropped wallet to its owner: honesty is the privilege of the rich).

- The routines of the workers in Louis's factory are directly analogous to those we saw in the prison workhouse (industry is a prison, workers are slaves; schools may teach that "Work is Liberty," but it does not compare to lazing about in a field of flowers).

- Émile tries to hang himself in despair, but in his attempt to do so, he accidentally pulls the bars out of the cell window, escapes, and gets a job, as chance would have it, in Louis's factory. There unintentionally he disrupts the dehumanized assembly line (Fordian capitalism is not only fascist but unutterably boring; any sign of intelligence or independence is unacceptable).

- Louis and Émile meet; Louis assumes his prison past will now come to light, and tries to buy Émile off or shoot him (the selfishness of capitalism is incompatible with mateship and affection).

52. Jean Mitry, quoted in Prédal, *La Société française à travers le cinéma*, 117.

- Reconciled, the mates go to a posh soirée where they wreak havoc (upper-class elegance and propriety are antithetical to the workers' spontaneity and vivacity).

- A real gang of thieves has discovered Louis's prison past and blackmails him for all he has. He tries to get away with his money, but the thieves get hold of it, are caught by the police, and leave it on the roof (money and greed rule both the business world and the underworld).

- Knowing the police are now on to him, Louis, the boss, makes a final speech to the workers: his latest industrial developments will obviate the necessity of ever working again, since machines will do all the work. He gives the factory and its profits to the workers, who spend their new-found leisure fishing, or playing cards and pétanque, while he and Émile hit the road.

The analogy of workhouse and assembly-line, and the craving for liberation from both, constitute the central moral theme of the film. Due to the Depression and numerous financial scandals, the identification of businessman and crook was to become one of the commonplaces of 1930s cinema. The final sequence, in which "progress" and the mechanization of production that had hitherto made the workers' lives hell is suddenly discovered to have been transformed by the boss's genius into their salvation, can seem contradictory and unconvincing, but should rather be read as a fantasized "happy ending" in which the long-suffering workers at last receive their just deserts.

The dominant tonality is a sort of anarchistic irreverence, and Clair acknowledged that the film was intended as an attack on capitalism as a mode of social organization.[53] Within that satirical framework, many of Clair's trademark techniques appear. First, we see the love of chases and enchained sequences, as the thieves, the mates, and the police all chase one another and the money passes from hand to hand. The process is repeated later when the money blows off the roof into the yard where the audience is listening to Louis's speech; the audience rapidly disintegrates into a wild yet neatly choreographed ballet of greed. More generally, here and elsewhere, we see Clair's slightly hectic comedy, which is not always as convincing now as it was then.

Second, the treatment of sound is typical: a film that would have been readily comprehensible if silent has had grafted onto it fragments of synchro-

53. In a discussion with Léon Moussinac, quoted in Billard, *L'Âge classique du cinéma français*, 190.

French Cinema—A Critical Filmography

nized dialogue and a complex noise-and-music track. The theme song of the title recurs at intervals, and there are moments of playfulness between sound and image: at one moment, the protagonist believes the attractive woman is singing on her balcony until the (concealed) gramophone winds down; at another, the boss rehearses his speech silently to imagined applause on the soundtrack.

Third, Clair's modernist credentials are on show, both with Georges Auric's almost continuous music track commenting on the action and with Lazare Meerson's monumental art deco factory. Effectively the factory set is

> a co-star in the film . . . taking its cue from the notions of efficiency, regularity, order and community cohesion implicit in the modernist construction ethos. Charting Louis's progress through the consumerist technological world, . . . its featureless walls both inside and out confirm the anonymity of mass production, while its gigantic proportions dwarf the individual. . . . Modernism is thus used against itself to express a dystopian vision of French society.[54]

Finally, gender characteristics and relations are similar to those in Clair's previous films. The two female subplots have been omitted from the sequences listed above since the women's roles are inconsequential, if not downright derogatory. The woman admired by Émile prefers a handsome hunk, and Louis's mistress is unfaithful, abandoning him when his financial collapse seems imminent. But the film makes it clear that the two mates are better off without them. Marriage would be just another form of prison. More importantly, neither of the friends are "heroes" but rather "little men," played by second- and third-level actors—unremarkable individuals, with no particular intellectual, cultural, or physical distinction. As R. C. Dale remarks, rather than two distinct personalities, the contrasting mates can be seen as two tendencies within a single personality, which must be "rebalanced," pruned of its materialist greed. Their departure at the end as they hit the road may recall the similar departure of many of Charlie Chaplin's protagonists—indeed the whole film recalls *Modern Times*—and Clair was in fact urged by Tobis to join them in suing Chaplin for plagiarism. He refused, saying that Chaplin had given him and the world so much that he was happy to think he might have given something in return.[55]

54. Bergfelder et al., *Film Architecture*, 184–187.
55. Charensol and Régent, *Un maître de cinéma*, 129. See also Dale, *The Films of René Clair*, 1:198, 205.

13. *Le Sang d'un poète*

Blood of a Poet
France, 1932, 65 min, b&w

Dir and Scr Jean Cocteau; *Asst dir* Michel Arnaud and Louis Page; *Prod* Vicomte de Noailles; *Cinematog* Georges Périnal; *Music* Georges Auric; *Art dir* Jean d'Eaubonne; *Sound* Henri Labrély; *Act* Enrique Rivero (the poet), Lee Miller (the statue), Pauline Carton, Féral Benga (black angel), Jean Desbordes, and Odette Talazac.

In 1929, the Vicomte de Noailles provided Jean Cocteau, Luis Buñuel, and Man Ray with a million francs each to produce whatever films they wanted to in total liberty. Buñuel produced *L'Âge d'or* (#3); Cocteau produced *Le Sang d'un poète*. Initially an animated film had been proposed, but Cocteau rapidly came to see that the necessary techniques were complex and would take much of the control out of his hands. He decided to make a film exploring visually and dynamically the same themes that he had been exploring in his literary works and sketches. His desire for total personal control made him one of the first and most outspoken advocates of what was later to be called auteurism: "A work written by one man and brought to the screen by another is merely a translation. . . . A writer must not let someone else interpret a work written with his left hand, but rather plunge both hands into the work and *construct an object* in a style equivalent to his writing style."[56]

Like *L'Âge d'or*, the film was shot during 1930 (April–October) though not screened until over a year later. And whereas Buñuel's film was politically explosive, a Freudian bomb hurled at contemporary bourgeois complacency, which consequently aroused violent opposition from right-wing activists, Cocteau's film, initially entitled *La Vie du poète*, was an act of self-promotion setting out his personal mythology. It is partially autobiographical and totally obsessed with the glorious vocation of artists such as himself. He liked to speak of it as a sort of diving-bell or probe lowered into the depths of his being to explore the (inevitably rich and mysterious) creative processes at work there.[57] Equally inevitably, the film would be largely incomprehensible to the ordinary spectator, to whom

56. Cocteau, *Entretiens autour du cinématographe,* quoted in Leprohon, *Présences contemporaines,* 388.

57. In his presentation of the film of 20 January 1932, reprinted in Abel, *French Film Theory and Criticism,* 2:89–93.

the anguish and glory of such experiences would be foreign. Indeed, he sometimes represented the film as foreign even to his own understanding, since he was merely the channel for divine inspiration. "I can scarcely blame spectators if they don't understand a film which I so little understand myself," he said. Also, "If you understand what I mean then I must have said it very badly."[58]

The film is largely non-narrative, juxtaposing fragmentary scenes linked by association only and full of (not very complex) special effects. Rather than innovatory, therefore, as Cocteau liked to think, it is one final example of the rich and diverse experimental avant-garde cinema of the 1920s, which had largely been strangled by the high cost of sound film production. The various elements of the film can fairly readily be seen to relate to the following ideas, which Cocteau himself outlined in an interview the month after filming ended and again when presenting the film at its first screening:[59] there are prose-films and poem-films, and only the latter count; the poet who creates the latter is privileged to be in touch with a deeper level of reality, an underworld where he encounters eternal truths of life and (particularly) death, here represented as accessed through the mirror; the poet's creative struggle to produce his work is a struggle *with* his work, which confronts and wounds him, and which he therefore both loves and hates; poets, to live fully, must often die, but in dying, they become immortal. As the critic René Gilson says rather apologetically, all this can be resumed in the simple questions, "Where does poetry come from, what is the poet's role, and how does poetry work?"[60] The film of course does not try to answer these questions but rather to suggest that they are mysteriously unanswerable.

On the one hand, the film exploits a diversity of techniques (voice over, handwritten inscriptions, slogans, reworked music, statues coming alive, tilted sets to make movement in the alien world seem effortful, a mouth superimposed on a hand) that aim to astonish and dazzle the spectator, while, on the other hand, the filming is rather cold, slow-paced, and arguably "realistic." As Cocteau liked to say of it, the film is a realistic documentary of unreal events. And mixed in with this documentary of the poetic process are elements from Cocteau's own early life, leitmotifs that recur in various of his works and that serve to tie the magical world of creativity to his personal experience.

Many commentators have found the narcissism of this autobiographical bric-à-brac self-indulgent if not outright repellent, especially communists and

58. Gilson, *Jean Cocteau*, 147, 164.

59. Reprinted in Lapierre, ed., *Anthologie du cinéma*, 189–190.

60. Ibid., 65. Charles Pornon summarizes Cocteau's own answers in *Le Rêve et le fantastique*, 112–117.

surrealists (Ado Kyrou, Georges Sadoul, Jacques-Bernard Brunius), who preferred Buñuel's more intellectually respectable and politically committed text. They saw Cocteau's special effects as simply rehashed Méliès, the film itself "esthetic to the point of mannerism, subtle to the verge of corruption, a calculated and somewhat precious spectacle staged by an entertainer all too pleased with himself and with society."[61] For others, a vainglorious Cocteau here represented himself as Christ, martyred and bearing the cross of human suffering. More generously, Jean Epstein considered it (along with *L'Âge d'or*) as one of those rare films "which mark the first tentative steps towards representing on screen that deeper interior life with its constant shifts, its confusing digressions, its mysterious effusions, its secret symbolism, its gloom almost impenetrable to consciousness and to will, its disquieting dominance of emotion and instinct—that domain always new, always mysterious which everyone bears inside themselves and of which everyone learns sooner or later to be terrified. This is for many the laboratory where the Devil distils his potions."[62]

Despite the fact that Cocteau saw the Vicomte de Noailles's two productions as participating in "a dark flood that nothing now can stop," they were to be the last non-narrative feature-length films made in France for some twenty years. Brunius in his quasi-autobiographical and fundamentally sympathetic review of such cinematic experiments eloquently praises *L'Âge d'or* but dismisses *Le Sang d'un poète* sardonically as "les menstrues d'un poète" (the menstrual fluid of a poet). Under the title "Death of the Avant-garde," he begins his next section, "That was the end. There seemed to be general agreement that purely formal research was futile." But he acknowledges that aspects of past experimentation would find their way into a number of subsequent works by Prévert, Grémillon, Clair, Vigo, Renoir, and Feyder.[63] Writing in 1947, Brunius could not have foreseen Cocteau's own ambitious sequels, *Orphée* and *Le Testament d'Orphée*, where, as Cocteau himself said, he was to orchestrate the theme that he had in *Le Sang d'un poète* picked out clumsily with one finger.

14. *Les 5 Gentlemen maudits*

(*Five Cursed Englishmen*)
France, 1932, 87 min, b&w

61. Georges Sadoul, quoted in Chevallier and Egly, eds., *Regards neufs sur le cinéma*, 130.

62. Epstein, *Écrits sur le cinéma*, 1:357. André Maurois was also favorably impressed.

63. Brunius, *En marge du cinéma français*, 143–145.

Dir and Scr Julien Duvivier, from the novel by André Reuze; *Asst dir* Ary Sadoul; *Prod* Vandal et Delac; *Cinematog* Armand Thirard; *Music* Jacques Ibert; *Art dir* Lazare Meerson; *Edit* Marthe Poncin; *Act* Harry Baur (Monsieur de Marouvelle, the settler), René Lefebvre (Jacques Le Guérantec), Robert Le Vigan (Strawber), Marc Dantzer (Woodland), Georges Péclet (Captain Lawson), Jacques Erwin (Midlock), and Rosine Deréan (Françoise).

Julien Duvivier's second sound film, a remake of a successful silent film, further strengthens the argument for his ambition and technical virtuosity. A summary of the plot might make it seem just another Agatha Christie murder mystery, like *And Then There Were None*. On a cruise to Morocco, Jacques, a young Frenchman, meets up with four English tourists. While touring, they irritate a native sorcerer, who places a curse on them: they will die before the full moon, in a specified order, ending with Jacques. Sure enough, the first three die (one drowns, the pilot crashes, a third is stabbed), and Jacques just manages, by paying his gambling debts, to prevent the fourth from committing suicide. Subsequently, and largely by accident, Jacques uncovers the cause of the "deaths," pursues and catches the murderer, and departs with the settler's daughter he had been courting in the early sequences.

So far, so trivial. But to be effective the narrative must invest the sorcerer's curse with a degree of at least provisional diegetic plausibility, and the brilliance of the film derives from the procedures employed to achieve that end. Essentially, Morocco must be represented as totally alien—weird, incomprehensible, and menacing. At intervals during the first half hour, the local culture is presented in quasi-documentary fashion, but, departing from the standard documentary procedure, which aims to describe and explain, these segments avoid all explanation. The image-track shows a series of startling scenes, objects, and events that seem to demand explanation but do not receive it. Consequently, the spectator is saturated in an alien culture that escapes understanding. This might seem like a Brechtian alienation device but is not, because it effectively places the spectator in the same position as the protagonists—bewildered, uneasy, and more than a little horrified. As a result, the curse, when it comes, can seem almost normal, no more than another manifestation of a frighteningly incomprehensible culture.

This situation is in some ways analogous to the opening sequences of Duvivier's later and better-known film *Pépé le Moko* (#56), where the disturbingly alien nature of the Algiers Casbah is seen as weird by the rational and orderly European administration. But in that case, the images of the Casbah are contained between two lucid segments set in the police station, controlled by the police inspector's voiceover, and demystified by a wall map. Here, the spectators have no such reassuring aids to orient them. Behind the titles, hoarse shouts and quasi-native music, raucous and rhythmic, interact with the sorcerer's incantations, while numerous natives, each immersed in a strange, stone tublike basin, respond and react rhythmically. What is happening here?[64] A row of men bend and straighten in unity, moving to a chant then listening to a lengthy untranslated harangue from an imam. These visuals are extraordinary and unsettling, even when marginally comprehensible (a cavalry charge with ceremonial gunfire, a line of harvesters), and always accompanied by weird music, sometimes sourced, sometimes not. Gratuitous inserts of objects (ostrich heads, grain waving in the wind, an Arab carving, a wonderful scene in an Arab school with grotesque shots of the children) are never less than fascinating, but sometimes held longer than seems reasonable. Why are we being shown these, and why so insistently? As the horses charge, a fire-eater and dancers stamp or whirl and jump, leading up to the moment when one of the Europeans tries to unveil a woman and the curse is delivered. In context, it can be accepted as credible, as can Jacques's increasingly distraught state as his companions proceed to die in the order predicted by the curse.

Of course, it is all a fraud. Hunting the sorcerer through the crowded streets and markets, Jacques comes upon the fourth Englishman, Strawber, and overhears him arguing with his fellows—not dead, except for one who had tried to betray the plot to Jacques—about the division of the spoils (the enormous check with which Jacques has paid his supposed gambling debts). In the course of the argument, it becomes clear that we have been watching an elaborate extortion procedure organized by Strawber, and the film ends in joyous but anticlimactic fashion with a well-staged chase across rooftops and roof-terraces.

But both during Jacques's search and during the chase (indeed right from the beginning), there are astoundingly beautiful and strikingly patterned shots, especially of local architecture. Streets and markets are shaded by netting, and the filtered and striated light flickers and flashes in a quite hallucinatory way, especially when the camera is panning with running figures. However trivial the material, this is both visually and aurally one of the most exciting films to have been made in the decade. No doubt the great set decorator Lazare Meerson and the noted composer Jacques Ibert, a disciple of Claude Debussy, played a large part in this triumph. This was the first of Ibert's nineteen contributions to film music during the decade.

Several commentators have pointed out, however, that the effect of these mystifying strategies on the representation of Arabic culture is far from inno-

64. In fact, it is the tanners of Fez at work.

cent. The sorcerer and his curse were, in fact, hardly central to the evil machinations—no more than minor accomplices—but have been represented as guilty all along. As Michèle Lagny and others say in their useful description and analysis of this film, "Nevertheless the racist overtones remain, along with all this overwrought representation of the Arab world [as irrational], for which the murder mystery has merely served as a pretext. . . . This sort of quasi-fantasized representation of [North African] energies as both violent and irrational dispensed with any need to reconsider the principle of colonization."[65] Representing the Arab world thus was the standard means by which to justify France's "civilizing" intervention in that world, which took the superstitious backwardness of the culture as a base from which to move through several stages toward ultimate enlightenment and integration into the French empire as an equal partner.[66]

15. *Croix de bois*

(*Wooden Crosses*); remade as *Road to Glory* (1936)
France, 1932, 110 min, b&w

Dir Raymond Bernard; *Prod* Pathé-Natan; *Scr* André Lang and Raymond Bernard, based on the novel by Roland Dorgelès; *Cinematog* Jules Kruger; *Songs* marches militaires and caf'conc songs; *Art dir* Jean Perrier; *Sound* Antoine Archaimbaud; *Edit* Lucienne Grumberg; *Act* Pierre Blanchar (Gilbert Demachy), Aimos (Fouillard), Antonin Artaud (Vieublé), Paul Azaïs (Broucke), René Bergeron (Ramel), Raymond Cordy (Vairon), Marcel Delaître (Sergeant Berthier), Pierre Labry (Bouffioux), Geo Laby (Belin), J. F. Martial (Lemoine), René Montis (Morache), Marc Valbel (Maroux), Charles Vanel (Corporal Breval), Gabriel Gabrio (Sulphart), and Jean Galland.

In 1930, both Georg-Wilhelm Pabst's *Westfront 18* and Lewis Milestone's *All Quiet on the Western Front* appeared. Although made in the United States, this latter film was based on the German novel, so both films represented World War I from a German point of view. Since Abel Gance's *J'accuse* (1919), no French equivalent had been filmed except the largely documentary *Verdun, visions d'histoire* (1928), partly because of a 1928 ban on war films that was only lifted in 1931. In that year, Bernard Natan bought the rights to Roland Dorgelès's *Croix de bois*, the most popular French fictional account of the war, and asked Raymond Bernard

---

65. Lagny et al., *Générique des années 30*, 149–152.
66. For the succession of these stages, see *Le Grand Jeu* (#31).

to direct it. Bernard was the son of the famous playwright Tristan Bernard, and had made a name for himself during the silent period filming his father's plays, directing Max Linder films, and especially directing *Le Miracle des loups* (1924). He had just finished shooting the social realist melodrama *Faubourg-Montmartre,* also for Pathé-Natan, and it had proved popular in general release. Moreover, he had a reputation for managing crowd scenes, which would clearly be useful in this instance.

Dorgelès's novel was written from experience at the front and pulled no punches in its description of the horrors of war. In bringing it to the screen, as Bernard recorded in his memoirs, the whole cast and crew felt they were "engaged on a sacred duty, a great pacifist project. By revealing the true nature of war to all those unaware of it, we wanted to make it an object of hatred."[67] The aim was to send the spectators away shell-shocked and horrified, saying, "This must never happen again." To achieve that end, all involved felt that as accurate an account as possible would be most effective, so every attempt was made at a faithful recreation. It was filmed near Reims, where the original trenches in which Dorgelès and his comrades had fought fifteen years before could still be seen. These were re-dug after unexploded mines and shells had been cleared. During shooting, the decomposed remains of several corpses were uncovered. The blitzed countryside was still as bleak and treeless as it had been at war's end. The Ministry of Defense provided soldiers for the shoot, but Bernard found more than enough veterans of that campaign in the area willing to participate. Each wore the same uniform and bore the same weapon as during the war. The principal actors (Charles Vanel, Pierre Blanchar, Gabriel Gabrio), like Bernard himself, had all fought in the war, so, as Vanel remarked, they did not need to act, they only needed to remember. Natan committed a large budget to the recreation of the artillery barrage and assault scenes, and the resultant images—about half the film of continuous bombardment and devastation—are still extremely harrowing to watch. The sound is equally vivid, and Bernard recalls losing seventeen microphones in the artillery scenes to explosions and falling rocks. The sound was extremely complex for the time, recorded on twelve separate tracks before being melded into a master track.

There is little narrative drive to the film. The impression is of simple endurance, and the spectator is asked to endure along with the cast. There is also little characterization. We witness the war with a small squadron of men but cannot be said to get to know them as we would in a standard psychodrama. Much of the film takes place at night, when figures are little more than silhou-

67. Quoted in Prédal, *La Société française à travers le cinéma,* 30.

ettes; the air is constantly full of smoke and dirt, conversations are rudimentary and often indistinct, and there is an almost total absence of those psychologizing shot/reverse-shot close-ups that normally introduce us to the central characters as individuals. Rather than depend on character, the film focuses on a series of generic situations—recruitment, letters from home, the faithless wife, church services, risking one's life for a mate, and so on. Nevertheless, we can recognize elements of a narrative progression in the (deliberately chaotic) initial scenes of the announcement of war, recruitment, the arrival of the new recruit (Gilbert Demachy, played by Blanchar), his initiation into battle, heroism (rescuing Corporal Breval under fire), and his agonizing death in the final images. As one critic writes, "A compact group, setting out enthusiastically for the front, is progressively annihilated in the course of a war of which they come to recognise the absurdity and the horror."[68] Also we can see a progression in the intensity and duration of the battle scenes as they build up to the relentless horror of the last half of the film. Throughout the movie alternates between frontline trenches and lighter moments behind the lines—the somber and the jocular, the aggressive and the comradely, the tense and the relaxed, the blastingly loud and the sudden silence—though the latter moments become sparser as the tone darkens even further toward the end. Outbursts of singing provide another form of punctuation. There are occasional cutaways to the Germans (for instance, attempting to undermine and blow up the French positions) but with no perceptible sense of antipathy. Twice in the apocalyptic closing sequences we see superimposed lines of the marching dead traversing the screen—French and Germans united at last, if only in death—and twice we get subjective memory shots of home, but for the most part, the film disdains special effects.

Croix de bois was one of the chief box office successes of the 1931–1932 season. It was screened in February 1932, first for the survivors of the regiment about which Dorgelès had written, then for the League of Nations in Geneva, while in March the French president attended the official premiere in Paris. Surprisingly, the film proved open to radically different interpretations. Most people felt that, as Bernard had intended, "it showed the horrors of war the better to defend the peace."[69] One reviewer described it as "a bleak, stark sober film that exalts neither heroism nor butchering; it exalts pity, and evokes the horror of collective murder."[70] But Lucien Rebatet, the brilliant, right-wing critic who was later to engage in violent anti-Semitic propaganda and welcome the German invasion,

68. Daniel, *Guerre et cinéma*.
69. See Cartier, *Monsieur Vanel*, 240–243.
70. Review in *La Cinématographie française*, 19 March 1932.

saw the representation of the army in more nationalist terms, as "a discipline freely consented to and never automatic, a struggle between irreverent individualism and an obscure feeling for the nobility of arms and for the soil they are defending; . . . [and the] noisy candor of all virile communities—a frame of mind that emerges only in our race."[71] A key scene for these ambivalent readings is the march in which the bedraggled and dispirited soldiers gradually straighten up and regain a semblance of order and pride. Are we to read this positively, as Rebatet did, or to see the soldiers as once again being duped by their officers' appeals to heroic national myths? Do such moments justify Rebatet's seeing the film as inspirational rather than pacifist? Interestingly, it was banned in Germany in 1933. Raymond Bernard, however, was awarded the Légion d'Honneur largely for his work on this film—the first filmmaker to receive this highest of French awards.

16. L'Atlantide

The Mistress of Atlantis
France-Germany, 1932, 86 min (German version), 90 min (French version), 81 min (English version), b&w

Dir Georg-Wilhelm Pabst; *Asst dir* Herbert Rappaport, and Pierre Ichac for mountain scenes; *Prod* Nero-Film AG/SIC; *Scr* Ladislaus Vajda, Hermann Oberländer, Alexandre Arnoux, and Jacques Deval (French version), from the novel by Pierre Benoit; *Cinematog* Eugen Schüfftan; *Art dir* Ernö Metzner; *Music* Wolfgang Zeller; *Sound* A. Jansen; *Edit* Hans Oser; *Act (French version)* Brigitte Helm (Antinéa), Florelle (Clémentinéa), Pierre Blanchar (Saint-Avit), Jean Angelo (Morhange), Vladimir Sokoloff (Count Volosei of Jitomir), Mathias Wieman (Norwegian captain), Tela Tchaï (Tanit-Zerga), and Georges Tourreil (Lieutenant Ferrières).

It is not easy to understand why Georg-Wilhelm Pabst, who had just completed a leftist trilogy of films for Nero-Film, should undertake as his final film in Germany this Franco-German coproduction, a French colonial story that has misogynist and arguably racist right-wing overtones. It is, however, much easier to see why Nero-Film might think it a promising investment. Pierre Benoit's novel on which it is based had been published in 1919, when it won the Académie Française prize, and was immediately immensely popular. Jacques Feyder's 1921 silent film played in the prestigious Madeleine cinema for a solid year, with a success-

71. See Abel, *French Film Theory and Criticism*, 2:93–97, and Daniel, *Guerre et cinéma*, 120–121.

ful re-release in 1928. It was the only film of the time to compete on equal terms with the American imports that dominated the French market, and the distributor, Aubert, made a fortune from it. It was, therefore, inevitable that a sound film would follow. Nero-Film produced it in both German and French versions, with an English version the following year. It was shot in Algeria over eight months, and while not such a runaway success as its silent predecessor, it inaugurated a series of colonial films dealing mainly with France's "civilizing mission" to spread enlightenment throughout its empire (see *Le Grand Jeu, #31*).

L'Atlantide itself is only marginally interested in this mythic civilizing mission; it recounts how a young officer, dispatched on a more practical mission (namely to establish a route southward across the Sahara), under the influence of drugs, the desert, and a mysterious woman (Antinéa), murders his senior officer.[72] It is roughly based on a number of historical events. First, in 1899, a senior French army officer was indeed killed by his subordinates in West Africa. Second, the French sometimes fantasized that the Tuareg people were former Christians resisting the advance of Islam, their black robes and shields decorated with crosses recalling medieval knights. The film links such quasi-Christian crosses with that of Morhange, the murdered senior officer, who is reputedly based on the French père-blanc soldier-missionary Charles de Foucauld (see *L'Appel du silence, #50*). Third, the legendary Tuareg tribesmen who figure in the film did at times, as in the film, misdirect and kill French explorers and expeditions. An expedition to establish a rail route across the Sahara had recently been wiped out by them. In *L'Atlantide,* however, the two officers are not killed but captured and taken to the lost city of Atlantis, which is inaccessible not for the usual reason that it is beneath the ocean but rather because it is beyond the "impenetrable" desert. There the younger one, Saint-Avit, falls under the spell of Antinéa, goddess-queen of Atlantis, and in a drug-induced desperation to earn her favor (but unaware whom he is attacking), kills his senior officer, Morhange.

Metaphors and myths abound in this narrative. Antinéa herself can be read as the embodiment of that fascination with North Africa as the alien Other that so captured the French imagination between 1850 and 1940, while her lethal seductions recall the disappearance of those early French explorers and expeditions. But onto this mythologized Other the Pabst film grafts a seemingly incompatible body of Greco-Roman legends. Atlantis itself comes, of course, from Plato, though the translation of it to the heart of a desert seems to be Benoit's own. Moreover, Atlantis is here transformed into a sort of Underworld by Saint-

72. I have borrowed some phrases and information from Slavin, *Colonial Cinema and Imperial France.*

Avit's descent into its shadowy, stone-hewn, labyrinthine corridors, from where the outrageously intrusive cancan of Offenbach's *Orpheus in the Underworld* blasts out on a gramophone. The cancan later reappears in a flashback to explain Antinéa's parentage (in the marriage between a Tuareg prince and a famous Parisian dancer, Clémentinéa). But at the heart of this labyrinth we find not a Minotaur but Antinéa herself, the leopard woman, at once Circe and Medusa, seducing intruding Europeans and turning them to (gilded) stone. Indeed, underlying the narrative is an aggressive misogyny. Womankind is feared because she is almost irresistible. The animal fascination she exerts is intrinsically inimical to the male friendship that initially binds Saint-Avit and Morhange. She is outraged that Morhange should resist her wiles and counter them with a request that she release his comrade, Saint-Avit. She must destroy that friendship, and does so by deception. In the process, the film presents us with a further borrowing from Greek mythology—a reenactment of the Oedipal legend, or "primal scene," in which the austere and self-controlled father figure Morhange rejects Antinéa's seductions and is killed by his protégé-son Saint-Avit, who then replaces him in her affections. Karl Sierek argues for yet other Freudian implications. As in the primal scene, Saint-Avit sees Antinéa and Morhange embracing, but then seeming to "struggle" with one another. The father leaves, and the son replaces him, or imagines replacing him.[73]

The weird amalgam of materials listed above still does not take into account the somewhat contradictory connotations implicit in the names of Saint-Avit (possibly "the holy life") and Morhange ("the angel of death")—though Sierek prefers to see Saint-Avit as relating to Avidus (greed, desire), Morhange as "custom, law, order," and the whole film as reflexively deconstructing the process of subject-positioning typical of cinema and typically unstable in Pabst's films. Nor does the above help to explain the presence so far from the sea of the Norwegian captain whose fate largely prefigures that of Saint-Avit, or of the eccentric Polish Count Volosei who has been there for twenty years, or of the patronizing treatment of Antinéa's Arab maid, who finally helps Saint-Avit to escape. The whole film has been narrated by Saint-Avit to a co-legionnaire, but when the opportunity arrives, he heads off once again into the desert following the Tuareg back toward Atlantis. Whether still under the spell of Antinéa or with the intention of exacting revenge on her, his motives are left to the viewer's imagination. Such an amalgam of disparate materials should not work, yet it can still exert a slightly surreal fascination through its claustrophobic sets and hallucinatory atmosphere.

73. Rentschler, *The Films of G. W. Pabst*, 145.

17. *Les Gaietés de l'escadron*

(*The Squadron Lives It Up*)
France, 1932, 84 min, b&w

Dir Maurice Tourneur; *Asst dir* Henri Lepage; *Prod* Pathé-Natan; *Scr* Georges Dolley, from a play by Georges Courteline and Édouard Norès, from the novel by Courteline; *Cinematog* Raymond Agnel and René Colas; *Art dir* Jacques Colombier; *Sound* Antoine Archaimbaud; *Edit* Jacques Tourneur; *Act* Raimu (Captain Hurluret), Jean Gabin (Fricot), Fernandel (Vanderague), Charles Camus (Flick, the adjutant), Henry Roussell (the general), René Donnio (Laplotte), Pierre Labry (Potiron), Mady Berry (canteen lady), Paul Azaïs, and Julien Carette.

This film appears here not so much for its own sake, since it is a terrible film, but rather to represent an entire genre of terrible films, the military vaudeville, which deserves to be included in this filmography because of its immense popularity during the 1930s. It had flourished in the theater since the 1880s, and many comic authors and actor-singers had specialized in the stereotypical roles and situations that these films offered. The essential setting is a military barracks, and the focus is always on the common soldiers—larrikins who are disrespectful of authority, jocular, lubricious, ribald, sloppily dressed, always whinging about their food and their duties, and always in trouble. As in *Les Gaietés de l'escadron*, the generic hierarchy is immediately recognizable: the soldier is cunning or gormless, the adjutant dimwitted, the captain voluble but basically paternal, and the general exempt from the chaotic comic environment.[74]

Comedians and music-hall singers such as Georges Milton, Bach, Ouvrard, Fernandel, and Jean Gabin often featured in such theatrical entertainments, and later brought them to the screen. Maurice Tourneur, who directed this, had already directed a silent film version of it in 1912. Jean Renoir also had directed a military vaudeville some years before—*Tire au flanc*—but it was with the arrival of sound and music that the genre really took off in the cinema. Bach was established as a leading cinematic comic by the astounding success of *Le Tampon du capiston* and *En bordée* in the 1930–1931 season, the latter directed by Henry Wulschleger who went on to direct him in twelve more comic films, six of them military vaudevilles. *Le Train de 8h47* (1934), with over half a million viewers in Paris alone, was one of the top-grossing films of the 1933–1934 season, with the remake of *Tire au flanc* (1933) just behind. Other outstanding box office successes of the genre were *La Margoton du bataillon* (1933), *La Garnison amoureuse* (1933), *Trois de la*

74. The description here is from Jeancolas, *15 ans d'années trente*, 148–150.

marine (1934), and *Les Dégourdis de la 11e* (1937). These films were so popular that on occasion they were released late in July at the beginning of the "dead" (summer) season, to carry the cinemas through into autumn. Like Wulschleger, Maurice Cammage specialized in the genre, though his films—*Le Coq du regiment* (1933), *La Caserne en folie* (1934), *Les Bleus de la marine* (1934), and *La Mariée du regiment* (1935)—were never among the top ten of their seasons.[75]

On the whole, the genre was not a box office success in exclusive (first) release; it was rather in general release that it attracted vast numbers of spectators, in the suburbs and country towns. *Les Gaietés de l'escadron* is the exception because of its immensely successful Paris first release—like *Le Train de 8h47*, it netted over 500,000 and considerably more than that in general release, making it possibly the most successful military vaudeville of the decade. Viewing it now, this popularity is hard to understand. The genre always had a tendency toward the episodic structure of a review, and the assumptions that the filmmakers could make about audience familiarity with the conventions meant that no establishing, linking, or explanatory shots were considered necessary. Moreover, the stereotypical nature of the characters meant that they were not individualized or developed, or even introduced to us at the beginning. The resultant film can now seem clumsily structured and inconsequential.

Les Gaietés begins with a string of unrelated "comic" incidents, which are marginally comprehensible and minimally amusing, analogous to high-school "japes." Much shouting, gesticulating, and stagey acting ensues, out of which it emerges that, despite the evidence of our eyes, the other ranks (here Fernandel and Gabin) are to be viewed as sympathetic and the officers as ridiculous, except the Captain (Raimu), who is understanding, if touchy and unpredictable. As usual in this genre, there is a central interlude (the pretext here is a visit to a café) that provides an opportunity for a few raunchy or sentimental comic songs. The visit by a general inspecting the quarters generates an improbably moving ending. When Captain Hurluret explains his attitude toward his men, the regiment, and life as a whole, the general expresses his satisfaction: "Vous êtes un brave homme" (You are a fine man).

There was considerable debate even at the time as to whether this genre was symptomatic of an affectionate respect for the military, or whether, on the contrary, it served to undermine any such respect (compare the opposite debate around *Croix de bois*, #15). An unsuccessful attempt was made by a government minister in 1935 to ban the genre, particularly *Les Bleus de la marine*, while the

75. For a list of some thirty of these military vaudevilles, see Prédal, *La Société française à travers le cinéma*, 171–175.

Renaitour inquiry into the state of French cinema in 1937 heard reports of the Censorship Board's necessary precensorship of various comic military and maritime films. Nevertheless, the tone of the comments from the inquiry was tolerant: "French spectators can easily distinguish the element of fantasy in these films," and "they attach relatively little importance to the matter." What did matter, however, was the image of the French military abroad, and the minister insisted that an export visa would be refused to "all films tending to bring the army into ridicule or to diminish its prestige."[76] With the outbreak of war, the genre attracted some of the blame for the French collapse—it was a potentially debilitating moral virus that had sapped France's noble military traditions. *Narcisse* (1939, released April 1940) and *Ils étaient 5 permissionnaires* ("Five Soldiers on Leave," 1940) were the last made, but the latter was caught up in the total ban by Vichy of all military vaudevilles and was not released until 1945, when it bombed badly. In fact, for obvious reasons, the genre was never resuscitated after the war, and can be identified (without much pride) as being one of the truly distinctive genres of the 1930s.[77] Maurice Tourneur himself was not abashed at producing such nonsense, as long as it succeeded, considering the producer's investment as important as the director's creative prestige.

18. *Vampyr*

Vampire
France-Germany, 1932, originally 75 min (now runs 60 min), b&w

Dir Carl Dreyer; *Asst dir* Eliane Tayar; *Prod* Baron Nicolas de Grunzberg; *Scr* Dreyer and Christen Jul, from Sheridan Le Fanu's "Carmilla" in *In a Glass Darkly; Cinematog* Rudolph Maté and Louis Née; *Music* Wolfgang Zeller; *Art dir* Hermann Warm; *Edit* Tonka Taldy; *Act* "Julian West"/Baron de Gunzberg (David Gray), Jan Hieronimko (Dr. Marc), Rena Mandel (Gisèle), Sybille Schmitz (Léone), Henriette Gérard (Marguerite Chopin), and Maurice Schutz (father).

Carl Dreyer had made numerous silent films in Scandinavia but was best known for his last silent film, *La Passion de Jeanne d'Arc*, made in France. He followed it up with this genre film, based on Sheridan Le Fanu's short story "Carmilla." What connects the two is the focus on individuals under extreme stress, and the ambivalent presence of the supernatural, the spiritual. Those who knew

76. *Où va le cinéma français?* 213, 358, 362.
77. *La Cinématographie française*, 14 May 1932.

him well dismissed any idea of Dreyer as preoccupied with the religious or the mystical, insisting rather on his belief that the cinema was preeminently suited to exploring the overlap of the physical and the supernatural. The surrealists would not have disagreed. Dreyer happened to meet Baron Nicolas de Grunzberg at a masked ball and thought him appropriate as the protagonist, and when production foundered over financial problems, the baron agreed to fund the film himself.[78] Shooting took over a year, and the film was postsynchronized in July 1931 in three languages.

Originally called *Vampire,* it later became *Vampyr* purely because that spelling seemed more sinister. In the original Le Fanu story, there are significant lesbian overtones, and these to some extent subsist in Dreyer's film, where the vampire is a (curiously bishop-like) woman and her principal victim an attractive young girl. The even more attractive sister has been tied to an iron bedstead by the vampire to await her pleasure. It is hard to take seriously these days the generic conventions of the vampire film, which are here exploited at length, since they have been endlessly reproduced and parodied, but David Bordwell in a brilliant analysis of the film makes a very good case for its being nevertheless worthy of study. His main point is that the narrative line is rendered willfully obscure by the absence of any causal explanation of the events. Consequences are shown without causes, so that right to the end, the film can maintain an ambivalence as to whether there are rational or supernatural explanations for the events we witness. This ambivalence is exacerbated by the reliance for most of the film's duration on David Gray's viewpoint, since our proxy in the film is peripheral to the events and does not at first have any understanding of the significance of the characters whom he meets or the relationships among them. This allows Bordwell the neat summation, "Making Gray the protagonist makes gray the story."[79] Instead of constructing a coherent storyline, the film foregrounds secondary material whose sole purpose is to contribute to a sinister sense of foreboding. This digressive material consists primarily of objects with connotations of death—corpses, blood, skeletons and skulls, coffins and graves, guns and poisoned chalices, and mysterious nocturnal intruders muttering of death.

A further deliberate block to any easy understanding of the plotline is the camerawork and editing, which disrupts and renders mysterious the spatial relations of the diegesis. There is a certain irony in this, since Dreyer had been ex-

78. Dreyer, *Réflexions sur mon métier,* 151. Grunzberg adopted a pseudonym to placate his aristocratic family.

79. Bordwell, *The Films of Carl-Theodor Dreyer,* 93–116, 97 (quotation).

tremely scornful of studio sets, insisting on the importance of location shooting throughout—according to him, "the cinema must return to the streets."[80] He sent his assistant on endless expeditions to identify appropriate locations and objects. Likewise, rather than rely on costumes and makeup, Dreyer emphasized the need to assemble a cast of characters whose physiognomy was already appropriate to the roles they were to play. Yet having identified real locations and assembled nonactors for the roles, he undermined these potentially realistic elements by rupturing the continuity, cutting across the 180 degree line, obscuring the locations by means of grills, veils of fog, night, haze, glass, and (finally) flour. Consequently, the question, "Where is he or she at this moment, and how does this location relate to the previous location?" can rarely be answered reliably. "Working against Bazin's assumption of coherent space-time as a cinematic ideal," Bordwell notes, Dreyer rather demonstrated "that the camera need not be subservient to narrative causality, that a film may foreground the active role of the camera in constituting and questioning cinematic space."[81]

In short, that incoherence of the narrative line, which might easily be written off as incompetence, should rather be recognized as a systematic, theoretical exploration of certain cinematic parameters. The same might be said of the soundtrack, which shuns the conventional function of linking and explaining events. Indeed, it involves very little dialogue, relying mainly on atmospheric generic sounds such as dogs barking and wolves howling, and on music. Cumulatively, these techniques render the logic of the narrative events not just obscure but irrelevant, and it can be quite confronting to come across a critic's attempt to summarize (or rather reconstruct) the story-line in a "logical" fashion. Nevertheless, Bordwell makes a good case for the film's *having* a fundamental structure: he sees it as being divided into three major segments, thematically differentiated (giving in exchange for loyalty, then bleeding, then burial) but embedded in them, respectively, a series of inter-titles, excerpts from a book on vampirology, and David Gray's dreams. These embedded elements provide an authoritative "voice" for the text, initiating us into the film's weird world and guiding us through the apparently unrelated events.

One way of viewing the film might be as a struggle between the caring father and the vampire "mother" for possession of the daughter Léone—a confrontation between life and death that never takes place directly but always through a set of intermediaries and exchanges, until finally the stake is driven through the vampire's heart and her principal minion is buried alive in a vat of milled flour.

80. "Introduction," in Dreyer, *Réflexions sur mon métier.*
81. Bordwell, *The Films of Carl-Theodor Dreyer,* 97.

At that point, David Gray can accompany the daughter out of the world of night and fog and into a radiant future.

Reputedly first released in Denmark to great acclaim, the film was later booed in Berlin at its official premiere. When finally released in France where it had been shot, it screened for ten weeks in a series of small art theaters. An early reviewer foresaw for it practically no box office in France, "where such purely plastic and typically Germanic works are little valued," and despite a belated publicity campaign ("a poetic nightmare, a symphony of fear, a daring work stripped of any concession to human baseness, a masterpiece"), the prediction was correct.[82] As Charles Pornon says of all of Dreyer's explorations on the margins of the supernatural, they involve an estheticism "of a sort to fascinate such spectators as don't lapse into utter boredom."[83] Most lapsed. Dreyer's disappointment at this failure can be assumed from the fact that he made no further fiction films for twelve years, though when he did so, it was *Days of Wrath* (1942), another quasi-supernatural subject involving witchcraft and victimized women.

19. *Poil de carotte*

(*Carrot Top*)
France, 1932, 80 min, b&w

Dir and Scr Julien Duvivier, from the play that Jules Renard derived from his novels *Poil de carotte* and *La Bigote; Asst dir* Ary Sadoul and Gilbert de Knyff; *Prod* Vandal and Delac; *Cinematog* Armand Thirard; *Music* Alexandre Tansman; *Art dir* Lucien Aguettand; *Sound* Roger Handjian; *Edit* Marthe Poncin; *Act* Robert Lynen (François, called Poil de Carotte), Harry Baur (Monsieur Lepic), Catherine Fonteney (Madame Lepic), Christiane Dor (Annette), Colette Segall (Mathilde), Simone Aubry (Ernestine Lepic), Marthe Marty (Honorine), Colette Borelli (a young girl), and Jean and Claude Borelli (young boys).

Julien Duvivier directed his first film in 1922 at the age of twenty-five, and by the end of the silent era had made no fewer than nineteen. Writing in 1936, the film historians Maurice Bardèche and Robert Brasillach already saw him as past his peak, which had occurred with the advent of sound, between 1930 (*David Golder*, #8) and the present film.[84] Nowadays he is better known for his work in the late

---

82. *La Cinématographie française*, 8 October 1932, 10 December 1932.
83. Pornon, *Le Rêve et la fantastique*, 13–14.
84. Bardèche and Brasillach, *Histoire au cinéma*, 337–338.

1930s, from *La Bandera* (#42) to *Un carnet de bal* (#62), while after the war, his Don Camillo films were immensely popular. A case has already been made for his being more than the dependable, consistent, prudent, solid craftsman, the skilled technician with nothing personal to say, who merely applied his skills to whatever commercial project came his way. Ever modest, however, he tended to agree: "Genius is just a word; the cinema is a job—a tough job—that you pick up bit by bit."[85]

He had already made a version of *Poil de carotte* in 1925, adapted from a script originally written by Jacques Feyder. For this sound version seven years later, however, he prepared a transcription of his own that omitted some earlier material in favor of a focus on the father-son relationship, which was intensely meaningful for Duvivier (and, as it turned out, for Harry Baur).[86] The story is of an unhappy childhood in a remote rural community. "Poil de Carotte" (Carrot Top) is the nickname given to François by his shrewish mother, who systematically thwarts his small pleasures and blames him for all problems, notably those caused by his nasty older siblings. A late child, he was born after the husband and wife had long ceased to be a couple, and the father has withdrawn into a variety of manly pursuits and a pointed disdain of his wife. As in many films of the decade, a single elegant long take at the beginning of the film serves to establish this dysfunctional family: Monsieur Lepic treads heavily down the stairs, moves to the chimneypiece to lift down his gun, and takes a straw hat off the hook. On the soundtrack, we have been listening to two female voices commenting on this— Madame Lepic and the old servant, as it turns out—and Madame commends the choice of straw hat; unspeaking, he replaces the straw hat and goes out wearing another. The camera pans steadily around to Madame Lepic, complaining of his attitude. Within a single shot we have been introduced to "the rancour, the scorn, the silence that separates husband and wife."[87]

The breakdown of the family was to be a familiar thematic field for 1930s French cinema, and particularly the problematic relationships between fathers and sons. One thinks of the final scenes of *Fanny*, where Fanny's greatest scene is almost upstaged by the return of Marius to his father, and by the confrontation between biological and legal fathers over ownership of the baby son. In general, childhood was not of much interest to filmmakers in the early years of this decade, but the neglect of a son by his father was the one exception to this generalization. Suicide, or attempted suicide, was a common consequence of the break-

85. Leprohon, *Présences contemporaines*, 52.

86. Bonnefille, *Julien Duvivier*, 1:121–130; Le Boterf, *Harry Baur*, 93. See also Bessy, *Les Passagers du souvenir*, 48–52.

87. Jeancolas, *15 ans d'années trente*, 82.

down of paternal affection, with the reconciliation in extremis that we find in *Poil de carotte* not always resulting, or not always an unqualified success.[88] In *La Chaleur du sein* (1938), a film with analogous preoccupations, Gilbert's father treats him coldly (in contrast to his three successive stepmothers, who come to prefer him to the father); when a friend visits him in the hospital, where he is recuperating from an attempted suicide, he learns that his friend's parents were also difficult: his father had finally killed his mother, then committed suicide. "There must be lots of us in this situation. How difficult family life has become," Gilbert comments. Like Poil de Carotte, Gilbert is finally reconciled with his father: "Papa, all my life I've wanted to get to know you." Or, as François and his father agree, "Now there are two of us." Cumulatively, these narratives about distant and unfeeling males constitute an ongoing inquiry into the validity of traditional male values but also of gender relations and the family.

The wife, Madame Lepic, is one of the most relentlessly unpleasant women in all of French cinema. Unfortunately, both Catherine Fonteney, who plays her, and all the three younger actors are terrible. Duvivier was notorious for his misogyny; nevertheless, his direction is fundamentally inadequate here, and contemporary admiration for the young Robert Lynen, even by Lucien Rebatet, is hard to comprehend. (More recent lack of criticism may be due to Lynen's capture and execution by the Nazis as a resistant.) Aside from the woman playing the young maid, Harry Baur is the only actor to come out well from the film (he too was to die in the war, as a result of imprisonment and torture).

The narrative provides Poil de Carotte with two classic 1930s forms of escape from his torments—nature and a laundress. The young maid who befriends him is the focus of several key laundering scenes in the field nearby, and laundresses were mythic figures in this decade's cinema, connoting warmth, purity, and humanity (e.g., *Le Crime de Monsieur Lange*, #46, and *Zouzou*, #43). Nature too is (as always and everywhere) mythic, typically connoting as here a world purged of human malice and of the exploitation of one human by another. Sometimes as an episode in a somber drama, sometimes as a fundamental structural element, nature proves a source of transcendence, such that the pressures of daily life can be forgotten. *Une partie de campagne* (#55) is a classic example. Here, for François, the holiday on his godfather's farm provides such a moment during which, wreathed with flowers, he and young Mathilde process with their (edited in) retinue of farm animals. When he and his father are reconciled, they take a companionable stroll in the meadows against a backdrop of haymaking.[89] Interestingly,

88. Crisp, *Genre Myth and Convention*, 133–135, 153, 112 (on castrating matriarchs).
89. Ibid., 195–199.

neither the godfather nor the old servant, both of whom acquire considerable importance in this version by responding to Poil de Carotte's need for sympathetic understanding, had been present in the silent version.

The special effects that accompany François's moments of terror derive from Duvivier's affection for evoking supernatural connotations. They can seem rather clumsy nowadays, but were clearly important to Duvivier since we find them both in the expressionist *Le Golem* (1935) and in his version of Christ's crucifixion (*Golgotha*, 1935) with Jean Gabin as Pontius Pilate and Robert Le Vigan as Christ(!). In 1939, Duvivier aspired to a similar effect in *La Charrette fantôme*, where we are confronted by the Grim Reaper himself, in an insufficiently eerie chariot.

20. *Boudu sauvé des eaux*

(*Boudu Saved from Drowning*); remade as *Down and Out in Beverly Hills* (1986)
France, 1932, 89 min, b&w

Dir Jean Renoir; *Asst dir* Jacques Becker and Georges Darnoux; *Prod* Films Michel Simon; *Scr* Jean Renoir and Albert Valentin, from the play by René Fauchois; *Cinematog* Marcel Lucien; *Music* Raphaël and Johann Strauss; *Art dir* Hugues Laurent and Jean Castanier; *Sound* Igor Kalinowski; *Edit* Suzanne de Troeye and Marguerite Houllé-Renoir; *Act* Michel Simon (Boudu), Charles Granval (Monsieur Lestingois), Marcelle Hainia (Madame Lestingois), Sévérine Lerczynska (Anne-Marie), Régine Lutèce (a passerby), Jane Pierson (Rose), Max Dalban (Godin), Jean Gehret (Vigour), Jean Dasté (student), and Jacques Becker (poet).

After the success of *La Chienne*, Jean Renoir directed a largely incomprehensible film noir based on a Georges Simenon novel, *La Nuit du carrefour*, which understandably failed badly at the box-office. Meanwhile, Renoir had been looking for another role for Michel Simon, and saw in *Boudu* a sort of continuation of Simon's hitting the road as a tramp at the end of *La Chienne* (#11). Indeed, the film was funded largely by Simon, who could see the possibilities of the lead role, and it is not hard to understand why. As the tramp, Boudu, he had an opportunity to exploit his hoarse, strangulated voice and bulging eyes, together with an eccentric, disjointed walk in which arms and legs are thrown out energetically in all directions at random.

The tramp figure plays a narrative function dear to French culture: the outsider whose intrusion into a tight and apparently stable community reduces it to chaos and desperation. Very frequently in the 1930s, as here, the community into which he intrudes is composed of a highly proper bourgeoisie, and his ignorance of or disregard for the rules of the game shows up those rules as arbitrary and ridiculous. A great deal of the pleasure of this film derives from watching fastidious people being horrified by acts of crassness, vulgarity, and lubricity. Always comic, the consequences can also be fatal. It is not surprising that later, in Marcel Carné's and Pierre Prévert's *Les Visiteurs du soir,* such outsider figures should be labeled "agents of the devil."

Here the tramp's role is to remind the Lestingois family that their proprieties will always be ineffectual against the anarchic power of the id. The tramp's alliance in the opening images with the scruffy dog, Jacques, whose tightly curled hair he scratches just as he will later scratch his own, is enough to characterize him as an agent of animality, of the instincts. The subversive effect of introducing such a figure into the Lestingois household is rapidly apparent, as the abrasive Madame Lestingois falls prey to his unsubtle seductions.

A crucial feature of any such narrative is the satisfaction obtained in recognizing that, far from being an alien intrusion, the foreign element was already firmly ensconced in the community, though concealed. Monsieur Lestingois has an ongoing "understanding" with the maid, Anne-Marie, and it is in fact Boudu's disruption of his nightly visits to her bed that triggers the climactic revelations. Indeed, as with most comic critiques of the bourgeoisie, it is the hypocrisy of this proper establishment that must be exposed—a process delightfully managed as Madame Lestingois's insistent pawing of Boudu forces him back against Anne-Marie's bedroom door, which opens to reveal her and Monsieur Lestingois on the bed. The instincts are unquestionably asserted here to be more powerful than the rules of the social game by which the family claims to be guided.

In the original play by René Fauchois, the contrary proved the case, with Boudu the anarchic tramp much less attractive and less central (Fauchois reserved the central role of Monsieur Lestingois for himself), and he is conclusively reintegrated into society at the end through winning the lottery and marrying Anne-Marie. As reworked by Renoir and Albert Valentin, however, Boudu is central, resolutely ungrateful for the Lestingois largesse, and irrepressibly anarchic: he upsets the marriage boat and floats off with the stream, free once more— saved *by* "drowning." In a final clownish act, he exchanges his sodden wedding clothes for those of a scarecrow (on a cross, which as he carries it off disconcertingly evokes Christ carrying his cross) and rejoins the community of tramps as they process off across the countryside singing.

Technically, the film represents a transition for Renoir. Like *La Chienne,* it has a clumsy allegorical frame, with nymphs and satyrs and panlike flutes. But like most of his later films of the decade, it contains a number of long shots (down a corridor to a distant room, or across a courtyard through the frame of several windows) that make use of great depth of focus to integrate different planes of action. And the pan following Boudu's eccentric progress along the bank of the Seine, filmed from a first-floor window in the building opposite, is a delightful precursor of later long pans and travelings, not least because the passersby are unaware of the filming.

Clearly in this film Renoir and Michel Simon conspire to promote an anarchist antiestablishment ideology. They were so successful that, Simon reports, Jean Chiappe, the Paris préfet de police, summoned them and ordered them to cut the sardine-eating and flea-scratching scenes, which were causing disturbances in the audience. They refused, and the film was banned after three days, at significant cost to Simon. This was, of course, the year when the Depression finally struck home in France, and capitalism could seem a failed and destructive ideology. It was the year when the Groupe Octobre was founded (see #21 for more details), performing outrageous political satires and anticapitalist propaganda in streets and cafés. Jean Dasté (here the student) and Jean Castanier (set decorator but probably much more) were both associated with that group, as was Jacques Prévert, whose ironically titled *Vive la presse* they had just staged. Capitalism is the central (vilified) character of the performance, and the chorus in the film intones: "The truth is comrades, that / Dying for your country is dying for Renault / For Renault, for the pope, for Chiappe / For meat merchants, for arms merchants. . . . / The street doesn't belong to you / It belongs to the cops / It belongs to the priests. . . . / Workers of the world, unite."

One can see here in Renoir's amiable denunciation of the hypocrisies of the bourgeoisie the seeds of his later move from anarchy toward the political left and the Popular Front, a move that peaked with *Le Crime de Monsieur Lange* (1935, #46, scripted by Prévert from a three-thousand-word outline by Renoir and Castanier) and *La Vie est à nous* (1936, #49, commissioned by the Communist Party).

21. *L'Affaire est dans le sac*

(*It's in the Bag*)
France, 1932, 55 min, b&w

Dir Pierre Prévert; *Prod* Pathé-Natan; *Scr* Jacques Prévert; *Cinematog* A. Gibory and Eli Lotar; *Art dir* Lou Bonin, modifying the sets that Lucien Aguettand had created for *La Merveilleuse Journée; Music* Maurice Jaubert; *Sound* Louis Bogé; *Edit* Louis Chavance; *Act* Gildès, J.-P. Dreyfus (who for strategic reasons became J.-P. Le Chanois during the war), Étienne Decroux, Jacques-Bernard Brunius, Marcel Duhamel, Jacques Prévert, Lou Bonin, Guy Decomble, D. Gilbert, Louis Chavance, and Julien Carette (Clovis).

This anarchic comedy has become a cult film, which alone would justify its inclusion. The first film scripted by Jacques Prévert, and directed by his elder brother, Pierre, it was made on the cheap in the sets of a more conventional film during downtime and at night, before the sets were dismantled. It is doubtful, therefore, whether it ever had a budget, and its nominal producer rapidly disowned it (though probably not as its supporters would like to think because it was too subversive). Jacques wrote it in a week, and his brother shot it in a week, plus one day on exteriors. It looks like it. Everything about it is excessive and clumsy, reminiscent of a student prank, which is largely what it was. The music is ostentatious, the acting can best be described as comic expressionist, and the characters are all grotesques—lugubrious, robotic, somnambulistic, or manic. The plot, such as it is, involves the courting of a millionaire's daughter, but the timid man she chooses does not meet the approval of her father, who is bored and wants to be amused. A mad hatter who steals hats and sells them back to their rightful owners advises the suitor to kidnap the millionaire's son and ransom him in return for the daughter, but by mistake he kidnaps the millionaire himself. Fortunately Clovis, the hatter's assistant (played by Julien Carette), is able to amuse the millionaire, who consequently refuses to be ransomed. Chloroformed and rescued by force, he will bestow his daughter (and his son as a bonus) on anyone who can bring him Clovis.

Aspiring to emulate the quick-fire gags of American comedies, the film has neither the pace nor the precision to succeed. It flopped despite the attempts of some journalist friends to promote it by likening it to Mack Sennett, the Marx brothers, and Max Linder (it had a brief release in New York). André Brunelin (and later René Prédal) makes a good case for several buried references to right-wing figures of the time who are now largely forgotten; but its main interest today is not so much the strained satirical humor as the recurrent mocking of conventional establishment figures—the millionaire, the suitors, and a policeman who helpfully interprets a plan of the millionaire's apartment for the kidnappers.[90] Here we can see in retrospect the beginnings of that malicious revolutionary verve that Prévert was to bring to all of his later antiestablishment films—seven with Marcel Carné including *Drôle de drame* (#66), *Quai des brumes* (#78), *Le Jour se lève* (#94), *Les Visiteurs du soir*, and *Les Enfants du paradis; Remorques* (#100) and *Lumière d'été* with Jean Grémillon; and *Le Crime de Monsieur Lange* (#46) with Jean Renoir, not to mention two equally fine but less well-known works with Christian-Jaque (see #76). Throughout them, he championed the worker, the poor, the oppressed, and the outsider against the self-righteous forces of authority.

90. In *Cinéma 59*, no. 41, and Prédal, *La Société française à travers le cinéma*, 190–192.

Lazy, shiftless and brilliant, Prévert could usually be found in le Dôme, chez Lipp, or in his favorite café, "Les Deux Magots," "headquarters of heretical communists, of filmmakers resistant to everything commercial (and) of dissident surrealists."[91] From 1925 onward, he lived amid a shifting population of artists, actors, and writers—Yves Tanguy, Robert Desnos, Louis Aragon, André Breton, Georges Sadoul, Raymond Queneau, Maurice Baquet, Jean Tissier, Georges Bataille, Michel Leiris, and many others, earning a crust by taking bit parts in films and composing cinematic advertisements for clients of the Damour agency. Denise Batcheff (later Denise Tual) has described the riotous activities of the "Lacoudèmes" that the Prévert brothers formed with Tchimoukow (as Lou Bonin called himself), Pierre Batcheff, and her during these years.[92] Members of these groups were, if not anarchist, then openly communist, especially after 1930 when the split between surrealists and communists forced them to choose. As noted earlier, Prévert and his friends thereafter formed yet another, more libertarian group whose political activism initially took the form of street theater. From 1929, as the Prémices Group, then from 1933 as the Groupe Octobre, they brought a running commentary on contemporary politics to the streets of Paris. Their performances, involving sketches, mimes, chanted choruses, poems, and songs, were written by Prévert in a few hours, rehearsed overnight, then taken around to union meetings, cafés, schools, workshops, factories, and occasionally even conventional stages. The groups included Jacques-Bernard Brunius, Jean-Paul Dreyfus, Yves Allégret, Raymond Bussières, Lou Tchimoukow, and Louis Chavance, as well as Paul Grimault, soon to be famous as an animator.[93]

The general orientation of these pieces was provocative, even iconoclastic—antimilitarist, antiracist, anticapitalist, satirical, and parodic—and their target was the establishment: admirals, generals, capitalists, priests, and cardinals. They took several of their pieces, notably Prévert's montage-review *La Bataille de Fontenay*, to the Theatrical Olympics held in Moscow in 1933, and won first prize. This exhilarating political activism was to come to a head during the 1935–1936 crisis, which saw riots, strikes, and ultimately the election of the left-wing Popular Front under Léon Blum. All of Prévert's most famous film scripts were to be written in the decade following this crisis, and drew on it and its aftermath. *L'Affaire est dans le sac*, which had been made early in this turbulent decade and

91. Roger Leenhardt in *Premier Plan*, nos. 22–23–24, 171. See also *Esprit*, no. 38, November 1935.

92. Tual, *Au cœur du temps*, 108–143.

93. For more details, see Crisp, *Classic French Cinema*, 180–182, and Rachline, *Jacques Prévert*, 71–91.

in the shadow of the Depression, was banned by the censors. In this it foreshadowed innumerable problems that Prévert was to have with authorities both political and financial. The list of scripts that he produced for Grémillon, Carné, and Marc Allégret that never saw the light is depressingly long. As he said in *Spectacles,* "When truth is not free, one's freedom is not true: today's truths are those of the police."[94]

For Pierre Prévert, the failure of this film was to prove catastrophic, condemning him to continue his long series of assistant director roles under Renoir, Carné, Marc Allégret, Robert Siodmak, Richard Pottier, and René Sti. Only during the war was he able to direct a second film in his own right, to a script by Jacques originally written in 1932—*Adieu Léonard* (1943)—while his third and last, *Voyage-Surprise (Magical Mystery Tour),* the transcription of an operetta, had to wait until 1946. That the venom of the Prévert brothers had not been diluted can be recognized from the fact that this final film contains a scene in which a preacher is tricked into delivering a sermon-advertisement including the lines, "In that time did Jesus pass through Samaria on his way to Jerusalem on a Magical Mystery Tour . . . and he said to his disciples, 'I say unto you, since one must pass through this Valley of Tears nothing helps like a Magical Mystery Tour.'" The Catholic Church duly banned the faithful from seeing that film as well.

94. *Premier Plan,* no. 14, 12.

PART II

The Great Depression

22. Quatorze juillet

Bastille Day (The Fourteenth of July)
France-Germany, 1933, 97 min, b&w

Dir and Scr René Clair; *Asst dir* Albert Valentin; *Prod* Tobis; *Cinematog* Georges Périnal; *Music* Maurice Jaubert, André Gailhard, and Jean Grémillon; *Art dir* Lazare Meerson; *Sound* Hermann Storr; *Edit* René le Hénaff; *Act* Annabella (Anna), Pola Illéry (Pola), Georges Rigaud (Jean), Raymond Cordy (Raymond), Thomy Bourdelle (Fernand), Paul Olivier (Monsieur Imaque), Aimos (Charles), Jane Pierson, Maximilienne, and Odette Talazac.

Whether because of the relative financial failure of *À nous la liberté* (#12) or because, as René Clair himself claimed, after two films in which fantasy reigned, he wished to return to the Parisian world of which he was so fond, *Quatorze juillet* has neither the ideological substratum of *À nous* nor the reckless fantasy of *Le Million* (#9), but resembles to a remarkable extent his first sound film, *Sous les toits de Paris* (#2).[1] In it we find again the "little people" of Paris, the street scenes where those people meet and interact, the class contrasts that promote them as more human than the bourgeoisie and less ridiculous than the effete upper class, and the music that expresses their vitality and sentimentality. And again we find a lack of depth in all characters, such that the narrative lacks motivation and drive, depending largely on chance encounters and patterns of repetition and variation.

Anna, a flower-seller, and Jean, a taxi-driver, live opposite one another. They meet during preparatory celebrations for the French national day; are separated when Jean's previous girlfriend, a sensual foreigner, returns and reseduces Jean, introducing him to an unsavory world of pickpockets and thieves; and are finally reunited when his taxi, swerving to avoid running over someone, runs (gently) into her flower-cart. This is a graceful romantic comedy, with little substantive thematic material. Despite the fact that the whole film takes place within

---

1. Leprohon, *Présences contemporaines*, 86.

forty-eight hours around the French national day, there is no hint of nationalist themes. Despite the presence of crooks who lead the hero astray, there is no hint of anxiety about criminality. Despite the losses and betrayals, there is no hint of psychodrama. The film is not played for intensity or for audience identification, but for delight—a gamelike spectacle.

One aspect of the film that sets it apart in Clair's output is the focus on female characters rather than male. At the center of most of his films is male friendship, threatened or disrupted by women. Here the male lead has none of the sentimentalizing attributes of Clair's other male leads: without vitality or musical talent, he has only his rugged good looks to justify his role. Where Clair's women are usually poorly chosen and badly scripted, Anna the flower girl, as played by Annabella, brings a rare moment of credible characterization to the film. Her opposite number, the foreign vamp with connections to the underworld, is effective as a narrative role but overwhelmed by the clichés in which she is enmeshed. Annabella manages, however, to overcome an analogous web of clichés and engage credibly with the kids whose sentimental presence guarantees her humanity. Aimos, as one of the two crooks (small and sprightly by contrast with the heavy, somber one), also succeeds in bringing a little life to the narrative.[2]

It is perhaps an exaggeration to say that the film is without thematic interest, since rudimentary class priorities make themselves felt: the bourgeois family appears at intervals to be duly shocked by whatever the central characters are doing, and there is a delightful role for Paul Olivier as an elegant, wealthy drunk at an effete dance, which contrasts with the lower-class celebrations in the street. When he reappears with a gun (indeed with two, as it turns out) in a later scene and comically terrorizes the dance-room, he serves to provide Anna with that essential 1930s narrative mechanism, arbitrarily acquired wealth, which allows her to buy a flower-cart and thus sets up the final resolution.

Clair himself felt that *Quatorze juillet* was, in some ways, "the most remarkable success of our team, but it lacked action. It contains good gags, but ingenious details don't make a good film, and the subject matter is too tenuous."[3] The gags mostly relate to objects, which in default of character are what hold the narrative together. Hats are exchanged, umbrellas are exchanged; recurrent unmotivated appearances of the crooks, the elegant gentleman and taxis, the mechanical piano triggered accidentally or deliberately, and rain showers that interrupt play pattern the narrative. Sound matches and image matches link se-

2. Charensol and Régent, *Un maître de cinéma*, 132–133, 158–159.
3. Ibid., 131.

quences that might otherwise seem arbitrarily juxtaposed. In particular, the recurrence of the wonderful theme song in its various versions provides a spurious unity for the film. The music had been suggested by Jean Grémillon and elaborated by Maurice Jaubert, and has become one of the great sentimental celebrations of Paris:

Á Paris dans chaque faubourg	In Paris, in every suburb
Le soleil de chaque journée	Each day's sunshine
Fait en quelques destinées	Causes in certain lives
Éclore un rêve d'amour	A dream of love to bloom
À Paris quand le jour se lève	In Paris when day dawns
À Paris dans chaque faubourg	In Paris, in every suburb
À vingt ans on fait des rêves	At twenty you dream away
Tout est couleur d'amour.	Everything has the color of love.

It is easy to be critical of this film for its lack of ambition, but it is redeemed by its gentle, slightly dreamy mood, and by its sporadic outbursts of noise and good humor. Disdained by many critics at the time of its release, it was markedly more popular than *À nous la liberté* with Parisian audiences. Unable to bring to a satisfactory conclusion his next scenario for Tobis, Clair was commissioned by Natan to complete another of his scenarios—*Le Dernier Milliardaire*—which evolved into a comic, ideological critique of dictatorship along the lines of *À nous* but proved an embarrassing flop. Clair retreated to Britain, then to the United States, not returning to France until the war's end, when he made the wildly successful *Le Silence est d'or.*

23. *L'Homme à l'Hispano*

(*The Man with the Hispano*)
France, 1933, 95 min, b&w

Scr and Dir Jean Epstein, from the novel by Pierre Frondale; *Prod* Vandal and Delac; *Cinematog* Armand Thirard; *Music* Jean Wiener; *Art dir* Georges Wakhévitch; *Sound* Marcel Courmes; *Edit* Marthe Poncin; *Act* Jean Murat (Georges Dewalter), Marie Bell (Stéphane, Lady Oswill), Joan Helda (Madame Deléone), Blanche Beaume (governess), George Grossmith (Lord Oswill), Gaston Mauger (Monsieur Deléone), and Louis Gauthier (Maître Montnormand).

This is a film that deserves to be better known, first because it is perhaps the only sound film to have survived by Jean Epstein, one of the great silent and documentary filmmakers, but also because it deploys both sound and image with precision and delicacy, and uses one of the most popular stars of the day against the grain.

Jean Murat was already a popular star in the late 1920s; he was one of the three men in 1930 to be voted by readers of *Cinémonde* into the Académie du Cinéma Français (which never actually eventuated), and he was rated second after Henri Garat in 1933. By 1936–1937, however, Murat was near the bottom of the twenty most popular male stars. His image was as an active sporty romantic hero; he had been a pilot during World War I, and appeared in several war films where he played a role as an officer or a spy, a role analogous to that of James Bond thirty years later. He was thus older than many leading stars of the day, more substantial and forceful than them—one of that group of substantial, mature leading men that included Jean Gabin, Charles Vanel, Harry Baur, and Pierre Renoir. In romantic comedies, he was accustomed to winning the heart of the heroine effortlessly. He had just partnered Annabella in a romantic musical, *Paris-Méditerranée* (1931, released 21 February 1932), where, as the English Lord Kingstonly, he was mistaken by a salesgirl for the impoverished fellow who was to take her to the Riviera in a car won in a lottery. He happily accepts this new identity in order to enjoy the company of the attractive girl, but has difficulty explaining away the luxurious lifestyle that he cannot quite bring himself to renounce. Finally his lordly status is revealed to her, and her virtues have become apparent to him. They live happily ever after.

L'Homme à L'Hispano plays resolutely against this predecessor, paralleling but reversing various plot elements. This time it is Murat who plays an impoverished gentleman, Georges Dewalter, asked by a friend to drive his Hispano to Biarritz. In this borrowed glory, he encounters Lady Oswill, who assumes him to be one of their elegant set and falls in love with him. He happily maintains the fiction of his wealthy status and exhausts his meager funds living the feckless, elegant life of her circle. Her husband, Lord Oswill, is an extraordinary character, at once ridiculous and sinister, who cynically asserts that love is an illusion and that no one really cares for anyone else. He leaves his wife free to flirt, until the point when it seems as if her and Dewalter's passion might disprove his theories. He uncovers the truth of Dewalter's origins, and at a ball to celebrate Lady Oswill's birthday, threatens to denounce him publicly if he does not quit Lady Oswill definitively. Dewalter agrees, provided the husband will allow her to remain ignorant of his fiction, and organizes a suicide to look like an accident. As she dances gaily on in the ballroom, Dewalter's friend prepares to break the news to her that "her rich lover" has died in a terrible accident. Beginning as a bouncy comedy, with jaunty music and a piquant situation, the film ends as an anguished drama. This ultimate contrast of public gaiety and private tragedy was, as we have already seen, a commonplace of the decade's films, and this ending is not the only element that links it to *La Règle du jeu* (#95).

In some ways, the narrative is banal, involving the standard 1930s theme of borrowed plumage, whether dress or appurtenances, which delude others into thinking one is something other than what one is, and which calls into question the validity and sincerity of sentiments thus generated. But despite its banality, the film is elevated by the attention given to the esthetics of the visual image and the unusually elaborate soundtrack. In his silent films, Epstein had been renowned for the attention he paid to the form and texture of the image. This is apparent throughout *L'Homme à l'Hispano*, both the framing and shaping of each shot and the gradation of tone within the image making a delight of quite ordinary material. Pierre Leprohon quotes Epstein as saying that both this and his other 1933 film, *La Chatelaine du Liban*, were films made to order, and that his main pleasure was in finding small ways to make them his own: "For the rest— all that is not and cannot be one's own—one must depend on professional competence. . . . An architect would not necessarily want to live in the houses that his clients commission."[4] Thus even clichés about romantic encounters, involving moonlight on the water and curling waves, achieve an improbable grandeur. Soft focus and halo effects romanticize Lady Oswill's property in the Landes, and together with the glitter and flash of paintwork, make a central character of the Hispano itself.

The other mark of Epstein's filmmaking to survive from the 1920s is the love of montage. Several such sequences describe the trip to and arrival in Biarritz, but the most spectacular instance calls upon all the technical resources of the day to figure a romantic drive in the country—for several minutes, overlapping and superimposed images blend into kaleidoscopic multiple images until the Hispano seems to be sailing through the sky. All the formal elements of a car's construction further pattern the visual, which is accompanied by a sort of car symphony constructed of a combination of car noises and orchestral sound, the whole leading up to a moment when the two leads embrace. Jean Wiener, the composer who wrote the music for the film, had been an associate of the group of composers commonly known as "the Six"; he was also an entrepreneur who frequently put on concerts of recent works by Igor Stravinsky, Sergei Prokofiev, Alban Berg, and Anton Webern, and who, with Darius Milhaud and Jean Cocteau, opened around 1920 the club called La Gaya, and later Le Boeuf sur le Toit. Regular attendees at these clubs included Sergei Diaghilev and Pablo Picasso, Mistinguett and Maurice Chevalier, Raymond Radiguet, Georges Auric, and Fer-

---

4. Leprohon, *Jean Epstein*, 57.

nand Léger. As Carlos Rim recalled, "Rubinstein would stop in after a concert to play us some Chopin."[5] Wiener had often accompanied silent films, but this was his first commissioned film score, and it is a masterpiece. Sometimes atmospheric, sometimes insistently foregrounded, sometimes an implicitly diegetic piano or chamber group in the various public spaces and occasions, it does a lot of work in carrying and integrating the narrative.

Even the quality of the ambient sound in the film is unforgettable, its brittle clarity providing Robert Altman-like complexity and credibility to the public occasions. And the film's ending, intentionally or not, leaves open the possibility that Dewalter has faked both the accident and his suicide, and survived to depart for Senegal as he had initially intended.

24. *Théodore et Cie*

(*Theodor and Co*)
France, 1933, 97 min, b&w

Dir Pière Colombier; *Prod* Pathé-Natan; *Scr* René Pujol, from the play by Robert Armont and Nicolas Nancey; *Cinematog* Victor Armenise; *Music* Jacques Dallin and Jane Bos; *Art dir* Jacques Colombier; *Sound* Robert Teisseire; *Edit* Léonard Moguy; *Act* Alice Field (Gaby/Adrienne), Germaine Auger (Loulou), Raimu (Clodomir), Albert Préjean (Théodore), Pierre Alcover (Chénerol), Charles Redgie (Malvoisier), Félix Oudart (the senator), Georges Morton (the barman), Pierre Piérade, Léon Larive, Louis Pré Jr., Rip, and Charles Camus.

Itself an enjoyable film, *Théodore et Cie* here represents a whole genre of films exuding popular vitality that was consistently the most popular with French audiences between 1930 and 1933, though the bulk of them have unfortunately not survived. One of these—*Le Roi des resquilleurs* (#5)—was the stunning success of the 1930–1931 season, with over a million spectators in Paris alone. It has only survived in a 1945 remake, and its two most popular sequels seem also to have disappeared. In the same season, the transcription of a Marcel Achard comedy, *Jean de la Lune,* with René Lefebvre and Michel Simon, attracted nearly 800,000 spectators, making it the second most popular film of the year. Taking into account the wild popular success of the military vaudevilles of Bach and others, and the two comedies that Henry Wulschleger filmed with Bach (*L'Affaire Blaireau,* 1932, 350,000 viewers; *Bach millionaire,* 1933, 320,000), one can begin to appreciate the

5. Rim, *Le Grenier d'harlequin,* 150. See also Crisp, *Genre, Myth and Convention,* 150.

scale of profits that certain production companies were deriving from these comic genres. *Théodore et Cie,* by Pière Colombier and René Pujol from a recent play, was in turn the most popular film of the 1932–1933 season, with some 830,000 spectators in Paris alone. A slightly longer summary of the narrative helps to explain why.

It starts slowly, establishing Théodore (Albert Préjean) and Clodomir (Raimu) as down on their luck because of a misunderstanding at the races, and unable to pay their bills. With the help of Clodomir disguised as a police officer, Théodore cons his rich Uncle Chénerol out of 1,000 francs. Then it emerges that Chénerol's young wife, Aunt Adrienne, is having an affair with a wealthy lover. When the uncle discovers a provocative photo of her, he begins to suspect. Ever a defender of other con artists, Théodore proposes to his uncle that it is not his aunt but a showgirl who just happens to bear a remarkable resemblance to Aunt Adrienne. When the uncle goes to check the showgirl's address, Clodomir, now disguised as the house butler, presents Chénerol to (his own wife) Adrienne, now dressed as Gaby Follette, showgirl and tart. The uncle is rather attracted to this Gaby, who flirts outrageously with him. Théodore traps in the lift the senator who actually owns this flat and who returns inopportunely, and cons his uncle into believing that Aunt Adrienne has arrived, raging jealous. The uncle hides, and the aunt changes back from Gaby to Adrienne and stages a dramatic entrance. Her husband goes off with her, promising Théodore he will apologize to Gaby that night at the theater, where he has been led to believe she is performing.

That evening, the aunt, once again as Gaby, is in a hastily arranged star's loge at the theater. Apologetic, Uncle Chénerol bribes Clodomir, now disguised as a fire officer (and smoking furiously), to take a message to Gaby and (still not realizing she is his wife) argues that she should continue her affair with the lover. She has to appear on stage and sing but cannot, so she mimes to Théodore's falsetto. Unfortunately, his voice breaks in mid-song, but she saves the day by performing a raunchy belly dance, which the audience loves. Uncle goes to meet her backstage but finds Clodomir now disguised as a pantomime dame and claiming to be Gaby's old mother, Charlotte. Chénerol bribes her to let him sleep with Gaby, who finds the prospect of adultery with her own husband sufficiently intriguing to accept. But at the crucial moment, Théodore and the aunt's lover burst in on them, the latter claiming to be jealous of Chénerol's attentions to "his" Gaby. A duel must be fought.

The uncle takes Gaby to the Café de Paris, and she realizes that he has a permanent rendezvous there for his mistresses. Théodore arrives to announce that "the Emir" (don't ask) wishes to meet Chénerol, but the Emir turns out, of course, to be Clodomir, grotesquely disguised and speaking gobbledygook. He indicates that he wants Gaby, and she convinces Chénerol that they must sacrifice their love to a higher political cause. Clodomir takes her off, giving Chénerol a medal as he goes. In the climactic duel scene, Adrienne, now once more the aunt, pretends jealousy that her husband, and incidentally her lover, are fighting over a tart. All make up and depart amicably.

Two fundamental patterns underlie the plot: first, a working-class version of the vaudeville/boulevard comedy plot in which the man has a bit on the side while his wife cuckolds him with everyone in sight, preferably (in a boulevard comedy) men with titles; and second, the classic double identity plot in which Alice Field here plays two diametrically contrasting women, one respectable and the other a tart and belly dancer. Théodore and Clodomir are, respectively, the supreme con artist who can con anyone out of anything or make anyone believe anything, and the shape-changer who turns up successively as a police officer, butler, fire officer, pantomime dame, and the Emir. These plot elements return time and again in the comedies of the 1930s. The prankster figure is always desperately short of money and lower class (but never "working" class, since the mere thought of actually *working* to earn money is laughable). A larrikin, living by his wits, he frequents popular cultural venues (the races, boxing matches, football matches, cycling rallies, casinos, shows, and nightclubs) where easy money might be made. He may inherit, win, or lose abrupt fortunes—easy come, easy go—but despises those who seek his favor when wealthy. He is far from scrupulous about property and morality, nicking food or objects, lying, and slipping into events without paying. The line between the legal and the illegal is never clearly drawn in working-class films of the 1930s. Chance is not always on his side—indeed it seems to delight in thwarting him to see what tricks he will devise to circumvent it—but he always comes out buoyant as ever, perhaps even, as in *Bouboule 1er, roi nègre*, king of Senegal. However outrageous the activities of the amiable rogue(s) in these popular farces, we can safely identify with them since there is no one honorable among those they do down.

There is a certain resemblance between these films and the series directed by René Clair in the same years: the milieu and the cast are similar, though the raucous vulgarity is absent from Clair. It is interesting that Clair's last French film, *Le Dernier Milliardaire* (1934), was a box office disappointment, and that the present genre also began to fade in popular esteem after 1933.

25. Zéro de conduite

(*Nought for Behavior*)
France, 1933, 42 min (originally), b&w

Dir and Scr Jean Vigo; *Asst dir* Albert Riéra, Henri Storck, and Pierre Merle; *Prod* Jacques-Louis Nounez and Gaumont Franco Film Aubert; *Cinematog* Boris

Kaufman; *Art dir* Vigo, Storck, and Kaufman; *Music* Maurice Jaubert; *Sound* Royné and Bocquel; *Edit* Vigo; *Act* Louis Lefèvre (Caussat), Gérard de Bedarieux (Tabard), Gilbert Pruchon (Colin), Constantin Goldstein-Kehler (Bruel), Jean Dasté (Huguet, the teacher), Robert le Flon (Parrain, the monitor, aka Pète-Sec), Delphin (headmaster), and Blanchar (head monitor, aka Bec-de-Gaz).

Jean Vigo's father, Eugène Bonaventure de Vigo, an editor of anarchist and socialist newspapers, was frequently imprisoned for his outspoken articles. He adopted the pseudonym Almereyda (anagram of "y a la merde"/"it's all shit") and was finally imprisoned for treason in Fresnes, where in 1917 he was found strangled, almost certainly at the behest of the police or of politicians.[6] Jean Vigo himself is a classic instance of the doomed romantic artist: wracked by tuberculosis from the age of twenty-one, he was repeatedly thwarted in his creative endeavors by producers and by the censors, and died at the age of twenty-nine within a month of the release of his one feature film, *L'Atalante* (#32), which had been totally destroyed by the producers.

It is not hard to see how the death of his father, whose name he subsequently spent some years trying to clear, might have soured him toward authority and the existing establishment. His early diaries show a scorn for police, the military, and the church. His first short film, *À propos de Nice,* is an aggressive satire of the Côte d'Azur bourgeoisie. In his presentation of that film, he asserted the need for a social cinema that

> avoided technique for its own sake. . . . This social documentary is no ordinary documentary or weekly news review, because of the point of view that its author adopts. It demands that the spectator agree with it or reject it. . . . It aims to open eyes. . . . By the way it presents Nice, . . . it aims to pass judgment on a certain way of life. [It shows] the last convulsions of a society so embarrassingly unselfaware that it makes you sick, and pushes you irresistibly towards revolutionary action.[7]

Filmed neutrally, largely with a hidden camera, it depends on editing to construct Nice's "respectable" society as grotesque. An affected woman is juxtaposed with an ostrich, and soldiers on parade with a line of graves in a cemetery, while

6. See Salès-Gomès, *Jean Vigo,* for an account of this and, indeed, of the whole of Vigo's life and work.

7. See *Premier Plan,* no. 19, 40–50, and *Positif,* no. 7.

fast motion makes a mockery of a funeral parade. "This film is based on a double opposition . . . : Nice, town of the idle rich / Nice, town of the worker; and Abnormal / Normal. Mostly the 'abnormal' effects are reserved for the representation of the idle rich, [while the camera] becomes 'normal' when describing the working class."[8] The work is heavily influenced by Bertolt Brecht, by the modernist movements, and by Soviet montage theory, and film critic Jean-Georges Auriol found that the social satire was somewhat undercut by the insistent formalist editing of banal similarities and contrasts.

Vigo proposed several further short films but could not get backing, which is a shame, because the scenarios are wonderfully outrageous. Made three years later, *Zéro de conduite,* Vigo's first fictional work, is more autobiographical but clumsy to the point of incompetence. If it has been enthusiastically praised—indeed become a cult film—it is not remotely because of narrative coherence, but rather because it is seen as the ultimate anarchist gesture of scorn both for cinematic conventions and for all forms of authority.[9] Loosely based on his own and his father's childhood experiences (not to mention certain literary models), it was filmed without any preexisting formal scenario, and the film suffers as a result of this improvisation. Like Vigo's first film, it presents two worlds—that of the respectable authorities and that of the rebellious, then revolutionary, schoolchildren. It deals with a revolt in a boys' school that culminates in the disruption of a ceremonial speech day. The general opposition of children and teachers stands as a metonym for the wider society, evoking surrealist notions of social repression and the urgent need for a liberating revolution that will destroy the existing authoritarian structure. The headmaster is ridiculed as a bearded dwarf; the teachers are rocklike and insensitive, or furtive and malicious; a fire chief and other authority figures are ridiculed by being posed among grotesquely dressed side-show figures; the curate is mistaken for a woman; and the school surveillant, ridiculed as a sneak and a spy, is finally tied to his bed and clownishly "crucified" by the boys. To all these dignitaries the film says, like the effeminate boy pushed too far, "Je vous dis *Merde*" ("Fuck the lot of you"—the headline of one of Almereyda's articles). The only adult who comes out well is Huguet, the young staff member who can imitate Charlie Chaplin to perfection.

Four or five minutes of the film are worthy of its surrealist heritage, notably the introductory train journey as the boys return from holidays and the (very brief) pillow fight in slow motion, with music played backward then reversed

8. Borde et al., *Deuxième cinécure,* 25.
9. See, for instance, Henri Agel in *Premier Plan,* no. 19, 74.

when recorded. Indeed, whenever it occurs, Maurice Jaubert's music "saves" the relevant scene. Before it was sonorized with the music, it had been screened for the crew, who were reportedly dismayed by its incoherence: "lack of clarity, lack of action, inadequate linking shots, lack of rhythm, absence of découpage, lousy acting. In a word, amateurism."[10] It is possible to feel that this is still the case, for the greater part of the film, though recent commentators are more indulgent.

Like all the other experimental films from these years, it was funded by a patron—Jacques-Louis Nounez, a businessman who had seen a gap in the mid-length film market, and to whom Vigo had been introduced by a mutual friend (René Lefebvre). The funding was, however, inadequate, and the studio hire too brief, requiring Vigo to omit several key scenes and accept clumsy takes of several others. His failing health reduced the shooting time even further, so the resulting film bore little resemblance to the original concept, and several elements of the surviving scenes become incomprehensible without those omitted. Moreover, the film we see today is even more incomplete than that first screened. Presented to an invited public in April 1933, it was strongly supported by a few friends, passed over in silence by most critics, and viciously attacked by Catholic reviewers. *La Cinématographie française* said, "This film is unclassifiable: it vainly tries to ridiculize and stigmatize colleges and educational systems, it lacks visual beauty, has inexcusable technical imperfections, and shots so gray and badly composed they seem the work of an apprentice. The sound is confused, and the actors give an impression of amateurism. Merits a large Zero, full stop."[11] The Catholic daily *Choisir* said of it, "Realistic observations, subversive ideas and overall an unpleasant impression," while its colleague, *L'Omnium cinématographique*, was more severe: "This is the work of an obsessive maniac expressing his disturbed thoughts. Eroticism, moreover, and even scatology. . . . Totally lacking in delicacy of expression and poetic visuals. It is doubtful whether our censors will allow this film to be screened."[12] They were correct. It was banned in August, notionally at the request of the association of heads of families (Pères de Famille Organisés) but more likely on direct orders from the government.[13] Originally intended to accompany *La Maternelle* (#26), it was not screened commercially until released with André Malraux's *Espoir* in 1945, when it inaugurated the rediscovery of Vigo.

10. Salès-Gomès, *Jean Vigo*, 134, 154.
11. *La Cinématographie française*, 15 April 1933.
12. Quoted in Salès-Gomès, *Jean Vigo*, 157.
13. See Ibid., 157–160.

26. La Maternelle

(The Kindergarten)
France, 1933, 100 min, b&w

Dir and Scr Jean Benoit-Lévy and Marie Epstein, from the novel by Léon Frapié; *Prod* Benoit-Lévy; *Cinematog* Georges Asselin; *Music* Édouard Flament; *Art dir* Robert Bassi; *Sound* Jean Dubois; *Act* Madeleine Renaud (Rose), Mady Berry (Madame Paulin), Henri Debain (Dr. Libois), Alice Tissot (Directress), Edmond van Daele (Old Paulin), Sylvette Fillacier (La Mère Cœuret), Alex Bernet (Rector), Paulette Élambert (Marie Cœuret), Jany Delille (singer), and Aman Maître (Monsieur Antoine).

Marie Epstein was the sister of the avant-garde filmmaker Jean Epstein (see #22), who had collaborated for a while with Jean Benoit-Lévy. When her brother had to break off that collaboration, Marie "inherited" it and worked with Benoit-Lévy on a series of socially engaged ("humanist, progressive and leftist") films of which *La Maternelle* was the most influential.[14] Benoit-Lévy had established a production company called Films d'Enseignement et d'Éducation, with an overtly militant purpose. For him, "every film had to have a social utility, teach the spectator something, develop 'healthy' ideas."[15] "There still exist," he said, "morally unacceptable instances of social distress which we intend to translate in *La Maternelle* through 'slices of life.' Yes, it is life itself that we will try to reproduce on the screen, by evoking as vividly as possible the social role of the kindergarten."[16] Most of the films he had made thus far had been short documentaries, explicitly educational and even propagandist, often for various government ministries, together with two longer fiction films. This was the first of a number of sound features that he and Marie Epstein made during the decade.

The suffering of poverty-stricken children was a recurrent theme in their work, and in this case, a principal aim was to demonstrate the supreme importance of maternal love in early childhood. The novel on which they based the film was described by its author as aiming for "a more Equally-Distributed HAPPINESS." It concerns a middle-class woman abandoned by her heartless lover and fallen on hard times who takes a job as a kindergarten assistant ("kindergarten" is translated as *école maternelle* in French). She is shocked to discover

---

14. Andrew and Ungar, *Popular Front Paris and the Politics of Culture*, 324.
15. See Fonds Jean et Marie Epstein, 181 B40, Bibliothèque du Film Archives, Paris.
16. Andrew, *Mists of Regret*, 203–204. See also Vignaux, *Jean Benoit-Lévy*.

the extent of the suffering of poor children, becomes committed to her charges (particularly to one of her young pupils, who comes from a miserable home and looks on her as a substitute mother), and has to struggle to reconcile her responsibility toward them with a new relationship with the kindergarten doctor. She is, then, torn between two loves, maternal and sexual.

This melodramatic material was potentially explosive (bad mother, thuggish boyfriend, abandoned child, attempted suicide), a problem that several of the decade's socially committed films confronted less successfully. Epstein's and Benoit-Lévy's strategy was to de-dramatize and authenticate the material by the use of documentary techniques. They used slum children from Asnières and Courbevoie, who themselves came from broken homes and whose parents were in some cases drunkards and/or criminals. In *Les Grandes Missions du cinéma*, Benoit-Lévy has left a fascinating account of the lengthy process he engaged in to ensure the children were "uncorrupted" by the affectations of stage acting.[17] The directors spent weeks in the children's school before returning to reconstruct it in the studio—so effectively that critics assumed it was filmed on location. While shooting, the children moved back and forth between the stage schoolroom and a real schoolroom next door. The resulting naturalness of the children's acting was widely admired, especially that of Paulette Élambert, but a potential incongruity was the introduction into this naturalistic context of a well-known actress, Madeleine Renaud, who was therefore asked to interact as spontaneously as possible with the genuine slum children. In film historian Dudley Andrew's opinion, the result of these tensions is "a workable compromise between a kind of stark realism that had been largely effaced from the cinema since the coming of sound and a moving melodrama that could have come straight from Freud's notebooks." Elsewhere he labels it "an attempt to reconcile traditional realism with a corrosive realism that challenges every convention, including those of traditional realism."[18] A parallel problem that Andrew identifies is the tension between a "neutral" documentary style and the use of avant-garde technical practices to evoke the subjectivity (and the unconscious) of the young girl. Possibly influenced by her brother's work, Epstein introduced a variety of strategies to mimic a young girl's traumatized vision and to link internal and external worlds—manipulation of the camera, an obsession with reflective surfaces and windows, superimpositions, foregrounded frames, montage effects, and tilted framing (Dutch tilts).

17. "L'Interprétation," in Benoit-Lévy, *Les Grandes Missions du cinéma*, ch. 10. See also Fescourt, *La Foi et les montagnes*, 402–406.

18. Andrew, *Mists of Regret*, 201.

In several respects, therefore, the film performs a difficult balancing act. On its release, however, critics had no doubts about its supreme virtues—simplicity, truth, naturalness, sincerity. "Never before has the French cinema produced such a profoundly sincere and human work," claimed one review. "A grave and beautiful film which will mark a turning point in the French cinema," said another. And a third commented, "The truest and most moving of films, with an immeasurable social significance." The film was unusual in the early 1930s in achieving an impressive international release, and one American reviewer enthused, "These are real children—dirty, squalid, immensely pathetic; they tug at the heart-strings as no artificial child star from Hollywood possibly could. This is a work of great subtlety and almost unbearable power: a film of extraordinary insight, tenderness and tragic beauty. There ought to be a Noble [sic] Prize for this sort of work."[19]

More recently, Sandy Flitterman-Lewis has revived interest in La Maternelle (and in Marie Epstein's work in general), seeing this as a proto-feminist film subverting the Hollywood model by rewriting point-of-view structures. In Flitterman-Lewis's view, it shifts focus from the typically masculine Oedipal model, in which the male child is rebellious and anarchic, onto the female child's vision, and onto her longing for the mother, with the formation of the couple predicated on the young girl's acceptance of it. What results is a virtual society of women, where the focus is no longer on woman as femme fatale but rather as mother, while it is rather the men who are reduced to simple functions.[20]

Epstein and Benoit-Lévy were prevented from working after 1940 by anti-Semitic laws, but Benoit-Lévy (who had received the Croix de Guerre in World War I) was director of information for the United Nations from 1946 to 1949, and Marie Epstein was director of technical services at the Cinémathèque Française until 1977, living to witness the revival of interest in her work during the 1990s.[21] Jean Vigo's Zéro de conduite (see #25), which was supposed to constitute the first half of the program on the release of La Maternelle, is stylistically remote from this film to say the least, but Epstein and Benoit-Lévy would have been wholly supportive of his call in 1930 at the première of À propos de Nice for a social cinema in which characters must be surprised by the camera, their inner spirit revealed through its purely external manifestations. For all of these directors, the main function of the cinema was to put an entire society on trial.

19. All of these reviews can be found in Fonds Jean et Marie Epstein, 182 B40, Bibliothèque du Film Archives, Paris.

20. Flitterman-Lewis, To Desire Differently; La Maternelle, 184, box 6, Bibliothèque du Film Archives, Paris.

21. See Fonds Jean et Marie Epstein, 137 B31, Bibliothèque du Film Archives, Paris.

27. Cette vieille canaille

(*That Sly Old Fox*)
France, 1933, 90 min, b&w

Dir Anatole Litvak; *Prod* Cipar Films; *Scr* Litvak and Serge Veber, from the play by Fernand Nozière; *Cinematog* Curt Courant; *Music* Georges van Parys; *Art dir* André Andrejew; *Sound* William Sivel; *Act* Harry Baur (Dr. Vauthier), Pierre Blanchar (Jean Trapeau), Alice Field (Hélène), Christiane Dor (Suzanne), Madeleine Geoffroy (Germaine), Paul Azaïs (Jacques), Pierre Stephen (the history professor), and Madeleine Guitty (Hélène's mother).

Anatole Litvak was one of the wave of cosmopolitan filmmakers that moved through European film industries in the years 1920–1935, partly because linguistic limitations did not apply in silent films, but more specifically because of the disruptions caused by the Russian Revolution and later the rise of fascism. Augusto Genina (see #1) had made films in Spain and Italy before directing them in France and Germany (1930–1935), then Austria, Germany, and Italy again. Georg-Wilhelm Pabst (#7 and 16), born in what is now the Czech Republic, made films in Germany, France (1932–1939), and later the United States. Alexander Korda, born in Hungary, made films there, in Germany, and in the United States before working in France (1930–1931) and the United Kingdom. Max Ophüls was assistant to Litvak in Germany before moving to France (1933–1939), then Switzerland and the United States. Robert Siodmak and Arthur Robison, born in the United States, moved early to Germany where they made films until 1930, when they both moved to France until 1935. Fritz Lang, born in Austria, made films in Germany until Joseph Goebbels offered him the job of official filmmaker to the Third Reich; being of Jewish ancestry, he thought the risk too great, and moved to France where he made *Liliom*, reputedly to obtain passage money to the United States. Billy Wilder, also Austrian by birth, made films there and in Germany, and likewise one film in France (*Mauvaise Graine*, 1934) on the way to Mexico and the United States. Consequently, the French cinema between 1930 and 1935 was more cosmopolitan than at any other period.

Most Russian filmmakers who moved to France worked with Albatros Films, but Litvak moved from Russia to Germany in 1923, making films mostly in that country (notably with Pabst) though also in London and occasionally Paris, until 1933 when he moved to France for three years (1933–1936), then Hollywood. His earliest French sound film (excluding a French version of *Nie wieder Liebe*) was *Cœur de Lilas* (1931), a rather fine police thriller in which André Luguet plays a policeman who goes undercover to solve a murder, only to fall in love with the girl who proves to be the guilty party. There is an early role for Jean Gabin as an un-likable thug, and songs for him, for Fernandel, and for Fréhel—the latter one of the greatest of the "realist" singers of the decade. Both visually and aurally, the film is a treat far above and beyond what the storyline deserves, and the tragi-cally ironic ending is extremely moving.

Cette vieille canaille ("canaille" means "scoundrel," and the title might trans-late as "that old bastard," but there is often a hint of admiration in the phrase: "that cunning old bugger," "that sly old fox") revolves around an elderly surgeon whose obsession with a vulgar, raucous fairground girl leads him to "adopt" her, educate her in Pygmalion style, and send packing any admirers who get too close, until finally he has to admit defeat in the face of her attachment to her youthful acrobat boyfriend. Indeed, in the ironic finale, he has to use his unique surgical skills to save her boyfriend's life.

Both in Germany and in France, circuses and fairgrounds were viewed as sites of chaos and disorder in the 1920s and 1930s—or at least of exhilaration, ad-venture, and the extraordinary.[22] The transient population of fairgrounds does not observe conventional rules and proprieties; it is always night-time there, so bustling crowds, looming shadows, shafts of light, and frightening physical monstrosities make them places to avoid or to escape from, threatening sites of passion and sensuality. There is a magnificent long tracking shot early in the film, where Dr. Vauthier, splendidly played by Harry Baur as a solid, impassive, manipulative bourgeois, moves smoothly through the nocturnal fairground in search of his young "victim" while all about him wheels of light and crazy fair-ground stalls cross-dissolve in a confusion of incomprehensible activity. The choice he offers young Hélène—on the one hand, wealth, comfort, and security (but also himself as a staid old partner), and on the other, her current prospects of poverty, drunkenness, and violence (but also young love)—is finally accepted on his terms. Interestingly, there is no indication that Vauthier has sexual intentions toward Hélène: she is an attractive, prestigious companion, his creature, and he enjoys having power over her life. In this he differs from the many other older men who link up with much younger women in films in this and the next decade, where what might start out as a quasi-paternal relationship soon evolves into something distinctly more sexual. This film, then, prefigures the many overtly or implicitly incestuous relationships that constitute one of the most distinctive characteristics of French 1930s cinema.[23] At least eighty (Noël Burch and Genev-iève Sellier estimate three hundred!) such films were made in this decade, treat-

22. See Crisp, *Genre, Myth and Convention*, 167–171.
23. Ibid., 119–130; Burch and Sellier, *La Drôle de guerre des sexes*.

ing the age difference between a man of 50–60 and a woman of 18–25 as the central source of narrative fascination.[24]

A common resolution of this situation was for the older man to have to cede to a younger rival: Hélène finally opts for the acrobat and a circus life. The technical brilliance of the opening sequence is echoed at that point of resolution in an astonishing 3-minute montage of the circus's travels around the world, with the hurrying music hinting at the different countries visited. At the other extreme from such virtuoso effects, the film retains interest nowadays largely for its documentary moments—modes of transport (especially by air), "modern" automatic self-service bars, and the sorts of acts you might have seen (acrobats, magicians, trick cyclists, etc.) on a night out at the variety theater. The final images are among the most magical as, defeated yet triumphant, Dr. Vauthier leaves the operating theater with the nurse who has loved him all along, and strolls away through the arcades of the night streets. A film to treasure.

28. *La Rue sans nom*

(*Street without a Name*)
France, 1934, 82 min (now 78 min), b&w

Dir Pierre Chenal; *Asst dir* Roger Blin and Louis Daquin; *Prod* Les Productions Pellegrin; *Scr* Chenal, Blin, and Marcel Aymé, from the novel by Aymé; *Cinematog* Joseph-Louis Mundwiller; *Music* Paul Devred; *Art dir* Roland Quignon; *Sound* Jacques Hawadier and A. Puff; *Edit* Chenal; *Act* Constant Rémy (Méhoul), Gabriel Gabrio (Finocle), Paul Azaïs (Manu), Enrico Glori (Cruséo), Pola Illéry (Noâ), Dagmar Gérard (La Jimbre), Fréhel (Madame Méhoul), Paule Andral (Louise Johannieu), Robert Le Vigan (Vanoël), Marcel Delaitre (Johannieu), and Pierre Larquey.

This is a typical instance of "the street film," a subgenre inherited from the German cinema of the 1920s (e.g., Karl Grune, *The Street*, 1923; Georg-Wilhelm Pabst, *The Joyless Street*, 1925; Bruno Rahn, *Tragedy of the Street*, 1927).[25] It was to flourish in 1930s France, and the titles of surviving films are indicative of the genre's focus on harsh street life in the poorer quarters of Paris: *Faubourg Montmartre* (1931); *Dans les rues/On the Street* (1933); *La Rue sans nom* (1933); *Jeunesse/Youth* (1934); *Ménilmontant* (1936); *La Rue sans joie/The Joyless Street* (1938); and *L'Enfer des*

24. See Crisp, *Genre, Myth and Convention*, 19–20, 119–130.
25. See Mast, *A Short History of the Movies*, 174, for a concise account of these films.

anges/A Hell for Little Angels (1939). Typically this genre exploited the standard melodramatic conventions of such films as *Les Misérables* and *Les Deux Orphelines* but combined them with a raw realism often labeled "naturalism." The teeming, seething squalor of "the street" rendered all too credible the inevitable corruption of innocent youth that was often a central theme, and aimed to evoke not pity for the vulnerable poor, as in melodramas, but rather a sort of fascinated horror.

Marcel Aymé had published the book on which the film is based in 1931. Pierre Chenal, who had just established his credentials as a director with a first forgettable film, recounts his haste to buy the rights and consult with Aymé on the screenplay.[26] He was delighted when he found an authentically awful alleyway near the Porte de Clichy, in the 17th arrondissement, where he could film it, and which indeed had no apparent name—and no footpaths, just a channel down the middle to drain away the filth chucked from the windows that opened onto it.

In the film, Méhoul, who lives there in disgruntled discontent with his family, is disturbed by the arrival of an old mate, Finocle, who recalls a criminal past and prison years that Méhoul would rather forget; murder and betrayal are both on the cards. Moreover, Finocle brings with him his daughter, Noâ, who generates violent sexual eddies wherever she goes. One of the more honorable lads of the quarter, Cruséo, falls for her, but she is seduced or raped by Méhoul's son on the kitchen table (seduction and rape being here almost indistinguishable). Paralleling all this interpersonal violence, the whole quarter is due for demolition, to the anger and dismay of its residents. Then a neighbor's boy dies of the fever, and Noâ catches it too. Finally, Méhoul and Finocle get carted off to prison, hands clasped in a final reconciliation ("mates" after all), leaving Cruséo to look after Noâ.

Violence, treachery, and malice are all seen as interlinked and due to the grinding poverty that prevails. None of this is aestheticized or prettified: the only saving grace of workers and criminals is, as usual, music. Cruséo plays the accordion and sings a sad love song, while Madame Méhoul is played by that greatest of exponents of the chanson réaliste, Fréhel (who also appears in *Cœur de lilas*, *La Rue sans joie*, and *L'Enfer des anges*, but is best remembered for her appearance in *Pépé le Moko*, #56). Here, music offers the most oblique of escapes from daily violence, but there is a telling moment in the (gratuitously digressive) incident of the young lad's death when Méhoul attempts to distract him by stories of the foreign lands he has seen, promising to take the lad there when he is better. These

26. Chenal, *Souvenirs du cinéaste*, 9–10, 49–58.

evocations of escape to a better land "over there," so frequent in 1930s films, are the more moving the more awful the daily existence of the characters. Nature, of course, is the most common form of escape, and not just in these street films: in *Faubourg Montmartre*, a wonderfully effete poet rescues the victimized girl and takes her to the provinces; in *Dans les rues*, the only tender moment occurs during a stroll by the river; in the relentlessly glum *Jeunesse*, the unemployed man fantasizes about leaving for a new life in the colonies, but when he actually does so, his pregnant girlfriend tries to commit suicide. Even when he finally invites her to follow, she sinks back glumly, uncertain, leaving the ending inconclusive. In *Ménilmontant*, a group of workers find a valuable ring and return it to its rightful owner. She is amazed by their honesty and, like the rich bourgeoisie in *La Maternelle* (#26), is astounded to hear of the condition of poor children in Ménilmontant. She will fund the group to construct a "boys' town." But the project is appropriated by pompous administrators, the workers shouldered aside, their shacks bulldozed to make way for the boys' town, and old Chenille, the initiator of the project, dies agonizingly. "It's inhuman," says one. "Do you really expect people who are well off to be human," says the other. Cynicism prevails, especially about the wealthy.

Perhaps surprisingly, all of these street films did well on release, achieving around 300,000 spectators in Paris. In most cases, this was not due to the initial (exclusive) release in up-market cinemas but to general release in the suburbs. The one exception is the last of the street films, *L'Enfer des anges*, which attracted over 750,000 spectators on release in 1941 and was enormously popular both in exclusive and in general release. But it has to be remembered that few films were being made or released at that time, and occupied Paris had no other sources of entertainment. Nearly all films did exceptionally well during the war. Nevertheless, it was the second most popular film of the 1940–1941 season, and far from standard escapist fare. *La Rue sans nom* itself was well received by both audiences and critics when released in January 1934, and established Chenal as one of the most promising young directors of the time. The reviewer for *La Cinématographie française* spoke of a film "oozing poetic intensity," while describing it as no film for adolescents or families.[27] Michel Gorel's review of the film in *Cinémonde* also spoke of a poetic film—indeed a poetic realist film—revealing

> a world where the sun rarely shines, blotted out by squalor, gut-rot and boredom, by the lugubrious wail of the factory siren. . . . I spoke of "realism" but I also called it "poetic." Because even when dealing

27. *La Cinématographie française*, 6 January, 21 April 1934.

with this harsh brutal subject matter Chenal does not forsake poetry. And the finest scenes in the films are perhaps those in which
characters, worn down little by little, like the stones of their hovels,
strive to escape, some through love, others through wine, adventure, revolt, or again . . . by constructing elaborate fantasy worlds.[28]

29. *La Croisière jaune*

(*The Yellow Expedition*)
France, 1934, 95 min, b&w

Dir André Sauvage; *Prod* Pathé-Natan, then André Citroën; *Cinematog* Georges
Specht and Morizet; *Music* Themes transcribed by Maurice Thiriet, further music
from Claude Delvincourt; *Sound* William-Robert Sivell; *Edit* Sauvage, then Léon
Poirier.

La Croisière jaune was by all accounts the finest feature-length documentary
of the decade. Jean Vigo, Marcel Carné, and others produced ambitious shorter
documentaries, and later in the decade, the threat of war generated a series of
propaganda documentaries. But *La Croisière jaune,* released through standard
commercial channels, was the most widely appreciated of all, screening for fifteen weeks in exclusive release and still being advertised in general release seven
months later as "the film you should on no account miss, the trip you could never
have dreamed of taking." It had been commissioned by André Citroën supposedly to show how the automobile "abolished the cultural, political and geographic
frontiers of the world," but in reality as a spectacular form of publicity for his
firm.[29] At a time when the exotic nature of the mysterious Orient and Africa's
heart of darkness held a particular fascination for French viewers, Citroën saw
the advantage of organizing transcontinental expeditions to demonstrate the endurance and reliability of his vehicles. In 1924, he had sponsored an expedition
through Africa from Oran to Madagascar, which Léon Perrier accompanied, filming native rituals, sorcerers, dances, customs, religions, and races. This had been
screened as a silent feature-length documentary entitled, with unselfconscious
racism, *La Croisière noire (The Black Expedition, Expedition among the Blacks).*
For the (no less racist) "yellow expedition," Pathé-Natan appointed a young
documentarist, André Sauvage, together with a cameraman, a sound recorder,

---

28. *Cinémonde*, October 1933.
29. See Reynolds, *André Citroën,* for an extensive account of the expedition.

and a reporter, to accompany the main body of relatively light-tracked vehicles across Asia. Because the Soviets had refused to allow passage, the expedition was to travel the Silk Road, from Lebanon across Syria, Iraq, Iran, and Afghanistan, then over the Himalayas into Xinjiang. A second group with another cameraman was to leave Tianjin to cross the Gobi Desert and meet up with the main party at Kashgar and accompany them back to Beijing. Altogether the venture took eleven months, from April 1931 to February 1932, and was not surprisingly beset by numerous technical and political problems. Because of a revolution in part of Afghanistan, the main body had to reroute over the Khyber Pass through what is now Pakistan, then travel northward via Gilgit. At one point, the tracked vehicles had to be disassembled and carried on mule-back over a pass; much of their equipment had to be abandoned, and precipitous roads had to be reconstructed to take the remaining vehicles, but they too were finally abandoned. Having taken three months to complete these first 9,000 miles, the primary expedition then took another three months to complete their last 1,300 miles on horseback. The secondary expedition was beset by sandstorms and heat that exploded their petrol cans, and later snowstorms and temperatures of $-30°C$ that inhibited repair-work. Moreover, a misunderstanding with a local warlord who had been promised some of their tracked vehicles led to their being detained for three months until they fortuitously proved useful to him in his war against a group of Muslims. Finally, they met up with the main party at Aksu in Xinjiang and returned with them to Beijing.

Further misadventures befell the scores of rolls of film stock that the expedition brought back. Pathé-Natan was at that time facing a financial crisis, which ultimately led to Natan's bankruptcy, jailing, and death. In October–November 1933, while Sauvage was still editing the material down to a viable commercial length of about 6,500 feet, these financial problems obliged Natan to sell the rights back to André Citroën, who professed himself dissatisfied with progress and appointed Léon Poirier in place of Sauvage. It is difficult to know to what extent the final product was true to Sauvage's intentions, but an outraged account of this "assassination of a work" was published by René Daumel, who blamed Poirier for "censoring, falsifying and interpolating material without the slightest scruple," and thus transforming the documentary into "a work of franco-citroic propaganda." Indeed, when it was released in March 1934, there was no mention of Sauvage's major role in the production. Daumel saw Poirier as "trampling beneath his feet of gilded corruption a man who had dared to undertake in the cinema an honorable job of work."[30]

30. *La Nouvelle Revue française*, May 1934.

Unfortunately, it is hard nowadays to judge the validity of these accusations, since the film itself seems to have disappeared. The last reference that I can find to a screening was in 1944, or perhaps 1965, though Jean-Pierre Jeancolas seems to have viewed a print of it at some time.[31] A useful account is given by Pierre Leprohon in his book on *Exoticism in the Cinema*. Sauvage had clearly made every effort to document the countries and peoples through which the expedition passed, focusing, as was usual when dealing with the exotic, on the typical but also on the weird:

> As the expedition advances the spectator has the impression of penetrating into a hermetic world. . . . You sense through and beyond the images a whole universe looming up that is totally alien to our understanding, to our character, even to our imagination. . . . *La Croisière jaune* gives us an eloquent overview of the enormity of the Asiatic continent, the austere face of Afghanistan, the voluptuous life of the maharajahs, the volatility of China caught between its feudalism and its future, at the edge of the known world.[32]

Jeancolas speaks of

> a mix of information, of brief tableaux, of moments of high emotion. [André Sauvage] films a religious and military ceremony in Tehran, . . . the future Reza Pahlavi, and Highlanders garrisoned in India parading in a tropico-Scottish kit of the weirdest sort; then he becomes fascinated by the powdery light falling obliquely on the souks of Hérat. . . . He is carried away by the fabulous landscapes of the Himalayas, then circles round a Mongol princess who speaks in a deliciously dated French to Pierre Teilhard de Chardin, the ethnologist attached to the expedition.[33]

Unfortunately, this was Sauvage's last film: dispirited by being deprived of control over his film, he quit the cinema forever.

There is some controversy about the sonorization of the film: William-Robert Sivell must have recorded much of the soundtrack on the spot, and Jean-

---

31. Jeancolas, *15 ans d'années trente*, 177–182.
32. Leprohon, *L'Exotisme et le cinéma*, 75–80.
33. Jeancolas, *15 ans d'années trente*, 177–182.

colas insists that this direct sound recording limited Poirier's ability to manipulate Sauvage's material, but Leprohon recounts that the sonorization took place after editing, at least partly based on "musical themes noted on the spot by a member of the expedition and transcribed by Thiriet."[34] Claude Delvincourt was to extract a suite from the orchestral music that he provided for the film, no doubt based on these themes.[35] The initial intention was to produce some twenty-four further (shorter) films from the excess footage, but I can find no record of this ever having been done.

30. *Ces messieurs de la Santé*

(*Those Rascally Bankers*)
France, 1934, 102 min, b&w

Dir Pière Colombier; *Prod* Pathé-Natan; *Scr* Paul Armont and Léopold Marchand, from their play; *Cinematog* Curt Courant; *Music* Jacques Dallin; *Art dir* Jacques Colombier; *Sound* Robert Teisseire; *Edit* Jean Pouzet; *Act* Raimu (Gédéon/Jules Tafard), Lucien Baroux (Amédée), Edwige Feuillère (Fernande), Pauline Carton (Madame Genissier), Yvonne Hébert (Claire), Monique Rolland (Ninon), and Paul Amiot (police commissioner).

The Santé of the title is the prison where the central character, Tafard, a financier, is incarcerated at the beginning and end of the film. There is a nice irony in the word, which means of course both "health" and "asylum" (maison de santé), but is also used in the toast ("your health"), which the police and prison guardians propose to Tafard at the end. This is a story about a financier who has been imprisoned for (unspecified) corruption at the beginning of the film and is living the good life in prison (his "cell" could be mistaken for an up-market apartment), no doubt as a result of further corruption. He escapes, begins afresh as a humble night-watchman in the Genissier family corsetry, and, now calling himself Gédéon, rapidly works his way up to become once again a wheeler-dealer using the corsetry as a cover to trade in arms. He founds a bank but finally returns voluntarily to prison to orchestrate a yet greater coup. The Santé gentlemen of the title, then, are high-flyers for whom the Santé is a second home, a second office, a convenient rest-home in times of stress.

34. Leprohon, *L'Exotisme et le cinéma*, 75–80.
35. See Porcile, *La Musique à l'écran*, 45.

No one watching 1930s films can be in any doubt about the reputation of financiers and bankers. The human embodiment of the "Crise" that had so recently devastated Western society, they were almost universally despised and condemned. A series of famous scandals forms the backdrop to this film—the Oustric case; the Staviski case, which erupted into a bloodbath the month before this film was released; and the Hanau scandal, in which Madame Hanau, an unscrupulous banker, ruined numerous investors who had entrusted her with their life savings. Closer to home, the Gaumont and Pathé-Natan scandals that were to follow in 1934 (the year of this film's release) would transform the face of the French film industry. It is not therefore surprising that the police should remark to Tafard at the beginning of the film that "there are lots of bankers in (the Santé)," and even more delightful that they should apologize to him at the end for being a little officious, because "We have to be careful with all these corrupt businessmen about." That Raimu should play Gédéon/Tafard, first in the 1931 play and now in its film version, is particularly piquant since he himself had lost his life savings in just such a collapse. Yet there is no doubt that, despite both general and specific reasons for detesting financiers, the film manifests a sneaking admiration for Tafard—a certain guilty delight in the way his cunning, his ability to think on his feet, and his knowledge of the levers of finance, power, and human weakness allow him to rise and rise, finally to regain his "rightful" place in control of a business empire. Moreover, everyone else ultimately benefits from his rise. Like all confidence tricksters, by definition he inspires confidence. All the little people that he relieves of their money in an elaborate pyramid scam bless and support him, call him "an honest person in his way," name their children after him, or want to marry him, and the ending constructs him as their savior. Yet most of the film has depicted him as just the reverse—an escaped embezzler gaily conning and manipulating others as we suspect he had done before to earn his initial prison sentence, working at best on the margins of the law and at worst in total disregard of it. He falsifies mineral assays and engages in international arms-trafficking (machine-guns, bombers, . . . a submarine!), which is all "just doing business." As he says himself, he is simply an amoral money-making machine, that is how he gets his kicks, and we are led to believe that there is a natural hierarchy in which quick-witted con-artists such as him will always be able to manipulate the system to come out on top.

To complicate this representation, he explicitly represents "modern" business methods: he takes over a backward family firm, uses aggressive and deceptive publicity, and thinks big. It prospers. But the corruption Tafard generates has wider implications, since his financial dealings are enmeshed with the courts and with the legal system, which (rightly or wrongly) exonerate him of all wrong-doing, and indeed with the state itself through armaments and the state lottery. His final coup is to insist on serving his remaining month in prison so that the stock exchange, which has come to depend on his high-flying deals, will collapse, and he can buy up for a song everything that he does not already own. A similarly ambivalent view of bankers seems to have structured *La Banque Nemo* (1934).

The other topic of central importance for 1930s films that is foregrounded in *Ces messieurs de la Santé* is Jewishness. The negative connotations of Jewish usurers had been particularly apparent in *La Petite Lise* (#6) and *David Golder* (#8), and there is no doubt that the connection between Jewishness and finance was maintained throughout the decade. Greedy creditors and bloodsucking moneylenders tended, especially in the early 1930s, to be clearly stereotyped as Jews. But given the fact that anti-Semitic attitudes were deeply ingrained in French society, and that this prejudice against all those connected to finance was only exacerbated by the effects of the Depression, it is amazing to see how relatively rare and how relatively mild any criticism of Jews was in the rest of the decade.[36] Here, Tafard is not Jewish, but he works through a Jewish bank—Moïse and (Solomon) Duguesclin—since they will understand his financial adventures, and he attracts as his sycophantic assistant a young Jew who watches with delight as Tafard cons more and more money out of the Genissier family, gloating, "Our capital is growing nicely."

The film is, then, profoundly ambivalent. Until near the end, it could seem to be the rollicking exposé of a corrupt financier with Jewish connections, conning the poor and naive out of what little they have, but his vindication at the end (and Raimu's joyous performance) make of him almost the reverse—a financial mastermind of the sort that the poor and backward *need* if they are ever going to see their money multiply. Basically, the play and screenplay are exploiting common knowledge of bankers and financiers, but as commonly happens in these "satirical comedies," the comic presentation necessary to turn this into an enjoyable spectacle works against the critique. Nevertheless, what emerges from the film is a cynicism about the sort of society in which such con-artists can survive and even flourish. It is interesting to note that the play had to be toned down before it could be released as a film.

36. See Crisp, *Genre, Myth and Convention*, 69–71.

31. *Le Grand Jeu*

The Game of Fate (The Great Game)
France, 1934, 78 min, b&w

Dir Jacques Feyder; *Asst dir* Marcel Carné and Charles Barrois; *Prod* Films de France; *Scr* Charles Spaak and Feyder; *Cinematog* Harry Stradling; *Music* Hanns Eisler; *Art dir* Lazare Meerson; *Edit* Jacques Brillouin; *Act* Marie Bell (Florence and Irma), Pierre Richard-Willm (Pierre Martel), Charles Vanel (Clément), Georges Pitoëff (Nicolas), Françoise Rosay (Blanche), Line Clévers (Dauvile), Olga Velbria (Aïchouch), Camille Bert (the colonel), Pierre de Guingand (the captain), André Dubosc (Bernard Martel), Pierre Larquey (Gustin), Nestor Ariani (Aziani), and Louis Florencie (Fenoux).

Jacques Feyder began directing in 1919 and had completed some twenty films by the time he went to Germany in 1928, then to Hollywood the following year to direct five early sound films. But his reputation rests on the three films that he made on returning to France—*Le Grand Jeu* (1933), *Pension Mimosas* (1934, #36) and *La Kermesse héroïque* (1935, #45). In each of these, Feyder gave his wife, Françoise Rosay, a leading role. In *Le Grand Jeu*, she is patron of the bar frequented by a local garrison of the French Army stationed on the edge of the Algerian desert. This North African "frontier world" served much the same function in French mythology as the Wild West did in American mythology: it was at once so close geographically and yet so alien in climate, topography, and culture. The French had occupied Algeria in 1830, and over subsequent decades, in the face of a number of rebellions, had subjugated the native population and established a settler community. The representation of these North African colonies in the cinema can be summarized in a series of notionally successive stages:

- ✌ The *exploration* of hostile territory
- ✌ The *pacification* of that territory by military means
- ✌ The *conversion* of the heathen locals to superior Christian values
- ✌ The *civilization* of the country and the people by engineers, doctors, and teachers
- ✌ The *integration* of the region into an expanded France, by way of the fraternal cooperation of French settlers and their new indigenous friends.[37]

37. Ibid., 45–51.

In the accomplishment of these noble tasks, many French folk could be represented as finding a fulfillment unavailable at home. In particular, black sheep could redeem themselves by hardship honorably endured, or at the extreme, by the sacrifice of their lives for their country's good. In *Le Grand Jeu*, Pierre has been living life in the fast lane with Florence and embezzling the family firm's funds to support it. The family will see him through, providing he exiles himself. He enlists, but at the Algerian outpost to which his unit is posted, he encounters a girl named Irma who bears a remarkable resemblance to Florence, whom he cannot forget. She may indeed actually *be* Florence, since she "has been ill," bears a scar on her head, and seems to have lost her memory. The rest of the film is spent working out the very public (but off-screen) destiny of Pierre the soldier, engaged in a struggle to repress the rebel forces, and the more private narrative of his attempt to master his romantic past by deciding whether or not Irma is Florence and whether or not he loves her regardless. Pierre inherits some money and is about to return to France with Irma when he encounters Florence herself, escorted by a wealthy Arab. Distraught, all ambivalence now dispelled, he dispatches Irma to France and reenrolls for a further tour of duty. For Noël Burch and Geneviève Sellier, the whole focus of the film is the desperate defense of male fantasies, and the despair that takes over when Pierre can no longer sustain them.[38] The tarot cards, which in Blanche's reliable hands had already detected his past and foreshadowed the events of the film, now predict his death. He has understood: he shoulders his pack and marches off to assume his destiny.

Many of the sequences in the film involve stock conventions of French military dramas: the arrival of the new recruits, marching, maneuvers, road-building, mateship, the homesickness and depression, nights on the town, girls, trying to forget, and so on. Indeed, treated differently, many of these overlap with the conventions of the military vaudeville. So the "grand jeu," or full tarot, is an appropriate metaphor for a narrative structured on mythic and largely predictable conventions. But quite aside from the mythologization of colonial military activity, which is the centerpiece of the film, with its internationalism (Nicolas, Pierre's friend, turns out to be Russian; they sing "Unser Heimat" nostalgically together), *Le Grand Jeu* provides an opportunity for several well-loved tropes of French cinema: First there is the lottery, which, along with other gambling wins, proved a mainstay of the decade's narratives—related, of course, to the omnipresent if often unstated poverty, both on and off screen. Second, Marie Bell plays

---

38. Burch and Sellier, *La Drôle de guerre des sexes*, 57–62. They see Blanche (Rosay) as a sort of Greek chorus, commenting on the text.

that favorite double role involving contrasting identities—here both a vivacious high-living sensualist and a wan melancholic amnesiac. To capture Pierre's uncertainty about her identity, Feyder not only ensured that her appearance was radically different in the two roles but dubbed her voice as Irma. We are therefore caught up in his uncertainty, and in his attempts to force her to remember— a situation somewhat reminiscent of *L'Année dernière à Marienbad*. Finally, the encounter with Florence and her Arab protector, which decides Pierre to reenlist, generates that recurrent scene, the steamer that sails without him, its foghorn signaling the end of his hopes of recapturing the happy times of old.

This film is loosely based on an idea borrowed from Pirandello that Feyder had almost filmed in America, with Greta Garbo in the lead role. He had intended to dub an alien voice onto her character for part of that role, too, but the producers finally decided the subject was too intellectual.[39] In France, the technique caused a sensation, and the film reestablished Feyder as a major French director, attracting some 600,000 viewers in Paris and topping the year's box office. Readers of *Pour vous* gave it nearly twice as many votes that year as the second favorite, but then the 1933–1934 season was not a strong one. The industry was in turmoil, with both Pathé-Natan and Gaumont involved in financial mismanagement and scandal. Fewer films than at any time during the decade topped 300,000 spectators in Paris—12 percent as opposed to between 17 and 40 percent in other years. The optimism of the early sound years was waning, and commentators began to emphasize the fragility of the exhibition sector, where over a third of all French cinemas were not yet equipped for sound (and many of those never would be), while two thirds of the others held at most four screenings per week. Excepting two military vaudevilles, there were none of the riotous comedies that had marked earlier seasons, and *Le Grand Jeu* is typical of the move toward somber dramas that were to figure at the top of the annual tables near the end of the decade.

32. *L'Atalante*

Released under the title *Le Chaland qui passe*, then in 1940 as *L'Atalante*
France, 1934, 90 min, b&w

Dir Jean Vigo; *Asst dir* Albert Riéra, Charles Goldblatt, and Pierre Merle; *Scr* Vigo and Albert Riéra, from the novel by Jean Guinée; *Prod* Jacques-Louis Nounez

---

39. Feyder and Rosay, *Le Cinéma, notre métier*, 38–39. See also Arnoux, *Du muet au parlant*, 128–132.

and GFFA; *Cinematog* Boris Kaufman and Louis Berger; *Music* Maurice Jaubert; *Art dir* Francis Jourdain; *Sound* Royné and Baujard; *Edit* Louis Chavance; *Act* Jean Dasté (Jean), Michel Simon (père Jules), Dita Parlo (Juliette), Fanny Clar (Juliette's mother), Louis Lefebvre (cabin boy), Gilles Magaritis (huckster), René Bleck (groomsman), Raphaël Diligent (Juliette's father), and Pierre and Jacques Prévert (at Gare d'Austerlitz).

Despite the reception and banning of *Zéro de conduite* (#25), its producer, Jacques-Louis Nounez, had liked it and was willing to fund another film directed by Jean Vigo—a full-length film this time—and he convinced Gaumont to once more provide the facilities. But Nounez insisted on selecting the scenario himself and opted for *L'Atalante*. The narrative was not obviously in line with Vigo's interests, being a stock tale of a canal-boat skipper's wife seduced by the glamor of Paris and finally fetched back to her distressed husband by the skipper's mate, père Jules. More interesting is Vigo's treatment of this material, and perhaps the final film is the more effective for this being necessarily grafted onto a solid, independent narrative.

Vigo was granted permission to modify the story almost at will, and made several major changes in the scenario, such as Juliette's no longer being led astray by a young sailor but by a huckster. Vigo also departed from the original script during shooting, notably in the oddly undramatic wedding at the beginning and in the development of Michel Simon's character, père Jules, with his exotic cabin and his uneasy, ambivalently erotic relationship with Juliette.

Two elements of the final film are of particular importance. The first is the representation of Paris, which was to become a central structural element in dozens of 1930s films, normally in the form of an opposition between Paris and the provinces. Married to Jean, the skipper, Juliette is fascinated by two other men—the huckster who flirts with her and lures her away to the spurious glamor of the city, where she is quickly made aware of its unpleasant underside, and père Jules, whose canal-boat cabin is a magical surrealist world seething with cats and crammed with a weird collection of mementoes brought back from his travels in foreign parts. The opposition that is here established, then, is between the suspect desirability of Paris and the adventurous wandering represented by père Jules and the canal-boat. Ironically, Paris itself had initially attracted Juliette precisely because it seemed to stand for the wider world outside the confines of the canal-boat, but the film redefines it as something to be despised and rejected. It is appropriate that it should be père Jules, the only truly "magical" figure in the film, who rescues her, since it was through him, his weird antics, his tattooed body, and his exotic cavern that the canal-boat was represented as at once fascinating and faintly revolting.

The second matter of importance is the physicality of this fascination and revulsion. Of all 1930s films, *L'Atalante* must surely most intensely embody a sensual physicality. The initial wedding scenes establish this erotic rapport between Jean and Juliette, as does their sensual embrace the next morning. The bed scenes, a naked photo, and père Jules's body all maintain this aura of rich sensuality aboard the boat. The absence of it during the couple's night apart is underlined by their respective longing and desire, closely filmed and intercut in such a way that they seem to be responding to one another in their respective beds. When père Jules fetches Juliette back from Paris to the boat and to Jean, this sensuality erupts overtly in a passionate embrace that has them tumbling to the floor. The centrality of sexuality to surrealist liberation has perhaps never been so effectively instanced as by its powerful introduction into this basically conventional plot, where it might have seemed totally alien.

As with *Zéro de conduite,* however, Vigo's health interfered with the shooting schedule, as did the limited funds available. Jacques-Bernard Brunius has an amusing account of the efforts needed to film the final sequence, hastily assembling their friends to constitute the crowd at the station.[40] Several key linking scenes had to be omitted that in turn introduced inconsistencies into those already shot, which had assumed the presence of the latter. Perhaps because of this, the corporate presentation of the film in April 1934 was disastrous, and Gaumont was persuaded (and in turn persuaded the reluctant Nounez) of the need to radically recut and rename it after a currently popular song, "Le Chaland qui passe," in order to make it commercially viable. Despite (or because of) this reworking, the film was a commercial failure when released in September. Vigo died on 5 October, reputedly while a street musician was playing "Le Chaland qui passe" outside his window. Partially restored for a 1940 screening, then further restored in 1950, the film was available for decades in a variety of radically recut and abbreviated versions that were sometimes barely comprehensible. Paulo Emilio Salès-Gomès, who had seen several of them, said, "They literally ransacked the original version. Only one or two sequences remained intact; the insomnia disappeared completely, as did the presentation of the radiogram. And the debris of Vigo's film was constantly poisoned by Bixio's soppy tune, which seemed repulsively vulgar in conjunction with Jaubert's songs and waltzes."[41] Happily, something like the original version of *L'Atalante* was finally reconstituted using a miraculously preserved 1934 English copy of the original, which had not been transformed into *Le Chaland qui passe* presumably because

40. Brunius, *En marge du cinéma français,* 155–158.
41. For an extended account of all these changes, see Salès-Gomès, *Jean Vigo,* ch. 4.

that song would have been unknown in Britain. As Jacques-Bernard Brunius said, somewhat triumphantly, "C'est *Le Chaland qui passe*, c'est *L'Atalante* qui reste."[42]

33. Si j'étais le patron

(*If I Were Boss*)
France, 1934, 103 min, b&w

Dir Richard Pottier; *Asst dir* André Cerf; *Prod* Para-Film (or possibly Pathé-Natan); *Scr* Cerf, René Pujol, and Jacques Prévert; *Cinematog* Jean Bachelet; *Music* Henri Poussigue; *Art dir* Jacques Krauss and/or Claude Bouxin; *Sound* Jean Lecoq; *Edit* Pierre Méguérian; *Act* Fernand Gravey (Henri Janvier), Max Dearly (Monsieur Maubert), Pierre Larquey (Jules), Mireille Balin (Marcelle), Madeleine Guitty (Madame Pichu), Claire Gérard, Jane Pierson, Magdeleine Bérubet, Charles Dechamps, and Pierre Palau.

A summary of the plot immediately shows why this film constitutes an interesting comment on French industry and society of the time. The setting is a French car factory. Henri, one of the workers, has invented a revolutionary silencer, as has the firm's head engineer, and a running joke involves the disastrous failure of the latter in a series of progressively more explosive tests. Henri cannot get the management to listen to his own more justified claims; the director thinks he is a troublemaker and plans to fire him. The workers are frustrated in their jobs, and the firm is in financial crisis. The workers win a lottery but rather than divide it up, they decide to hold a communal celebration. An eccentric investor, Maubert, notes the management's incompetence and appreciates the workers' ability to enjoy themselves. They know how to live, whereas the bosses only know how to give orders. Maubert overhears Henri describing how the firm could be made profitable, and agrees to save the factory on condition that Henri be given the director's job. After a heavy night out with Maubert (who is incognito still), Henri wakes up in the director's office, and to his surprise, finds that he is being consulted on the way the firm should be run. Growing into the job, he discovers that the board has been rifling the workers' funds and that the accountant has been selling the plans of their forthcoming car to a rival firm. He demonstrates his silencer to a wealthy American client, who agrees to buy it for a vast sum. The firm is saved.

42. Brunius, *En marge du cinéma français*, 157.

Clearly this car company stands metonymically for the whole of French industry, in a state of crisis partly because of the Depression but also because of incompetence and graft in the upper echelons. As noted earlier (#30), this was the year of several high-level financial scandals in French firms. Thus in the film, the opposition between workers and bosses is unsubtle to say the least: the latter are authoritarian, greedy, and treacherous, the former joyous, willing and inventive. Their mateships and communal celebrations contrast with the selfishness of the bosses. As Henri repeats, if the workers ran the factory, it would be much more productive, and given the chance, he proves it. It is not hard to see why Jacques Prévert, who was then involved in the aggressively Marxist Groupe Octobre, might have been induced to contribute to such a film.

Although the matter of the film is socially significant, the manner is lighthearted, good-natured, and unpretentious. The firm is saved not only by Henri's invention but also by an eccentric millionaire (a hilarious performance by Max Dearly). A residue of the German original (*Wenn ich den König war,* When I Was King) subsists in the boss's name (Leroi) and in numerous mocking references to the monarchy and Napoleon that run through the film, while the inventive worker is named Janvier (January)—representative of a new epoch. Typically, the vitality and generosity of the workers is characterized by song. They like singing while they work, a practice that the bosses quickly stamp down on. Led by Henri, the workers perform a happy little song at the communal celebrations, and when he discovers that he has been made director, one of Henri's first acts is to install loudspeakers so he can pipe music to the men . . . and found a sports club—sports and music throughout the 1930s constituting the twin pillars of popular culture, and twin guarantees of popular integrity.

This film is worth considering in conjunction with Robert Siodmak's *La Crise est finie* (*The Depression Is Over*), which came out on 4 October 1934, a few weeks earlier, and which treats even more flippantly the impact of the Depression on French industry. Like Fritz Lang and others, Siodmak was en route from Germany, where Joseph Goebbels had just attacked one of his films, to Hollywood where he was to spend the war years. Organized around the desire of a group of musical comedy actors to put on a show in Paris (a common narrative schema of the decade), his film again sets up an opposition between bosses and workers. The star actress and the producers cause her understudy to be fired for insubordination, and the whole cast resigns in solidarity. They will put on a show of their own devising. But the project is countered by a nasty businessman who has his eye on the understudy's beautiful body, and who does his best to block their use of an abandoned theater. As the sole representative in the film of the bourgeoisie, he is systematically ridiculed and humiliated. The show that they devise is a musical with its title and key song, "La Crise est finie." Obviously the financial slump was not over, but the film asserts that it is more a state of mind than an economic reality—if you smile and sing along, all your troubles will evaporate. An optimistic attitude and optimistic productions such as this one will dispel the economic gloom enveloping the Western world.

Finally, it is worth noting that elaborate forms of punctuation are used throughout both of these films. This was normal for comedies at the time, since it was seen as contributing to the inherent gaiety of the genre.

Both films were well received by audiences in Paris but did not make the top thirty films of the season. The excitement generated by populist comedies in the early sound years was no longer apparent, and audiences were beginning to manifest a preference for more dramatic productions that was to last to the end of the decade.

34. Angèle

Angele
France, 1934, 150 min (less after cuts, currently 133 min), b&w

Dir and Scr Marcel Pagnol, from *Un de Baumugnes* by Jean Giono; *Prod* Films Marcel Pagnol; *Cinematog* Willy; *Music* Vincent Scotto; *Art dir* Marius Brouquier; *Sound* Jean Lecoq and Bardisbanian; *Edit* Suzanne de Troeye; *Act* Orane Demazis (Angèle), Jean Servais (Albin), Fernandel (Saturnin), Annie Toinon (Philomène), Blanche Poupon (Florence), Henri Poupon (Clarius), Édouard Delmont (Amédée), Andrex (Le Louis), and Charles Blavette (Tonin).

Marcel Pagnol's theatrical success with *Topaze, Marius* (#10), and *Fanny* led to three immensely successful films in 1931 and 1932. Although he allocated the direction to experienced directors, he retained supervisory control over each of them. The profits that thus accrued to him permitted him in the course of 1932–1934 to establish studios in Marseilles to develop and edit his own films; to establish distribution outlets in Paris, Lyons, Marseilles, Strasbourg, Algiers, and Casablanca; to buy a state-of-the-art Philips sound truck to permit location shooting, for which he became justly famous later; and to exhibit these and other films in his own chain of cinemas. Most of his location films were shot at a 100-acre site at La Treille near Aubagne, which he bought for that purpose. He would point out later to Pierre Leprohon, "There's where we built the village for *Regain;* further on, in a fold in the land, there are traces of the farm in *Angèle;* the cave for *Manon* was behind that line of rocks."[43] From 1933 on, Pagnol directed and pro-

43. Leprohon, *Présences contemporaines*, 218.

duced all of his own plays and scripts, producing also those of friends and colleagues, and published sporadically a film journal called *Les Cahiers du film* in which he outlined his evolving ideas on film. His production, distribution, and exhibition network became the stable center of filmmaking in Provence until war intervened, and the only integrated independent filmmaking company outside of Paris.[44]

One of the major ironies of Pagnol's career is that, having from the beginning allocated the direction of his own plays to others, when he came in 1933–1934 to take over the role of director, he applied his undoubted skills to the adaptation and direction of other people's works, and most notably the short stories and novels of his Provençal compatriot Jean Giono—*Angèle* from *Un de Baumugnes; Regain* (1937, #67) from the novel of that name; *Jofroi* (1933); and *La Femme du boulanger* (1938, #79) from *Jean le Bleu*. Some critics consider it even more ironic that, having recently engaged in a polemic with René Clair in which he is supposed to have proclaimed that the only valid use of cinema was to record and make more readily available the great theatrical works, he should now, in *Jofroi, Angèle,* and *Regain,* not to mention Renoir's *Toni* (#38), which he coproduced and distributed, establish a pattern of open-air production that was to make him in many commentators' eyes the father of neorealism and the New Wave. In fact, his thoughts on these matters had always been more sophisticated than his critics wished to represent them (see #10).

Despite its artificiality, the fake Provençal village at La Treille provided a credibly "authentic" meridional atmosphere for many of his films. Further contributing to this sense of authenticity, he used in these films his established Provençal actors—Charpin, Édouard Delmont, Charles Blavette, Maupi, and of course Raimu. Fernandel, whom Pagnol also used in several of these films, against the grain of that actor's comic performances, was likewise from the region. The result is a series of films that exude a "parfum de terroir" (feel for the land).[45]

The storyline of *Angèle* celebrates this "terroir." It is organized around one of the principal structural oppositions of the decade (and beyond), namely city and country. Angèle is a farmer's daughter, desired by Le Louis, a cad from the city, and by Albin, a lad from the remote village of Baumugnes. Le Louis represents urban sophistication and seduces Angèle with flowery compliments. Despite Albin's warnings, she allows herself to be whisked away to Marseilles where Louis puts her to work as a prostitute; she is saved by Saturnin, the farmhand, but has had a baby. Her father, overcome by shame, shuts her and the baby away

44. See Peyrusse, *Le Cinéma méridional,* 32–33, 37–40.
45. Leprohon, *Présences contemporaines,* 218.

in a cellar. Albin's mate discovers her whereabouts when a storm flushes her out of the cellar, and rescues her, but rather than fleeing with her, he returns to confront the father and ask formally for her hand. All are gruffly reconciled, and the couple and "their" baby head for Albin's village in the mountains.

As the fierce old father, almost insane with grief, says, "Nothing but shame comes from the city. . . . This is the worst thing that could ever have happened to us." Albin, from the remotest of villages, is, as his name suggests, unremittingly pure. A scale of altitude supports this opposition: from the farm, Angèle goes *down* to the village where she meets Le Louis, and he takes her *further down* to the coast, where corruption is rife. Albin comes from the high mountains, and once Angèle has been purified by her suffering, he takes her *back up* there.[46] And where the harsh strictures of Angèle's father, Clarius (whose arm, incidentally, has been in a sling throughout this sexual shame episode), are represented as excessive, the forgiveness and charity manifested by Albin are represented as a step higher in the moral chain.

Angèle was enormously popular everywhere in France, earning double its production costs in the first month of release, but there are aspects of it that grate today. The story of seduction, illegitimacy, and sequestration is wildly melodramatic, and the agony is frequently overplayed. Only the final scenes, gruff in their understatement, come across as truly moving (until Fernandel is allowed to revert to his "rustic idiot" act). The music, which later Pagnol was to use more discretely, is surprisingly clumsy for Vincent Scotto, and it is here clumsily applied and heavily foregrounded. Moreover, the story is surprisingly devoid of action: Pagnol's theatrical predisposition transforms it into a series of highly dialogued tableaux. Nevertheless, this film (with its mid-length predecessor, *Jofroi*) sees the beginning of that simple yet powerful set of sacramental elements—conservative and even regressive, but richly moving—that were to run through all the best of Pagnol's films, namely Provençal life and character, the high harsh interior, the sun, the soil, water, and a hard-won fertility.

35. L'Hôtel du Libre Échange

(*The Free Exchange Hotel*)
France, 1934, 106 min, b&w

Dir Marc Allégret; *Asst dir* Paul Allemen and Pierre Prévert; *Prod* Or-Film; *Scr* Prévert and Allégret, from the boulevard comedy by Georges Feydeau and Mau-

---

46. Peyrusse, *Le Cinéma méridional*, 117.

rice Desvallières; *Cinematog* Roger Hubert; *Art dir* Lazare Meerson, Alexandre Trauner, and Robert Gys; *Edit* Denise Batcheff and Marguerite Beaugé; *Act* Fernandel (Boulot the boot-boy), Raymond Cordy (Bastien), Saturnin Fabre (Monsieur Mathieu), Pierre Larquey (Pinglet), Mona Lys (Marcelle Paillardin), Marion Delbo (Angélique Pinglet), Ginette Leclerc, Raymond Bussières, Alexandre Trauner, Serge Grave, Jacques Prévert, Lou Bonin, and Paul Grimault.

This amusing film is included here primarily as a typical example of an enormously popular theatrical genre, the boulevard comedy or vaudeville (the former term normally reserved for plays depicting the upper crust, the latter for satirical farces centering on bureaucrats and lesser creatures). At its zenith between 1880 and 1920, the genre was principally associated with the playwright Georges Feydeau, but also Robert de Flers and Gaston de Caillavet, Maurice Hennequin, and later Georges Berr and Louis Verneuil. At least one hundred of their productions were transcribed to film in the 1930s (i.e., about 8% of total output), often appearing in the lists of the year's most successful films. The best-known are perhaps Feydeau's *La Dame de chez Maxim's, Occupe-toi d'Amélie,* and *On purge bébé* (and three others); Flers and Caillavet's *Le Roi, L'Habit vert,* and *Miquette et sa mère* (and nine others); Hennequin's *Compartiment de dames seules* and *Le Monsieur de 5 heures* (and nine others); and Verneuil and Berr's *Arlette et ses papas* and *Mademoiselle ma mère* (and twenty-two others). Just as they had their regular authors, they had their regular actors in regular roles: Elvire Popescu as the provocative blonde vamp, Fernandel as the gormless naïf, Victor Boucher as a count or baron, André Lefaur as a stuffy bourgeois, Françoise Rosay as a licentious character with a pompously respectable facade, but also Gaby Morlay and Raimu, not to mention Saturnin Fabre, Jules Berry, and Michel Simon to provide over-the-top comic performances.

Three that have survived and that give a good overview of the genre are Verneuil's *Ma cousine de Varsovie* (Gallone, 1931), Yves Mirande's *Sept hommes . . . une femme* (1936), and Feydeau's *L'Hôtel du Libre Échange* (Marc Allégret, 1934). In this last, there seems to be a ghost in Room 12, and an architect is called in to investigate. As chance would have it, his wife and his nephew have both arranged a wicked weekend in this very hotel, while a lawyer friend and his four nubile daughters, unable to stay with the architect, also put up there. What follows is an elaborately choreographed ballet in which people are put in the wrong rooms, try but fail to organize their illicit affairs, spy on one another, discover or nearly discover their wife (husband, daughter, nephew) in compromising situations, burst in on embarrassing scenes, hide in wardrobes and alcoves, barricade themselves in bedrooms, scramble up the chimney, and so on. There is ample opportunity for the display of feminine flesh and comic moments of mistaken identity, notably when the police arrive. Essentially the plot of these films assembles a group of frustrated and dissatisfied bourgeois and has them attempt (unsuccessfully) to realize their basically libidinous desires. All make fools of themselves in the process. No real denouement is possible since the spectators, unlike the characters themselves, have been kept in the know from the start, and much of the pleasure derives from their expectations of the confrontations and revelations that must inevitably happen. At best, the characters end up as they started, relieved not to have been found out, though occasionally one young couple is allowed a relatively happy ending.

The main point of the genre, then, would seem to be the dissatisfactions, tensions, and frustrations occasioned by bourgeois values and forms, and particularly by bourgeois family life. None are happy with what they are or have, but cannot imagine anything radically different, merely a change of partner or a minor reversal of role. Sexual desire is used as a sort of safety valve to vent these frustrations without the need to modify social values or forms—novelty without change. Cuckoldry, duplicity, and impersonation are essential plot devices, and the trick of the narrative is not to let anyone except the audience know who is tricking whom. Moreover, the implication of the cast-list is that nothing is of importance unless it is happening to the rich, the famous, the powerful, or the noble, yet much of the pleasure derives from seeing these "worthy" figures make idiots of themselves. That, no doubt, together with its hysterical pace, is why the genre so delighted the Prévert brothers and the fiercely left-wing Groupe Octobre, who figure prominently in the credits of the present film.

The earlier boulevard comedy mentioned above, *Ma cousine de Varsovie*, establishes a typical generic situation: a gormless older banker with an attractive young wife is being cuckolded by a young painter friend; then his provocative blonde cousin from Warsaw arrives and reorients all the desire lines. Two illicit but shifting relationships develop, with all the expected amorality and insincerity, but nicely mocked in the lyrics of the comic operetta composed by the banker. Finally, the cousin departs, leaving the original threesome having the same pointless conversation as at the beginning. The later boulevard comedy *Sept hommes . . . une femme* is of particular interest because it parallels in many ways Jean Renoir's *La Règle du jeu* (#95), thereby reminding us of the extent to which that great film is underpinned by generic conventions with which the audience would have been totally familiar. A recently widowed countess, discovering with dismay her late husband's infidelities, abandons herself to the rules of a new game: assembling her seven suitors in a country house, she resolves to test their worthiness as husbands. They include an impoverished childhood friend, the Comte de Brémontier (Fernand Gravey), a novelist, a politician (Saturnin Fabre), a marquis, a composer, and a more modest man whose father was a poacher (Pierre Larquey). During the hunt that forms the centerpiece of the narrative, the widow is discovered, as in *La Règle du jeu,* by the count in the embrace of one of his rivals. That evening, again as in *La Règle,* bedtime rituals take place in the elaborate, tiled corridors of the chateau. Above and below stairs, events parallel one another, until all suitors except the count and his humble friend have been subjected to the test of greed and found wanting. The latter offers the former the funds that he needs to marry the widow and stands aside.

Quite apart from any parallels with *La Règle du jeu,* however, this film is a pleasure to watch in its own right. It was scripted directly for film by Yves Mirande, rather than adapted from a preexisting play—one of seven that he directed in the late 1930s and one of forty-eight that he scripted or adapted during the decade, nearly all lighthearted comedies.

36. *Pension Mimosas*

(*The Mimosa Boarding House*)
France-Germany, 1935, 109 min, b&w

Dir Jacques Feyder; *Asst dir* Marcel Carné and Ary Sadoul; *Prod* Tobis; *Scr* Feyder and Charles Spaak; *Cinematog* Roger Hubert; *Music* Armand Bernard; *Art dir* Lazare Meerson; *Sound* Hermann Storr; *Edit* Jacques Brillouin; *Act* Françoise Rosay (Louise Noblet), Paul Bernard (Pierre), André Alerme (Gaston), Lise Delamare (Nelly), Arletty (Parasol), Ila Meery, Nane Germon, Sylviac, Paul Azaïs, Jean Max, Raymond Cordy, and Pierre Labry.

Pension Mimosas was commissioned to exploit Françoise Rosay's immense success in *Le Grand Jeu* (#31). Funded by Tobis, it was made without any of the financial anxieties that beset Jacques Feyder's previous film. It focuses on two thematic fields that were omnipresent and immensely popular in the years 1930–1945, namely gambling and (usually implicit) incest. The pension (boarding house) of the title is a rather elegant establishment not far from the casino. Its proprietors, the Noblets, are childless, and take over as their own son Pierrot, the son of a lodger sent to prison. Released, the lodger reclaims him and he grows up in bad company, obsessed with gambling (at which he loses catastrophically) and with an "unsuitable" woman, Nelly. Attempting to save him, his (adoptive) mother enters into an overt rivalry with Nelly for his affections. To refinance him, she herself gambles and wins big, but too late: Pierrot has committed suicide and dies in her arms.

The Noblet family is at once intensely involved in the world of gambling and intensely threatened by it. The husband, a former croupier, runs a training school for croupiers, and the pension thrives on the presence of addicted gamblers patronizing the casino nearby. The fantasy of unimaginable and unearned wealth runs through the film, as it runs through the cinema of the decade. Early on, the adopted son wins money in some minor gambling at school, and is punished for it as a threat to the family's honor. Indeed, when the narrative resumes some ten years later, Pierrot (nicknamed "Baccara" and never without a pack of cards) is mixing with low company, has been beaten up by Nelly's current lover, and has conned the Noblets out of thousands of francs to pay his debts. Madame Noblet pawns her jewelry to refinance him but returns to find him rifling her chest of drawers. Now a car-salesman, Pierrot fraudulently gambles away the proceeds of a car he has sold. Desperate, ruined, he takes poison, and the money Madame Noblet has won for him comes too late.

This is altogether a more thorough exploration than usual of the milieu of gambling and the fantasies of unearned wealth that are an insistent theme of the decade. The documentary element is high, due to the procedures employed by Feyder and the scriptwriter, Charles Spaak, when developing the storyline: "Both of us felt that what was essential was not so much the story . . . as the milieu where it would unfold. Every great film has a documentary aspect which is primordial." They believed that every region of France, every Paris suburb, had its potential characteristic film, and to generate a script, they would study a map of France, debating the landscape, the climate, and the human activity typical of the area until a storyline arose out of these. "This game amused us greatly, and we considered various regions of France, ending up in Menton. That's where *Pension Mimosas* was born."[47]

But perhaps even more interesting than the documentary aspect is the obsessive, quasi-sexual relationship between Madame Noblet and her "son." These quasi-incestuous passions are so common in this period as to have inspired one of the major books on the cinema of the period.[48] Most commonly, the relationship is between a father-figure and a younger girl. On a few occasions, the relationship is fully incestuous, but more usually the proprieties are preserved by having the daughter not a true daughter but a stepdaughter, daughter-in-law, or young employee regarded as a daughter. Equally as often the narrative involves a case of mistaken identity, wherein someone finally turns out not to be a daughter after all. Frequently the narrative ties itself into knots denying the reality of incest while nevertheless evoking it as a real possibility. Clearly all such "pretext" narratives depend for their fascination on evoking forms of illicit sexuality. They

47. Marion, ed., *Le Cinéma par ceux qui le font*, 107–108.
48. Burch and Sellier, *La Drôle de guerre des sexes*.

were extremely common between 1930 and 1945: As mentioned earlier (#27), at least eighty such films were produced in the course of the decade.

Instances of an older woman's incestuous passion for her "son" are fewer but still common—about twenty in the decade, most notably Henri Bataille's *Maman Colibri* (filmed 1921 and 1937). Françoise Rosay was to figure in at least two other such films, *Fauteuil 47* (Fernand Rivers, 1937) and Marcel Carné's first film, *Jenny* (1936, #52), where she runs a nightclub and is passionately involved with a younger man whom (as often happens) a young rival, in this case her own innocent and unsuspecting daughter, steals from her while trying to win him over to the path of righteousness. In *Pension Mimosas*, the younger girl, Nelly, is a casino-hand. Distraught with jealousy at Pierrot's attachment to Nelly, alternately raging at Pierrot and rocking him in her arms, Madame becomes "more than a mother to him," as Nelly complains. Ultimately Nelly decamps with her former lover, and the film ends with Madame cradling the dying Pierrot in her arms, and at his request (thinking her Nelly), kissing him passionately. The film is astonishingly explicit in its representation of an older woman's passion for a younger man who is legally her son, and it is hard to credit Françoise Rosay's protestations that she saw her character as simply displaying maternal solicitude.[49]

Pension Mimosas was as successful at the box office as *Le Grand Jeu*, so it is interesting that both Jacques Feyder and Françoise Rosay have almost entirely written it out of their memoirs. Many critics are slighting of it, too, seeing it as starting splendidly with the establishment of an unusual milieu but steadily deteriorating from gritty realism to reprehensible melodrama.[50] It is possible to argue, on the contrary, that it starts slowly and a little clumsily, only really taking off as the melodrama of the incestuous relationship and of Pierrot's ruined life are worked out.

37. *Le Bonheur*

(*Happiness*)
France, 1935, 105 min, b&w

Dir Marcel L'Herbier; *Asst dir* Jean Dréville and Eve Francis; *Prod* Pathé-Cinéma; *Scr* L'Herbier, with Michel Duran, from the play by Henry Bernstein; *Cinematog* Harry Stradling; *Music* Billy Colson; *Art dir* Guy de Gastyne; *Sound* Robert

49. Rosay, *La Traversée d'une vie*, 197.
50. See, for instance, Roger Leenhardt, "Chroniques de cinéma," *Esprit*, March 1935, 70–71.

Teisseire; *Edit* Jacques Manuel; *Act* Gaby Morlay (Clara Stuart), Charles Boyer (Philippe Lutcher, aka le Chacal/The Jackal), Michel Simon (his manager), Jaque Catalain (Clara's husband), Paulette Dubost (Louise), and Jean Marais.

Le Bonheur was Marcel L'Herbier's twenty-second feature film. The fourteen that he had made during the silent period had established him on a level with Abel Gance, Jean Epstein, Louis Delluc, René Clair, and Germaine Dulac as a leader of the cinematic avant-garde. More interested in the plasticity of the image than in the relationship between shots, he became well-known for the modernist sets he commissioned and the distortions he effected on the image. An esthete, mixing with the wealthy and the aristocratic, he liked to call on all of the most ambitious, modernist artists of the day. His *L'Inhumaine* (1923) includes in its credits Pierre MacOrlan, Fernand Léger, Robert Mallet-Stevens, Alberto Cavalcanti, and Darius Milhaud.

As we have seen, for such an experimental filmmaker the transition to sound was sure to be difficult, and cost pressures forced L'Herbier to take on commercial projects in an attempt to fund more personal films. This disappointed many critics of the time: Georges Sadoul dismissed those early sound films as "obscure incoherent mediocrities."[51] By L'Herbier's own account, this period can be considered "a decline," though in his autobiography, he defended some aspects of it as "a quite new venture."[52] After two years without work (1931–1933), he turned in desperation to the canned theater promoted by Marcel Pagnol and Sacha Guitry, which was certainly in demand, as witnessed by the remarkable success of Pagnol's own plays and of Marcel Achard's *Jean de la Lune* (1931). Although clearly embarrassed at having to film theatrical works by "minor authors," L'Herbier still found favor with the public. Indeed, throughout the decade, despite or because of the compromises he felt obliged to make, his films consistently attracted large audiences. *Le Bonheur* was the fourth of his "canned plays" and the one he felt (as did the playwright) that he had transposed to greatest advantage. It allowed him to bring together Charles Boyer and Gaby Morlay, whose first sound films had in both cases been earlier L'Herbier films (and who enjoyed acting together in the theater), along with Michel Simon, who had acted the same hilariously camp manager in the original theatrical cast, and L'Herbier's friend ("almost son") Jaque Catelain.

Le Bonheur is at once a play of ideas and a reflexive work. Boyer's character is an anarchist cartoonist sent by a daily newspaper to do a sketch of Gaby Mor-

51. Quoted in Jeancolas, *15 ans d'années trente*, 160.
52. L'Herbier, *La Tête qui tourne*, 218–223.

lay's Clara Stuart, an actress/singer/film star. He attends her show that night, listens sardonically as she sings her current hit song ("Happiness is not just a dream, it's right here, within reach"), waits at the stage entrance, and shoots her. The scene of the arrival of the star at the Gare St. Lazare is a classic 1930s scene—night, the train draws in with clouds of hissing steam, clamorous surging crowds, reporters' flashbulbs—which will occur in various media before its most famous manifestation in the opening shots of the plane's arrival in *La Règle du jeu* (#95). At his trial, when asked why he shot her, the anarchist asks quizzically, "Why not?" or "Who should I have shot?" ("Qui tuer?"). The act is seen as partly motivated by financial envy but more importantly by the facile sentimentalism of her song. Certainly one can see how this queasy popular culture might have seemed to L'Herbier an appropriate target for an assassin: star or sporting hero, both could seem to him, as to the anarchist, to dispense cheap dreams of glamorous wish-fulfillment to the masses who can never realize them in real life, and thus prevent them from ever calling into question the system that enslaves them. Benefiting gratuitously from popular adulation, they were both eminently disposable.

The long central section in which the star (who has survived his assassination attempt) pleads for the anarchist's release, meets him at the prison gates, and takes him under her wing is less interesting. He lends himself to the process reluctantly, unwilling to compromise with "la bêtise humaine" (the crass stupidity of humanity). A recurrent theme during this section, almost irresistible to scriptwriters when dealing with actors, involves the impossibility of knowing when, if ever, actors are being sincere (for instance, sincerely in love), since their whole lives are performance.

The film picks up again when the anarchist overhears a discussion of Clara's next film, which is to be *Le Bonheur*—a sentimentalized dramatization of his anarchistic attempt to kill her. He discreetly attends the filming at the Gare St. Lazare, where the initial "arrival of the star" and the theater shooting are amalgamated into a sensational and poignant scene designed to best show off Clara's melodramatic acting skills. Feeling betrayed, or that in lending himself to this nonsense he has betrayed his own principles, he decides he must leave her and regain a scornful detachment from such populist idiocy.

The earlier reenactment during the trial of his "assassination" has also been packed with ironies of this sort, as Clara puts on for the court a persuasive act to get his sentence reduced, then, reproached for such histrionics, performs it again in "a more sincere" version. And the anarchist's final departure likewise involves accusations from him that her "pleading that he not leave her" is a particularly effective scene, which she might well include after the station scene in her current film. Finally, he leaves the "real" star, the better to appreciate her re-corded performances, which will be all the more convincing for her heartbreak at his departure. The film cuts from her pleading "Chéri" as he leaves, to her per-forming the same farewell on screen in her film *Le Bonheur,* histrionically plead-ing "Chéri" as he watches sardonically from the stalls.

Finally, the circularity of the narrative is typical of the decade, and reminds us of numerous other circular narratives in these years where the abstract formal pattern implies an extratextual fatality whose decisions are irrevocable and whose pleasure it is to mock the petty plans of humankind—for instance, *Toni* (#38), *Sous les toits de Paris* (#2), *La Petite Lise* (#6), and later *Trois Valses* (#90). Such tropes can reasonably be read as a manifestation of the inescap-able nature of the characters' social destinies in a time of economic crisis and collapse.

38. *Toni*

Toni
France, 1935, 100 min (currently 85 min), b&w

Dir Jean Renoir; *Asst dir* Georges Darnoux; *Prod* Films d'Aujourd'hui; *Scr* Renoir and Carl Einstein, from case notes drawn up by Jacques Mortier (aka Jacques Levert); *Cinematog* Claude Renoir; *Music* Paul Bozzi; *Art dir* Marius Brouquier and Léon Bourrely; *Sound* Bardisbanian and René Sarrazin; *Edit* Marguerite Houllé-Renoir and Suzanne de Troeye; *Act* Charles Blavette (Antonio Canova, aka Toni), Édouard Delmont (Fernand), Célia Montalvan (Josépha), Jenny Hélia (Marie), Max Dalban (Albert), Andrex (Gaby), André Kovachevitch (Sébastian), Paul Bozzi (Primo, the guitar-player), and many nonprofessionals.

Toni is undoubtedly one of the most radical cinematic undertakings of the 1930s. Not a great film, it is nevertheless astonishingly rigorous in its determi-nation to push documentary realism to the limits. For this reason, it earned the admiration of the Italian neorealists (Luchino Visconti was a trainee on this film and on *Une partie de campagne*) and of the New Wave, though it is doubt-ful if those movements ever produced its equal. The form its realism takes is as follows:

- ↗ It is based on real events that happened some twelve years before to people such as those shown in the film, as reported to Jean Renoir by the Martigues police chief.

- ✕ It deals with "ordinary," unremarkable people, largely without charisma, whom the camera does not single out and psychologize in *plan américain* (waist-up shot) or close-up.[53]

- ✕ It shuns studio sets, being filmed entirely on location (except for a few linking shots) in the area where the events actually happened.

- ✕ It refuses all star actors, relying on little-known professionals (from Marcel Pagnol's troupe, mostly drawn from the caf'conc world of Marseilles) and on nonprofessionals.

The storyline concerns Italian and Spanish immigrants in the Martigues area of the south of France, between Marseilles and the Camargue. Toni works in a quarry and lives with a group of coworkers in Marie's house; he has become her lover, but falls for Josépha, a sensual Spanish woman. She, in turn, gets involved with Albert, the quarry foreman; marries him; is badly treated; and kills him. Toni covers for her and is killed while fleeing the police. There is enormous dramatic potential in this storyline, but it is resolutely resisted. "Our ambition," Renoir stated, "was for the public to imagine that an invisible camera had filmed each stage of the conflict without the participants being aware of its presence."[54] Social realism of a sort was not uncommon in 1930s films when representing sordid circumstances, but was usually urban rather than rural, and combined with a sentimental melodrama that emoted over the plight of the characters— abandoned orphans, seduced maidens, and so on. Here the events are de-dramatized, treated as existential phenomena, free of psychologization, suspense, or other plot mechanisms beloved of classical narrative. It has therefore the feel of a realist documentary or a filmed reportage. (The one exception is Marie's attempted suicide by drowning, which has rightly been criticized for disrupting the elsewhere-prevalent understatement.) We do not see Josépha shoot her husband, and when Toni is surprised by the police trying to set up a fake suicide for Albert, the drama is again played down:

> POLICEMAN: "Oh. Did you kill Albert?"
> TONI (after a long pause): "Yes. I did. You can arrest me. I'll come quietly."

53. See Peyrusse, *Le Cinéma méridional,* 152–156.
54. *Cahiers du cinéma,* no. 60, June 1956.

Throughout, the dialogue has this extreme sobriety. Looking back on his output, Renoir said of the film, "With the passage of time I now see more clearly what was characteristic of *Toni:* the absence of any star. Not just any star actor, but any star setting or star situation."[55] The film shuns the picturesque. This Martigues area was particularly favored by Impressionist painters because of the quality of its light, but you would never know it from Renoir's film.[56]

One of the most crucial aspects of the film is that it implies, by its focus on an underprivileged group of unremarkable foreign immigrants, that their experience is of central importance to French society. It also implies that nationality is not as important as class. As Renoir was to say later, "[*Toni*] allowed me to dwell on a theory that has always been dear to me, namely that the people of this earth are not divided into nations but are rather divided into work categories. *What we do* is our true nation."[57] In this respect, *Toni* constitutes a step beyond the anarchism of *Boudu* (#20) in the direction of the socialism of *Le Crime de Monsieur Lange* (1936, #46) and the Communist Party activism of *La Vie est à nous* (#49), which, in turn, leads into Renoir's great humanist films of the late 1930s (and, alas, the sentimental pantheism of his old age). In its focus on a close-knit group of male workers, it foreshadows numerous films of the years 1935–1938 that focus on such a group whose friendships make of them the microcosm of a harmonious society, ultimately undermined by the twin serpents of women and bosses. When Toni is accused of treating Marie badly, his coworkers stand up for him: he is "a good lad, a colleague." "I know Toni; he's my mate / I work with him." As usual in this period, the guarantee of the group's virtue is their appreciation of popular song. Primo's Italian and Corsican songs linger in the background of at least a dozen scenes in the film. And Josépha's "betrayal" of Toni is all the more bitter in that she betrays him with Albert, their foreman—nasty, tight-fisted, and with an eye for the main chance—whom old Sébastian (now reluctantly Albert's father-in-law) nicely characterizes when apologizing to him for preferring Toni: "Don't take it too hard, Albert; here on the land you just haven't got what it takes. . . . The earth only has to hear your footsteps approaching, and it becomes lazy." It is a sentiment that Pagnol would have recognized. Bosses are unproductive, and persecuted workers throughout the 1930s dream as here of fleeing their persecution to the idealized liberty of South America.

Clearly such an understated film was not going to appeal to commercial producers, and since the financial disaster of *La Petite Marchande d'allumettes* (1928),

---

55. Renoir, *Ma Vie et mes films*, 75.

56. *Toni, Avant-Scène cinéma*, nos. 251–252, 33.

57. Renoir, *Renoir on Renoir*, 215.

Renoir had been struggling to fund his own productions. Moreover, his four preceding films had been relative failures at the box-office. These were frustrating days in which his cinematic career seemed in doubt, until his friend Pierre Gaut managed to assemble half the necessary funding and persuade Pagnol to provide the rest, partly through providing facilities and personnel from his production unit. When released, *Toni* was neither a commercial success nor an outright failure. Most critics, especially left-wing critics, admired it (notably Georges Sadoul), while right-wing critics despised it (notably Lucien Rebatet).[58] The surviving copies lack a key scene in which Josépha and Toni wheel along in her laundry cart the body of the husband she has just killed, concealed beneath clothes, while jocular Corsican charcoal-burners accompany them unawares. Most critics seem to believe it was excised by the producer (who denied it). Subsequently, Renoir seemed to acknowledge that he himself had cut and then lost it, possibly in an attempt to make the film more commercial, though his account is of doubtful reliability.[59]

39. *Justin de Marseille*

(*Justin from Marseilles*)
France, 1935, 95 min, b&w

Dir Maurice Tourneur; *Asst dir* J. P. Dreyfus; *Prod* Pathé-Natan *Scr* Carlo-Rim; *Cinematog* Georges Benoit and René Colas; *Music* Jacques Ibert; *Songs* Vincent Scotto; *Art dir* Lazare Meerson; *Sound* Antoine Archaimbaud; *Act* Berval (Justin), Pierre Larquey (le Bègue), Alexandre Rignault (Esposito), Paul Olivier (Achille), Aimos (le Fada), Guislaine Bru (Totone), Line Noro (La Rougeole), Milly Mathis, and Tino Rossi.

That most famous of French cinematic styles, poetic realism, is normally associated with the extraordinary collaboration from 1935 to 1947 between Jacques Prévert and the directors Marcel Carné, Jean Renoir, and Jean Grémillon, and was often embodied in the doomed outsider figure played by Jean Gabin. It is salutary to be reminded that poetic realism has a prehistory, and that some of its precursors involved none of the above individuals and none of the expected settings. *Justin de Marseille* was created by the far-from-prestigious team of script-

---

58. See *Premier Plan*, nos. 22–23–24, 155–164.
59. See *Cahiers du cinéma*, nos. 60 and 78.

writer Carlo-Rim (real name Jean-Marius Richard) and director Maurice Tourneur (real name Maurice Thomas). Tourneur had been involved in all aspects of
the French theater from 1903 to 1909, then the cinema as an actor and director.
From 1914 to 1926, he had managed Éclair's U.S. subsidiary, directing some sixty
films and introducing modernist techniques to the American cinema. Back in
France, he had directed some of the best and worst of the late silent and early
sound films. His last film was to be the splendid *Impasse des Deux Anges* (1949).
Justin was, however, Carlo-Rim's first scenario, though he was to contribute to
fourteen others in the course of the decade, and to write and direct a number of
additional movies after the war, becoming president of the International Fed-
eration of Film Authors. A reporter in the early 1930s, he developed an article
on "Ma belle Marseille," which he felt could form the basis of a script organized
around the Corsican boss of the Marseilles underworld, Venture. A happy accident earned him Venture's permission.[60]

In the film, Justin is that gang boss, beloved of all of the citizens of his
quarter because he runs it as an orderly community. Berval, who plays Justin,
had acted in minor roles until 1932–1933, when he succeeded in the title role of
Maurin des Maures and *L'Illustre Maurin* as a womanizing Robin Hood, a Provençal folk hero who makes fools of the constabulary. The role of Justin, the benevolent criminal, was a logical extension of this, though written for someone else.
The introductory segment, in which his assistant, Le Fada, leads a group of kids
singing through the Marseilles streets indicates that this will not be a typical
film noir but a benign, meridional version in which shots of night and rain-
glistening streets are at odds with more optimistic shots, bathed in sun and good
humor. Any violence takes place off screen, conveniently eliding those aspects of
Justin's activities that might have offended the moral authorities, or Venture.[61]
Of course, relations between criminality and the working classes had always
been viewed sympathetically in film. It worked very differently from criminality associated with the bourgeoisie, which was normally symptomatic of their
inherent corruption hidden behind a hypocritical facade of respectability, and
therefore viewed extremely negatively. In connection with the working classes,
such criminality is seldom condemned, often tolerated, and occasionally celebrated.[62] In the early 1930s, it took three forms: (1) the picturesque apache, a
colorful figure in his striped shirt and beret, who fascinated all the women and

60. Rim, *Mémoires d'une vieille vague*, 39–70.
61. See Peyrusse, *Le Cinéma méridional*, 112–113, 127, 146.
62. See Crisp, *Genre, Myth and Convention*, 82–88.

beat them up a bit, but they loved him all the more for it; (2) the social realist delinquents—working-class men and women in urban slums who often found themselves forced into criminality to pay the rent or feed their families; and (3) the sentimental petty crook and con-man, found notably in René Clair's films and often played by Albert Préjean, amiable, bumptious, and full of *joie de vivre*. These three were to come together in the latter half of the decade in the famous poetic realist films, but *Justin de Marseille* is a key transitional film leading into *Pépé le Moko* (#56) two years later.

There is more than a little of the apache in Justin—a bit brutal with the girls, he will not take "no" for an answer, dragging one resisting girl through the mud to the hotel. Yet they love him for his masterful ways—the African's girl is so ashamed that her man works for Esposito rather than Justin (he has even tried to knife Justin) that she kills him for it. Justin's realm is the docks, the streets, the brothels, the restaurants, and the nightclubs of the city heart, which he polices as the gendarmes never could. (One such scene in a nightclub provides Tino Rossi with his first cinematic opportunity.) The central narrative concerns an attempt by a rival gang run by Esposito to muscle in on Justin's territory (namely drug trafficking). There is a nice scene where a coffin stuffed with drugs is unloaded at the docks: a "grieving" cortege of the two rival gangs winds through the city with the coffin, until Justin's men snatch it and the police give chase. Thereafter, various members of Esposito's gang try to do away with Justin, but he leads a charmed life. It is not just the womenfolk but the whole community who greet Justin warmly as a mate. He is a good family boy with a code of honor, and even the police hope for everyone's sake that he will triumph over his rapacious rivals, who are *not even French* (Italian, Chinese, African—the film is more than a little xenophobic), as he in fact finally does, disposing of Esposito in a knife fight on a cliff, casually rescuing his current flame, and parading her around his patch. No such happy end was to await his fellow marginals later in the decade.

The film opens with locals proudly promoting their city to a journalist (effectively, Rim's persona in the film): "Marseilles isn't at all like you think," they say, "it's a bit like Chicago. Take Justin, for instance. When you understand him you'll understand Marseilles." The journalist later publishes an article comparing the two cities. It was no doubt this overt characterization of the city as a criminal's fiefdom that aroused the ire of the city's mayor, who banned the film there in 1935, as did the mayor of Tarbes. It was one of the fifty-six "depressing, morbid and immoral" films banned at the outbreak of World War II, along with *Hôtel du Nord* (#89), *Gueule d'amour* (#64), and most of Renoir's films. Honorable company.

40. *Quelle drôle de gosse*

(*What a Crazy Kid*)
France, 1935, 85 min, b&w

Dir Léo Joannon; *Prod* Metropa-Film; *Scr* Yves Mirande; *Cinematog* Robert le Fe-
bvre; *Music* Jean Lenoir and Georges van Parys; *Sound* Marcel Courmes; *Edit*
Jacques Grassi; *Act* Danielle Darrieux (Lucie), Albert Préjean (Gaston), Lucien
Baroux (the butler), Jeanne Helbling (Bertrande), Suzanne Desprès (Madame
Gaudoin), André Roanne (Paul), and Jean Tissier.

The inclusion of this little-known comedy would be justified by its simple
entertainment value alone. It is the nearest the French cinema ever came to
matching the great American screwball comedies of this decade. Danielle Darrieux, who had debuted in the cinema four years before at the age of fourteen, is
astonishing as the outrageous, volatile female, resembling Katharine Hepburn
in her slightly masculine narrative agency combined with a feigned and manipulative femininity.

The screenplay, written by the amazingly prolific Yves Mirande (forty-eight
films in this decade as scriptwriter and/or director) is an astute variation on the
boulevard comedy in which Mirande specialized. It has Darrieux as Lucie, a secretary in love with her boss, but he feels he could never marry an employee, so
he fires her, intending to propose to her the next day. Not realizing this, however,
she throws herself in the river but is saved by a passing drunk named Gaston,
who turns out to be wealthy. The inevitable happens: there is an immediate antagonism between them, which the audience knows must lead to their getting
together at the end. Essentially, the scenario has three acts: (1) she is fired by Paul,
her boss; (2) she is saved from drowning by Gaston and taken back to his elegant
pad, where a party is in progress; as a result of her drunken and near naked ca-
vorting on the roof (don't ask) the party progressively degenerates into a chaotic
brawl, with her and some chess-players as the sole still center; and (3) Gaston
honorably intercedes with Paul to take her back, but when she encounters Paul
again, she realizes how stuffy he is and sneaks back to Gaston.

The opposition, such as it is, is therefore between a smug, self-centered businessman who considers a firm hand is needed with any prospective wife, and
a partying wastrel who is capable of recognizing her qualities. There is a wonderful role for Lucien Baroux as Alfred, the butler, whose task it is at one point
to keep her from leaving the flat again to commit suicide. Enraged at not being able to wrest the key from him, she exclaims what, in context, is one of the
funniest lines in all of French cinema: "You're exploiting the fact that I'm just a

feeble woman!" The climactic scene, of course, has her and Gaston discovering that they love one another. "Just as well," she says, "or I would have thrown myself in the river." But on hearing that she is going to stay, the butler groans that *he* is going to throw himself in the river. The helter-skelter pace and the delightful patterning of the narrative into a series of repetitions with variations make this a film well worth viewing.

This was the season in which the French cinema began its rapid recovery from the crisis years of 1932–1934, and *Quelle drôle de gosse* was one of the thirty films that attracted over 300,000 spectators in Paris alone. This must have been a great relief to Léo Joannon, whose previous films had been so unsuccessful as to be, in two cases, completely untraceable in release. Of the seventeen films he directed or supervised in the course of the decade, only three achieved any measure of success—this one, *Alerte en Méditerranée*, and *Vous n'avez rien à déclarer*—despite having in some cases such stars as Pierre Renoir and being released into major cinemas such as the Rex and the Gaumont Palace. Even the risqué *On a trouvé une femme nue* flopped badly. This by-current-standards extraordinary career pattern was not at all unusual in the context of a chaotic production system to which the astounding profits of the first two years of sound cinema had attracted profiteers and mountebanks. Numerous untalented individuals directed film after film, sometimes continuing throughout the decade without a single success. Others despaired and quit the industry after one, two, or five failures.

Here, however, Joannon had the advantage of a highly popular lead actor in Albert Préjean. Twenty-three-years older than Darrieux, he had nevertheless partnered her in six films from 1933 to 1935. All were lighthearted, sentimental comedies, often musicals. Their successful pairing was largely due to the sense of spontaneous gaiety that they generated and which contemporary commentators attributed to their nontheatrical origins. Nearly all of the acting fraternity on which the cinema depended during this decade belonged to one of the theatrical troupes run by Antoine, Gémier, Baty, Copeau, Dullin, and Louis Jouvet, making occasional forays into cinematic work when time permitted or to fund their less viable theatrical performances.[63] The acting style that they commonly brought to their films, designed to carry in the theater, was generally thought to be inappropriate in the cinema, coming across as grandiloquent, forced, and artificial. Préjean on the other hand, son of a suburban bistro owner, had been a cyclist, boxer, and aviator before getting a workman's job in the cinema and working his way up to stardom. He was not, as he acknowledged, the Valen-

---

63. See Crisp, *Classic French Cinema,* 154–157.

tino type of young lead, slender and romantic; his popularity was due to "a sympathetic face, constant acrobatics and a permanent smile."[64] Danielle Darrieux likewise did not come from the theater. A music student specializing in singing and the cello, she was, with Michèle Morgan, the only young girl to enter the French cinema and become a star without passing through the theater. By the age of twenty-two, in 1939, she had already figured in thirty films and was still appearing in them fifty years later. Perhaps her first nonfrivolous role was opposite Charles Vanel in *Abus de confiance* (1937, #69), which won the Grand Prix du Jury International at the 1937 Paris Exhibition.

41. *Crime et châtiment*

Crime and Punishment
France, 1935, 110 min, b&w

Dir Pierre Chenal; *Prod* Général Production; *Scr* Chenal, Christian Stengel, and Wladimir Strijewski, from the novel by Fyodor Dostoyevsky; *Cinematog* René Colas and Joseph-Louis Mundwiller; *Art dir* Aimé Bazin; *Music* Arthur Honegger; *Sound* Guy Moreau; *Edit* André Galitzine; *Act* Harry Baur (the judge), Pierre Blanchar (Raskolnikov), Madeleine Ozeray (Sonia), Lucienne Le Marchand (Dounia), Alexandre Rignault (Razoumikhine), Marcelle Géniat (Madame Raskolnikov), Sylvie, Magdeleine Bérubet, Catherine Hessling, Aimé Clariond, and Georges Douking.

The French cinema of the 1930s was heavily influenced by two groups of immigrants: the German contingent fleeing Hitler, which arrived in the early 1930s, and a Russian contingent that had fled the Russian Revolution and was already well established. In 1920, J. N. Ermollieff, who had been Pathé's agent in Russia, formed a production company in France that evolved into Albatros Films and later Ciné-France-Film, making many of the greatest French films of the 1920s. Aside from production itself, the principal areas of filmmaking that were affected were directing (Volkoff, Tourjansky), cinematography (Toporkoff, Bourgassoff, Roudakoff), set design (Lochakoff, Bilinsky), and acting (notably Mosjoukine), though the arrival of sound generated language difficulties for the actors. Later East European immigrants such as Lazare Meerson, Alexandre Trauner, André Andrejew, Eugène Lourié, Georges Annenkov, Georges Wahkévitch, and Léon Barsacq dominated set and costume design and determined the visual and ar-

64. Cadars, *Les Séducteurs du cinéma français*, 90.

chitectural direction of the French cinema for the next thirty years. Many more directors arrived, notably Trivas, Ozep, Granowsky, Strijewski, and Litvak, directing between them over forty films in the course of the decade. Willy and Kauffmann (brother of Dziga Vertov) joined Bourgassoff and Toporkoff to film between them 109 of the 1,300 films of the decade. Invariably artistically ambitious, often grandiose, the films of this Russian contingent figure among the most widely admired of the age. It would be difficult to overestimate the contribution that Russian immigrants made to French sound cinema. Inevitably, many of these productions demonstrate a preference for Russian themes and history, often as mediated through the great works of Russian literature.[65]

Along with *Les Bas-Fonds, Crime et châtiment* is the most successful and well-known adaptation of a Russian novel from this decade. Produced by Kagansky's production company, adapted by Pierre Chenal in conjunction with Wladimir Strijewski, and filmed by Mundwiller, whom Pathé had sent to Russia to look after cinematography there, this film was guaranteed a high degree of authenticity. Moreover, it featured Harry Baur, whose massive physical presence seems to have appealed to both French and Russian directors as "typically Russian"—he appeared as Tsar Paul I in *Le Patriote* (Maurice Tourneur, 1938), Tarass Boulba in the film of that name (Granowsky, 1936), a prosperous Volga wheat merchant in *Les Nuits moscovites* (Granowsky, 1934), and Rasputin in *La Tragédie impériale* (Marcel L'Herbier, 1938, #75). Here he is Judge Porphyre, investigating the deaths of a usurious pawnbroker and her daughter—murders that he (rightly) suspects were committed by Raskolnikov.

The focus of the novel, of course, is the religious implication of an opposition between faith and the intellect—the latter leads one astray, and one must pay the price of suffering to obtain redemption. Inevitably this theme still underpins the narrative: Raskolnikov is obsessed with "ideas," and knowing himself more intelligent than his fellows, feels that he should not be bound by their moral prejudices and conventions. He has written an article on criminality asserting that exceptional individuals should not stop at murder in the exercise of their will. "There is no god," he whispers to Sonia, the true believer who has been forced to prostitute herself to feed her family. Only cowards accept the social conventions deriving from faith, and he has to murder the pawnbroker to prove himself not a moral coward. But he also half wants his act to be known and acknowledged. For Chenal, "what mattered most was not the murderer's progress towards redemption but the psychological confrontation between a cunning

65. For details, see Crisp, *Classic French Cinema*, 160–174.

civil servant and an arrogant masochistic student, both playing a devilish game of cat and mouse."[66] The narrative is punctuated by three wonderful scenes exploring this confrontation, in which Raskolnikov and Porphyre engage in a psychological game of traps and evasions, which should culminate in Raskolnikov's admitting what they both know he did. Despite the false confession of a simpleminded workman and other delaying mechanisms, this is what, prompted by Sonia, ultimately happens.

Porphyre here can be read as the embodiment of divine justice, or at least of Destiny, pursuing Raskolnikov in much the same way that, a year before, Javert, also played by Baur, had embodied Destiny pursuing Jean Valjean in *Les Misérables*. But then, such destiny figures were to appear with disturbing regularity in French cinema for the next ten years, culminating in the rather too explicit appearance of Destiny in Marcel Carné's *Les Portes de la nuit* at war's end. For Pierre Blanchar, the role of Raskolnikov was one in a series of what André Sallée has characterized as those "obsessed, disoriented and hallucinatory roles" in which the actor came to specialize. "He built his career on uneasiness, whether experiencing it or engendering it. His best roles were those in which he played misunderstood characters and visionaries, often dangerous."[67] This present performance won Blanchar the Coupe Volpi at Venice in 1936. Indeed, *Crime et châtiment* can be seen as one of the films that began the progressive conquest of foreign markets by the French cinema. Admired in Japan, it was deemed the best foreign film of 1936 by the U.S. National Board of Review, beating *La Bandera* (#42), *La Maternelle* (#26), *Maria Chapdelaine,* and *Le Dernier Milliardaire.*

42. *La Bandera*

Escape from Yesterday (Foreign Legion)
France, 1935, 100min; b&w

Dir Julien Duvivier; *Prod* Société Nouvelle de Cinématographie; *Scr* Duvivier and Charles Spaak, from the novel by Pierre MacOrlan; *Cinematog* Jules Kruger; *Music* Jean Wiener and Roland-Manuel; *Art dir* Jacques Krauss; *Sound* Robert Teisseire; *Edit* Marthe Poncin; *Act* Jean Gabin (Pierre Gilieth), Robert Le Vigan (Lucas), Pierre Renoir (Captain Weller), Annabella (Aïsha), Margot Lion, Reine Paulet, Viviane Romance, Gaston Modot, Aimos, and Charles Granval.

66. Le Boterf, *Harry Baur*, 115–117.
67. Sallée, *Les Acteurs français*, 84–85.

La Bandera was Julien Duvivier's first unequivocal popular success. To that point, while no film had failed, and while critics praised his films as competent and meticulous, the general public had not followed. *Maria Chapdelaine* alone stood out a little above this run of modestly successful box-office results. Moreover, even the critics expressed confusion at the eclectic nature of his subject matter—psychodramas, adaptations of Simenon thrillers, religious blockbusters, and now a foreign legion story. Add to this the fact that no one could identify any stylistic continuity in his output and we can understand Roger Leenhardt's notorious auteurist review of *La Bandera*:

> It's hard to see any integrity in a director who can make *Le Petit Roi, Maria Chapdelaine* and *Golgotha* one after the other. The production of a director has value so long as a unity of tone, style and atmosphere . . . convey a particular way of thinking, a personal vision of the world. Consequently whatever they might produce we should always expect a lot from a Clair, a Feyder, a Renoir or a Chenal—nothing from a Duvivier. I find completely ridiculous the garbage spoken of this worthy craftsman, this honest workhorse of the French cinema.[68]

Yet as we have seen, Duvivier's early sound films were sometimes startlingly inventive (#8 and 14), and arguably, *La Bandera* was contributing to establishing just that thematic continuity that Leenhardt thought absent, manifesting yet again what was to prove a characteristic pessimism, the sense of an ineluctable fatality. The setting is familiar from *Le Grand Jeu* (#31): Gilieth, a disgraced individual, a killer on the run from the police, joins the foreign legion where he acquires the fraternal solidarity of the military and redeems himself through a noble death. But whereas *Le Grand Jeu* focuses on the personal anguish of the legionnaire faced with the ambivalent resurgence of a past love, and indeed with his resignation and despair as he reenlists and marches off to his death, *La Bandera* focuses rather on the exaltation of fraternity and the nobility of self-sacrifice inherent in colonial military duty. Like many other films of the decade, it provides an embodiment of Destiny in the figure of Lucas (Le Vigan), perhaps an agent of the law, certainly a bounty hunter attracted by the 50,000 francs reward placed on Gilieth's head. Lucas recalls a number of such figures of doom from the period 1930–1945, notably the two played by Harry Baur—

---

68. See Leenhardt, *Chroniques de cinéma*, 67.

Javert from *Les Misérables* (1933), hounding Jean Valjean through his multiple transformations of identity, and the judge from *Crime et châtiment* (1935, #41). Symbolizing at once Gilieth's past guilt and future tragic destiny, Lucas comes finally to appreciate Gilieth's nobility in the last fatal encounter with the rebel forces. As the lone survivor of the troop, he intones the names of those martyred in the national cause.

Leenhardt is surely correct to see this as a right-wing film, which, even though nominally set in the Spanish foreign legion, implicitly exalts France's civilizing mission in the colonies, and the esprit de corps of the African battalions that carry out that mission. Noël Burch and Geneviève Sellier are no less sardonic about the final apotheosis of the martyred heroes, "drawn out to unconscionable length" as Le Vigan "tells the rosary" of fallen martyrs.[69] Right-wing critics had been demanding "un cinéma viril" (a macho cinema, a cinema with guts), and this film was recognized as an appropriate response. It was taken from a novel by Pierre MacOrlan, who had begun as a nonconformist—*Quai des brumes* (#78) was adapted from one of his novels—but had moved steadily to the right, had just written *Verdun*, and had taken to appending his name to imperialist manifestoes. If further evidence were needed, the film was originally released with a dedication, "To General Franco and the soldiers who served their time in the Haff and Uest mountains." Nine months later, when Franco staged a coup to overthrow the Frente Popular, that dedication was strategically withdrawn.

There is a certain irony in the fact that Jean Gabin's screen persona should have begun to accrete definitively around a character in a right-wing film. The roles that were to further define this persona were all tentatively or resolutely left-wing, and called into question certain of the values asserted here—none more so than *Quai des brumes,* where his character is a deserter from the French Army that is here implicitly glorified. In the early 1930s, Gabin had acted in roles that earned him the appellation "un rude gars" (a tough guy) and "un chic type" (a good bloke), but when *La Bandera* was released, *Pour vous* published a series of articles on his new persona, best summarized in a *Ciné-Miroir* article:

> No one is better fitted for this role of a black sheep transformed into a superbly courageous soldier. Indeed, Gabin has preserved from the company he kept as a young man and from his military service the impression of being a man of the people. He likes to assume the air of a free-thinker, he uses slang, he shrugs his shoul-

69. Burch and Sellier, *La Drôle de guerre des sexes,* 58.

ders, he's simple, frank and open . . . and when the occasion calls for it he knows how to send trouble-makers unceremoniously about their business. Jean Gabin could be said to have created on screen a character type that didn't exist before his arrival—the bad lad with a heart of gold, mocking, sardonic, sensitive and generous, all of a piece, conscious of his strength but capable of putting it to use in the name of something higher.[70]

Twenty years later, of course, André Bazin also was to explore and summarize this mythic persona. He identifies a malevolent fatality that hounds "Gabin," his stoic and solitary endurance of it, the glimpse of a possible salvation in the form of a woman, the disillusion caused by her impurity or betrayal, the outburst of anger that places him in thrall to a fatality that he thought he had outdistanced, as personified in "that secular arm of contemporary destiny, the law—cops," and his final submission to that destiny.[71] We may witness the progressive definition of Gabin's persona in entries relating to *La Belle Équipe* (1936, #51), *Pépé le Moko* and *Gueule d'amour* (1936, #56 and 64), *Quai des brumes* and *La Bête humaine* (1938, #78 and 91), and *Le Jour se lève* and *Remorques* (1939, #94 and 100).

43. *Princesse Tam-Tam*

(*Princess Tam-Tam*)
France, 1935, 77 min, b&w

Dir Edmond Gréville; *Asst dir* Robert Bips; *Prod* Arys; *Scr* Pepito Abatino and Yves Mirande; *Cinematog* Georges Benoit; *Music* Elixo Grenet and Jacques Dallin; *Art dir* Lazare Meerson and Pierre Schild; *Sound* Antoine Archaimbaud; *Edit* Jean Feyte; *Act* Josephine Baker (Aouina), Albert Préjean (Max de Mirecourt), Robert Arnoux (Monsieur Coton, his secretary), Germaine Aussey (Lucie de Mirecourt), and Viviane Romance (Odette).

Josephine Baker was one of the few Americans to figure prominently in 1930s French culture. Of African American extraction, she was already notorious in French music-halls for her risqué performances (notably in the Revue Nègre in 1925, and her outrageous banana dance at the Folies Bergère) when

<hr>

70. *Ciné-Miroir*, no. 630, 1935.

71. André Bazin, 1947, reprinted in Chevallier and Egly, eds., *Regards neufs sur le cinéma*, 146–163.

she made her two feature films, *Zouzou* (released 14 December 1934) and *Princesse Tam-Tam* (1935). Not surprisingly, they capitalize on the two factors that distinguished her in the public's mind—her risqué performances and her negritude. *Zouzou* employs the much-loved structure of "the discovery of a star": the white actress is petulant and walks out; Zouzou, a laundress who does the washing for the theater, is overheard singing the show's songs; "Who is that girl?" exclaims the producer, and despite losing her man, she goes on to sing her heart out, grief transmuted into art.[72] The film is awash in concepts mythic to the decade: she and Jean Gabin are orphans, an improbable white brother and black sister separately adopted by circus folk; she loves him but he loves her fellow laundress, Claire. Negritude, art transcending grief, orphans, laundresses, a quasi-incestuous love—it could not fail at the box-office, and did not, rating tenth in its season.

Princesse Tam-Tam is, in mythic terms, even more interesting than *Zouzou*, if only for the fundamental opposition that it elaborates between nature and culture, savagery and civilization. This was one of the most intensely exploited oppositions of the decade, because it could be used to figure many of the conceptual problems being debated in the cinema and society, notably Paris versus the provinces, industry versus agriculture, the future versus the past, the relations between metropolitan France and the colonies, parenthood and childhood, spontaneity versus sophistication in art, and the common people (so simple and spontaneous in their tastes) versus their masters (often seen as too cunning and sly for their own good).

As with all structural oppositions, there was nothing inherently simplistic about the form that these debates took: the provinces could be figured as naive, backward, and boring, or as a site of all that was most beautiful, true, and sincere—or, indeed, as was often the case, as a complex mix of both. Most commonly, however, when a 1930s film with an urban setting allows its characters to visit the countryside, that visit is figured as a moment of idyllic transcendence, when the routines of daily existence can be momentarily put aside. Even a stroll in the park can serve this purpose, while a visit to a guinguette on the banks of the Marne was to become the archetypal goal of workers on their days off. This opposition was, of course, well-established long before the 1930s, but made its most prominent appearance then in the colonial and exotic genres, especially in documentaries dealing with far-flung colonies. Again the debate can be com-

---

72. See Crisp, *Genre, Myth and Convention*, 175, for other such instances, notably Mistinguett and Tino Rossi.

plex: the colonial and exotic can be ugly, barbaric, archaic, even lethal, or it can be a source of ease, tranquility, and serenity.[73]

Princesse Tam-Tam explores these oppositions by way of an Arab girl, Aouina, played by Josephine Baker, whom a sophisticated French writer suffering from writer's block discovers while touring in Tunisia. Dancing for kids in her typically extrovert, spontaneous, native way, she contrasts with the effete, sulky white women accompanying the writer. A "bête sauvage" (wild creature), she finds European ways (wearing shoes, using knife and fork) distasteful, a loss of liberty. Nevertheless, we next see her being transformed into someone capable of holding her own in polite society—a Pygmalion process involving dress and manners, learning to play the piano and to appreciate sculpted nature—"more beautiful than nature itself." The writer, Max de Mireville (Albert Préjean again), takes her to Europe, promotes her as a native princess, and promenades her around Paris high society, where of course she shows up the hypocrisy, malice, and deceit of his compatriots. This contrast between Africa and Europe is more effective in that, whether intentionally or not, Max is played by Préjean as a giggling, supercilious fop. Aouina becomes immensely popular, especially when seduced into an extrovert song and dance in a nightclub. This is surprisingly well choreographed, and worthy of an American musical. Josephine Baker's own dancing is not terribly impressive, but her voice is more than passable, or would be were it not for the insistent tremulous vibrato that had become a sort of trademark for her.

Aouina falls for Max and believes he feels the same for her, but Max's secretary disillusions her and advises her to return to Africa. At this point, we learn that the whole Pygmalion/princess/Paris segment, which we have just been watching, has simply been part of the novel that Max has developed around her personality. The status of the central part of the film turns out to be hypothetical, and we are left retrospectively groping for the moment when the film abandoned "reality"—probably the Pygmalion moment. This reflexive intellectual notion of a film containing different levels of reality without signaling them is typical of Edmond Gréville, who was one of the most intelligent and ambitious of the 1930s directors, now largely forgotten. With Pierre Chenal, he was in 1933–1934 seen as a coming force in French cinema, but faced with relative lack of box-office success (perhaps largely because of his intellectualism), he abandoned France for Britain, returning only in 1939 to film a fascinating premonitory *Menaces* (#98).

---

73. See ibid., 67, 92, 233–236, 255–257; also Leprohon, *L'Exotisme et le cinéma*. For a discussion of the sets, see Bergfelder et al., *Film Architecture*, 191–198.

In *Princesse Tam-Tam,* Max's new novel based on the fantasized transformation of Aouina has been titled *Civilization,* and the final scene of this humble film is one of the great moments of 1930s French cinema: we cut from Max signing copies of it in Europe to Aouina herself, with an indigenous husband and cherubic child somewhere in the Tunisian landscape. Their donkey comes upon a copy of *Civilization;* curling its tongue appreciatively around the title page, it gathers it up into its mouth and, in close-up, munches meditatively upon it and all it stands for.

44. *L'Équipage*

(*The Crew*); remade as *The Woman I Love* (1937)
France, 1935, 110 min, b&w

Dir Anatole Litvak; *Prod* Pathé-Natan; *Scr* Litvak and Joseph Kessel, from the latter's novel; *Cinematog* Armand Thirard; *Music* Arthur Honegger; *Art dir* Lucien Aguettand; *Sound* William Sivel; *Edit* Jean-Paul Le Chanois and Henri Rust; *Act* Charles Vanel (Lieutenant Maury), Jean-Pierre Aumont (Jean Herbillon), Jean Murat (the Captain), Annabella (Hélène/Denise), Suzanne Després, Pierre Labry, and Roland Toutain (fellow airmen), Serge Grave (Jean's young brother), Raymond Cordy, and Aimos.

Between 1930 and 1934, war films had not been frequent, and only two of those made achieved popular visibility—*Croix de bois* (1931, #15) and *La Bataille* (1933). *L'Équipage* is the first (and one of the finest) of the growing number of war and spy films made in the progressively more anxious years from 1935 to 1939. Expensive to make, they nevertheless promised rich returns to those producers willing to invest in them, since seventeen of them achieved significant box-office success in those years. Moreover, the military soon realized the propaganda potential of the two genres, and began to subsidize their production.

Most such war films, like *L'Équipage,* were set during the First World War. Jean Herbillon is a young airman just beginning an affair with Denise. Joining his new squadron, he befriends and comes to admire Lieutenant Maury, whose gunner he becomes, only to discover that his beloved Denise is in fact Maury's wife, Hélène. Distraught, he is torn between his passion for Denise and the fraternal loyalty that reigns in the squadron, between love and duty. He ignores Denise's appeals and departs with Maury on a dangerous mission, in the course of which he is killed. Maury, having come to understand the nature of his gunner's distress, tactfully lies to Hélène about Jean's final moments, allowing her to think he himself was unaware of their affair, and that Jean had died with the name of his love on his lips—"Denise."

Based on a 1923 novel by Joseph Kessel, who was himself a wartime fighter pilot, *L'Équipage* draws on personal experience for some key plot elements, and Kessel invited old colleagues (Carretier, Mermoz) onto the set to check authenticity. The plot, like so many 1930s plots, is distinctly Oedipal. Jean discovers that, unaware, he has made love to his "father's" woman. In the context of war films, this plot had already served in *La Bataille*, where during the Russo-Japanese war, a young English officer, in love with a Japanese girl (Annabella again), joins a ship's crew captained by her husband. He is killed in battle, and the Japanese officer, having come to understand what has occurred, commits hara-kiri. Charles Vanel and Jean-Pierre Aumont were to enact a similar situation in 1936 when they starred in *Roman d'un spahi,* and the same plot elements were to reappear in *Légions d'honneur* (1938), where a young French officer falls in love with the wife of his commanding officer (Vanel again), who wrongly believes him guilty of seducing her, and wounds him in a fight. Rather than betray his superior, the young officer allows himself to be accused of self-mutilation through cowardice. All three of these films—*L'Équipage, La Bataille,* and *Légions d'honneur*—were immensely popular. Not only was the love triangle among a woman, a young man, and an older military man of guaranteed fascination to the public of the day, with its themes of masculine friendship, anguished betrayal, and high-minded self-sacrifice, but the finer points of honor that emerged in such plots melded well with the heroic representation of the military that was being systematically constructed during this period. The French military was noble, fundamentally peace-loving, but strong to act when strength was needed.

Aspiring to be a patriotic statement, *L'Équipage* was provided by Pathé-Natan with the funding to qualify as a quality product, and is thus symptomatic of another crucial move within the French film industry at the midpoint of the decade, toward a level of technological sophistication that attracted the attention of international audiences. Moreover, it typified a further trend already mentioned, namely the move away from popular comedies toward powerful dramas. The acting is reserved, underplayed, and sober, where the plot might easily have led to melodramatic excesses. Unusually, even the young actor playing Jean's younger brother is effective and credible. The photography throughout is admirable, exquisitely sharp and well-framed. The music by Arthur Honegger borrows usefully from Richard Wagner to support the battle scenes. The atmosphere of collegiality and affection among the men of the squadron is brilliantly constructed, and the découpage effectively evokes the alternation between a somber awareness of danger and a hectic letting-off of steam. This alternation, in turn, is often brutally asserted through abrupt juxtapositions, as grotesque can-cans erupt into meditative moments (e.g., *L'Atlantide*, #16). Elsewhere, sound bridges of diegetic piano or superimpositions of clasped hands elide breaks and unite scenes in a lyrical forward movement. The three brief outbursts of ground warfare recall *Croix de bois* in their violence—atmospheric shots involving night and fog are suddenly interrupted by blasts of sound and light—while the aerial warfare, largely using back-projection, is unusually credible. This is filmmaking controlled by an expert director.

Not least interesting is the use of Vanel against type. Acting in films since 1912, he had figured in thirty-nine silent films, and this was the twentieth of his forty-four sound films from the 1930s (about 140 sound films altogether). Solid, taciturn, tough, and often sinister, Vanel was usually seen in "films policiers," where he might be on either side of the law but always a force to be reckoned with. Here he is quite the contrary: disliked and marginalized by his fellow airmen, introverted and socially inept, he makes of Lieutenant Maury a vulnerable figure who contemplates suicide and only blossoms when speaking of his wife or when in the company of Herbillon—the two people who, the one knowingly and the other unknowingly, are to betray him. His shrewd understanding of this situation at the end is a fine piece of acting.

In his wartime anti-Semitic diatribe, Lucien Rebatet lists the director of *L'Équipage*, Anatole Litvak, among the filmmakers responsible for French decadence and defeat. Litvak had made seven films in France, from *Cœur de Lilas* (1931) to *Mayerling* (1936), and all those that have survived are worthy of admiration (see #27). But being Jewish, he had to move on as the threat of Nazi invasion loomed. Fortunately, *L'Équipage* proved so popular that Litvak was invited to Hollywood to remake it as *The Woman I Love* (1937), and he did not return to France until the 1950s, at which point he made a further five films.

45. *La Kermesse héroïque*

Carnival in Flanders
France-Germany, 1935, 150 min, b&w

Dir Jacques Feyder; *Asst dir* Marcel Carné; *Prod* Tobis; *Scr* Charles Spaak and Feyder; *Cinematog* Harry Stradling, Louis Page, and André Thomas; *Art dir* Lazare Meerson, Alexandre Trauner, and Georges Wakhévitch; *Sound* Hermann Storr; *Edit* Jacques Brillouin; *Act* Françoise Rosay (Cornélia), Micheline Cheirel (Siska), Jean Murat (the Duke), André Alerme (burgomaster), Bernard Lancret (Jan Breughel), Alfred Adam (butcher), Louis Jouvet (chaplain), Arthur Devère, and Pierre Labry.

Although well-known and well-liked, this is a rather tedious one-joke film in fancy dress. The one joke concerns the wives of the councilors of a Flemish town occupied by the Spanish army, who, disgusted by their husbands' cowardice (to avoid facing the invaders, the burgomaster pretends to be dead), welcome the Spanish officers into their homes and their beds. Charmed by this civil gesture, the Spanish officers withdraw their soldiers, leaving the town unharmed and the husbands shamed. It is interesting to contrast the tolerant amusement shown by the French toward this Belgian instance of "horizontal collaboration" with their attitude ten years later toward French women who so indulged an occupying army.

As with Jacques Feyder's two previous films, the script for *La Kermesse héroïque* was written for Feyder by Charles Spaak, a fellow Belgian. With Jacques Prévert, Spaak was the most important scriptwriter of the decade, scripting some thirty-four films in the period 1930–1939 (and sixty altogether between 1928 and 1959)—four for Julien Duvivier, including *La Bandera* (#42), *La Belle Équipe* (#51), and *La Fin du jour* (#93); three for Jean Grémillon, including *La Petite Lise* (#6) and *Gueule d'amour* (#64); two for Jean Renoir, including *La Grande Illusion* (#60); and others for Marcel L'Herbier and Christian Jaque. Spaak had a particularly close understanding with Feyder, whom he thought of as a bitter man (he was also a drunkard according to Charles Vanel—a man who "needed a little doping up to keep going; Rosay had to keep a constant eye on him on set"[74]). For Spaak, Feyder was a fantasist who did not believe in anything much, and a great cynic who took pleasure in portraying failed lives: "Around all his great characters there floats a fog of dreams, of nostalgia for lost paradises. . . . He had a liking for human wrecks. . . . For his protagonists, fine feelings are difficult to sustain; events, daily life conspire to bring them low, to corrode them."[75] In this respect, *La Kermesse héroïque* is an exception, standing out from his other 1930s films as a more sunny and apparently unproblematic film. "I wanted a bit of light-hearted relief after all those grim films," Feyder wrote, "and to relax a bit with something of a farce."[76] Spaak had written a brief script for *La Kermesse héroïque* some ten years before, and it was taken up now because Tobis saw it as an appropriate film for Feyder's wife, Françoise Rosay. Originally entitled "The Six Bourgeois of Alost," it was not specific to time or place, and its original aim was to make a sardonic comment on the national heroics that followed World War I. Setting it back in sixteenth- and seventeenth-century Flanders allowed Feyder to commission sets

74. See Charles Vanel's contribution to *Jacques Feyder, ou le cinéma concret*.
75. See Charles Spaak's contribution to *Jacques Feyder, ou le cinéma concret*.
76. Feyder and Rosay, *Le Cinéma, notre métier*, 40.

from Lazare Meerson that recalled the Flemish painters of that age. Meerson was one of the most influential set-decorators of the French cinema, producing sets for thirty-six French sound films before his premature death in 1938. His best-known work was done for René Clair and Feyder. It is hard to believe now, but Meerson claimed to see his task as essentially self-effacing: his sets had to establish an atmosphere that lent credibility to the film, and that credibility would be compromised if the sets drew attention to themselves: "The most difficult thing is to compose an atmospheric décor which, unnoticed, underlines the action and confers credibility on it, rather than a super-architecture before which the jaw drops in awe."[77] In this aim, it could be argued that he fails precisely in the films of Clair and in *La Kermesse héroïque*. In the latter, critics noted the sheer plastic beauty of the sets, which are based on paintings of the period but which tended to distract from (or compensate for) the rather tenuous and slow-moving action.[78] Others, noting various discrepancies and inconsistencies, have asserted that "what Meerson and his team succeed in creating is less a copy of a Flemish town than a fictional space that, in nostalgia for other kinds of texts, corresponds to . . . the popular conception of such a site."[79]

Most critics thought the film insubstantial and complained that so many millions of francs had been spent on such trivia. Nevertheless, the set design earned the film first prize for Best Set Decoration at the Venice Biennale in 1936. For other critics, it was rather the political and ideological implications of the film that attracted reservations. Feyder's assumption that a film set in such remote times would not attract the outrage of certain of his earlier films was entirely misplaced. Flemish nationalists saw it as mocking the inadequacy of their resistance against the German invasion of Belgium in World War I. Feyder and Rosay recalled that "screenings were interrupted every night: wild shouts, stink bombs, seating destroyed, rats being released in the theatres; 38 arrests in Antwerp, police baton charges, 27 arrests in Amsterdam, police reinforcements in Brussels, banned in Bruges, demonstrations in Gand."[80] As Spaak remarked, "Caesar praised us Belgians as the bravest of races; I don't remember him praising our sense of humour."[81]

But the Flemish were not the only ones to see the film as unduly flattering to an occupying army. Henri Jeanson, ever provocative, claimed to detect a

77. *Ciné-Magazine*, 21 January 1927.
78. For critics, see Ford, *Jacques Feyder*, and Bachy, *Jacques Feyder*.
79. Bergfelder et al., *Film Architecture*, 217–218, 234–242.
80. Feyder and Rosay, *Le Cinéma, notre métier*, 42–43.
81. Marion, ed., *Le Cinéma par ceux qui le font*, 113.

scent of Nazi ideology in it (Feyder sued him for slander but lost, reputedly on the grounds that "Nazi" was not an insult), and others wondered if the anticlericalism implicit in Louis Jouvet's chaplain did not perhaps derive from Joseph Goebbels's Kulturkampf. The general public in France was under no such apprehension, and the film attracted audiences as large as Feyder's two preceding films. Interestingly enough, it was particularly popular in Germany, though to identify the reason for this it would be necessary to analyze the German version, which though shot at the same time, used a largely different cast. Contemporary accounts suggest that the change of cast modified drastically the relationships among characters, with resultant thematic implications.[82]

After a film in Britain, Feyder returned to France to make *Les Gens du voyage,* another in the gritty realist-cum-melodrama style of *Le Grand Jeu* (#31) and *Pension Mimosas* (#36), then *La Loi du Nord* (1939), released during the war as *La Piste du Nord,* which unfortunately seems to have disappeared. His last film was made in Switzerland during the war, though two years before his death, he was technical adviser (and probably much more) to Marcel Blistène on the wonderful and much underrated film *Macadam* (1946).

82. For the best account of these differences, see Rosay, *La Traversée d'une vie,* 205–206.

PART III

The Rise of Poetic Realism

46. *Le Crime de Monsieur Lange*

(*Mr. Lange's Crime*)
France, 1936, 83 min, b&w

Dir Jean Renoir; *Asst dir* Pierre Prévert; *Prod* Films Obéron; *Scr* Jacques Prévert, based on an outline by Renoir and Jean Castanier; *Cinematog* Jean Bachelet; *Music* Jean Wiener, with a song by Joseph Kosma, to words by Prévert; *Art dir* Castanier and Robert Gys; *Sound* Guy Moreau; *Edit* Marguerite Houllé-Renoir; *Act* Florelle (Valentine), René Lefebvre (Lange), Jules Berry (Batala), Nadia Sibirskaïa (Estelle), Marcel Levesque (concierge), Sylvia Bataille, Odette Talazac, Claire Gérard, Janine Loris, Marcel Duhamel, Henri Guisol, Maurice Baquet, Jacques-Bernard Brunius, Jean Dasté, Sylvain Itkine, Edmond Beauchamp, René Génin, Guy Decomble, and Fabien Loris.

Monsieur Lange's crime is to kill his boss, a strategy that the film finds perfectly comprehensible. This is a great film, that every film-lover should see, whatever his or her political orientation. Made by left-wing film personnel at a time of high optimism, "It is," as Noël Burch and Geneviève Sellier note, "a utopian film par excellence, proclaiming the end of capitalist exploitation and the dawn of a new era."[1] Initially entitled "Sur la cour," it deals with a close-knit community of working men and women living around a courtyard, many of them employed in Valentine's laundry or Batala's printing shop. Batala, the emblematic capitalist boss, is played with genius by Jules Berry at his most sinister—voluble, slimy, gesticulatory, exploitative. To evade financial ruin, he takes advantage of a providential train crash to exchange his identity for the vestments of a dead priest, thus allowing the film's anticapitalism to flow over into anticlericalism. In Batala's absence, one of his workers, a mild-mannered fantasist called Lange, reorganizes his printing shop as a workers' cooperative, which flourishes on the profits from Lange's *Arizona Jim* tales. Batala reappears (still as a priest) and de-

1. Burch and Sellier, *La Drôle de guerre des sexes*, 45.

mands the proceeds; Lange shoots him. The story is told in flashback at an inn on the Belgian border, where Lange and Valentine are seeking refuge. The innkeeper and his clients have understood and wave them through.

This is the high point of enthusiasm for workers' cooperatives. The curve can be traced from *Tumultes* (1931), where cooperatives are little more than a front for criminal activities, through *Si j'étais le patron* (1934, #33), where an eccentric millionaire ensures that cooperation replaces competition and that the workers' inventiveness is no longer stifled by greedy bosses, to *Lange*, and then *Hercule* (1937), in which an enlightened newspaper proprietor comes to recognize the cynical and ruthless exploitation that his workers endure, and hands the paper over to their cooperative. After 1936–1937, however, the attitude toward such cooperatives in film was not always so optimistic.

The energy and optimism of *Lange* derive in large part from the participation in its production of members of the Groupe Octobre (see #21), a left-wing avant-garde theatrical group. It was one of that group, Jean Castanier, who devised with Jean Renoir the initial scenario, which was subsequently made over and extended by the Groupe Octobre's principal scriptwriter, Jacques Prévert. For René Lefebvre, who plays Monsieur Lange, Prévert, not Renoir, was the true author of the film, while Bernard Chardère argues that it should be considered a Groupe Octobre film with Renoir as technical director.[2] Jacques's brother, Pierre, was assistant director, while all of the actors in the Groupe Octobre have roles in the film. Unquestionably much of the film's exuberant iconoclasm comes from Prévert and the group, but reined in and given direction by Renoir in a way that would have benefited the group's earlier effort *L'Affaire est dans le sac* (#21). Renoir himself acknowledged that the film evolved day to day in intense collaboration between himself and Prévert, with help from the actors.[3]

The political argument is outspoken: daily life and work under capitalism is intolerable. Its advertisements for Ranimax pills insult the intelligence, while its billboards block out the sun from a sick man's room. Lange's Arizona Jim fantasies provide an archetypal instance of the escape to a better land, "Mexico, where the sun always shines," and where a popular hero kills off a few villains from time to time, just as the innkeeper and his anarchist client would like to. Arizona Jim's foreshadowed confrontation is with the fascists, and we know how he will fix them—just as Lange fixes Batala, who threatens their idealistic social experiment. The values here opposed are community and selfishness, altruism and greed. The exuberance of the film, however, comes not just

2. *Premier Plan*, nos. 22–23–24, 165.
3. Renoir, *Renoir on Renoir*, 85, 227.

from its political aggression and optimism but from its constant technical inventiveness. This had not always been Renoir's strong point, and it is easy, for instance, to see *La Nuit du carrefour* (1932), based on a Georges Simenon novel, as incompetent to the point of incomprehensibility. One technical area for which Renoir has become celebrated, and on which he came to pride himself in later life (when, incidentally, he no longer practiced it), was the preference for long takes and deep-focus camera work, which signaled a resistance on his part to the intense psychological editing then being used by American filmmakers to attract identification with the central characters (see #11). André Bazin was to promote these long takes as a key "realist" technique, to be admired because they respected the integrity of diegetic space-time.[4] And it is true that, whereas the average shot length (ASL) of French films descended steadily from about 15 seconds in the early 1930s to 8–10 seconds at war's end, as French filmmakers came to accept American practices, Renoir maintained throughout the 1930s an ASL of about 18 seconds. Indeed, *Le Crime de Monsieur Lange* has an amazing ASL of 24 seconds. The film is broken up into less than half the number of shots of its contemporaries.

A crucial question, however, is whether this succession of deep-focus long takes really "respects reality." There are famous instances where it does, serving to integrate the characters in the foreground into an ambient and sometimes distant bustle of action. In *Lange,* when the camera is in Charley's sickroom as the billboard is torn down, we see Charley in bed in the foreground, the courtyard and Charley's mates beyond, then Estelle in the distance being brought forward to greet him; or again when Batala storms out of the room through door after door, room after room beyond. But much more often the use of long takes tended to seduce Renoir into elaborate camera movements within the shot in order to keep the action in frame without cutting or privileging any one character's subjectivity. These camera movements come across as foregrounded technical virtuosity rather than realism. There had been, for instance, a long, dizzy tracking shot in *La Chienne* (1931, #11), and complex pans and tracks in *Boudu sauvé des eaux* (1932, #20) as Boudu is rescued from the water. But these are as nothing compared to the astounding, unmotivated pan and track, for a time against the grain of the movement, in *Lange* from Valentine and Batala in the courtyard up to Lange's window, then following him through window after window and down stairs toward Valentine and Batala, then quitting him to circle back and reframe him as he corners and kills Batala. And this is only one of several such

4. Ibid., 228; Bazin, *Jean Renoir,* 36–43, thought his description of the techniques used by Renoir is simply wrong.

rhetorical flourishes that must amaze any modern spectator watching this film: at times the screen appears to be torn open to reveal what's behind, and when the *Arizona Jim* magazine sells well, we see a montage flurry of superimposed editions, which momentarily turns into whirlpools of magazine covers. Again, the connection between Jim's disposing of a few villains and galloping off and Lange's disposing of Batala and driving off is made by way of galloping music that in the finale accompanies Lange's car to the frontier. However Bazin might attempt to justify such moments in terms of realism, they come across as inventively avant-garde to the point of formalism. Despite this exuberance, Peter Harcourt is perceptive in noting that the finale is qualified by melancholy, in that Lange's freedom is at the cost of exile: "To take a stand is to isolate yourself from society and happiness."[5]

47. *Razumov* or *Sous les yeux d'Occident*

Under Western Eyes
France, 1936, 90 min, b&w

Dir Marc Allégret; *Asst dir* Yves Allégret and Françoise Giroud; *Prod* André Daven; *Scr* Hans Wilhelm, H. G. Lustig, and Jacques Viot, from the novel by Joseph Conrad; *Cinematog* Michel Kelber; *Music* Georges Auric; *Art dir* Eugène Lourié; *Sound* Marcel Courmes; *Edit* Yvonne Beaugé; *Act* Pierre Fresnay (Razumov), Jean-Louis Barrault (Haldin), Jacques Copeau (Mikulin), Pierre Renoir (police inspector), Michel Simon (Lespara), Gabriel Gabrio (Nikita), Danièle Parola (Nathalie), Roger Karl (His Excellency), Wladimir Sokoloff, Aimos, and Jean Dasté.

Histories of the French cinema are full of dismissive remarks about Marc Allégret. He is frequently accused of a lack of personality (or at least an inability to stamp it on his films), a flaccidity in the direction of actors, and a lack of ambition. The only talent that critics then or since have consistently recognized in him is his ability to spot potential star quality in the young, and a concomitant fascination with the theme of youth, or regret for lost youth. Critics might also, however, have acknowledged an ability to spot a potentially profitable scenario. Of the fifteen films that he directed during the decade, none flopped, and eight are included in this filmography, for a number of reasons always including box office success: *Fanny* (#10), with 664,000 viewers in Paris; *L'Hôtel du Libre Échange*

5. Harcourt, *Six European Directors*, 83–85.

(#35), c. 280,000; *Zouzou* (#43), 430,000; *Razumov* (#47), 300,000; *Gribouille* and *Orage* (#63), 404,000 and 471,000, respectively; *La Dame de Malacca* (#65), 321,000; and *Entrée des artistes* (#82), 529,000. All of these box office figures would have secured their respective films places among the principal successes of the year, and if box office were the sole criterion, nearly all of his other films would figure here also—*Mam'zelle Nitouche* (1931), 405,000; *La Petite Chocolatière* (1932), 450,000; *Lac aux Dames* (1934), 478,000; *Sans famille* (1934), 364,000; and *Les Beaux Jours* (1935), 323,000.

His critics might also have recognized in him an ability to surround himself with prominent collaborators who assured his films high visibility among the social and cultural elite. His familiarity with most of the great figures of the age originated to some extent in his longstanding relationship with André Gide, as protégé and "nephew," from about 1918 until 1937 (at which point he left Gide's residence to marry). As secretary and part-time cameraman, he had accompanied Gide to Africa, and brought back a feature-length documentary, *Voyage au Congo* (1926), which brought Allégret to the attention of the film world.[6] Early sound films with his friends Raimu and Pierre Braunberger recommended him to Marcel Pagnol, who invited him to direct *Fanny* (#10). A series of cultural soirées that appear to have flopped nevertheless earned him the friendships of Pablo Picasso and Man Ray. Conversations with Philippe de Rothschild at cocktail parties and dinners led to the latter's funding the production and distribution of Vicki Baum's latest novel, *Lac aux Dames,* and Rothschild brought to that production Colette, Georges Auric, Jean-Georges Auriol, and Lazare Meerson.[7] A wild success at the time, it is nevertheless little more than a Mills and Boon romp, with a distant hint of Éric Rohmer. This degree of patronage and friendship guaranteed him the ability to choose his scenarios and actors in a way many better-known directors must have envied, and in 1935, he chose Joseph Conrad's *Under Western Eyes,* with an astonishing cast of Pierre Fresnay, whom he had directed in *Fanny;* Michel Simon; Pierre Renoir; Jean-Louis Barrault, who had just begun to appreciate that he could fund his theatrical enterprises more effectively if he dabbled in cinema from time to time; and that other great theatrical director Jacques Copeau, who in the prewar years had founded, with Gide (among others), the NRF (Nouvelle Revue Française), then the Vieux Colombier troupe of actors, several of whom appear with him here—Barrault, Fresnay, and Copeau's son-in-law, Jean Dasté.

6. Gide reputedly wrote *Les Faux-Monnayeurs* for Allégret.
7. See Andrew, *Mists of Regret,* 189–192, and Houssiau, *Marc Allégret,* 189–192.

The story is, at least overtly, the most aggressively political that Allégret was ever to direct. His brother Yves, his assistant here and on most of his 1930s films, was the more political of the two, participating in the activities of Prévert's Groupe Octobre, and was subsequently to make a series of more aggressively intellectual films. But Marc confined himself normally to social and psychological situations. In *Razumov*, Barrault, friend of libertarians and anarchists, is appropriately cast as Haldin, a Russian revolutionary who assassinates the prime minister. He takes refuge with a former friend, Razumov, who is apolitical but reluctantly agrees to shelter Haldin and contact his friends. Due to a misunderstanding, however, and to save his own skin and career, Razumov betrays Haldin to the police chief, Mikulin. A further misunderstanding, fostered by the police chief, leads the group of revolutionaries to believe that Razumov has actively participated in the assassination, and he is warmly received by them. The plot revolves around Razumov's progressively more intolerable situation as an apolitical caught up in dangerous political games, wrongly believed by Haldin's colleagues to be a revolutionary, and manipulated by the police chief to provide inside information on the revolutionary group. More and more distraught, he finally cracks and confesses to the group his betrayal of Haldin. When one of them follows him down a sordid urban alleyway and guns him down, his dying words are to thank the assassin for relieving him of his guilt.

Conrad's Eastern European heritage here brings him close to Fyodor Dostoyevsky's *Crime and Punishment*, filmed the year before by Pierre Chenal (#41), where another Russian student guilty of murder is hounded by a police chief, or for that matter to *Les Misérables* (Raymond Bernard, 1933), where the police chief Javert similarly embodies a relentless fatality. The film also constitutes Allégret's gesture toward the rich stream of Russian material in French interwar cinema originating with the contingent of filmmakers who migrated to France after the Russian Revolution and set up Les Films Albatros. But *Razumov* is raised above these influences by the strong storyline and brilliant acting. In particular, Jacques Copeau, whose theatrical acting (as opposed to his management of the troupe) seems to have often attracted slighting references, is here astounding as Mikulin, implying by the slightest of sly glances and gestures his appreciation of the situation and of the advantage he can extract from it. Perhaps the close attention of the film camera better suited his acting style than the auditorium, and it is a great pity he made so few appearances in the films of the decade (five, including two as a judge).

As this account makes clear, however, though nominally a political film, the real focus of attention is the psychological trauma and crisis suffered by Razumov, and the political context is more a pretext than a central element.

48. *La Terre qui meurt*

(*The Dying Land*)
France, 1936, 88 min, Francita Color Film

Dir Jean Vallée; *Prod* Paris-Color-Film; *Scr* Charles Spaak, from the novel by René Bazin; *Cinematog* Marcel Lucien; *Music* Jane Bos; *Art dir* Roland Quignon; *Sound* Jacques Hawadier; *Act* Pierre Larquey (Old Lumineau), Simone Bourday (Marie Rose), Jean Cyrano (Jean Nesmy), Line Noro (Éléonore), Germaine Sablon (Félicité), Mady Berry (la Michelonne), Marcelle Monthil, Alexandre Rignault (Mathurin), Robert Arnoux (François), Robert Goupil, Romain Bouquet, Georges Flamant, Noël Roquevert, and Sinoël.

La Terre qui meurt has two main claims to our attention: it was one of the earliest French color films, and it is a principal prewar instance of the "retour à la terre" (back to the land) ideology that was to be so heavily promoted by the Vichy government.

"Back to the land" already implies a fundamental structural opposition between the countryside, which is being abandoned, and the city, which is seducing away the younger generation with its lure of excitement, social mobility, liberty, and individual self-realization. The city represents the future, whereas generations of the same family tilling the same land represent the past. The storyline of *La Terre qui meurt* embodies these oppositions in a farming family from the Vendée: the land is dying as the old mother has died; the old father is grief-stricken because two of his five children have left for the city; a third has sailed away to seek his fortune in Brazil; and while the eldest son, a hulking bully, is possessive of his future inheritance, he has, alas, no love for it. Only the young daughter has a feel for the land, but she loves Jean, from the marshy coastal areas, which the old father despises almost as much as the city. To make matters worse, the farm is in hock to that most sinister of all city creatures, a lawyer, who is looking to foreclose on them as he has on many others. After a series of crises, the old man comes to recognize and accept the commitment of Jean and his daughter to the farm's future, and hands over control to them. The eldest son, mad with malevolent rage, asserts that no one will have the farm if not him, and in trying to set fire to the haystacks, accidentally brings about his own death. A final panel informs us that

> Thus, despite everything
> The soil of France will live again
> Through the Love and Labor
> Of its children.

And another generation of children will be able to engage in the twee folkloric rituals and round-dances with which the film opens.

Interestingly, the film is not Manichean in the choices it offers the five children: given the death-in-life poverty, frustration, and boredom of their life on the farm, it is perfectly understandable that three of them should look for fulfillment elsewhere. François and Éléonore run a bistro in town; later, François is seen covered in grime in an industrial setting, and Éléonore is trapped in a difficult relationship with a callous man. Neither are rich, but despite their trials, neither regrets the choice to leave the farm. The city, after all, is precisely the place where choices are available. So while the overall message of the film concerns the necessity for generational continuity and love of the land, the problem is not simplified out of existence.

The other principal prewar films to promote this essentially conservative ideology were those made by Marcel Pagnol from the novels and stories of his Provençal compatriot Jean Giono—*Jofroi* (1933), *Regain* (1937, #67) and *La Femme du boulanger* (1938, #79). They, however, did not benefit from the use of color. *La Terre qui meurt* was one of only two color feature films made in France during the 1930s, the other being *Jeunes filles à marier* (1935), also directed by Jean Vallée. When one considers the rate at which Hollywood was producing color films, especially after the commercialization of the Technicolor process in 1928, this tardiness in the French cinema industry can seem surprising. Of course, there had been hand-painted color films—in fact, by 1910 Pathé had a workshop with four hundred workers devoted to it—and tinting and toning of film-stock was routine practice during the silent period. Moreover, a number of more sophisticated additive or subtractive color processes had been developed in France—histories mention at least seven, the first formulated as early as 1895—but patents for the two most promising, developed by Berthon and Keller-Dorian, were bought out by American and German firms, and by the late 1920s, their developers were both working for Kodak. A crucial factor, as always in France, was the lack of investment capital available to the industry. In this respect—early development, late implementation, lack of investment capital, bought out by foreign firms that then commercialized it and charged French firms heavily for the right to use it—color technology is typical of all the "new technologies" of the period, including sound itself. Similarly, cinemascope was developed by Professor Henri Chrétien and used in 1927 by Claude Autant-Lara to film *Construire un feu*, but then bought up by Fox and finally commercialized in 1953.[8]

---

8. See my account of these processes in Crisp, *Classic French Cinema*, ch. 3, esp. 134–146.

The color system used by Vallée for his two films was the Francita-Realita process, a three-color additive process that split the image into three separate black-and-white images by means of blue, red, and green filters. At the point of projection, the film was reconstituted using a special lens to recreate a single color image. Unfortunately, the only surviving copy of the film found is a black-and-white contratype, so the effectiveness of the use of color can no longer be judged. Contemporary accounts suggest a problem with the predominance of blue, but that a convincingly realistic representation of the colors of the countryside had been obtained.

Finally, it is rather surprising to find that the screenplay for this film was written by Charles Spaak, who was to write, adapt, and/or produce dialogue for no fewer than thirty-four films between 1930 and 1939, for Jean Grémillon, Julien Duvivier, Jacques Feyder, and Pierre Renoir, not to mention Marc Allégret, Pierre Chenal, Georges Lacombe, Léonide Moguy, Robert Siodmak, Marcel L'Herbier, and Christian-Jaque (see #44). One of the most prolific and respected of French scriptwriters, Spaak's most famous scripts are unreservedly left-wing and humanitarian in their ideological orientation, so *La Terre qui meurt* looks distinctly out of place in the list. Nonetheless, as a journeyman scriptwriter, Spaak also produced less well-known scripts in every conceivable popular genre, such as those for *Adémaï au moyen âge; Aloha, le chant des îles; Les Gaietés de la finance; Il a été perdu une mariée;* and the spy story *Les Loups entre eux*. He was nothing if not versatile.

49. *La Vie est à nous*

(Life Belongs to Us)
France, 1936 (not commercially released until 12 November 1969), 62 min, b&w

Dir and Scr (in alphabetical order) Jacques Becker, Jacques-Bernard Brunius, Marcel Carné, Henri Cartier-Bresson, Jean-Paul Le Chanois, Jean Renoir, Pierre Unik, P. Vaillant-Couturier, and André Zwobada; *Technical Supervision* Renoir; *Prod* Parti Communiste Français; *Cinematog* Jean-Serge Bourgoin, Alain Douarinou, Claude Renoir, and Jean Isnard; *Act* Julien Bertheau, Jean Renoir, Le Chanois, Becker, Jean Dasté, Brunius, Max Dalban, Charles Blavette, Gaston Modot, Nadia Sibirskaïa, Madeleine Sologne, Gabrielle Fontan, Madeleine Sylvain, Claire Gérard, Simone Gulsin, Madeleine Dax, Muse Dalbray, Yolande Olivieiro, O'Brady, Marcel Duhamel, Sylvain Itkine, Roger Blin, Fabien Loris, and Pierre Unik.

The inclusion of a piece of political propaganda such as this in the midst of a series of fictional narratives might seem incongruous, but in the context of the times, this film is very much in line with a number of politically oriented feature films made by members of the production team. It is, moreover, a brilliant piece of propaganda. For those who thought that, working around 1970, Jean-Luc Godard and Jean-Pierre Gorin had no predecessors on which to draw except the Russian filmmakers of the 1920s, *La Vie est à nous* comes as a revelation. It is in three parts, the first of which is the most innovative and intellectually exciting— a juxtaposition of documents, interventions, and satirical reworkings of existing material—while the second consists of three brief scripted fictions of "typical" contemporary sociopolitical situations, and the third a series of addresses and exhortations from French Communist Party (PCF) leaders.

The strategy of the first section is to set up a schoolroom presentation relating to the industrial and cultural wealth of France, then to question it as the schoolchildren themselves do: where is this national wealth, so obviously absent from their deprived lives? All in the hands of the wealthiest two hundred families, we are told, who are then mocked and ridiculed in a variety of ways:

- Board members mouth hypocritical regrets while laying off workers to save money.
- Bosses complain about workers' demands while gambling in a casino.
- The rich indulge in shooting practice, gunning down silhouettes of workers.
- Newsreels of fascist parades have comic music, animal noises, and machine-gun fire associated with them.
- Fascist bombing runs have skull and crossbones superimposed.

And all this is interspersed with chants, cheers, intertitles, cartoons, newspaper headlines, and shouted slogans. Other newsreels of the fascist riots of 6 February 1934 and of police repression lead to the question, "Can nothing be done?" In answer, the audience is called upon to unite behind the PCF, and the section ends with stunning images of a mass demonstration. Jacques-Bernard Brunius, requested by Renoir to edit this material to a predetermined commentary, was able to explore a set of contrapuntal montage techniques that he had been contemplating for some time.[9]

9. Brunius, *En marge du cinéma français,* 131. For the results, see *Avant-Scène Cinéma,* no. 99, January 1970.

By comparison, the central section is a little anticlimactic, though the three episodes are strategically chosen to target urban workers (an old man is laid off and his pension refused, but with the help of the PCF, his mates pressure the management into doing the right thing), farmers (a bankrupted farming family is contrasted with the life of luxury led by those in the chateau; when the farm is put up for sale, the PCF sees that it is bought back for next to nothing), and intellectuals/technicians (an engineer is scapegoated and fired; humiliated, he is saved by the PCF, and the sketch ends in a general celebration).

These fictions are acted out mostly by the members of the Groupe Octobre—indeed, we witness one of their performances at one point—and it is Gaston Modot who leads the final march of the people, singing and chanting, ever increasing in numbers, to the accompaniment of images of French productivity recognizable from the opening shots but now reclaimed for their rightful owners, the working people of the nation.

It was immediately after the release of *Le Crime de Monsieur Lange* (#46) that the PCF commissioned from the group that had collaborated on it a militant propaganda film to promote the Communist Party candidates at the forthcoming elections of 26 April 1936. (Carné later claimed it had been offered to him first.) It has been suggested that *Lange* can best be seen as a film authored by the Groupe Octobre with technical supervision by Renoir. No one could doubt that this is the case with *La Vie*. It was financed by a collection among party members (about 70,000 francs, some 5–10% of the cost of a commercial film), while ideas for the various segments were contributed by different individuals, using as a template Maurice Thorez's report to the PCF Congress of 22–25 January. Sections of it were filmed by several different teams, and clearly it must have been shot and put together very rapidly.[10] It was not submitted for a commercial visa, since it was meant to be screened "privately," in party meetings, informal gatherings, and local halls (ironically, the Popular Front government, which it had helped to elect, later refused it a commercial visa). It may seem surprising now that the film is so silent about the clergy's conservative role, but this too was related to Thorez's speech, which, as a strategy to ensure election, urged the need for unity between workers, Catholics, and peasants.

An informal group called Ciné-Liberté was formed in March to organize these private screenings, sometimes in actual cinemas where spectators would

10. For details, see Jeancolas, *15 ans d'années trente*, 196–207; Courtade, *Les Malédictions du cinéma français*, 135–136; and Vincendeau and Reader, *La Vie est à nous*, 48–53.

"pay for their seat" by subscribing to the bulletin put out by the group.[11] The list of filmmakers on one or another of the management committees of Ciné-Liberté, which itself remained in existence until the summer of 1937, is perhaps even more astounding than the membership of the Groupe Octobre. The bulletin's editorial board consisted of Renoir, Henri Jeanson, and Léon Moussinac, while Feyder, Germaine Dulac, Chenal, Modot, Lefebvre, Duvivier, Dasté, Nino Frank, and Charles Spaak contributed to it or to a series of talks sponsored by it. Others made politically committed short films, while in July or August 1937, Pierre Unik, who had contributed to the script of *La Vie est à nous,* scripted another film, called *Le Temps des cerises,* to be directed by Jean-Paul Le Chanois, with the same political orientation as *La Vie est à nous,* closer to an episodic fictional narrative but still including titles, choruses, documents, caricatures, and satirical juxtapositions. Shot in sixteen days and intended to promote the Popular Front in the October 1937 local elections, it was screened "commercially" on 22 November, but with no perceptible commercial success. Forgotten, believed lost, *Le Temps des cerises* was rediscovered in 1976.

Also forgotten and believed lost, *La Vie est à nous* itself was rediscovered and screened (commercially, for the first time) in 1969, following the social upheaval of May '68. Reviewing that re-release, Jean-Louis Bory noted that the film is "an election speech in the form of a long dramatic tract, [proclaiming] that happiness, a concept new to Europe at the end of the 19th century, has never been anything but an idea for most people, and that it is time for it to become a reality—a political reality. That was the great drive behind 1936. The PCF was at that time the party of the people's happiness."[12] The film is a manifestation in concrete form of this mood of exhilaration and expectation.

50. *L'Appel du silence*

(*A Vow of Silence*)
France, 1936, 109 min, b&w

Dir and Scr Léon Poirier; *Prod* SACIC; *Cinematog* Georges Million; *Music* Claude Delvincourt, J. E. Szyfer, and a Chopin study; *Sound* Maurice Menot; *Act* Jean Yonnel (Charles de Foucauld), Pierre de Guingand (General Laperrine), Thomy

---

11. For the history of Ciné-Liberté, see Courtade, *Les Malédictions du cinéma français,* 130–136.

12. *Le Nouvel Observateur,* cited by Vincendeau and Reader, *La Vie est à nous,* 51.

Bourdelle (a general), Pierre Juvenet (a colonel), Jacqueline Francell (Mademoiselle X), Alice Tissot, Suzanne Bianchetti, Pierre Nay, Fred Pasquali, André Nox, and Alexandre Mihalesco.

L'Appel du silence acts as a useful reminder that right-wing films were at least as common as the more celebrated left-wing films during the Popular Front years, and that they were routinely more popular. This film can usefully be compared to Jean Renoir's *La Marseillaise* (#73), commissioned by the PCF the following year, since both were to be funded by subscription. But whereas, despite the enthusiastic support of government and unions, *La Marseillaise* raised less than a third of the required 3 million francs (and finally cost 10 million), such that the workers' cooperative had to be transformed into a standard production company controlled by the workers' union (CGT), Léon Poirier's film, backed by the National Catholic Confederation, reputedly met its subscription target with ease.

It is readily recognizable as a right-wing film: by way of a biography of Charles de Foucauld, it celebrates the French colonization of North Africa and the spiritual mission of the Catholic Church that accompanied it. Certainly the life of de Foucauld was a rich source of material, which had already been exploited as the basis for Lieutenant Morhange in *L'Atlantide* (#16) in 1932, and indeed earlier, in 1921, but, while still fictional, *L'Appel du silence* remains truer to the original. It sketches de Foucauld's frivolous immoral life as a cadet at Saint-Cyr, where he befriended Laperrine (later General Laperrine), then follows him to North Africa with his regiment. There his commanding officer discovers that de Foucauld's supposed wife is in fact his mistress; he is told to get rid of her, refuses on a point of honor, and resigns. Hearing of war in Tunisia, he reenlists but again resigns in order to undertake an unofficial reconnaissance to the interior of Morocco, disguised as a Jewish trader, with a view to France's future colonization of that country. More and more attracted to the silence and immensity of the desert, de Foucauld has a religious vision, symbolically burns his materialist past, and devotes himself to the service of the church. With a view to converting the Tuareg, he joins with his old friend Laperrine on a combined military/religious expedition ever farther southward into the desert. Befriending the Tuareg, he builds a church in their territory, but treachery leads to misunderstandings, a revolt against the French presence, and de Foucauld's death. Laperrine returns to bury him by his hilltop church, and later is himself buried there—a soldier of the faith beside a soldier of the nation.

Poirier, the director, was a survivor of the "First Wave," the directors of the silent cinema. One of the brilliant group of Gaumont directors before World War I, he had made a number of fiction and documentary films shot (at least notionally) in exotic Asian and (more authentically) African locations—*La Croisière noire* following the 1924 rally down through Africa (see #29), *La Brière* in Madagascar, *La Voie sans disque* in Ethiopia. But, as Charles Ford notes, "From 1920 onwards he put his talent to work in the service firstly of France, secondly of Christianity. On occasion the two coincided, as in *Verdun, visions d'histoire*, in *Soeurs d'armes*, and especially in *L'Appel du silence* which is one of the most characteristic of Léon Poirier's films."[13]

One of the great strengths of the film is its powerful location shots of the bleak interior of Algeria, Tunisia, and Morocco. Inserted into successive episodes of de Foucauld's North African experience, they lend credibility to his reputed fascination for the silence and majesty of the desert, such that both his military and spiritual vocations can at times come to seem mere pretexts to attain the solitude, silence, and stillness that the desert represents for him. Then in the latter half of the film, the narrative begins to underline the parallels between his experiences and biblical events, notably the life of Christ, that ultimate model for all spiritual biographies—the vision, the retreat into the desert, the hill from which he surveys the land where God has called him, the "miraculous" cures of the locals, the Judas figure who betrays him, and the martyrdom at the hands of the Tuareg. Numerous premonitions of his forthcoming end provide that element of predestination without which no spiritual biography is complete.

The one episode in his life that clearly posed problems for the biographer was his mission to Morocco as a spy disguised as a Jew. The central event of his "military" reputation, this expedition nevertheless involves an element of deception, and the somewhat racist representation of de Foucauld's decision to adopt the guise not of an Arab but of a Jew. Both of these sit uneasily with the rest of the film. François Garçon sees this episode as betraying Poirier's instinctive anti-Semitism, typical of right-wing attitudes in France throughout the period.[14] Yet perhaps even more surprising is the relatively little space given to such Jewish stereotypes in the films of the decade, and the consistent refusal of the French cinema later under the occupation to pander to German anti-Semitism.[15]

L'Appel du silence was by far the most popular film of the 1935–1936 season, attracting nearly 900,000 spectators in Paris alone. This was a good year for right-wing populist triumphalism, with several other military and colonial films sharing the honors—*La Bandera* (#42, 2nd), *Veille d'armes* (4th), *L'Équipage* (#44, 6th), the spy story *Deuxième Bureau* (7th), and *La Route impériale* (12th). *L'Appel*

---

13. Ford, *Le Cinéma au service de la foi*, 132.
14. Garçon, *De Blum à Pétain*, 178.
15. See Crisp, *Genre, Myth and Convention*, 68–71.

du silence won the Grand Prix du Cinéma Français for 1936, an award founded in 1934 by the film industry and attributed by a panel overseen by the minister. In the spirit of the times, a number of "independent" critics were so outraged by the conservative orientation of this award that they founded a counter-award, which they called the Prix Louis Delluc. Its first beneficiary, in 1937, was Renoir for *Les Bas-Fonds,* not so much (as Lucien Rebatet grumpily but justifiably observed) recognizing the artist Jean Renoir as recognizing the antifascist Jean Renoir. It also perhaps served to counter the award of the 1937 Grand Prix to Maurice Gleize's *Légions d'honneur,* which blends aspects of the narrative of *L'Appel du silence* and *L'Équipage.*

51. *La Belle Équipe*

They Were Five (A Great Team)
France, 1936, 101 min (downbeat end), 99 min (upbeat end), b&w

Dir Julien Duvivier; *Prod* Arys; *Scr* Duvivier and Charles Spaak; *Cinematog* Jules Kruger and Marc Fossard; *Music* Maurice Yvain; *Art dir* Jacques Krauss; *Sound* Antoine Archaimbaud; *Edit* Marthe Poncin; *Act* Jean Gabin (Jean), Charles Vanel (Charles), Aimos (Raymond), Charles Dorat (Jacques), Raphaël Médina (Mario), Micheline Cheirel (Huguette), Viviane Romance (Gina), Marcelle Géniat, Michèle Verly, Marcelle Yrven, Fernand Charpin, Raymond Cordy, Charles Granval, Jacques Baumer, Robert Ozanne, Robert Lynen, Roger Legris, and Maupi.

This film was contentious even before it was screened, not least because two different endings were filmed for it—the pessimistic one originally planned by Charles Spaak and Julien Duvivier, and the optimistic one requested by the producers and preferred by the public. Given that the film dealt with a number of concepts central to the rise of the Popular Front, this ambivalence was ideologically explosive: Was the film as originally planned a cynical exploitation of trendy left-wing ideas, or a sardonic dismissal of them? Should it be read as a premonition of the inevitable disillusion that reality would inflict on the ideals of the Front, or did it totally misread the current mood of the French viewing public? These questions were felt with particular intensity because the film was shot precisely in the two months following the Front's taking of office, when popular expectations of improved living and working conditions, such as the forty-hour week, collective bargaining, and paid holidays, were still high.[16]

16. Or, according to one source, the two months preceding it.

As Geneviève Guillaume-Grimaud says, the narrative encapsulates all the mythology of 1936: having won a lottery (itself a mythic event at the time), a group of unemployed men decide to found a cooperatively run guinguette (a sort of bar-restaurant) on the banks of the Marne, called "Chez Nous" (Our Place) and symbolized by clasped hands (the emblem of the trade union movement). There, urban workers could spend a day in the country exploiting their new-found leisure.[17] The opening images set up several crucial themes in a concise fashion:

- Mateship: Comradeship is evoked repeatedly, as the four men become a unit then propose to include Mario, an illegal refugee from the Spanish Civil War. The idea of pooling their resources scarcely needs justifying, since it is taken for granted that happiness and liberty can only be attained communally.

- Nature: At the beginning, girls are seen fabricating paper flowers for sale, and an enormous holiday poster ironically invites workers on a skiing holiday. What the guinguette will offer is a genuine "escape to nature" for the worker.

- A better world: An equivalent dream of escape to a better land beyond the seas obsesses one of the mates, Jacques, who early opts out of the enterprise.

- Women: As usual in such films, misogyny is omnipresent. Jean becomes interested in Charles's wife, and Jacques in Mario's girl. Women are divisive, *effortlessly* divisive, and in the original scenario, they wreck the enterprise.

- Financiers: No film of the time about workers could ignore class opposition. Here, the former owner of the land to whom they become indebted threatens to repossess the guinguette: "Having done none of the work, they think they can just move in and take over."

So the exhilaration of becoming self-employed patrons and providing an enjoyable venue for day-trippers suffers a series of reverses: Raymond falls to his death while raising the flag on opening day, Jacques departs for Canada, Mario is arrested by the police, and the two remaining—Jean and Charles—come to

17. Guillaume-Grimaud, *Le Cinéma du Front Populaire*, 68. See also Prédal, *La Société française à travers le cinéma*, 253–255.

blows over a woman. In the original scenario, Jean shoots Charles and is led off by the police saying, "It was a fine idea, too fine ever to succeed." The solidarity of the group and the idealism of their venture have collapsed under the pressures of "reality." In the alternative, upbeat ending, Jean slaps Charles's wife, saying, "There are things between us worth more than any woman," and reads out a telegram from Jacques congratulating the team and announcing his imminent return.

Anyone who knows Duvivier's other films constructed around Jean Gabin will recognize the bleak fatalism that hounds any attempt to establish a life worth living, and will see the pessimistic ending as more consistent with those narratives. Duvivier's political allegiance was uncertain, but his fatalism was ingrained, and Spaak wrote for his directors. In the eyes of Charles Vanel and Raymond Chirat, what resulted was a negative version of *Le Crime de Monsieur Lange* (#46), which put an end to any illusions that might still subsist about workers' cooperatives. But at the corporate screening, theater managers felt that the filmmakers had misjudged the public mood; the producer agreed, and commissioned the alternative "happy end." Duvivier and Spaak suggested a public test to decide between the two, and the public voted 305 to 61 in favor of the happier ending. It was, therefore, this version that was commercialized in France, though the grim ending was preserved in at least some export copies. When that version is viewed these days, it sometimes has German subtitles.

Georges Sadoul clearly had the negative version in mind when he was reviewing *La Belle Équipe* in his account of recent French films characterized by realism: "Realism implies an understanding of this world of ours, an acknowledgment that this world contradicts the highest aspirations of man and particularly of the engaged artist, a sense of revolt against the society which has produced this inhuman world, and hope in the people who wish to free mankind." He is referring of course to the Communist Party, of which he was a member, having broken with the surrealists along with Louis Aragon and Pierre Unik. This is why he goes on to say, "It's undoubtedly for this reason that our best directors are discovering their place in the ranks of Ciné-Liberté."[18] Renoir, of course, had done just that, and it is interesting to speculate what Renoir might have made of this scenario if his offer to allow Duvivier to direct *La Grande Illusion* in return for his directing *La Belle Équipe* had been accepted. Almost certainly he would have wanted to see it end on an upbeat note, as in *Lange* and *Les Bas-Fonds*, where, like Charlot and Boudu, the protagonists end up hitting the open road to freedom.

18. Abel, *French Film Theory and Criticism*, 2:218–223.

52. Jenny

Jenny
France, 1936, 105 min, b&w

Dir Marcel Carné; *Prod* Réalisations d'Art Cinématographique; *Scr* Pierre Rocher, Jacques Prévert, and Jacques Constant; *Cinematog* Roger Hubert; *Music* Lionel Cazaux and Joseph Kosma; *Art dir* Jean d'Eaubonne; *Sound* Joseph de Bretagne; *Act* Françoise Rosay (Jenny), Lisette Lanvin (Danielle), Albert Préjean (Lucien), Charles Vanel (Benoit), Jean-Louis Barrault (the Dromedary), Sylvia Bataille (Florence), Roland Toutain (Xavier), Robert Le Vigan (the Albino), René Genin, Margo Lion, Génia Vaury, Louis Blanche, Roger Blin, Joseph Kosma, and Marcel Mouloudji.

This was the first feature directed by Marcel Carné, then an unheralded critic who had held positions as assistant cameraman and assistant director (to Jacques Feyder, 1927–1935, and to René Clair 1930) but who within two years was to become one of the leading French directors, his name indissolubly linked to that of Jacques Prévert, Jean Gabin, and the school of filmmaking known as poetic realism.[19] Poetic realism was essentially a poetic mythologization of contemporary reality but not, of course, just any aspect of contemporary reality: it involved the mythologization of the working class as the true focus of human worth—as oppressed, alienated, forever dreaming of realizing its aspirations, either "here and now" or in a vaguely defined better land "over there," but doomed to be forever disappointed. Aside from these thematic aspects, which implied certain character types from an already well-established populist/underworld cast-list, and certain equally well-established environments (working-class suburbs, slums, and streets; boarding houses; canals; Sunday visits to the country; and guinguettes on the banks of nearby rivers), the films commonly recognized as poetic realist employed a range of technical practices to evoke the atmosphere of fatalistic doom—set-design combined with lighting, camerawork, and fog/night effects to conjure up bleak worlds in which working-class protagonists briefly glimpse salvation, usually in the form of a woman. Pierre Leprohon summarizes these themes as "the sense of an implacable Fatality and of Solitude, a relentless Destiny determined to separate humans one from another, and the triumph of Love over Death."[20] At least one hundred films made

19. For his background and training, see Chazal, *Marcel Carné*, 12–15; Quéval, *Marcel Carné*; Landry, *Marcel Carné*; and Carné, *La Vie à belles dents*, 75–83.

20. Leprohon, *Présences contemporaines*, 227.

between 1934 and 1939 have for one reason or another been associated with this school,[21] and it has commonly been linked to socioeconomic conditions exacerbated in the years 1937–1939 by the decay of the Popular Front and premonitions of approaching war. Three films, however, are central to the canon—*Quai des brumes* (#78), *Le Jour se lève* (#94), and *Remorques* (#100), all scripted by Prévert and the first two directed by Carné, the outer two with Jean Gabin and Michèle Morgan.

Jenny is not only the first film directed by Carné but the beginning of his ten-year collaboration with Prévert. There is considerable disagreement as to how Carné came to be associated with this film and came to collaborate with Prévert. Most commentators assert that *Jenny* was supposed to be Jacques Feyder's next film after *La Kermesse héroïque* (#45), but when he was obliged to leave for London to film *Knight without Armour*, he recommended Carné, who had met Prévert while making comic film ads with Jean Aurenche and Paul Grimault. In his painfully self-serving and therefore probably unreliable memoirs, Carné tells an entirely different story: a producer, impressed by the success of Carné's short film *Nogent, Eldorado du dimanche*,[22] suggested they make a feature film, and they settled on a ten- to fifteen-page outline by Pierre Rocher. Carné summarily refused supervision by Feyder (and by Jean Stelli, officially credited as technical advisor) and chose Prévert as his collaborator without having met the man, on the basis of Prévert's Groupe Octobre work.

Rocher's outline seems to have centered on "a girl who unwittingly becomes the mistress of her mother's lover," but Prévert set about introducing a range of more picturesque secondary characters—Dromedary, the brutal hunchback; the Albino; and the peaceable arms-merchant with a love of flowers and little birds. In the original script, Jenny, the mother, runs a brothel with a sexy lingerie shop as a front, but Gaumont, pretexting censorship problems, managed to get this house of ill-repute changed to a high-class nightclub cum gambling joint. This modification rather detracts from the force of the plot, not least because when Danielle, the daughter, a successful pianist from whom Jenny has managed to conceal her louche activities, visits her mother's business and discovers with horror the nature of that business, her reaction is somewhat less credible than it should have been (though, admittedly, even as it is, she has just been mistaken for one of Jenny's available "girls"). While there Danielle meets and is rescued by Lucien, her mother's young lover, and an idyll begins between

---

21. See, for instance, Guillaume-Grimaud, *Le Cinéma du Front Populaire*, 198–213.
22. Which had also poeticized the Sunday exodus of Parisians.

them (the countryside, of course, the banks of the Ourcq, and talk of "escaping from all this"), which, grimly, Jenny is obliged to accept. The final sequence contains a nicely ironic contrast between Jenny, wandering disconsolate and potentially suicidal across a smoke-wreathed railway bridge, and the cheerful offer of the taxi-driver whom she subsequently hires to take her "to Jenny's place, it's the gayest place in town."

A point of particular interest in the film is the reverse Oedipal quality: normally in this decade's films, an older man is obsessed by a younger woman but regretfully sacrifices this relationship when she falls for a younger rival, often his son. The other well-known film to exploit the same reverse plot as *Jenny* is *Pension Mimosas* (#36), again starring Françoise Rosay, on which Carné had been assistant director to Feyder. A second point of interest is Lucien's underprivileged background, which the film uses to explain why he has gone wrong—before becoming a gigolo he had been imprisoned in Belle-Île (which, incidentally, was the setting for a 1936 scenario, based on a real-life revolt by young prisoners, for which Carné and Prévert were unable to find a producer).

For a first film, *Jenny* is remarkably assured. Carné had surrounded himself with an experienced crew who were to stay with him for years. The long opening shot (105 seconds) is a classic, as are the series of shot and reverse shot exchanges during interactions, while the edit rate (ASL) of 13.3 seconds is exactly the norm for the day. Carné had assimilated and was to perpetuate the form of psychological filmmaking developing in France in the aftermath of the introduction of sound, and his edit rate was to progressively increase toward 10 seconds, due mainly to clusters of these brief shot/reverse shots. *Jenny* was well-received by critics and the public alike, losing only by twelve votes to ten to *Les Bas-Fonds* for the first Prix Louis Delluc. According to the producer, it returned to him seven times his investment.

53. *Le Roman d'un tricheur*

The Story of a Cheat
France-Germany, 1936, 100 min, b&w

Dir and Scr Sacha Guitry; *Prod* Tobis; *Cinematog* Marcel Lucien; *Music* Adolphe Borchard; *Art dir* Jacques Gut and Henri Ménessier; *Sound* Paul Duvergé; *Act* Guitry (the cheat), Serge Grave (the cheat as a boy), Pierre Assy (the cheat as a young man), Jacqueline Delubac (the woman), Marguerite Moréno, Rosine Deréan (the thief), Pauline Carton, Fréhel, Henri Pfeiffer, Pierre Labry, Gaston Dupray, and Roger Duchesne.

Most film historians mention Sacha Guitry only to record his profound scorn for the cinema as a medium. The son of Lucien Guitry, a famous man of the theater, Sacha was likewise a devotee of the stage. He wrote (and acted in) his first play in 1905 at the age of twenty, and was subsequently to write and act in over 150 more. Along with another playwright, Marcel Pagnol, he is notorious as the principal exponent of cinema as canned theater ("théâtre en conserve"). Cinema was "the most dangerous enemy of the theatre, because it panders to the public." Its only saving grace was that it could immortalize those great theatrical performances that were otherwise regrettably ephemeral. "I am the first person," he declared, "to have dared to film plays from one end to the other without changing a word . . . to have brought to the screen texts conceived, written and directed for the stage."[23] Certainly, technicians working with him on these projects recorded his exclusive preoccupation with the actors' performances, dismissing the rest with a brusque, "Now, record that for me."

He was, however, not the first to do this. Such was the popularity of the new sound medium that producers were desperate to get more films before the public, and theatrical works were ideal for this purpose: they were the right length, the scripts already existed, the actors were already rehearsed. Consequently, a flood of canned plays was presented to the public, to the dismay of proponents of the particular virtues of the cinema as a medium. Such "runts, born of a dangerous half-caste mismarriage of screen and stage," constituted a "sub-theatre" that "could have no artistic future," it was "a false and bastard genre, in decline before having really found its feet."[24] Yet in the early 1930s, about one quarter of French production originated in theatrical works, more or less literally transcribed, and many of the resultant films were extremely popular. They had the virtue of introducing working-class cinemagoers to a theatrical culture that had previously been beyond their financial or cultural reach.

This brief review of the situation makes the specifically cinematic conception of *Le Roman d'un tricheur* almost inexplicable. It seems likely that a principal factor directing Guitry's attention to filmmaking was his third wife, Jacqueline Delubac, who here plays "the woman," surrounded by numerous personae of Guitry himself. Until his marriage to her (1935–1937), he had only allowed one of his plays to be filmed as a talkie, whereas from 1935 to 1938, eleven were so filmed, all starring Delubac (except *Pasteur*, 1936, where there are no female

23. From a talk in 1932–1933; see Guitry, *Le Cinéma et moi*.

24. See Icart, *La Révolution du parlant*, and Crisp, *Classic French Cinema*, 284–293, 285–286 (quotation).

roles). In nine of them, as here, Guitry plays opposite her. Perhaps out of deference to the film technology that did not interest him, Guitry initially codirected his films with other more experienced directors, but he took sole responsibility for *Tricheur*.

Its storyline is based on a single jocular anecdote: our young protagonist, guilty of a petty theft, is deprived of the privilege of mushrooms with his dinner; he is thus the only survivor, as his whole family is poisoned by the mushrooms and subsequently carted off in coffins. Deducing that honesty and morality are fatal, he devotes his life to ever more numerous forms of cheating, notably gambling. His fortunes expand accordingly; but shamed by the example of an honest man who had saved his life during the war, he renounces cheating—regrettably, since by gambling honestly, he loses everything. The main interest of the film is in the novel and surprisingly effective way in which this anecdote is told: it is in the form of an autobiography, written at a café table by our bespectacled protagonist (now an adult, played by Guitry himself). The image-track illustrates his past life, but as a silent film with only Guitry's autobiographical voiceover providing a commentary, occasional dialogue, and stage directions for his characters. There is also a crude "silent film" musical accompaniment littered with comic "synchronisms" that comment on the action. Synchronized sound is used solely for a cabaret scene in which Fréhel sings one of her songs. The film returns sporadically to the café table where our man is writing the words we have just heard in voiceover.

On first viewing, this unusual treatment of the narrative can still impress, though with repeated viewings, the self-congratulatory complacency of the commentary becomes wearing. But then Guitry's complacent self-presentation was central to all his work, of whatever sort. Here, the very format of autobiography, the patronizing voiceover, the numerous guises in which he appears in order to demonstrate his brilliance as an actor, his dominating presence, seducing women right and left, including (while disguised) his own wife, his effortless ability to dupe the other gullible players—all this vainglorious self-representation serves to promote his own masterful personality. He had played and was to play many brilliant men, notably Napoleon and diverse kings and emperors, but rather than "play" them, he demonstrated his close kinship to and understanding of them. He was naturally on intimate terms with genius and royalty.

Most of Guitry's other films with Delubac were relatively direct transplants of the boulevard comedies ("comédies mondaines") that were the mainstay of his output, with flippantly presented adultery, misogyny, and mild implications of incest, the more titillating for being played out between aging husband and young wife. Of these, *Désiré* (#68) is particularly interesting, with its Freudian overtones and plot foreshadowing *La Règle du jeu* (#95). All of them, including *Le*

Roman d'un tricheur, were box-office successes, but by far his most popular were two films, *Les Perles de la couronne* (1937) and *Remontons les Champs-Élysées* (1938, #88), modeled in form on *Tricheur* and in content on his play *Histoires de France,* recounting by way of dialogued tableaux with professorial voiceover the history of France.

54. César

(*César*). Part 3 of a trilogy remade as *Port of Seven Seas* (1938) and *Fanny* (1960)
France, 1936, 132 min (a longer version has been located), b&w

Scr and Dir Marcel Pagnol; *Asst dir* Pierre Méré; *Prod* Films Marcel Pagnol; *Cinematog* Willy; *Music* Vincent Scotto; *Art dir* Marius Brouquier; *Sound* Julien Coutellier; *Edit* Suzanne de Troeye; *Act* Raimu (César), Pierre Fresnay (Marius), Orane Demazis (Fanny), Milly Mathis (Aunt Christine), Alida Rouffe (Honorine), André Fouché (Césariot), Robert Vattier (Monsieur Brun), Fernand Charpin (Panisse), Paul Dullac (Escartefigue), Édouard Delmont (doctor), Doumel, Maupi, and Rellys.

Since he had begun directing his own productions, Marcel Pagnol had had only one unqualified success—*Angèle* (1934, #34). Deciding to capitalize on past successes such as *Marius* and *Fanny* (#10), which had been directed by others and were still being screened and rescreened, he suggested to Raimu a third play in that series, but problems with assembling the cast led to its being filmed, unlike the other two, before ever seeing the stage. This had both advantages and disadvantages. It had not been test-driven on the stage, so has a less declamatory style, though still heavily indebted to static, dialogued tableaux, and by comparison with the first two episodes it is less physically restricted, more open to the outside world (the hills around Marseilles, Toulon, the calanques). Pagnol's films are always wayward, given to digressions, delighting in the exploration of uneventful moments, of "temps mort," but this film seems to take a long time to get going, and feels every minute of its 2 hours and 12 minutes.

Nevertheless, it provides a fitting conclusion to the earlier episodes. It focuses on three melodramatic events—Panisse's deathbed, Césariot learning who his true father is, and his consequent engineering the reconstitution of the genetic family. These hackneyed situations ought to be less moving, but Pagnol's great talent lay in the humanizing of melodrama, the reinvigoration of hackneyed situations. Bewildered by precisely this talent, Pierre Leprohon protested that Pagnol manifested "a total lack of critical sense," "a scorn for the most elementary and unchanging rules of filmmaking," but that "his errors, his naivety, his weaknesses are more sympathetic than any faultless technique."[25] Thus Panisse's deathbed, his public confession of sins, his "moral testament" are intensely moving, not least because interspersed with comic moments like César's hope that Panisse will meet up with an appropriate God, rather than a Native or Chinese divinity to whom he might not be able to make himself understood. These comic moments—the discussion about lying, César's claim that his son Marius is effectively guilty of patricide, the rock in the bowler hat, and Panisse's empty chair at the card-game (which, though dead, he wins)—are cunningly interspersed with the humanized melodrama of Césariot's learning who is his true father, meeting with him, believing him a crook, then having the misunderstanding cleared up. Pagnol manages to wring every ounce of sentiment out of these situations, out of Fanny's romantic description of the Marius she first knew, and out of the rage that Marius finally gets to express at the twenty years of injustice he has had to endure.

The reinstatement of Marius as father closes a trajectory that began, as Claudette Peyrusse notes, with the temptation of new horizons, the craving for distant lands that had to be exorcized before he could settle down once again where he began, where he belonged—in Marseilles, "the one true world that he ought never to have left."[26] In the meantime, Fanny has formed that archetypal 1930s relationship with an older man, her lover's father's friend, arguably a displaced marriage to his father, César, himself. The generational change that results from Panisse's death and his replacement as husband by Marius, argues Peyrusse, represents the definitive defeat of the closed world of archaic patriarchal structures and their replacement by the "modernity" of oceanographic and automotive technology. She reports that in an extended version held by the Cinémathèque de Toulouse, Césariot is destined to marry the daughter of the owner of Bremond Motors. Incidentally, as well as generational change, in Marius Fanny is also replacing the comfortable small business world of the bourgeois Panisse family with a working-class man, a mechanic. This class conflict comes to a head in the final scene, where their reconciliation might have been scuppered by this class difference but for the cunning of old César.

More important, however, than either family reunification, generational change, or class conflict is the constant foregrounding of regional character. One of the aces that Pagnol was most skilled at playing was the meridional ambiance. A lot of the pleasure of the film arises from meeting again old Provençal friends—not just Raimu, Fernand Charpin, and (elsewhere) Fernandel,

25. Leprohon, *Présences contemporaines*, 218, 222.
26. Peyrusse, *Le Cinéma méridional*, 122, 130.

but Raimu's great mate Maupi, together with Édouard Delmont, Paul Dullac, Charles Blavette, Henri Poupon, Milly Mathis, and the "foreigner" (from Lyons!) Robert Vattier. As Pagnol's troupe, they lived and worked as a family, leaving moving accounts of the affectionate links that bound them together and of the oddly casual and superficially inefficient pattern of each day's filmmaking. "The day over, the studio hands stayed on to play boules with the cast or with the boss." "With Pagnol," said Fernandel, "making a film involves a trip to Marseille, a dish of bouillabaisse with a mate, idle conversation, then sooner or later, if there's any time left, shooting a scene."[27] Pagnol himself mucked in at whatever task was most urgent—"fabricating a rake, moving a table, sawing down an inconvenient pine-tree. There is no hierarchy, no specialisation; they work as a team." Pagnol agreed: "I lived in the studio: we ate in the canteen every day . . . the table was always crowded—the actors, the technicians, the studio hands. We would talk about the afternoon's work. . . . The studio hands were always there for the rushes. They lived close by. Our cinema was a family affair."[28]

Released four and five years respectively after *Marius* and *Fanny*, *César* offered Pagnol the opportunity (even the obligation) to rehearse the backstory of the earlier films, as Césariot learns of his origins little by little (and not always reliably) from César, Marius, Dromard, and Fanny. In later years, the three films were customarily screened as a trilogy, as if initially conceived as a unitary whole.

55. Une partie de campagne

A Day in the Country
France, 1936 (released in 1946), 40 min, b&w

Dir Jean Renoir; *Asst dir* Jacques Becker, Claude Heymann, Jacques-Bernard Brunius, Yves Allégret, Luchino Visconti, and Henri Cartier-Bresson; *Prod* Les Films du Panthéon; *Scr* Renoir, from a short story by Guy de Maupassant; *Cinematog* Claude Renoir; *Music* Joseph Kosma; *Art dir* Robert Gys; *Sound* Joseph de Bretagne; *Edit* Marguerite Renoir; *Act* Sylvia Bataille (Henriette), Jeanne Marken (Madame Dufour), Gabriello (Monsieur Dufour), Georges Darnoux (Henri), Brunius (Rodolphe), Paul Temps (Anatole), Gabrielle Fontan, Marguerite Renoir, and Jean Renoir (innkeeper).

27. These two quotations are from Leprohon, *Présences contemporaines*, 216.
28. Ibid., 220; *Cahiers du cinéma*, no. 173.

For many critics, *Une partie de campagne* is Jean Renoir's best film. They wax lyrical about the way it captures "la douceur de vivre" of the Belle Époque, a particular enchantment exercised by the banks of the Marne, by flower-garlanded guinguettes and elderberries, men with rods and the gentle motion of the waters where Parisians come on Sundays to row their pleasure-crafts.[29] For J.-P. Jeancolas, too, it is "a film about happiness, about the wind in the poplars, the song of the nightingale and the scud of rain on the surface of the river. A film about the present instant."[30] Likewise, Alexandre Astruc delights in Renoir's sly ability to seduce and enchant us with his "mad painter's sensuality, the way he revels in the landscape, wallowing in it like a drunken faun, and splashing us with diffuse luminosity that glitters gloriously through the foliage."[31] It is easy to interpret the moody aspects of the film evoked by these quotations as a homage by Renoir to his father's paintings and the period atmosphere they capture, not least because the film was shot in a region painted frequently by Auguste Renoir.

Yet this can also seem an odd film. First, it is so short. Renoir did not make short films, and his attempt to explain this one retrospectively as one of three intended to constitute a film of vignettes (a trend he would thus have initiated) is unconvincing. The evidence suggests it was always intended as a standalone film motivated by his love of de Maupassant's work, of the Belle Époque, of impressionist painting, and of the mythic riverside setting. Although he insisted it was complete as it stood, the titles at the beginning and before the final sequence seem to replace (perhaps relatively unimportant) scenes projected in the initial scenario. Pierre Braunberger, his producer, who personalized all commercial operations and later reminisced nostalgically about the 1930s as a period when producers were on intimate terms with the rich intellectual and cultural brew of the cinematic and theatrical worlds, and when it was normal for producers to sleep with their stars, agreed to fund it because he was obsessed with Sylvia Bataille. He implied that Renoir was equally obsessed with her. Introduced to Renoir by a mutual friend, Pierre Lestringuez, Braunberger immediately found himself in sympathy with the director, and gives a hair-raising account of himself and a group of friends (Jean and Pierre Renoir, Lestringuez, Louis Jouvet, Jean Giraudoux) heading off to a brothel to plan their next film,

---

29. From a review by Jean Rougeul, April 1946, quoted in *Premier Plan*, nos. 22–23–24, 213.

30. Jeancolas, *15 ans d'années trente*, 213.

31. Quoted in *Premier Plan*, nos. 22–23–24, 220.

sitting naked around a table while the prostitutes crouched under it working on them.[32]

But *Une partie de campagne* is odd not just because of its length and origins but because it is a lyrical and relatively asocial film made at a time when Renoir was at his most socially committed. He had just made *Le Crime de Monsieur Lange* (#46), then *La Vie est à nous* (#49) for the Communist Party, and the following year, he was to make *La Marseillaise* (#73) as a celebration of popular revolution. Yet *Une partie de campagne* contains little trace of this passionate left-wing commitment. Of course in the 1930s, the riverside setting, the guinguette, and the day in the country were becoming mythic for the working class, and were to become more so with the paid leave inaugurated by the Popular Front. But these are not working-class people; they are petty bourgeoisie for whom the same had been true fifty years before. Equally clearly, evidence of left-wing tendencies could be deduced from the fact that the petty bourgeois parents are not treated respectfully: the shopkeeper and his assistant (and future son-in-law) are heavily satirized, and the mother's seduction by a riotous Rodolphe is treated in the comic mode, with gentle irony. Their daughter Henriette's tentative exploration of the possibilities of a relationship with Henri is treated in an altogether more delicate and poignant manner, the more moving for our final view of her later in life when she daydreams every night about that brief encounter, her most treasured memory. Rather than being related to the social films that Renoir was making before and immediately after it, *Une partie de campagne* looks forward to the sensuality and "naïve pantheism" of his postwar films.[33] At most we can say, with Geneviève Guillaume-Grimaud, that the film is political in that the romance sketched out here comes to nothing because Henri and Henriette are not of the same class—and because, as Marcel Martin notes when describing the long retreating track across rain-spattered water that interrupts the boating party, the film denies any possibility of fulfillment within such a society.[34]

The fourth oddity about the film is its editing. In general, critics have admired the invisible technique of this film (if one excepts the swinging camera

32. See Braunberger, *Cinémamémoires*, especially 48–83, and "À quoi servent les producteurs?" *Cinéma 61*, no. 54, March 1961. See also Crisp, *Classic French Cinema*, 274–277.

33. The quote is from Jacques Doniol-Valcroze. See *Premier Plan*, nos. 22–23–24, 223.

34. Guillaume-Grimaud, *Le Cinéma du Front Populaire*, 60–61; Martin, *Le Langage cinématographique*, 171–172.

in the swing scene), but in fact, the film is highly edited. At a time when the average shot length of Renoir's films was 18 to 24 seconds, this one averages less than 12. A likely explanation is its delayed editing and release. Braunberger did not release it in 1936 because it lacked the final scenes, and because he admired it enough to want to extend it to feature length. Prévert worked on possibilities that came to nothing, and the film was finally edited by Marguerite Renoir in 1946, while Renoir himself was still abroad. What we now think of as his film, then, was edited a decade after shooting, when editing practices had changed radically, and by Marguerite Renoir, who was then editing films for Renoir's former assistant, Jacques Becker, who expected much more intensive editing. It would probably have looked very different if edited in 1936 with Renoir present.[35]

Finally, as a partial corrective to the myth of genial Jean Renoir, the amiable bear, who prided himself on his relationship with his actors, it is worth quoting Sylvia Bataille's account of her rage when the film's shooting, repeatedly delayed by rain, was abruptly terminated (she clearly implies that several scenes remained to be shot):

> It wasn't pretty, let me tell you, those last days. People couldn't stand one another; there was hatred in the air. . . . Then one day Renoir turns up and tells us he's abandoning us, that he's just signed to shoot *Les Bas-Fonds*. Well! I couldn't help it, I called him all the names in the book. . . . What he did was unpardonable. . . . Really it wasn't easy. . . . Imagine working with someone drunk every morning. After the war when Braunberger showed us the edited version, without music, no-one thought it was screenable. . . . But in fact when Kosma constructed his great score for it the film suddenly came together as a coherent whole. . . . It was a complete surprise.[36]

56. *Pépé le Moko*

(*Pépé le Moko*); remade as *Algiers* (1938) and *Casbah* (1948)
France, 1937, 93 min, b&w

Dir Julien Duvivier; *Asst dir* Robert Vernay; *Prod* Paris-Films Productions; *Scr* Henri Jeanson, from the novel by Detective Ashelbé; *Cinematog* Jules Kruger

---

35. Crisp, *Classic French Cinema*, 402–404.
36. *Premier Plan*, nos. 22–23–24, 225–226, from *Cinéma 61*, no. 58.

and Marc Fossard; *Music* Vincent Scotto and Mohammed Yguerbuchen; *Art dir* Jacques Krauss; *Sound* Antoine Archaimbaud; *Edit* Marguerite Beaugé; *Act* Jean Gabin (Pépé le Moko), Mireille Balin (Gaby), Lucas Gridoux (Inspector Slimane), Line Noro (Inès), Fernand Charpin (Régis), Saturnin Fabre (Grandfather), Gabriel Gabrio (Carlos), Marcel Dalio (Arbi), Gilbert-Gil (Pierrot), Gaston Modot (Jimmy), Roger Legris (Max), Charles Granval (Maxime), Fréhel (Tania), Olga Lord (Aïcha), and Renée Carl (la mere Tarte).

In these final years of the decade, a mythic persona accreted around the actor Jean Gabin, and *Pépé le Moko* is a key film in the construction of that persona. Gabin had been acting in films ever since the point when the coming of sound had generated a need for popular singers (his parents were from music-hall and operetta backgrounds, and during the 1920s, he had appeared in revues and operettas, and at the Moulin Rouge with Mistinguett). Until 1934, however, even when he was acting the tough guy, his films had been lightweight entertainment. Then Julien Duvivier took him up, and after playing a somewhat grotesque Pontius Pilate, cast him in roles where he was basically a good bloke who came to unfortunate ends (*La Bandera*, #42, and *La Belle Équipe*, #51). *Pépé le Moko* added to this mix the themes of alienation and exile, together with a more explicit sense of tragic fatality. We discover Pépé as the leader of a gang in the Casbah, safe in the impenetrable labyrinth of alleyways but unable to leave them—protected by the Casbah but also trapped in it. Attempting to escape, he is betrayed, captured, and commits suicide.

In the series of films that followed this one, the "Jean Gabin" persona rapidly crystallized into that of a tough but vulnerable man of the people, living at best on the margins of the law, often on the run because of an understandable and almost justifiable murder. A charismatic leader and lover, he is fated to be betrayed by those around him, notably by women, and ends up alone and trapped, hounded by fate to a tragic death. This mythic persona was consecrated by his roles in *Gueule d'amour* (#64), *La Bête humaine* (#91), *Quai des brumes* (#78), *Le Jour se lève* (#94), and *Remorques* (#100). (I omit the recently rediscovered *Récif de corail* because in that incongruous and distinctly inferior film, he and his girl are permitted by "fate" to escape to their idyllic coral isle.) Around him, idealistic dreams are constructed based on male friendship and female love, but an ineluctable fatality dooms them to disaster. As J.-P. Jeancolas notes, however different these films may be from one another, they all embody the same desperation, the same sense of tragic hopelessness. This is perhaps the first time that such a tragic persona had ever been constructed around a man of the people. "It doesn't take a great scholar to recognize the link between the multiple deaths that scriptwriters and public imposed on Gabin from the autumn of 1936 onward . . . and contemporary disillusionment with the failures and divisions of the Popular Front."[37]

In many of these films, in narrative terms, it is the love of a woman that proves his downfall, but in *Pépé le Moko* it is not Gaby who betrays him but the police informers Régis and Arbi, together with his native woman, Inès. All of these three are "natives" (though played by Europeans). Several critics have seen this as indicative of a racism implicit in many of Duvivier's films, or at least of a typical representation of humanity (and particularly women) as having a dark treacherous side. This ambivalence is most obviously present in the wonderfully named Slimane,[38] yet another Arab, who alone is able to move easily between the white world of authority and order and the labyrinthine Arab Casbah, and who embodies Pépé's fate through repeatedly predicting it. This opposition of two worlds is brilliantly established in the opening sequences where the police are debating how to capture Pépé: the cutaway to the Casbah as they talk about it systematically contrasts it with the orderly police station through editing (rapid montages/long takes), camera angle (steep/level), camera movement (violent/slow), and the soundtrack (Mohammed Yguerbuchen's Arab music/synchronized dialogue). The narrow steep winding alleys of the Casbah constructed in the studio by Jacques Krauss, where the camera picks out exotic and picturesque details, admirably complement these technical practices, evoking vividly the atmosphere of the elaborate trap in which Pépé languishes. His desire to escape it, symbolizing in Graham Greene's eyes the craving of the human spirit to escape its prison, is captured most intensely in his visit to Tania, played by the aging *chanteuse réaliste* Fréhel.[39] Herself back in France after fifteen years of exile, with alcohol and drugs bloating her figure, she gazes grimly at a photo of herself in younger, happier days and accompanies her own recorded younger voice singing of a lost paradise, in a song recalling François Villon's "Mais où sont les neiges d'antan" ("Where are the snows of yesteryear?"). This exile's longing for yesteryear and otherwhere is equally captured in the exchange between Gaby and Pépé concerning Paris, and the familiar stations of their metro line, that have them meeting at La Place Blanche, a name that acquires an unbearably heavy weight of connotation both here and in Fréhel's song.

The urgency of Pépé's need to break out of his prison and sail away back to France with Gaby, to the "home" she has come to symbolize, is captured by the

37. Jeancolas, *15 ans d'années trente*, 223–225, 269.

38. A variant of Solomon but implying here a sly man, a slippery hissing name. See Slavin, *Colonial Cinema and Imperial France*, 175–184.

39. Ibid., 172.

magical unreality of that final descent to the port where the steamer and Gaby await: behind him, as he descends into town, deliberately unrealistic painted backdrops cross-dissolve into one another, while ahead of him, equally impossible crashing waves promise purification and salvation. For all its poesy elsewhere, this is the one moment when the film transcends the real, not just suggesting but *demanding* that it should be read on a metaphorical level. It stands with the execution of the traitor Régis (who, as he cowers in terror, triggers a mechanical piano that accompanies his death with a hectically gay tune) as one of the unforgettable scenes in a great film. *Pépé le Moko* has deservedly acquired the status of a cult film—a key to understanding the mood and attitudes of the people as the decade drew to its close.

Inevitably, on its release right-wing critics were outraged at the celebration of such a persona: "In *Pépé le Moko* France is admitting it is unworthy of possessing a colonial Empire, and incapable of administering it," noted one reviewer.[40] Indeed, during the war such poetic realist films were seen not as symptoms of prewar distress but as the cause of it, and accordingly banned. As Lucien Rebatet said, "Gabin portrays an abject puppet, reducing humanity to the level of the animal, where freewill counts for nothing . . . , a crapulous individual, adrift in a squalid fatality."[41]

57. Messieurs les Ronds-de-Cuir

(*The Red Tape Fraternity*)
France, 1937, 100 min, b&w

Dir and Scr Yves Mirande, based on characters from Georges Courteline's *Messieurs les ronds de cuir* and *Friends' Wives; Prod* Paris-Ciné Films; *Cinematog* Charles van Enger; *Music* Armand Bernard; *Art dir* René Renoux; *Sound* Wilmarth; *Edit* Maurice Serein; *Act* Lucien Baroux (Lahrier), Pierre Larquey (Conservator), Gabriel Signoret (Monsieur Soupe), Saturnin Fabre (Letondu), Roger Duchesne (Chavarax), Jean Tissier (Nègre, the director), Armand Lurville (La Hourmerie), Georges Bever (Ovide), Josette Day (Madame Chavarax), Arletty (La Hourmerie's sister-in-law), Betty Spell, Jeanne Véniat (Madame La Hourmerie), and Simone Chobillon.

40. Vuillermoz, quoted in *La Cinématographie française*, 12 August 1938.
41. 1941, quoted in Sallée, *Les Acteurs français*, 134. For a fuller account of the Gabin persona, see Ginette Vincendeau, "Community, Nostalgia and the Spectacle of Masculinity," *Screen* 26, 1985, and Crisp, *Genre, Myth and Convention*, 273–277.

The terminology for describing the wide range of comedies and satires from this and preceding decades is confusing. Such generic categories as were used are far from watertight. At one extreme, boulevard comedies such as *L'Hôtel du Libre Échange* (#35) assemble a cast of frustrated bourgeois and minor aristocracy, and mock their attempts at adulterous licentiousness. At the other extreme, in military vaudevilles such as *Les Gaietés de l'escadron* (#17), army recruits engage in farcical encounters with the military authorities. In between, innumerable comedies satirized all possible social institutions—not just the army but the church, the press, the academy, trade unions, the government, business, finance and banking, or (as here) the bureaucracy. Farcical in tone and episodic in structure, they usually originated in theatrical productions of the years 1890–1930, written by Paul Armont, Flers and Caillavet, Courteline, Verneuil and Berr, Hennequin, or Veber, but also Jules Romains and Marcel Pagnol (see #35).

In all cases, it is establishment figures who are the butt of the satire. In the context of the Depression, this ridiculing of the establishment, seen as responsible for the socioeconomic collapse, became even more astringent. Greed and self-interest is represented as these figures' sole obsession, and human relations suffer as a result. Families collapse, lovers are parted, and corrupt bankers become stock villains. As Pagnol proposed in *Topaze*, this is a financial world in which the dishonest flourish. In an even more cynical film, *La Banque Nemo,* an arriviste banker dabbles in shady deals but, protected by friends in high places, enjoys the fruits of his criminal activities. Nothing, it seems, can stop the rich and powerful, who have police and politicians in their pockets. Geneviève Guillaume-Grimaud lists ten films made in 1936 attacking and/or satirizing the bourgeoisie in these terms.[42] Moreover, the immense success enjoyed in November 1936 by Pière Colombier's version of *Le Roi* generated a renewed interest in the genre. *Messieurs les Ronds-de-Cuir* followed early in 1937, and the 1937–1938 season saw good box-office returns for *Mademoiselle ma mère, L'Habit vert, Hercule,* and *La Présidente.*

Messieurs can be compared to two other films from the decade that specifically mock the bureaucracy, *L'École des contribuables* (1934) and *Monsieur Coccinelle* (1938, #83). In the first of these, the taxation department is the butt of an ongoing joke involving a school that teaches taxpayers systematically to fiddle their returns. Finally it is taken over by the taxation department itself, the better to train its own staff. *Messieurs les Ronds-de-Cuir* opens with a wonderfully sardonic prologue stating that, "just as in his military vaudevilles Courteline did not ridicule

---

42. Guillaume-Grimaud, *Le Cinéma du Front Populaire,* 132. See also Crisp, *Genre, Myth and Convention,* 81–82.

the army, so here he does not ridicule public servants. After all, he was himself in the army and the public service." What better justification, one might ask, for undertaking the demolition of a social institution, and what better vantage point than from within. The setting is a government department manned by staff who delight in thwarting their clientele by means of red tape, laziness, and procrastination. A song whose theme is "It's not easy to do nothing" sets the tone. Dossiers pass from office to office, absenteeism is the norm, and the staff are eccentric to a man, not least Letondu, played by Saturnin Fabre, inseparable from his hunting horn. Lucien Baroux who here plays the lead idiot was one of the mainstays of the genre (47 films during the decade) as were Fabre (41 films), Jean Tissier (44 films), and Pierre Larquey (99 films). Here Baroux plays Lahrier, a feckless employee of the Bureau of Gifts and Legacies who, since he has little official work to occupy his time or energies, is writing a revue for the Folies Boutonnières. Members of the Folies come to collect it, which provides an opportunity for scanty costumes, songs, and attendance by the staff at a rehearsal (held, naturally, in the ministry itself). The head of the bureau doing his rounds discovers disturbing numbers of his staff engaged in frivolous and time-wasting activities. His direction to his assistant to get rid of all wastrels, if followed rigorously, would have emptied the offices. The essence of the opposition thus set up is, of course, the stuffy conventional view of the public servant versus the exuberant licentious vivacity of the Folies—two mythic aspects of French culture that can be simplistically represented as Death versus Life. At the end, Lahrier resigns his post at the ministry to devote himself exclusively to writing lyrics for the Folies.

The "Ronds-de-Cuir" of the title are the circular (leather) cushions used by fat cats in the office while doing their "cushy" jobs. Yves Mirande, writer and director of this film, was to sum up this rich seam of social satire in another of his films, *Derrière la façade*, in which a police inspector investigating a murder committed in a Parisian apartment building handcuffs one after another of the buildings tenants, since all from the lowest to the highest are hiding guilty secrets that make them likely murderers. These scenarios, in which Mirande specialized, are symptomatic of a profound cynicism that saw all forms of authority as hiding crapulous secrets behind the facade of respectability.

58. *L'Homme de nulle part*

The Late Mathias Pascal
France-Italy, 1937, 95 min (now 90 min), b&w

Dir Pierre Chenal; *Asst dir* Louis Daquin; *Prod* Ala-Colosseum Film/General Production; *Scr* Chenal, Christian Stengel, and Armand Salacrou, from the novel *Il fu Mattia Pascal* by Luigi Pirandello; *Cinematog* Jean-Louis Mundwiller; *Music* Jacques Ibert; *Art dir* Guido Fiorini; *Sound* Giovanni Pari; *Edit* Chenal; *Act* Pierre Blanchar (Mathias Pascal, Adrien Méis), Robert Le Vigan (Papiano), Isa Miranda (Louise Paleari), Catherine Fontenay (the widow Pescatore), Ginette Leclerc (Romilda), Margo Lion (the corporal), Maximilienne (Scholastique), Charlotte Barbier-Krauss (Madame Pascal), Sinoël (Paleari), Pierre Palau, Pierre Alcover, Marcel Vallée, Jean Hebey, Charles Granval, René Génin, Douking, Yvonne Ima, and Paquita Claude.

It is not hard to find directors who are passionately committed to causes in this decade, nor directors who are skilled technicians, but almost the only true intellectual among them was Pierre Chenal. He made many fine films, most of which did well at the box office, yet along with Edmond Gréville, and for similar reasons, he is one of the least appreciated directors of the decade. After a rebellious childhood during which he was thrown out of three high schools, he found a soulmate in Jean Goetgheluck (Jean Mitry). Together they explored the avant-garde literary, theatrical, and cinematic milieus of the 1920s, linking up with the Deux Magots group (Jacques Prévert, Jacques-Bernard Brunius, Paul Grimault, etc.).[43] Talented in the visual arts, Chenal provided sketches of actresses for various periodicals (and jazz for his mates) but discovered a preference for the spatio-temporal dynamism of the cinema. Once he had proved himself with some shorts and the commissioned *Martyre de l'obèse*, he was able to choose scenarios based precisely on those "great ideas" that Renoir shunned, filming work by Marcel Aymé (#28), Fyodor Dostoyevsky (#41), Jack London, here Luigi Pirandello, and later James M. Cain, Unamuno, and Richard Wright. Other projected films based on Stendahl, Thomas Hardy, Simone de Beauvoir, and Vladimir Nabokov came to nothing. Pirandello's fascination with identity was clearly the sort of theme to attract Chenal: the protagonist, Mathieu Pascal, escapes accidentally from a disastrous marriage when he discovers that he is believed to have drowned himself in despair at his mother's death. He assumes the identity of the actual drowned man—a tramp called Adrien Méis—and moves into a boarding house in the city. In that more amiable community, he meets and begins an affectionate relationship with Louise. But a malevolent and jealous fellow boarder comes to suspect his identity and makes life difficult for him, so he reluctantly fakes his own death (deliberately this time) and returns to his village. His sudden reappearance shocks and dismays his wife, who has remarried (bigamously, as it now turns out) the mayor's gormless son. In return for tactfully disappearing

43. Chenal, *Souvenirs du cinéaste*, 15–25.

(yet again), Mathieu blackmails the new husband into providing "genuine" identity papers for his new persona. Now he can return to the pension, face down his persecutor, and marry Louise.

The narrative thus provides for a constant play with identity, a sort of extended existentialist metaphor in which the protagonist learns to define the person he wishes to be (or to be known as). In one sense, the film suggests that identity is superficial, as in the case of clothes and appearances—a mere matter of plausibility and appropriate documentation—but in another, it suggests that what we normally take for a personality is the dead weight of an involuntary past into which we have been unwillingly socialized, and which must be shrugged off so that we can begin to construct a more authentic personality from zero. This play with identity leads to a particularly satisfying narrative structure: at the end of "act one," Mathieu dies unintentionally, apparently drowned; at the end of "act three," he seizes the opportunity to die once again, intentionally this time, also by drowning. His village life had become unendurable, and he is saved from it by a benign "fate figure" who directs him to the casino and limitless wealth. His communal life in the pension is idyllic, but he is driven out of it, this time by a malign "fate figure" who steals that wealth. The film ends with him explaining to Louise what has happened by narrating the beginning of the film we have just seen. It is clearly the mark of an intellectual filmmaker to be attracted to such a structure of repetition, variation, inversion, and circularity.

The formal structure, however, frames a very common 1930s theme—a critique of the petty bourgeoisie. As Chenal himself noted, it constitutes "a fable about the lord god Money."[44] Mathieu's wife and mother-in-law are grasping shrews who extort all the money they can from the Pascal family, driving his mother to the grave. The village mayor also exploits Mathieu, paying him far less than his due and keeping the rest for himself. The win at the casino, the theft of that money by the sinister Count (Robert Le Vigan) whose presence and greed introduce the one element of evil into the pension (the Count covets Louise because of the dowry she will bring with her), Mathieu's recovery of the money— throughout the narrative, money determines the course of relationships. There is a sense in which the film outlines a generational change from kindly caring people to weak people governed by malevolence, cupidity, and self-interest. Yet despite this, the film ends optimistically, with a newly assertive Mathieu winning Louise and triumphing over the weak and the wicked. This is an uncharacteristically happy ending for a Chenal film.

44. Ibid., 97.

The atmosphere of the shoot in Rome was particularly agreeable, and numerous cast members (Chenal mentions Pierre Palau, Margo Lion, Douking, and Pierre Alcover) requested the privilege of working with Chenal again whenever possible. Indeed, the recurrence of cast and crew on his 1930s films is striking—Louis Daquin as assistant, Christian Stengel as cowriter/coproducer, Joseph-Louis Mundviller on camera, Pierre Blanchar and Harry Baur, then Louis Jouvet and Erich von Stroheim, together with Gabriello, Alexandre Rignault, Fréhel, and Sinoël as actors. The most surprising of these recurrences is Le Vigan, a very close friend, who acted in *La Rue sans nom* (#28), *Les Mutinés de l'Elsinore, L'Homme de nulle part,* and *Le Dernier Tournant.* "My old mate," Chenal called him, "who hadn't yet entered his pro-German period"—the period when he was to publish vitriolic anti-Semitic articles that must have pained Chenal as a man of Jewish birth.[45] Renoir, too, who used Le Vigan in *Les Bas-Fonds,* admired him as "not just an actor but a poet," wonderful in ambiguous and sinister character roles. When he was condemned at war's end to ten years hard labor and "permanent national shame," Chenal rang him to say, "You acted like an idiot, but you've done your time, you've paid, no? Now *you're* the Jew."[46]

59. *Marthe Richard au service de la France*

(*Marthe Richard, a Spy in the Service of France*)
France, 1937, 95 min (now 80 min), b&w

Dir Raymond Bernard; *Prod* Paris Films; *Scr* Bernard Zimmer, from the memoirs of Commandant Ladoux; *Cinematog* Robert le Febvre; *Music* Arthur Honneger; *Art dir* Jean Perrier; *Sound* Antoine Archaimbaud; *Edit* Charlotte Guilbert; *Act* Edwige Feuillère (Marthe Richard), Délia Col (Mata Hari), Erich von Stroheim (von Ludow), Jean Galland (von Falken), Fernand Bercher (Marthe's fiancé), Marcel André, René Bergeron, and Marcel Dalio.

Also *Mademoiselle Docteur* or *Salonique, nid d'espions* (*Salonica, Nest of Spies*), directed by Georg-Wilhelm Pabst, with Dita Parlo, Viviane Romance, Louis Jouvet, Charles Dullin, Pierre Fresnay, Pierre Blanchar, and Jean-Louis Barrault.

Improbable as it may seem today, *Marthe Richard* was one of the most successful spy stories of the decade. It opened on the same day as another spy story,

---

45. Ibid., 91, 74.
46. See Mazeau and Thouart, *Les Grands Seconds Rôles,* 209–214.

Georg-Wilhelm Pabst's *Mademoiselle Docteur,* in a year when the proliferation of such stories was beginning to draw comment—no less than seven were released, of which six were outstanding commercial successes and two (including *Marthe Richard* itself) exceeded half a million entries for Paris alone. There had been a scattering of spy stories in the first half of the decade, but none had achieved this level of success. The first to signal the developing popularity of the genre had been *Deuxième Bureau* (1935) featuring Jean Murat as the French agent Captain Benoit. Such was its success that the novels by Charles-Robert Dumas relating the fictional exploits of this Captain Benoit of the Secret Service (Deuxième) Bureau during World War I experienced a merchandizing boom analogous to that of Ian Fleming's James Bond thirty years later. Three more of them were adapted to film—*Les Loups entre eux* (1936), *L'Homme à abattre* (1937), and *Capitaine Benoit* (1938)—together with two by Pierre Nord—*Double Crime sur la Ligne Maginot* (1937) and *Deuxième Bureau contre Kommandantur* (1939). In addition, four spy films were made loosely based on the real-life exploits of Anne-Marie Lesser (*Mademoiselle Docteur*), Marthe Richard, Mata Hari (*La Danseuse rouge,* 1937), and the network run by Louise de Bettignies and Léonie Vanhoutte (*Sœurs d'armes,* 1937).[47]

As this list implies, a particular fascination surrounded female spies, partly because such narratives built on gender myths of the duplicitous nature of the female, but equally because of the potential for licentious scenes in which the spies used their sexuality to seduce and corrupt. Vera Korène and Viviane Romance became typecast in this role for some years, though Renée Saint-Cyr, Mireille Balin, and Edwige Feuillère also took it on at least once. Typically the plot of these films involved the need to procure the plans of some sinister enemy prototype—a revolutionary airplane engine, the formula of a deadly poison gas—or to steal documents. Here the main aim is to identify the whereabouts of a foreign submarine base. The seductive female temptress was most usually foreign, and determined to thwart the heroic French agent, but was often distracted from her devious designs by his male magnificence, perhaps ultimately sacrificing herself to save him. Sometimes, however, as in *Marthe Richard,* the seductive spy is French, and successfully deceives the Germans. But whether French or foreign, male or female, the central characters always at some crucial juncture find themselves torn between love and duty, obliged to sacrifice either their principles, their patriotism, or their partner. Spy and counter-spy, plot and counter-plot, regularly involved deception and treachery, disguise and alias, real and apparent turncoats, with the result that it is not always merely the enemy who are deceived and confused but often the spectator too—especially at a distance of sev-

47. See Courtade, *Les Malédictions du cinéma français,* 165–166.

enty years. Contributing to this confusion of identity is the fact that the setting is often Alsace or Belgium, where history has created divided allegiances within and between families. And as befits such a theme, technical codes are often mobilized to reflect and heighten the confusion, with night-time shots, Dutch tilts, flickering searchlights, and rapid montage.[48] In *Marthe Richard,* the use of mottled, barred, and shafted light, especially in moments of violence, is unquestionably expressionistic.

This film was directed by Raymond Bernard, whose *Croix de bois* (#15) had been a groundbreaking war film, and the montage of combat scenes has here a documentary credibility reminiscent of that earlier film, let down only by some crude submarine-base models late in the film. Marthe Richard, an Alsatian who speaks German fluently, has lost family and, she believes, her fiancé in the war, so applies to become a spy and infiltrate the German command (von Ludow, supported by Mata Hari) in Spain. She succeeds with the help of a colleague (both at this stage pretending to be German spies), and when they strip off their disguises, she finds her fellow-spy is her supposedly dead fiancé. In the final conflagration that she has initiated, she watches French warplanes bomb the German submarine base. But any simplistic nationalism is undercut by von Stroheim, who plays von Ludow: realizing he has been deceived by Marthe, he injects poison, strips off his insignia, and sits at the piano to play his own funeral dirge. "I believed," he says, "that we were living a great adventure, but you are just another petty spy after all." This show-stealing scene, which positions the audience solidly behind the German commander, is typical of a genre that does not belittle or condemn the former enemy but treats their national rivalry rather as a continuation of "the great game." Perhaps to combat the implicitly unpatriotic mood thus established, however, the film ends with a flourish of crass triumphalism as U.S. troops (their ships saved by Marthe) disembark, the battle is won, and victory celebrations are held, complete with a parade on the Champs-Élysées.

Mademoiselle Docteur, released the same week, is even more resolutely understanding of the German cause, and not just because it was directed by Pabst or because all of the German agents and spymasters are played by famous French actors who invite identification. For the most part, Anne-Marie Lesser's largely successful exploits are recounted by her German colleagues, whose narrative position the audience is invited to share. As a German spy infiltrating the French in Salonica, she seduces and lives a romantic idyll with the French Captain Carrère. This generates for both of them at different moments the conventional conflict

48. For the conventions of the genre, see Crisp, *Genre, Myth and Convention,* 52–54, 115, 192.

between love and duty, which in her case momentarily inhibits her normal ruthless efficiency. Nevertheless, she steals crucial documents, gets messages through enemy (French) lines, and calls down (as her French rival did in the other film) a climactic German air attack on the French base. Amid the chaos of exploding bombs and sweeping searchlights, she escapes in a car, only to be killed by her lover, Captain Carrère, who grimly fires the fatal shot that causes her to crash.

At the time of the release of these two films, Émile Vuillermoz worried that they and their like "tended to establish a powerful war-time psychology and to arouse hatred and a desire for vengeance. They inflame passions that are all too ready to flare up everywhere in Europe today"—an odd attitude, he thought, for a nation to promote when it was currently holding a Universal Exhibition aimed precisely at bringing together those same peoples.[49]

60. *La Grande Illusion*

(*The Great Illusion*)
France, 1937, 113 min (95 min in some versions), b&w

Dir Jean Renoir; *Asst dir* Jacques Becker; *Prod* RAC (Rollmer); *Scr* Renoir and Charles Spaak; *Cinematog* Christian Matras and Claude Renoir; *Music* Joseph Kosma; *Art dir* Eugène Lourié; *Sound* Joseph de Bretagne; *Edit* Marguerite Houllé-Renoir and Marthe Huguet; *Act* Jean Gabin (Maréchal), Pierre Fresnay (de Boïeldieu), Erich von Stroheim (von Rauffenstein), Marcel Dalio (Rosenthal), Dita Parlo (Elsa), Julien Carette (artist), Jean Dasté (teacher), Gaston Modot (engineer), Sylvain Itkine (poet),Georges Péclet, and Jacques Becker (an English officer).

La Grande Illusion was from the start an immense success. Georges Sadoul said of it, "This film has achieved the greatest moral and material success of any French film of the last ten years."[50] It attracted more than a million viewers in Paris alone, putting it in the same league as *Les Enfants du paradis* at war's end. It was awarded the Jury Prize at the 1937 Venice Biennale for most artistic film—an award invented for the occasion to avoid awarding the Coupe de Mussolini to such an ideologically inappropriate film. It was also named best foreign film in 1938 by the U.S. Board of Review, and ranked among the ten best films of all time at the Brussels Convention of 1958. While still impressive, it can now seem

---

49. In *Le Temps*, 24 April 1937, cited by Courtade, *Les Malédictions du cinéma français*, 165.
50. Quoted in Abel, *French Film Theory and Criticism*, 2:276.

a ramshackle, incoherent film with little continuity between prison and farm-house segments. But arguably it is precisely this incoherence that allowed a film dealing with all of the most contentious topics of the day—nationalism, class, and racism—to be read as acceptable by quite divergent sections of the audience.

One source of this multivalency is the shift that took place between Charles Spaak's script and Jean Renoir's final film.[51] Renoir based his first outline partly on his own experiences in World War I, where he was (like Maréchal) an airman in a reconnaissance squadron. He was saved on one occasion by a fighter pilot, Pinsard, and escaped perhaps seven times from German prisons. Like Rosenthal, Renoir ended up with a permanent limp. He handed all this material to Spaak to shape into a scenario, but at a later stage, he replaced the young intellectual whom Spaak had written into the script (a role intended for Robert Le Vigan, who refused it) with the character of Rosenthal (now a Jew), and at an even later stage, as a result of getting to know Erich von Stroheim, vastly expanded the role of von Rauffenstein (and consequently of de Boïeldieu; the two roles origi-nally intended for Louis Jouvet and Pierre Renoir). Spaak's scenario had focused throughout on Maréchal (Gabin), who is still present in the opening and closing images of the film, but now cedes center-stage to others for much of the time. The original scenario would have minimized the disjunction of mood and focus at the moment of escape.

Nevertheless, a central thematic concern remains: this is primarily a paci-fist script, which asserts that national differences are much less significant than class differences. Or as Renoir was wont to say, "Vertical divisions are more sig-nificant than horizontal divisions."[52] That, he subsequently asserted, was the one story he had told and retold all his life, varying and expanding it from film to film. The lower ranks are shown as inhabiting a quite different France from that of the aristocrat and career officer, de Boïeldieu. On the one side, irreverence, vulgar-ity, and mateship; on the other, formality, distance, correctness, fastidiousness, honor, and duty—the difference, as the film notes, between on the one hand a Strauss waltz, Fouquet's, and Maxim's, and on the other a music hall, a popular song, and the bistro on the corner. Maréchal says "tu" to everyone; de Boïeldieu says "vous" even to his wife. "Clearly, everything separates us," as Maréchal ac-knowledges. But if everything separates classes, nothing separates the same class across national boundaries: "Nature couldn't care less for frontiers; they can't be seen, they're an invention of man." Across national boundaries, de Boïeldieu

51. For a brief but fine account of this, see Ferro, *Cinéma et histoire*, 184–190; also Renoir, *Renoir on Renoir*, 90–93.

52. See *Premier Plan*, nos. 22–23–24, 238, 245, and Renoir, *Renoir on Renoir*, 136.

and von Rauffenstein recognize one another as of a kind, sharing acquaintances and relations, international haunts and languages, even dalliances with the same courtesan, Fifi, at Maxim's. Likewise across national boundaries, the German guard's compassion saves Maréchal from madness, and on the run, Maréchal and Rosenthal find refuge with a well-disposed German widow in a farmhouse near the frontier. The film's most explicitly pacifist and internationalist moment occurs at this point, when the widow bitterly lists her menfolk who have been killed at Verdun and other "great victories." Maréchal and the widow establish a liaison, and he will return at war's end. Language may separate them, but (so the film implies) fellow-feeling links the peoples of different countries. The cow moos in agreement. Right from the beginning (when we witness von Rauffenstein's courtesy, hospitality, and tact as the Germans prepare a wreath for the dead French airman), every attempt is made to present the Germans in a respectful light and to minimize national hatreds.

But if this pacifist, internationalist message runs through much of the film, it was blurred by the expanding role given to von Stroheim—wonderfully stiff in a neck-brace that makes of him something between an astronaut and a Dalek out of *Dr. Who*—and the consequent sacrifice of de Boïeldieu (also a late addition) to allow Maréchal and Rosenthal to escape. The nobility of this gesture, and von Rauffenstein's quietly spoken but moving speech in favor of patriotism, soften Renoir's intended satire of the aristocracy. At the same time, this and the French prisoners' jumping to attention to sing the Marseillaise at the news of the recapture of Douaumont shift the balance from class toward nationalism, and thus produce a somewhat schizophrenic film. This conflict is exacerbated by the introduction of Rosenthal, whose actions and background, while primarily aimed at promoting "the good Jew," allow for a reading involving cultural knowledges of rich privileged Jews whose wealth knows no frontiers—knowledges that give internationalism a bad name. Glossed over and finally reconciled, they could nevertheless appeal to quite a different ideological constituency.

The change in emphasis has another consequence: where the original script's (and Renoir's) preference was for "the people," von Rauffenstein's and de Boïeldieu's meditations on the imminent doom of their class acquire an improbable poignancy. The value of democracy and the French Revolution are called into question, and we almost regret the passing of an aristocracy that views war, as François Truffaut was to say, "as a form of chivalry, as one of the fine arts, or at least as a sport, an adventure."[53] Thus, almost despite its authors, the film's argu-

53. Quoted in *Premier Plan*, nos. 22–23–24, 244–246.

ment became more complex in the course of production, such that right-wing critics, militarists, and anti-Semites could still praise it as glorifying France. Italian critics saw the supposedly "sinister pacifism" ("communistoid and patriotard") as not all that dangerous after all, and Lucien Rebatet noted that, "Without Renoir realising it, *La Grande Illusion* turned into a sort of exaltation of war, viewed as ennobling man."[54] Indeed, the sense of the title itself is no longer clear-cut: what exactly is the great illusion? That this war was to end wars between nations—no longer credible in 1937? That national divisions and enmities are the central determining factor in society? Who exactly are the deluded people here? André Bazin saw the initial meaning as deriving from Maréchal's and Rosenthal's promise to meet again at Maxim's at war's end, but failing to do so—the illusion of mateship had fallen through. But this whole episode was dropped during production. Now the notion of "illusion" has diffused through various elements of the film—love, sexuality, freedom, peace, escape—all those illusions, good and bad, that inspire human beings to passionate action. Bazin ends up deciding that the most satisfactory interpretation of "illusion" is rather those fanaticisms and hatreds that divide peoples who are in reality not distinct at all—frontiers, war, race, and class.[55] Even the value of "freedom" apparently achieved at the end is after all only affirmed ambivalently, since it involves separation from a loved one, and the somewhat melancholy departure through the snow at the end recalls Lange's ambivalent departure into exile at the end of *his* adventure.

At the technical level, this film confirms Renoir's filmmaking procedures by returning to a slow average shot length of 18.8 seconds. This is achieved despite a series of conventional shot/reverse shots whenever de Boïeldieu and von Rauffenstein converse, and a transitional series of brief shots as the soldiers are moved from camp to camp. Central to Renoir's longer ASL are 39 shots each longer than 45 seconds, of which 14 are between 1 and 2 minutes in length. Nevertheless, refuting Bazin's claims, where Renoir's earlier and later films were undoubtedly shot with great depth of field, a surprising number of shots occur here with out-of-focus distant events, or with racked focus between participants in an event. The photography was by Christian Matras, whom Renoir had not used before and was not to use again.

54. Ibid., 246–250; *Action française*, 11 February 1938, quoted in Abel, *French Film Theory and Criticism*, 2:241–245.

55. Bazin, *Jean Renoir*, 50–60. See Ferro, *Cinéma et histoire*, 184–190, and Prédal, *La Société française à travers le cinéma*, 256.

61. *Sarati le terrible*

(*Sarati the Terrible*)
France, 1937, 89 min, b&w

Dir André Hugon; *Prod* Hugon; *Scr* Jacques Constant, from the novel by Jean Vignaud; *Cinematog* André Bayard; *Music* Vincent Scotto, Jacques Janin, and Mahieddine; *Art dir* Émile Duquesne; *Act* Harry Baur (César Sarati), Georges Rigaud (Gilbert de Kéradec), Jacqueline Laurent (Rose), Rika Radifé (Concetta), Marcel Dalio (dock worker), Jean Tissier (Sarati's woman's brother), Charles Granval (Hudelo), Jeanne Helbling, Nadine Picard, and Yvonne Hébert.

Sarati le terrible is a rich, weird, and fascinating film, noteworthy both as a colonial film and as a source of debate on traditional patriarchy. It is also a central film for any appreciation of the place of Harry Baur in the cinema of the 1930s. The role he plays as a brutal dock boss in Algiers, overtly interested in an incestuous relationship with his niece, has been well analyzed by Michèle Lagny and colleagues in *Générique des années 30*. Wielding his vicious club, Sarati is brutal with all of his workers but especially with Arabs, Africans, and his homosexual "brother-in-law," systematically exploiting them as dock boss, landlord, and hash-house proprietor. In *The Colonial Cinema and Imperial France*, David Slavin sees the film's invitation to us to identify with such a man as an attempt to justify "the rough work of conquest that prepares the civilising mission, [which] requires just such atavistic qualities as this sexually obsessed abusive colonist demonstrates." Noël Burch and Geneviève Sellier in *La Drôle de guerre des sexes du cinéma français* focus rather on gender relations in the film, seeing it as key to understanding the whole period—an attempt by the patriarchal imagination to sketch a possible evolution from exploitative nineteenth-century capitalism toward a more benign form, and as a prefiguration of the cinema of the war years. These three books have more than adequately summarized the significance of *Sarati le terrible*, and what follows is based on their propositions.[56]

The novel on which it is based was written by Jean Vignaud in 1919. It won a literary prize, was a bestseller, and was first turned into a film in 1923. Vignaud was a right-wing novelist who took as his subject matter the French colonial experience in Algeria, of which he later wrote a history. He manages to make of the odious Sarati a tragic figure, his despicable characteristics elevated into

---

56. Lagny et al., *Générique des années 30*, 195–200; Slavin, *Colonial Cinema and Imperial France*, 25–29; Burch and Sellier, *La Drôle de guerre des sexes*, 40–43.

tragic flaws. In a manner similar to the American Western, Sarati's violence and ruthlessness are represented as an inevitable byproduct of the initial confrontation between Europeans and "the wilderness." Such men, we are led to suppose, cannot be judged by European standards. Opposing him for his niece Rose's affections is Gilbert, a typical ne'er-do-well younger son of the aristocracy whose reckless debauchery, gambling losses, and near murder of his brother have led to his exile in the colonies. We witness his gradual rehabilitation under Rose's influence and his subsequent alliance with the more enlightened gang-boss, Hudelo, in a project to modernize the Algiers dockside and introduce a less exploitative brand of capitalism. Sarati's double defeat, as a male and as a boss, leads him in the novel to slash his own throat, while in the early (silent) film he drowned himself. In this remake, entering Gilbert and Rose's nuptial chamber while Gilbert is absent, wracked with jealousy, he flourishes a knife over his sleeping niece, then uses it on himself—in a gesture interpretable as either killing or castrating himself.

As Burch and Sellier note, "In the 1930s the Rule of the Father manifested itself first of all in the possession, symbolic or actual, of a young woman who is (actually or symbolically) his own daughter."[57] In these Oedipal narratives, it is normal for the father-figure to encounter a young rival whose aim is to oust the older man from his role as protector of the young woman, but most commonly, it is the older man who, through experience and social position, wins out. Sarati is a pivotal figure in that he foreshadows a generation of older men who in their defeat by their younger rivals signal the passing of the old order, "the collapse of a certain archaic form of the patriarchy."[58] Yet here the defeat is felt as tragic because the audience is invited to identify with Sarati. Even his incestuous craving is almost excused both in the book and in this film version by the provocative behavior of Rose: strolling in the grounds of Sarati's country house, she suddenly (and uncharacteristically) flings herself to the ground in an attitude of abandon that leaves her blouse gaping. She could seem to invite the gesture that exposes her breast, only to recoil when it eventuates. While both Christianity and Islam reject such a desire as incestuous, Slavin notes that colonial attitudes might well see such "patrilineal endogamy" as preferable to mixed-race relationships, and that Mediterranean peoples have never been entirely averse to it since it serves to prevent the fragmentation of landholdings.

Michèle Lagny and her coauthors see Harry Baur as the ideal actor to embody Sarati, since of all the older male actors who dominated the cast-lists of

57. Burch and Sellier, *La Drôle de guerre des sexes*, 90.
58. Ibid., 41.

the decade, Baur most convincingly and consistently portrays emblematic figures of brute power. Often his role requires him to manifest "an excessive masculinity," "a dangerous animal force"; he is "a disturbingly solitary beast," a male deprived of females, to whom his narratives systematically deny any marital or paternal relationship.[59] Whether in North Africa or Russia, Baur's characters seem not just foreign but *alien,* monstrous. He inevitably ends up excluded in some painful way from the forms of belonging he seeks, either through suicide or death, in deprivation and degradation. Often he is sacrificed either to cleanse or save society, but for whatever reason, he must die. "It is as if the cinema of the 1930s, unable to suppress or to assume this excess, could only destroy it."[60]

Fascinating as it is, *Sarati le terrible* was not the success at the box-office that one might have expected. André Hugon, who directed it, was a journeyman director who had made twenty films since the coming of sound (he made what was arguably the first French sound feature, *Les Trois Masques*) without any significant success except two lighthearted films in 1930 and 1932. Perhaps his most inexplicable decision here was to mobilize a bewildering array of punctuation devices, which cumulatively disrupt the narrative tone of the film. Typically employed in riotous comedies as an aid to comic momentum, they are completely incongruous in this somber drama. Nevertheless, for its ideological significance, this is a film to be viewed.

62. *Un carnet de bal*

(*A Dance-Card*); remade as *Lydia* (1941)
France, 1937, 125 min, b&w

Dir and Scr Julien Duvivier; *Asst dir* Charles Durat; *Prod* Sigma; *Adapt* Duvivier, Jean Sarment, Pierre Wolff, Yves Mirande, Bertrand Zimmer, and Henri Jeanson; *Cinematog* Michel Kelber; *Music* Maurice Jaubert; *Art dir* Serge Pimenoff; *Sound* Jacques Carrère; *Edit* André Versein; *Act* Marie Bell (Christine Surgère), Françoise Rosay (Madame Audié), Harry Baur (Alain Regnault), Pierre Blanchar (Thierry), Fernandel (Fabien Coutissol), Louis Jouvet (Pierre Verdier/Jo), Raimu (François Patusset), Pierre Richard-Willm (Eric Irvin), Robert Lynen (Jacques), Milly Mathis (Cécile), Jeanne Fusier-Gir (newspaper seller), Sylvie (Gaby), Pierre Alcover, Andrex, René Génin, and Roger Legris.

59. Lagny et al., *Générique des années 30*, 195–200.
60. Lagny et al., *Générique des années 30*, 200.

This movie has been recognized as "the first great film to be based on a se-ries of sketches," a genre that was to flourish in France for the next thirty years.[61] Here, a woman returning from her husband's funeral rediscovers the dance-card from her first ball and sets out to find the men with whom she had danced that night. The storyline consists of nine relatively autonomous episodes in which she and the audience discover what those men have now become. The idea for the script seems to have been Julien Duvivier's own, perhaps inspired by *Cav-alcade* (Frank Lloyd, 1933), which had used an analogous pretext to elaborate the characteristic virtues of Britishness. Indeed, episodic narratives came to be seen as opportunities to set aside the individualism inherent in Western culture since the eighteenth century in favor of portraying a collectivity. Duvivier was to make another such in 1940—*Untel père et fils*—which elaborated the character-istic virtues of Frenchness, followed by three episodic films in America—*Lydia* (four lovers), *Tales of Manhattan* (six episodes centering on a frockcoat), and *Flesh and Fantasy/Obsessions* (based on Oscar Wilde's works). No less than five writers helped Duvivier to develop the nine episodes of *Carnet,* and one of these, Yves Mirande, was quick to see the advantages of the genre: it lent itself to star turns by famous actors, and to a series of generic pastiches. Already in 1934 he had or-ganized a script around the episodic "adventures" of a thousand-franc note (as had René Clair, *Le Chapeau de paille d'Italie* and *Le Million,* #9), while *Derrière la façade* (1939) is episodic, working through a series of vignettes. During the war, Mirande was to devise a whole series of such scenarios consisting of episodes within a loose framework.

In *Un carnet de bal,* the loose framework of the dance-card soon gives way to more thematic linkages. We first see Christine returning home from the fu-neral of her husband. With him dead, how is she to give sense to the rest of her life? The loneliness that has always threatened her, not least because of her child-lessness, suddenly looms larger, and a friend urges her to explore the past repre-sented by her first ball. It was a time of dreams, of hopes, and of ideals, now fur-ther romanticized by nostalgia. Her quest will be an attempt to recapture these qualities, and to overcome the loneliness she dreads. But her nine encounters with past dancing partners will decisively disillusion her. The most disturbing are the crooked lawyer (Louis Jouvet) who mistakes her for a corrupt client, and the dissolute doctor straight out of Graham Greene (Pierre Blanchar) who mis-takes her for a patient seeking an illegal abortion. All are in one way or another disappointing—they have committed suicide, in fact or in effect; have commit-ted crimes of the nastiest sort; or have at least retreated from life (into the church,

61. Leprohon, *Présences contemporaines,* 54.

into the snowy heights). As she says to the one to whom she is still attracted (Pierre Richard-Willm), "All I've found are dead men, or the living dead," and, as Michèle Lagny and colleagues point out, mad or murderous women.[62] Moreover, most often the men's "deaths" have been occasioned by her rejection of them that night at the ball. A cruel disillusionment comes when the most jocular of them (Fernandel) takes her to the very ballroom where that magical event took place, and in a genuine masterstroke, it turns out to be a banal, unlovely dance hall where another such glum "ball" is even now taking place, equally magical for the double of her young self that she meets. There is no hope for her in the past.

But if not the past, perhaps the future? Her quest has been largely triggered by the absence of a child, and in several episodes, this absence is explored and confirmed. Mademoiselle Audié (Françoise Rosay) has been driven to madness by being deprived of her son who committed suicide because of Christine. The abbot (Harry Baur) has retreated to the church because of her indifference but also because of the death of a son from his tumultuous youth. The village mayor (Raimu) has adopted a son who has gone bad, and whom we see trying to blackmail him and being whipped close to death. Lastly, the corrupt doctor's weary abortion routine sums up this infertility theme. Finding her final partner has been ruined and also committed suicide, she adopts his abandoned teenage son and will prepare him for his first ball—a final tentative glimmer of hope after a trajectory dominated by childlessness, aging, grief, despair, disillusion, failure, corruption, criminality, and death. It is easy to see why J.-P. Jeancolas should see Christine's bleak "tour de France" as a whole generation being put on trial and condemned.[63] For other critics, the film merely confirmed Duvivier's pessimistic view of humanity.

But watching the film is not at all depressing: the varied moods and genres provide constant interest, and the technical quality is masterly. This was a key film in the move toward "quality filmmaking" that marked the years 1937–1939 and earned the French cinema a reputation overseas. Sets, lighting, framing, and atmosphere are a constant delight, and the virtuoso set pieces are unforgettable. As Christine begins to drift into memories of the ball, her subjectivity is evoked by a very slow cross-dissolve mobilizing superimposed images of the ball, slow motion, soft focus, distorted sound, close-ups of her remembering head, and whispers of past dialogue. One reason for this flurry of technical activity is, of course, that contemporary audiences were still relatively unaccustomed to transitions in time, so needed redundant signifiers to orient them. But

62. Lagny et al., *Générique des années 30*, 56–91, esp. 74.
63. Jeancolas, *15 ans d'années trente*, 274.

no such defense need be made of the astounding panning back and forth of an angled camera during the ship's doctor's episode. Partly echoing a ship's rolling, it is better seen as exteriorizing the mental instability of the Blanchar character, who, as Christine leaves, has an epileptic fit and seems about to murder his female companion. Philippe Agostini has left a vivid account of the violence done to him as he tried to control the twisting camera.[64]

It is easy to see why such an ambitious "quality film" was judged Best Foreign Film at the 1937 Venice Biennale.

63. *Gribouille*

(*The Old Fool*); remade as *The Lady in Question* (1940)
France-Germany, 1937, 95 min, b&w

Dir Marc Allégret; *Prod* ACE; *Scr* Marcel Achard; *Cinematog* Georges Benoit; *Music* Georges Auric; *Art dir* Alexandre Trauner; *Sound* William Sivel; *Edit* Yvonne Martin; *Act* Michèle Morgan (Natalie Roguin), Raimu (Camille Morestan), Gilbert Gil (Claude Morestan), Jean Worms (the president), Jacqueline Pacaud (Françoise Morestan), Oléo (Henriette Clovis), Jeanne Provost (Louise Morestan), Pauline Carton (the other Natalie Roguin), Julien Carette (Lurette), Marcel André (prosecuting lawyer), Jacques Grétillat (defense lawyer), Jacques Baumer (Marinier), Andrex, René Génin, Pierre Labry, and Bernard Blier.

Also *Orage* (*Storm*)
France, 1938, 98 min, b&w

Dir Marc Allégret; *Scr* Marcel Achard, from a play by Henry Bernstein; *Cinematog* Armand Thirard; *Music* Georges Auric; *Art dir* Serge Pimenoff; *Sound* Marcel Courmes; *Edit* Yvonne Martin; *Act* Michèle Morgan (Françoise Massart), Lisette Lanvin (Gisèle Pascaud), Charles Boyer (André Pascaud), Jean-Louis Barrault (L'Africain), Robert Manuel (Gilbert), Jean Joffre, and René Génin.

As mentioned earlier, Marc Allégret is seldom singled out for mention as an auteur. Pierre Leprohon did so in a dismissive way, quoting the sardonic judgment of Charles Spaak, who when working with Allégret found him "indecisive, without constancy or weight, . . . transparent, odourless, tasteless."[65] Yet the box-office returns of even his relative failures during this decade would have

---

64. See Crisp, *Classic French Cinema*, 398–399.
65. Leprohon, *Présences contemporaines*, 157.

gladdened the heart of most contemporary directors (see #47). The one quality all commentators recognized in him was his ability to spot young talent. He gave their first major roles to numerous young actors who later became stars—Simone Simon and Jean-Pierre Aumont in *Lac aux Dames*, Jean-Louis Barrault in *Les Beaux Jours*, Odette Joyeux and Bernard Blier in *Entrée des artistes* (#82), and Gérard Philipe and Danielle Delorme in *Les Petites du Quai aux Fleurs*. Reputedly he saw Michèle Morgan sunbathing on the beach and approached her with the hackneyed line, "With those eyes you ought to become an actress," hence the title of her autobiography, *Avec ces yeux-là*. Certainly he gave her her first major role at the age of seventeen opposite Raimu in *Gribouille*, followed by another opposite Charles Boyer in *Orage*. The former was written by Marcel Achard (initially for Louis Jouvet's theatrical company), the second adapted by Achard from a Henry Bernstein play, and several subsequent joint successes suggest that Achard and Allégret formed a team with compatible sensibilities.

Morgan was thus, with Danielle Darrieux, one of the few female stars to come directly into the cinema without passing through the theater, thus avoiding the tendency toward exhibitionism that the theater encouraged. Although she took acting lessons from René Simon, the most famous acting coach of the day, Jonathan Driskell reports that Simon was wise enough to encourage her "more nuanced and naturalistic style," which comes across as more intensely felt, especially in contrast to Raimu, whose expansive and exuberant theatricality registers (appropriately enough in context) as suspicious.[66] The narrative of *Gribouille* involves Camille Morestan (Raimu) doing jury service in a case where Natalie (Morgan) is being tried for the murder of a wealthy man's son. Largely through his efforts she is acquitted, and Monsieur Morestan offers her a job to reintegrate her into society. In doing so, though, he conceals her origins from his wife and son, pretending she is the daughter of a friend. Thus, a certain ambivalence is preserved throughout the second half of the film as to whether his motives are entirely altruistic. His son certainly comes to believe they are not. This offers an opportunity for two classic tropes of the decade—the old man nervously attracted to a woman much younger than himself, then an Oedipal rivalry between father and son for her affections. Ultimately, Natalie finds herself trapped in precisely the same situation for which she had earlier been tried. In what could be interpreted as a jealous rage, Morestan, believing her to be fleeing with his son and the shop's takings, batters her over the head with a statue and believes he has killed her.

66. Jonathan Driskell, "The Female Metaphysical Body in Poetic Realist Film," *Studies in French Cinema* 8, no. 1 (2008): 57–73.

From her very first starring role, then, Michèle Morgan embodied a femme fatale, though of a new type—as the involuntary cause of disruption to the family and even of death to those men unfortunate enough to be fascinated by her. A nice analysis of her screen persona by Jonathan Driskell, as mentioned above, notes the combination of sensual physical intensity and ethereal otherness that is established in this film and in *Orage*, a combination that was to accompany her throughout her career. A waif and outcast, always already grieving when we meet her, her tragic past often related to victimization by males, she yet seems with her unworldly off-screen gaze to aspire to transcend this harsh reality, and to offer a parallel transcendence to the men (notably Jean Gabin in his many roles opposite her) who are drawn to her. Driskell notes the saintly link with Joan of Arc established in *Gribouille*—the trial, plus the fact that the statue with which Monsieur Morestan knocks her out is of the nation's patriotic saint. Driskell also points out that the posters for both these films represent her face pale and disembodied, above and beyond the men she attracts.

Several commentators have remarked on the fact that Natalie is Russian, and that the film licenses several characters to voice a xenophobia that flourished in these last prewar years. François Garçon notes that a jury member in the initial scene is outraged that she should talk disparagingly of the lice you can pick up in French railway stations, while film scholars Noël Burch and Geneviève Sellier see Morestan as guilty of a double disavowal, suppressing awareness of both her foreignness and his desire for her.[67] This they see as consonant with the crisis of national identity that was often to find expression as xenophobia in the films of these years.

In *Orage*, Morgan plays opposite Charles Boyer, an actor again twenty years older than her, but one who despite his years in the theater was capable of the same stillness and intensity as her. Consequently their joint performance is more powerful than that in *Gribouille*. Again she is an involuntary yet kindly femme fatale, Françoise, capable of devotion and self-sacrifice; again she is rescued by the protagonist and drawn into an ambiguous relationship with her rescuer, again finding that the disastrous situation from which he had rescued her is reproducing itself in their own relationship. Again her own happiness is opposed to that of a family and found to be incompatible with it: believing André and his wife are to have a child, she decides she must die. This time another trope familiar to students of the decade is woven into the narrative: Boyer plays an engineer happily established with his family in the provinces, while Morgan's involuntary femme fatale is associated with the disorder of Paris. Despite

---

67. Garçon, *De Blum à Pétain*, 184; Burch and Sellier, *La Drôle de guerre des sexes*, 38.

their attempts to refashion an idyll in the provinces, her urban past cannot be denied. Perhaps the most moving and astonishing scene in the whole film has Françoise meeting the engineer's wife to discuss their common love for André, an encounter painful to both of them, which would normally have been exploited for its gesticulatory melodramatic effect. Instead, as elsewhere in this admirable film, all is understated, underacted, the emotion implied rather than expressed.

64. *Gueule d'amour*

(*Lover-Boy*)
France-Germany, 1937, 90 min, b&w

Dir Jean Grémillon; *Asst dir* Louis Daquin; *Prod* UFA/ACE; *Scr* Charles Spaak, from the novel by André Beucler; *Cinematog* Gunther Rittau; *Music* Lothar Bruhne; *Act* Jean Gabin (Lucien Bourrache, aka Gueule d'amour), René Lefebvre (René), Mireille Balin (Madeleine), Marguerite Deval (Madeleine's mother), Jane Marken (Madame Cailloux), Jean Aymé (Madeleine's valet), Henri Poupon (Monsieur Cailloux), Pierre Etchepare (hotel proprietor), and Robert Casa (Monsieur Moreau).

So catastrophic was the reception of *La Petite Lise* (1930, #6) that Jean Grémillon spent five years in the wilderness. Most of his succeeding films were chores accepted to continue working, though *Pour un sou d'amour* (1931–1932), is no less inventive than *La Petite Lise* in its initial technical strategies: after an opening act set on a cruise liner and integrated by a series of musical themes, it develops into a conventional romantic comedy involving exchanged identities, but uses some amazing vertical camera angles and allows for the introduction of a number of musical items. It concludes with an extended public/private contrast in which, in the middle of a joyous dance scene, the villain out of jealousy tries to knife the hero.

In 1935, however, Grémillon joined Raoul Ploquin in Germany, where Ploquin had begun producing the French versions of German films for UFA, and was soon to initiate purely French productions. UFA already had a French production arm at the Épinay studios outside Paris, which specialized in high-quality films by reputable directors (René Clair, Julien Duvivier, Jacques Feyder) with all the best-known French actors, many on long-term contracts.[68] In the Berlin studios,

68. For a list of these, see Courtade, *Les Malédictions du cinéma français*, 66, 106–108.

Henri Clouzot, Henri Decoin, Henri Chomette, and others had already scripted or directed dozens of French versions, but from 1935, Ploquin began a more ambitious program there. Ultimately some 11 percent of all "French" films from this decade were produced by UFA or its French production arm, the Alliance Cinématographique Européenne (ACE). Ploquin insisted that the choice of scenarios, directors, and actors be exclusively his responsibility, and he had no difficulty attracting them to the Neubabelsburg studios. J.-P. Jeancolas explains this massive transfer of personnel as a consequence of the lack of adequate funding available in France. An anonymous and highly ironic pamphlet circulated in 1934 tends to confirm this but suggests that the "international co-operation" that resulted was not uniformly appreciated by French cinema personnel.[69]

It was not just money that attracted them. The studios were incomparably better equipped than any in France. André Beucler, whose novel Charles Spaak adapted for *Gueule d'amour*, attended the shoot and came away overawed by the technological superiority, the aspiration toward perfection, and the international camaraderie that united French, German, and other nations in Neubabelsburg. As Jeancolas says, "For ten years a veritable colony of Frenchmen were working in Berlin: directors, scriptwriters, technicians, actors, all lived in the capital of the Weimar Republic, then with the same ease, it seems, in that of the Third Reich."[70] It was in this benign climate that Marcel L'Herbier and Albert Valentin made films, and that Grémillon directed a French version of *Königswaltzer* (*La Valse royale*) and the adaptation of a French play (*Pattes de mouche*) before finally in 1937 making *Gueule d'amour*, the film that was to restore his reputation with the French public and inaugurate for him a decade of ever greater successes.

It is not hard to see why Beucler's novel should have seemed an appropriate vehicle for Jean Gabin at this stage of his career, since it brings together and capitalizes on elements from several of his previous successes, notably *La Bandera* (#42), *La Belle Équipe* (#51), and *Pépé le Moko* (#56). Gabin plays Lucien, called Lover-Boy, a spahi (soldier of the North African cavalry regiment), object of the admiration and lust of all the women of Orange, where he is stationed. He casually picks up Madeleine, who equally casually gambles away all of his money and abandons him. Her unpredictability and independence provoke him, the more so as his resignation from the spahis deprives him of that charisma and confidence that had effortlessly attracted women. Now an uncharismatic printing

69. See Crisp, *Classic French Cinema*, 177–180.
70. Jeancolas, *15 ans d'années trente*, 21–26, 31–35, 270–274.

worker, he pursues Madeleine more and more desperately, abjectly, dramatically. This then is a portrait of a femme fatale and kept woman who cannot imagine renouncing her power over men and over the wealth that results, seen through the eyes of a victim who once treated women as she treats men (though the film's male gaze condemns her as it would not have thought of condemning him). He endures the alternating hopes and disappointments until he discovers that his best mate is another of her victims. At that point, his rage explodes: he strangles her, and the final images are of his departing once more for North Africa, no doubt to reenlist. As Geneviève Guillaume-Grimaud says, *"Gueule d'amour* finishes where *La Bandera* had begun."[71]

The film is typical of 1930s femme fatale films in two important respects. First, it assumes the overwhelming significance of male friendship as the natural basis of any stable community, and the primary crime of any femme fatale is to provoke fissures in that idyllic male relationship. It is when his mate René is humiliated that Lucien erupts in that trademark outburst of righteous rage which will prove his downfall, and the embrace as Lucien and René part—the passionate kiss on the neck—constitutes a surprisingly explicit assertion that the male-male bond is the highest form of human relationship. Second, as Noël Burch and Geneviève Sellier rightly complain, Spaak and Grémillon have grafted a left-wing class critique onto Beucler's novel. Furthermore, their film is characteristic of its time in that it is a rich female, with her combination of nymphomania and calculation, who is portrayed as the symbol of all that is destructive and decadent in the wealthy.[72]

The film begins on a high note, with an early comic scene borrowed from *Le Roi des resquilleurs* (#5), in which Lucien and René con a café proprietor into providing a free meal, but ends with a disastrous scene, out of character with Gabin's persona and beyond his acting ability, in which, weeping copiously, he pleads for his mate's help to escape from France. Throughout, however, the sophisticated quality of the image is a delight: the abstract patterns of the spinning wheel, the bottles, and the urns in the opening shots; the overhead shot of sheep crossing a bridge; the recurrent use of shadows, mirrors, reflections, and repetitions; the angles and quizzical unmotivated sideways slides of the camera; and the neat transitions such as that from Paris to Orange. Critics were not overly impressed with the film, but the public flocked to it, perhaps largely attracted by Gabin's developing persona and reputation.

71. Guillaume-Grimaud, *Le Cinéma du Front Populaire*, 146.
72. Burch and Sellier, *La Drôle de guerre des sexes*, 49–52.

65. La Dame de Malacca

(*That Woman from Malaya*)
France, 1937, 113 min (now 98 min), b&w

Dir Marc Allégret; *Asst dir* Armand Léon and Jean Huet; *Prod* Régina; *Scr* H. Lustig and C.-A. Puget, from the novel by Francis de Croisset; *Cinematog* Jules Kruger; *Music* Louis Beydts; *Art dir* Jacques Krauss; *Edit* Yvonne Martin; *Act* Edwige Feuillère (Audrey), Betty Daussmond (Lady Lyndstone), Gabrielle Dorziat (Lady Brandmore), Pierre Richard-Willm (Prince Sélim), Jacques Copeau (Lord Brandmore), Jean Debucourt (Sir Eric Temple), Jean Wall (Major Carter), Liliane Lesaffre (Lady Johnson), Foun-Sen (the servant), Ky-Duyen (a Japanese), William Aguet (Gérald), and Alexandre Mihalescu (Sirdar Raman).

For *La Dame de Malacca*, Marc Allégret selected as leads a couple who were beginning to register with the public as an appropriate romantic duo: Pierre Richard-Willm and Edwige Feuillère, who had already acted together in *Stradivarius* and *Barcarolle* (both 1935). Here their romantic attachment is across racial boundaries, with Richard-Willm's skin discreetly darkened to make of him a Malay, while Feuillère plays an English schoolteacher now married to an army officer. But rather than seeing this cross-racial liaison as a daringly liberal gesture, we should see it rather as mobilizing for dramatic purposes two standard French myths concerning sexuality, associated respectively with the British and Asian characters (or, indeed, any colonial of swarthy appearance). The former were routinely portrayed as sexually inhibited, the latter as sexually provocative and threatening. The erotic and the exotic were always, so to speak, intimately linked, though seldom is "the dark side" of the human personality so unambiguously celebrated and triumphant as here.[73] In their discussion of the ways in which the dark-skinned races are effectively elided from the decade's films, Michèle Lagny and colleagues note that when minorities were not reduced to an anonymous seething mass then either

1. Native actors were simply not mentioned in the credits, even
   when as in *Les 5 Gentlemen maudits* (#14), *Les Hommes nouveaux*,
   and *L'Homme du Niger* their roles are central to the plot; or

---

73. Much of this entry is a condensed version of my account in Crisp, *Genre, Myth and Convention*, 42–45.

2. The roles of natives are played, as here, by European actors, often of foreign birth. It is a Romanian Jew (Lucas Gridoux) who plays Slimane in *Pépé le Moko* (#56), Dalio who plays the Maltese in *La Maison du Maltais* (#81), Annabella who plays Aïcha in *La Bandera* (#42), Brigitte Helm who plays Antinéa in *L'Atlantide* (#16), and Jean Grétillat who plays Belkacem in *Bourrasque;* or

3. If by any chance a mixed-race child eventuates from such a relationship, then it must be purged of its darkness, as in *Le Blanc et le noir* and *La Maison du Maltais.*[74]

Richard-Willm is then merely following this tradition, but unlike most dark-skinned roles, the character he plays is not represented as slimy, sinister, or superstitiously backward but rather as nobler than the whites, whom he displaces in Audrey's affections. This was, of course, always an option in the representation of exotic, where "Nature" could be seen as threatening and lethal or as the abode of the noble and pure.

We first meet Audrey as a young English teacher in Le Havre. A dominating shrew of a headmistress drives her to escape into a loveless marriage with a stuffy English army doctor obsessed with career advancement who is posted to Malaya. Interestingly, her habit of smoking cigarettes, which triggered her resignation from the teaching establishment, is used insistently to characterize her as bravely modern and unconventional, as opposed to the bridge parties that are used to characterize "respectable" French/English society as old-fashioned, rule-governed, and boring. (The smoking of cigarettes was often used in this way in films of the decade—see, for instance, *Les 5 Gentlemen maudits,* #14.) Dreaming of romance and the jungle, whose combined forces might just possibly subvert the propriety and convention that is tightening around her, Audrey meets on the ship taking her and her husband to Malaya the Prince Sélim. The usual metaphoric storm, which disrupts the Englishmen's card game but which she finds exhilarating, facilitates her acquaintance with the prince. We find out that he had been to England to study but could never get close to the English because of their formality and because they despised his "dark blood." "The heart speaks more truly," she whispers. Once in Malaya, and despite her husband's warning that all natives are thieves, she immediately finds herself in sympathy with the life of the Malays. The identification between Malaya and sensuality is made clear in such scenes as that in which Prince Sélim is showing her the exotic flower that blooms

74. Lagny et al., *Générique des années 30,* ch. 4.

for one night only. As they speculate about the possibility of their own relationship blooming, a brief, quasi-subjective shot shows several bare-breasted native women flashing past. It is clear, however, that Malaya represents for her not just release and sensuality but something more violent—or rather, that conventions broken and sensuality unleashed is represented as being not just exhilarating but also potentially destructive, if taken to excess. When she abandons her husband, the Malay streets through which she escapes are characterized by seedy bar-hotels, cock-fights, drunken sailors, and prostitutes. Sexuality is closely allied to chaos, and nearly leads to her death. She must learn to navigate between the extremes of formality and sensuality, both of which are represented as intolerable in their pure states. The prince marries her and engineers her rehabilitation, such that she can now lord it over the desiccated expatriate Englishwomen who have sought to destroy her.

This is a film of fantasized fulfillment. Unlike many of her contemporaries, trapped in one or another stultifying French institution, Audrey does escape, sailing out of Le Havre on that fabled steamer bound for exotic lands "over there," where (in contrast with France) all dreams *can* be realized. In this sense, *La Dame de Malacca* is an anti–poetic-realist film, or if not anti-, perhaps ante.

66. Drôle de drame

Bizarre, Bizarre
France, 1937, 95 min, b&w

Dir Marcel Carné; *Asst* Pierre Prévert and Walter; *Prod* Corniglion-Molinier; *Scr* Jacques Prévert, from *His First Offense* by J. Storer Clouston; *Cinematog* Eugen Schüfftan, Louis Page, and Henri Alekan; *Music* Maurice Jaubert; *Art dir* Alexandre Trauner; *Sound* Antoine Archaimbaud; *Edit* Marthe Poncin; *Act* Michel Simon (Irwin Molyneux and Félix Chapel), Louis Jouvet (Archibald Soper, Bishop of Bedford), Jean-Pierre Aumont (Billy, the milkman), Jean-Louis Barrault (Willian Kramps, the mad cyclist), Françoise Rosay (Margaret Molyneux), Nadine Vogel (Eva), Pierre Alcover (Inspector Bray), Agnès Capri (street singer), Jane Lory (aunt), Henri Guisol, René Genin, Marcel Duhamel, Sinoël, Pierre Prévert, and Jean Marais.

Drôle de drame represents a second attempt by Jacques Prévert to introduce Anglo-Saxon slapstick humor into mainstream French cinema. Having failed, both financially and arguably artistically, with *L'Affaire est dans le sac* (#21), he came very close to succeeding in this collaboration with Marcel Carné, whose meticulous control of all aspects of production provided the sort of rigor that

slapstick needs, and that had been notably lacking from the earlier film. Moreover, Carné assembled perhaps the most astounding cast—Louis Jouvet, Michel
Simon, Françoise Rosay, Jean-Pierre Aumont, Pierre Alcover, and Jean-Louis
Barrault—ever assembled for any film in the decade (though see *Un carnet de bal*,
#62, and *Salonique*, also from this year). The script was based on a farcical En-
glish novel, and the brief, twenty-three-day shoot is described with affection by
several concerned (Simon, Carné, Aumont) as a magical collaboration despite (indeed partly because of) several marked antagonisms (Prévert and Rosay, Simon
and Jouvet). Carné later said of Michel Simon's performance that if ever he had
encountered genius, it was then and there.[75]

Difficult to summarize, the narrative contains scenes and situations that
once seen will never be forgotten: the Bishop of Bedford salivating over an affectionate dedication from a music-hall actress ("to Baby Bedford, in memory of our
night of madness"); his cousin Molyneux, a timid botanist, doubling incognito as
Félix Chapel, the crime writer; their wonderful conversation ("Bizarre, bizarre."
"You said 'bizarre'?" "I said 'bizarre'? . . . How bizarre." etc.); Molyneux accused
of supposedly murdering his wife, hastily disguised as Félix Chapel, and asked
to write articles on the murderer (i.e., himself); the bishop trying to recover his
incriminating music-hall program while disguised as an uncomfortably short-
kilted Scotsman, who is himself then arrested for supposedly murdering Molyneux (the bishop's "If you don't respect me, at least respect my vestments" becoming ever more hilarious as his vestments do); the animal-lover and crazed
cyclist William Kramps, who kills butchers (the pleasant life—"A little money,
a butcher from time to time, the sun . . .") and is besotted with Madame Molyneux, who comes upon him bathing naked in her fish-pond; the milkman who
turns out to be the brains behind Molyneux/Chapel's writings; and the burly
policeman disguised in drag who arrests them one after another for supposedly
murdering one another.

Of course, one can see here, as heavily disguised as the characters, certain of
Prévert's well-known social preoccupations—a delight in ridiculing the law, religion, and the bourgeoisie, whose facade of respectability hides licentious if not
downright illegal behavior; all creativity residing in the working class; and the
suggestion that the latter are on the side of nature and purity (animals, flowers,
milk), which the middle classes despise or corrupt. Guy Jacob points out other
analogies with later films—Eva, like Nelly in *Quai des brumes* (#78) and Françoise in *Le Jour se lève* (#94), is an orphan; again, as in *Le Jour se lève*, there is a love
scene in a conservatory; William Kramps, the poetic murderer, is clearly a blood

75. Carné, *La Vie à belles dents*, 88.

brother of Lacenaire, the murderous poet; and the novelist or playwright who encounters his own fictional characters is a recurrent trope.[76] All these thematic preoccupations are, however, here concealed beneath the burlesque surface of a hectic plot, whereas in his other scripts of the period, they are the cornerstone of the plot. Arguably they are the more effective here for the indirection.

Given the riotous atmosphere that prevailed during production, none involved were prepared for the critical and financial catastrophe that followed. For the purposes of self-dramatization, that box-office disappointment has been somewhat exaggerated: genius is, after all, supposed to meet inevitably with misunderstanding from the masses. Reputedly the audience booed and shouted insults during the premiere, nearly all reviews except that in *Le Merle blanc* panned it, and the gullible Édouard Corniglion-Molinier, who had financed it reputedly lost his total investment.[77] It is interesting to see so late in the decade one of the few eccentric and risky films still depending on an individual patron for funding. Carné rather complacently likened the film's public rejection to that of *L'Atalante* (#32) and *La Règle du jeu* (#95) in the same cinema. In fact, however, there were several other favorable or partly favorable reviews, and the film ran for six weeks in exclusive release at the Colisée, which is not a charitable institution, and in general release screened in no less than forty-three cinemas in the Paris suburbs. This equates to a Paris audience of nearly 250,000, which was above average for the day.

Fifteen years later, at its 1951 re-release, *Drôle de drame* was greeted with the enthusiasm it deserves, and it has remained a cult film ever since. It was at the time, however, a relatively low point in Carné's career. Fortunately, it did not deter him from working over the next decade with Prévert and the crew he was building up around him—Prévert in *Jenny, Drôle de drame, Quai des brumes, Le Jour se lève, Les Visiteurs du soir, Les Enfants du paradis* and *Les Portes de la nuit,* and for most of these the cameramen Eugen Schufftan and Roger Hubert, the set-decorator Alexandre Trauner, and the composers Maurice Jaubert (until 1940 when he was killed in the war) and Joseph Kosma. His preference for working with those he had come to know and trust was undoubtedly a product of lack of confidence, due to a background more culturally deprived than that of (say) Jean Renoir and Jean Grémillon, but it made for a stable and efficient team, collaborating over a number of films within a cinema where such collaborations had been rendered extremely difficult by the fragmentation of production into small units that no longer offered long-term contracts either to stars or technicians.

76. *Premier Plan,* no. 14, 22.

77. Carné, *La Vie à belles dents,* 85–91; Barrault, *Memories for Tomorrow;* Aumont, *Le Soleil et l'ombre;* Loubier, *Michel Simon,* 150–157.

67. Regain

(Regrowth)

France, 1937, 121 min (reports of other versions 90–160 min), b&w

Dir and Scr Marcel Pagnol, from the novel by Jean Giono; *Asst dir* Léon Bourrely; *Prod* Films Marcel Pagnol; *Cinematog* Willy; *Music* Arthur Honegger; *Art dir* Marcel Brouquier; *Sound* Jean Lecoq; *Edit* Suzanne de Troeye; *Act* Orane Demazis (Arsule), Gabriel Gabrio (Panturle), Fernandel (Gédémus), Édouard Delmont (Gaubert, Jasmin's father), Charles Blavette (Jasmin), Marguerite Moreno (la Mamèche), Odette Roger (Alphonsine), Milly Mathis (la Belline, Jasmin's wife), Henri Poupon (l'Amoureux), Robert Le Vigan (local police chief), Marguerite Chabert (Martine), and Paul Dullac.

Regain recounts the regeneration of a dying Provençal village, Aubignane, that initially has only three remaining inhabitants: Panturle; Gaubert, an old man who is reluctantly leaving for the city; and an old woman, la Mamèche. The regeneration is initiated by the reestablishment of a fertile couple—Panturle and Arsule—who reassert the fertility of the land. Like *Angèle* (1934, #34), this film came about as a consequence of Marcel Pagnol's exploration of the literary oeuvre of his Provençal countryman, Jean Giono, which had reoriented Pagnol from his coastal fringe trilogy toward the drier interior regions of Haute Provence. As in *La Terre qui meurt*, the drift of the young to the cities has left the land unproductive and the villages deserted. Gédémus, the knife-grinder (Fernandel used against the grain of his comic persona as a brute), acts as a parodic spokesperson for this "modern" ideology of mechanization and industrialization, and his exploitation of Arsule (who out of the generosity of his heart he takes under his wing and allows to pull his grinding machine over hill and dale) stands as a low-key metaphor for the exploitation of workers in the industrialized world. Constantly on the move, he has lost all contact with the land. Panturle, on the other hand, stands for "the soil": fertility, renewal, belonging. As he says later, with Gaubert gone and la Mamèche dead, he has to stay in Aubignane because, "As long as I'm there, it's still a village." Earlier, la Mamèche has herded Gédémus and Arsule toward Aubignane, so that Panturle can rescue Arsule and work with her to once again render the land productive, using a plough hand-fashioned by old Gaubert. He then waits patiently in the market for customers to recognize the superiority of his "old-fashioned" hand-milled wheat. So this film purveys a rigorously conservative ideology in which to abandon the land (like Panturle's father) results in paralysis, while to rediscover it leads to fruitfulness. In the final sequence, Jasmin, Gaubert's son, accepting the validity of Panturle's morality, abandons his stationmaster's job and concomitant uniform to work a plot of inherited land—"In general, uniforms are worn by people who obey, not by people who do real work." In fact, the film exhibits throughout a deep distrust of all systems, laws, rules, and regulations, all politics and hierarchies. This is right-wing anarchism at its most forceful and affecting. Inevitably, at the end, Arsule is discovered to be pregnant, as productive as the land (and her goat!).

One of the most controversial aspects of the film was its treatment of Arsule, who at the beginning is used sexually by a gang of charcoal-burners, then becomes a beast of burden for Gédémus, a replacement horse. Feminists, but not only feminists, saw this as an unacceptable manifestation of conservative patriarchal ideology, not least because when Gédémus rediscovers her now living with Panturle, he demands compensation. Panturle apparently acknowledges his claim, providing money for a mule to replace her labor. The film is not, however, as most commentators have claimed, effectively accepting the commercial equivalence of woman and animal: it makes clear that Panturle is lovingly committed to Arsule; his face steely with scorn, he is merely paying off the avaricious Gédémus so that Arsule and he can start anew.

For other commentators, the film involved, as had Pagnol's previous adaptation of a Giono novel, the redemption of a fallen woman, implying that it is primarily women who need redeeming. This criticism is more defensible. Arguably, however, Arsule's initial sexual degradation is represented as so extreme primarily in order to underline the limitless redemptive power of the land. Nevertheless, it might be seen as dubious practice to use the gang-rape of a helpless woman for narrative and structural convenience. As in *Angèle,* the redemption takes place against a typically Gionoesque scale of altitude, the coastal cities being the source of all evil and the interior village heights the sites of salvation.

The other main debate concerning *Regain* is whether it was not simply a foretaste of the Vichy ideology of 1940–1944, which likewise promoted the soil, family, and local roots ("Famille, Travail, Patrie"—family, work, community).[78] Certainly it joins *La Terre qui meurt* (#48), *Hercule,* and other late 1930s films in giving voice to values that were to be officially consecrated as necessary for the regeneration of the whole country after the catastrophe of 1940. But where Vichy also promoted the Catholic faith as an essential co-requisite of this "return to the land," *Regain* is more ambivalent. Again many commentators have been too extreme, asserting that the film proposes a violent rejection of Catholicism: they point out that la Mamèche early on curses the Virgin Mary and hurls a bowl of liquid at her statue, and that at the end, others are joining Panturle and Arsule in

78. Crisp, *Genre, Myth and Convention,* 195, Jeancolas, *15 ans d'années trente,* 267; Peyrusse, *Le Cinéma méridional,* 139.

the regeneration of the village but not of the church.[79] This is inaccurate, since the church tower is prominent on the village hilltop in the final sequence, and arguably there are several signs of reverence or prayer, notably from la Mamèche, in the course of the film. It can, however, be said with confidence that the film is antagonistic to any *institutionalization* of religious feeling, displacing reverence from the church toward the practical essentials of everyday survival, and thus toward a form of pantheism in which soil, seed, and bread are central.

Perhaps appropriately, given the nostalgic ideology it embodies, the film resists any sophisticated use of technology. The titles and credits are primitive, and the editing is rudimentary, with blocks of time juxtaposed brutally. It has been described as a cinema without relief, without perspective, "flattened out." This has led commentators to liken it to naive painting, or even because of its sacramental simplicity, to a medieval film, analogous to a fabliau, *chanson de geste,* or medieval altarpiece. J.-P. Jeancolas goes so far as to label it "a Neolithic film," while for Bazin it was the rediscovery of a form of epic narration analogous to that practiced by the troubadours.[80]

68. *Désiré*

(*Désiré*)
France, 1937, 93 min, b&w

Dir and Scr Sacha Guitry, from his own play; *Asst dir* Gilles Grangier, Guy Lacourt, and Albert Sandberg; *Prod* Serge Sandberg (Cinéas); *Cinematog* Jean Bachelet; *Music* Adolphe Borchard; *Art dir* Jean Perrier; *Sound* Norbert Gernolle; *Edit* Myriam; *Act* Sacha Guitry (Désiré), Jacqueline Delubac (Odette), Arletty (Madeleine, the housemaid), Pauline Carton (Adèle, the cook), Alys Delonde (Madame Corniche), Geneviève Vix (the countess), Jacques Baumer (Montignac), and Saturnin Fabre (Corniche).

Also *Bonne Chance* (1935); *Mon père avait raison, Faisons un rêve,* and *Le Nouveau Testament* (all 1936); *Quadrille* (1937); and *L'Accroche-cœur* (1938).

A principal reason for watching Guitry's filmed version of *Désiré* is to appreciate an unmistakable source for that greatest of all 1930s films, *La Règle du jeu* (#95). Guitry plays a valet de chambre engaged by an actress who is the mis-

---

79. See, for instance, Jeancolas, *15 ans d'années trente*, 267.
80. See ibid., 265–267, and Leprohon, *Présences contemporaines*, 222–223.

tress of a government minister. The patterns of action above and below stairs are nicely paralleled and markedly similar to those of Jean Renoir's film; the bedtime rituals evoke those of La Colinière, and the cook's husband, a policeman, plays a role analogous to that of Schumacher. In particular, the central episode, where the characters leave for a stay in the country, recalls the parallel episode in *La Règle du jeu*.

But it was natural that *Désiré*, like most of Guitry's "comédies mondaines" (worldly, or boulevard, comedies), should deploy the well-known conventions of the genre, which included such above- and below-stairs interactions in elegant establishments. The audience expected fast-paced, elaborately choreographed action involving adultery, misunderstandings, disguises, and confusions of identity. Arguably this genre, in which Guitry specialized, proposed a cynical view of human nature in general and a no less cynical view of bourgeois family life in particular. Of the thirteen films scripted by Guitry between 1935 and 1939, some seven bear the marks of this genre. Four are transcriptions of his plays (*Mon père avait raison* and *Le Nouveau Testament* in 1936, *Désiré* and *Quadrille* in 1937), while three were written specifically for the cinema (*Bonne Chance* in 1935, *Faisons un rêve* in 1936, *L'Accroche-cœur* in 1938). All are worth viewing because they encapsulate many of the tropes of the decade: *Bonne Chance* is constructed around a romance between an artist and a blanchisseuse[81] (who turns out to be an orphan and wins a lottery), while *L'Accroche-cœur* is constructed around a romance between a society woman and a thief who masquerades as a respectable gentleman to steal her money and jewels, but falls in love with her, and incidentally gambles away all her money at Monte Carlo. Guitry's plays and films are a compendium of the decade's favorite tropes.

But the two 1930s conventions that are most intensely present in Guitry's comedies are misogyny and Oedipal sexuality. The misogyny is omnipresent: women are pretty little things but inherently weak and treacherous, and any female who poses a threat to male superiority is put in the wrong, or in a state of ignorance. Her subsequent humiliation may not be so severe as in *Le Blanc et le noir* (1930), where the female lead has the black male baby to which she has just given birth (which was conceived in the dark without her being aware of its parentage) exchanged for a white female baby without her knowing, but there will always be some patronizing decisions made for her by men who understand all too well her feeble nature, and can see better than she can what is best for her. In *Le Nouveau Testament*, a doctor becomes aware in the initial sequence that his

---

81. A washerwoman, but I retain the French, which has more flattering connotations.

wife is having an affair with the son of a friend—a knowledge that he ruthlessly exploits thereafter to humiliate her (though he himself has fathered an illegitimate daughter). In *Mon père avait raison*, the belief in male superiority is articulated more explicitly than ever: successive generations of sons are brought up by their fathers indoctrinated to despise women, to see love and the family as delusions, and to exploit women merely for sensual pleasure. Solitude, and the occasional male companion, is the secret of happiness. Admittedly the play's ending sees the current son dismiss this moral in the name of "having confidence in life," while nevertheless acknowledging its objective truth.

This patronizing view of womankind is exacerbated by the age difference between lead actors: Guitry always cast himself and his third wife, Jacqueline Delubac, in these plays, and she was twenty-five when they married. This age difference provided Guitry with material for mildly perverse titillation, which several of these films exploit to the full. In *Le Nouveau Testament*, his character engages a young secretary and proceeds to play on his wife's doubts as to whether she is his daughter or his mistress, or indeed both. In *Bonne Chance*, the money from the lottery win allows a trip to the Riviera, as "brother and sister." The pleasure of the young woman's company leads the protagonist to propose adopting her as his daughter. Very soon, however, their relationship becomes a sexual one, and the marriage that she had arranged with a younger man is appropriated for their own use. Their relationship, then, has passed from brother and sister to father and daughter to man and mistress and finally man and wife. In *Désiré*, however, the sexual frisson depends not on a father-daughter relationship but a "son"-mother relationship. Guitry as the butler is discovered to have regularly developed an overwhelming erotic desire for the lady of each household in which he has served, and they for him. This displaced mother fixation is played out yet again in the present instance, in which both he and the mistress of the house experience erotic dreams about one another. Horrified, she rushes out to buy Freud's *The Interpretation of Dreams*, only to find when she comes to read it that the butler has got in before her and cut out the relevant section. She has been reading it in bed; laying it aside to sleep, she "doesn't notice" that it rests on the bell that summons the butler.

All these films were more successful than the average for the day, and must have made a fortune for Serge Sandberg, who produced nearly all of them. He had worked for Pathé in Russia before emigrating like so many other film personnel to France, where he was instrumental in having the La Victorine studios constructed in Nice.[82] All of the above films depend heavily on theatrical dia-

82. See Crisp, *Classic French Cinema*, 168.

logue, since Guitry was and remained a theatrical man who loved to hear the sound of his own voice. When talkies were introduced, they were often promoted as "100% parlants" (100% talking); as Georges Neveux notes wryly, Guitry's films are better described as "100% bavards" (100% talkative).[83]

69. *Abus de confiance*

(Abuse of Trust)
France, 1937, 91 min, b&w

Dir Henri Decoin; *Prod* UDIF; *Scr* Pierre Wolff; *Cinematog* Henri Burel; *Music* Georges van Parys; *Art dir* Roger Hubert; *Edit* Marguerite Beaugé; *Act* Danielle Darrieux (Lydia), Charles Vanel (Monsieur Ferney), Valentine Tessier (Madame Ferney), Yvette Lebon (Alice), Jean Worms (the president), Pierre Mingand (Pierre), Gilbert Gil (a student), and Jean Marais.

This film and *Battement de cœur* (1939, #99) were central to establishing Henri Decoin's credentials as a commercial director. Obsessed by sports from a young age, he was a boxer and champion swimmer, then an aviator during World War I, emerging with the Légion d'Honneur and the Croix de Guerre (nine citations). Subsequently a journalist, novelist, and playwright, his first screenplay (*Un soir de rafle*, 1931), set in boxing circles, was an immense success. Eight others followed in the course of the 1930s, two of which, on aviation and boxing, he himself directed. A period in Germany adapting and subdirecting French versions brought him into contact with Danielle Darrieux, whom he married in 1935 (his third marriage, the second also having been to an actress, Blanche Montel). The relationship lasted until 1941 and resulted in five films with Darrieux in the lead role. The first of these, *Mademoiselle ma mère*, from a Verneuil boulevard comedy, is typical of the genre—lighthearted, Oedipal, and risqué. It involves a girl whose parents are tired of her rejecting numerous fiancés, so she finally marries, a little at random, a much older widower, but locks him out of her bedroom. His son falls for her and finally wins her, thus marrying his ex-stepmother, who is still, however, a virgin.

The material out of which *Abus de confiance* is fabricated also lends itself to this sort of risqué interpretation: Danielle Darrieux plays Lydia, a poverty-stricken and recently orphaned girl who convinces Monsieur Ferney, a much older man, that she is his daughter by an earlier mistress. She is accepted into his household

---

83. Quoted in Courtade, *Les Malédictions du cinéma français*, 82.

and brings a touch of spring to everyone; Ferney's secretary falls for her, but Ferney's wife is suspicious and finally uncovers the truth. Nevertheless, she decides to conceal the falsity of Lydia's story out of consideration for the happier family environment now developing. The bleak initial sequences in which Lydia is exposed to one form of masculine predation after another—a typically melodramatic fate for a newly vulnerable and attractive girl—serve to represent men (and particularly mercenary predatory petty bourgeois males, as Noël Burch and Geneviève Sellier note) as callous and unlovely. Under the influence of a street-singer's sentimental ballad, she almost succumbs to their persuasions.

Lydia has been studying law before being thrown to the wolves. With the Ferney's help, she resumes her studies, and the final sequence has her defending a girl who has abused the trust of a family just as she herself had been doing. Lydia defends her in terms that apply directly to herself before she encountered the Fernys, who are there in court, attributing the crime to poverty and social pressures rather than to a flawed personality. The judge, already established as crusty but kind, is moved to pardon the girl. This focus on young women whose morally dubious deeds are diversely interpreted—by hardliners as crimes that must be punished in an exemplary fashion, and by liberals as failures of an unjust society that on the contrary require understanding and help ("It's the parents who should be punished")—was to form the basis of two other important prewar films and numerous wartime acknowledgments of the older generation's culpability. Overall, this focus on poverty, male predation, and criminality lends the film a weight that makes of it a *comédie dramatique*—that genre much beloved of French commentators—rather than a *comédie sentimentale* like other Decoin-Darrieux productions.

As the above summary suggests, the film represents men in negative terms and focuses primarily on the female protagonist, which could be read as pointing to an awareness of increasing female emancipation. Even with the rise of young female protagonists embodied by Darrieux, Michèle Morgan, and Edwige Feuillère, it was rare to find a narrative built as here primarily around their problems. Despite this progressive element, however, Burch and Sellier see the film as embodying a fundamentally conservative ideology.[84] Indeed, they classify it with the many other 1930s films that insist on the need for a firm hand from the patriarchy in dealing with uppity young women. They see Ferney as a typical older man laying claim to a young woman and in Oedipal rivalry with his secretary/son for that woman. The relationship between Monsieur Ferney and Lydia

84. For their comments on this film, see Burch and Sellier, *La Drôle de guerre des sexes*, 28–30.

is characterized by them as implicitly incestuous, with the secretary as a substitute for Ferney, his final marriage to Lydia serving merely to displace the incest taboo. Moreover, Ferney is a historian studying the ancien régime, and this is seen as further evidence for a nostalgic longing for the old order underpinned by a benevolent monarchy. While I usually find Burch and Sellier convincing, this is surely going too far. First, Monsieur Ferney's historical field of study can better be seen as simply a way of setting up an effective contrast between the old and new, and there is next to no indication in the film of any sexual interest in Lydia on his part. Second, there is little evidence of any "marriage" in the final sequences. Finally, the ending of the film is scarcely conservative, "seeking to maintain patriarchal control," since the feminist element is there triumphant, the film leaving Madame Ferney and Lydia in a complicitous tête-à-tête preparing to "manage" their men.

Very few of the films of this decade, once the cost of production had squashed the residual avant-garde tendencies of the 1920s, can claim to be of interest for their technical practices. Yet this one foreshadows Jean-Luc Godard in some surprising moments. At a conventional level, there are several brisk montage segments, with agitated musical accompaniment, that punctuate the text. One in particular, figuring Lydia's subjectivity as she stumbles blindly through a nocturnal fairground with superimposed images of the day's crises evoking her distress, increases in speed progressively to culminate in her collapse. At another moment, during her torment by predatory males, the image is "torn" or "burned" open several times in succession—an aggressive foregrounding of punctuation found previously in this decade, to my knowledge, only in *Le Crime de Monsieur Lange* (#46). Most surprising, however, is the series of images of film posters and of cinemas that she passes as she stumbles through the fairground, including one poster that proclaims, "Abus de confiance."

Earlier, as Lydia was being rejected from job after job, another such poster had announced the 1937 Paris Exposition then being held. *Abus de confiance* in fact was recognized as the best fiction film in the competition organized for that exposition, and went on to be, by my calculation, the third most popular film of the 1937–1938 season.

70. *Naples au baiser de feu*

(*Naples Touched by Fire*)
France, 1937, 89 min, b&w

Dir Augusto Genina; *Prod* Paris-Films; *Scr* Henri Jeanson, Marcel Achard, and Ernesto Grassi, from the novel by Auguste Bailly; *Cinematog* Robert le Febvre;

Music Vincent Scotto; *Art dir* Guy de Gastyne; *Sound* William Sivel; *Act* Tino Rossi (Mario), Mireille Balin (Assunta), Viviane Romance (Lolita), Michel Simon (Michel), and Marcel Dalio (Francesco).

This film was designed around Tino Rossi, one of the most successful music-hall stars to make the transition to cinema. From 1936 through to the 1950s, he was immensely popular with the public, and with some justification, since his voice was purer, truer, and more controlled than those of his cinematic colleagues. He was the French equivalent of a crooner but in a higher register. Unfortunately, his ability to act was negligible, as he readily admitted. In 1934 and 1935, he had played walk-on roles as a nightclub singer and a troubadour in six films but hit the big time in 1936 with *Marinella*, where, appropriately enough, he played a singing painter-decorator who is "discovered" when the star falls ill during rehearsal (yes, again) for the gala opening of a nightclub. This cinematic success was to lead to three further starring roles during the 1930s: *Au son des guitares* (1936), *Naples au baiser de feu* (1937), and *Lumières de Paris* (1938), followed by a number of wartime successes, including a quite impressive drama, *Fièvres*. Being Corsican by birth, he had a pronounced southern accent which largely determined the musical roles that scriptwriters produced for him over the next twenty years. After Tino the Corsican painter-decorator, there was Jeannot the Corsican fisherman, Tonio the Meridional fisherman, Carlo Ferrari the fashionable singer, Ramon the Basque singer, Bicchi yet another singing Corsican fisherman, Sylvio the fashionable singer traveling incognito, and Julien the singing Portuguese fisherman, then, somewhat incongruously, in 1948, Franz Schubert.

In *Naples au baiser de feu*, he is Mario the caf'conc singing waiter. The songs he is given to sing in these films were composed, often specifically for him and the film, by the best popular songwriters of the day, notably Vincent Scotto and Maurice Yvain. Scotto, composer for this film, was the sole French film-composer of the decade not to have had a thoroughly classical training in music composition. Well-known to the others and liked by them, he could nevertheless not even write musical notation, so depended on friends and neighbors to transcribe the operettas and the thousands of songs he produced. Like all of Tino's films, this one, then, is worth viewing for the songs alone, and not least Michel Simon's parodic rendering of a Neapolitan serenade.

Many of the plots of Rossi's films focus on the discovery of a singer/star, the trials and tribulations of stardom, masked and incognito singers, and the mounting of a performance. Unlike female singers of the day, who were frequently *chanteuses réalistes,* and who fitted naturally into the squalor of urban poverty, Rossi and other male singers such as Charles Trénet avoided association with the city and the seedier nightclubs, generating rather a set of scenarios that emphasized their association with the open air and with the Mediterranean sun and sea. The essential simplicity of the country lad is normally attributed to Rossi (despite his incongruously suave appearance and voice), and in his 1930s films, he is most at home at a guinguette on the banks of the Marne, or nostalgic for his Corsican lifestyle, or trying to realize a dream of peace and happiness by the sea, or fleeing his sycophantic urban fans to discover true love with a simple country girl.

Typically these narratives involve a crisis in which Rossi is seduced, or almost seduced, by a brazen female who embodies the selfishness and treachery of the urban world he is fleeing. This seductress role, commonly known in French as a *garce* (tart or vamp), was of course not original to the 1930s or to the cinema, but was reasserted most insistently in the late 1930s by two actresses, Ginette Leclerc and Viviane Romance. Both were presented as dark, fleshy, and aggressively sexual, flaunting their often near-naked bodies. But whereas Leclerc was trapped in this role indefinitely, Romance strategically moved across to play purer roles during the prudish Vichy period. The vamp figure that they embodied during the 1930s was typically represented as a force of nature, a creature of instinct who threatens all social bonds. She evokes a male fear of the assertive, aggressive female, and her bid for dominance must be thwarted at all cost. Here, as in *La Belle Équipe* (#51), which established Romance as a lead actress and a *garce*, one of her main functions is to disrupt a potentially idyllic situation dominated by an alliance of males. She plays Lolita, a stowaway who compulsively fictionalizes her past life to suit her audience, and whose sultry eyes, extreme déshabillé, and overt sexuality seduce Mario from his fiancée such that he abandons poor Assunta at the altar. Lolita's sexuality overwhelms both love and friendship. But having won Mario, she cannot resist seducing other men—all other men—not because she likes them but to demonstrate her power over them. As Noël Burch and Geneviève Sellier note, in films of this decade she must be taught a lesson, and here she is finally thrown at a distraught Dalio in a humiliating comic scene.[85] These vamp roles, recurring in *L'Étrange Monsieur Victor* (#77), *Le Puritain* (1937), *Le Joueur,* and *La Maison du Maltais* (1938, #81), made Viviane Romance the highest paid of all French actresses in the late 1930s.

Interestingly, the role of Assunta, the simple waitress whom Mario abandons in order to run off with Lolita, is played by Mireille Balin, who both in *Pépé le Moko* (#56) and in *Gueule d'amour* (#64) had herself played the more sophisti-

85. Ibid., 52–53.

cated vamp (the rich *garce* as opposed to the poor *garce*). During shooting, gossip columns were full of the real-life amours of Tino Rossi and Mireille Balin, and Rossi acknowledged having spent two happy years with her. Because of their wartime activities and sympathies, most of the cast of *Naples* fell afoul of resistance strictures when France was liberated. Like Leclerc, and more specifically Arletty, Mireille Balin was to spend time in a *camp d'épuration* for indulging in horizontal collaboration with an enemy officer, while Rossi, suspected of the more conventional vertical sort, also spent a brief period in such a prison. This, however, in no way hindered his popularity, especially with female fans, and he was one of the very few French actors to have his own fan-club in the 1950s.

71. *L'Alibi*

Alibi for Murder
France, 1937, 84 min, b&w

Dir Pierre Chenal; *Asst dir* Pierre Blondy; *Scr* Chenal, Marcel Achard, and Jacques Companeez, from an idea by Achard; *Prod* Buchovzer and Nash, and Tellus Film; *Cinematog* Ted Pahle; *Music* Georges Auric and Jacques Dallin; *Art dir* Eugène Lourié and Serge Pimenoff; *Sound* Igor Kalinovski; *Edit* Heidenheim; *Act* Erich von Stroheim (Professor Winkler), Jany Holt (Hélène), Louis Jouvet (Inspector Calas), Albert Préjean (André Laurent), Margot Lion, Florence Marley, Foun-Sen, Odette Talazac, Roger Blin, Philippe Richard, Jean Temerson, and Maurice Baquet.

L'Alibi is not a great film; it is a quality genre production, but without any great depth, a policier blessed by impeccable casting and an extravagant performance by Erich von Stroheim. It focuses on a nightclub where a telepath, Professor Winkler, played by von Stroheim, performs nightly. One night after the show, he pursues and murders a businessman who once stole the woman he loved, then pays one of the nightclub hostesses, Hélène, to provide him with an alibi. Such tension as exists derives from our uncertainty as to when Hélène's deceptive alibi will be revealed as a lie under the relentless moral and emotional probing of Inspector Calas, played by Louis Jouvet. Neither we as spectators nor the police are in any doubt as to Winkler's guilt, and having failed to convince Hélène to recant by direct means, the police inspector calls on one of his men, André Laurent (Albert Préjean), to get to know her and court her. Once she is emotionally committed to André, Calas fakes evidence that implicates him in the murder. Fearing for the man she now loves, she finally confesses to having lied about Winkler's alibi.

One nice point of casting is the use of Préjean as the policeman/suitor. He contacts Hélène in a bar and plays the frivolous, superficial charmer to perfection. So he should, since this is the role in which he had become typecast over the preceding seven years. But here he is "only acting it" while in reality conducting a murder investigation and, incidentally, falling in love with his intended victim. When she discovers his deceit, she is distraught and rushes out into the street, where Professor Winkler's henchman guns her down.

This plot mobilizes numerous tropes that either had already proved successful with 1930s audiences or were beginning to do so, which is no doubt why it was so popular at the box-office. The actor who can act sincerity all too credibly—the fake suitor who begins to genuinely fall in love with his victim, the revelation of his insincerity just as he is beginning to become sincere, and the necessity to overcome doubts caused by his deceit—were a regular phenomenon of films in the mid- to late 1930s.[86] No less mythic is the day in the country that André and Hélène spend with the thugs Jojo and Dany (in the car Jojo has stolen—he genially offers the undercover policeman a piece of the car-theft action): the riverside picnic, the unsourced accordion, the pleasure-craft that they row on the river all evoke the recurrent trope captured so well the year before in *Une partie de campagne* (#55). By contrast, the elegant nightclub where much of the action takes place had long come to characterize Paris in the provincial imagination. As the focus of all insidious moral corruption, it was at once fascinating and frightening. Like the casino, it was normally represented as a site of violence and chaos, the performers inherently suspect, first because of their showmanship and second because they are never quite what they seem.[87] Among the performers here, the tastefully naked balloon-dancer and the black jazz band recur insistently as signifiers of trendy but suspect morality. Between 1937 and 1939, every cinematic nightclub had its resident black saxophonist, pianist, singer, or band, their negritude speaking of spontaneity and improvisation, of letting oneself go, and perhaps according with the darkness of the night that characterized the city as an extended underworld, an antiworld by contrast with the sunny purity of nature.

A nightclub, then, is an ideal setting for the weird telepath played by von Stroheim. Between his arrival in France in late 1936 (when his first films were *La Grande Illusion*, #60, and *Mademoiselle Docteur*, #59) and his departure for America in 1940 (when his last films, *Macao*, #101, and *Paris–New York*, had to be reshot with other actors before the Germans would permit their release), von

86. Crisp, *Genre, Myth and Convention*, 198–199.
87. Ibid., 64, 67, 85, 175, 347.

Stroheim acted in nineteen films. In all of these he is the charismatic center of attention. No one other than Louis Jouvet had such an inherently magnetic screen persona, and *L'Alibi* would be fascinating if only for their dual presence as antagonists, not least because of their contrasting physiques. Because of his physique and his accent—soft, sibilant, and curiously foreign in every language he speaks—von Stroheim tended to play eccentric and exotic characters. He reputedly cultivated this persona on set also, and preferred (as in this film) to organize his own costume and setting to underline the effect. Sometimes elaborately caped, sometimes curiously monastic in his appearance, he is here attended by his Chinese maid and his implicitly homosexual servant, and surrounded by cabalistic signs and astrological paraphernalia. There is a nice irony when he hears that young Gérard can disprove his alibi. In his sacramental garb, he raises worshipful eyes to heaven and says, "I don't believe he will talk," then makes sure he does not. As for Jouvet, Pierre Chenal, speaking with affection of the actors he had directed, characterizes him nicely: "He never entered into the skin of his characters: he condescended to let them partially enter into his, then pounced on them and devoured them [*les phagocytait*]."[88]

The film would undoubtedly have been better without the perfunctory happy ending in which we discover that Hélène, who has been gunned down, is not dead but recuperating on the beach with a devoted André. The tone of this final sequence is totally inconsistent with the tenor of the film, which was clearly leading up to Hélène's death in parallel with Winkler's suicide. Chenal reports that the happy end was imposed by the producers as a precondition of the film's release.[89] No doubt in purely financial terms they were correct: one of the top five films of the 1937–1938 season, *L'Alibi* was screened in 1938 in London and in 1939 in New York—one element in the increasingly successful export drive organized by the French film industry in these final prewar years. It fell two votes short of winning the Prix Louis Delluc in February 1938, losing out to Jeff Musso's *Le Puritain*. Incidentally, Florence Marley (real name Hana Smekalova), who plays Gordon's girlfriend, had just become the director Pierre Chenal's wife, and Jany Holt (real name Vladesco Olt), Romanian by birth, had just (briefly) married Marcel Dalio, who convinced Chenal to cast her here. In parallel with her very successful wartime career, she was to be active in the Resistance, which earned her the Croix de la Libération at war's end.[90]

88. Chenal, *Souvenirs du cinéaste*, 71.

89. Ibid., 101–107.

90. For an entertaining account of Dalio's life and films, see Dalio, *Mes années folles*.

72. Mollenard

Hatred
France, 1938, 91 min, b&w

Dir Robert Siodmak; *Asst dir* Rodolphe Marcilly and Pierre Prévert; *Prod* Corni-glion-Molinier; *Scr* Charles Spaak and Oscar-Paul Gilbert, from the book by Gilbert; *Cinematog* Eugen Schüfftan; *Music* Darius Milhaud and Jacques Dallin; *Sets* Alexandre Trauner; *Edit* Léonide Azar; *Act* Harry Baur (Mollenard), Albert Préjean (ship's mate), Jacques Baumer (director of shipping company), Pierre Renoir (Bonnerot), Gabrielle Dorziat (Madame Mollenard), Elisabeth Pitoëff (Marie Mollenard), Robert Lynen (Gianni Mollenard), Maurice Bacquet, Marcel Dalio, Gina Manès, and Foun-Sen.

Francis Courtade includes *Mollenard* in his canon of five Popular Front films —*Le Crime de Monsieur Lange* (#46), *La Vie est à nous* (#49), *La Belle Équipe* (#51), *Les Bas-Fonds,* and *Mollenard*—"which are powerfully expressive of the social effervescence of the time and of the aspirations of millions of working men."[91] Few would question the other four, some would wish to add to the list, but most would be greatly bemused by the inclusion of *Mollenard.* Geneviève Guillaume-Grimaud, in a useful book devoted specifically to the cinema of the Popular Front, does not once mention *Mollenard.* Certainly there is in the film no direct reference to political events, class conflict, cooperatives, or the plight of the workers. Courtade defends its inclusion on the grounds that Captain Mollenard, a man of the people married as chance would have it to a representative of the propertied class, is "a sort of rock standing out against the interests of the great trading merchants, the hypocritical façade of official ceremonies, that 'respectable bourgeois society' whose collusion with the Church had never since *Lange* been so openly decried."[92]

Indeed, this is the systematic set of oppositions constructed by the early scenes of the film: Mollenard is a bluff cargo captain beloved by his crew, boisterous, rambunctious, disrespectful, rough-talking, hard-drinking, operating always on the margins of the law. The ship's owners, on the other hand, are respectable and officially disapprove of all this but are happy to profit from his activities and quick to disown him. His wife's family has roots in the same "respectable" society as the ship's owners. The atmosphere at home is hostile, and his periods back in port are a trial both for him and for his harridan wife. A key

91. Courtade, *Les Malédictions du cinéma français,* 139.
92. Ibid., 134.

scene for any argument about the film's Popular Front credentials occurs when he returns from a successful gun-running trip to the Orient to a hero's welcome —disembarking, he ignores the provincial dignitaries and their official reception, just as he (and everyone else) ignores his wife's official homecoming reception, preferring to join his mates in the local bistro, where, as J.-P. Jeancolas notes, strong analogies appear with the popular demonstrations supporting the Front. As he says, in effect agreeing with Courtade, while this is basically a standard exotic adventure story, it is "touched by the grace of 1937 politics in its vicious attack on the provincial bourgeoisie."[93] It sets up an opposition between, on the one hand, the mediocre and the hateful, embodied in the shipping company executives and Mathilde Mollenard, and, on the other, the adventurers—Mollenard himself, his crew, and their Asian contacts. The opposition is most forcefully expressed when he asserts, "I may be a monster, but it's your fault, you and your world . . . we belong to a different race; you made us like this." Worn down, humiliated, and reduced almost to suicide by the malice of the company and of his wife, he is reinstated in quasi-piratical fashion by his crew, and dies at their head at sea. The critique of social and commercial respectability is incessant, such that gun-running comes to stand for mocking official procedures and the establishment, for a brutal realism that contrasts with the firm's hypocrisy, and thus arguably for a desire not just to circumvent but to subvert the existing social order. This justifies Jeancolas's claim that the ending in which (like so many other working-class protagonists of these years) he dies is not a defeat but rather an affirmation of independence and of liberty.

This grandiose positioning of the film is radically at odds with Noël Burch and Geneviève Sellier's view of it. Typically, they shift the focus onto gender issues, seeing Mathilde Mollenard as just another misogynistic masculine misrepresentation of "Woman as Virago" drawn from the banal repertoire of 1930s French cinema's stock images, while Mollenard himself becomes yet another stock figure—the pathetic male victim fleeing his wife into "virile" adventures in the Orient, until old age and death deliver him once again to his tormentor. For them, then, this film constitutes sick masculine wish-fulfillment rather than an inspiring call to liberty and independence.[94]

The production history of *Mollenard* is interesting for a number of reasons. Siodmak, though American by birth, had begun his filmmaking in Germany, including making French versions of three German films for UFA, but being of Jewish origins, he moved definitively to France in 1933 where he was to make

93. Jeancolas, *15 ans d'années trente*, 221–223.
94. Burch and Sellier, *La Drôle de guerre des sexes*, 36, 56, 122.

eight more films. At the outbreak of war, he moved on again, like many of his colleagues, to the United States, returning to Europe (and particularly Germany) in 1952. Until *Mollenard,* his regular producer in France had been Nero-Films, which Seymour Niebenzahl, a fellow Jew, had transferred to France from Germany in 1933. Here, however, Siodmak was funded by Corniglion-Molinier, who had tried but failed to enter the navy, then had a remarkable career as an air ace in World War I. An airforce general thereafter, he was to be General Charles de Gaulle's personal pilot and a commander of the Free French Airforce during World War II, then a minister in the Fourth Republic. The films he decided to fund during the 1930s were never less than interesting, and usually related to his passion for the sea and air—perhaps *Courrier-Sud* from Antoine de Saint-Exupéry's novel, certainly *Les Jumeaux de Brighton* from a script by Henri Cartier-Bresson, Marcel Carné's *Drôle de drame* (#66), and *Espoir* from André Malraux's Spanish Civil War novel, as well as *Mollenard.* Siodmak was having trouble getting Carné's film distributed but managed to negotiate its release as a prerequisite to the distributor's obtaining the rights to *Courrier-Sud* and *Mollenard.*

73. *La Marseillaise*

(*The Marseillaise*)
France, 1938, 135 min, b&w

Dir Jean Renoir; *Asst dir* Jacques Becker, Claude Renoir, Claude Renoir Jr., Jean-Paul Dreyfus, Demazure, Marc Maurette, and Antoine Corteggiani; *Prod* Soc La Marseillaise, supplemented by public subscription; *Scr* Jean Renoir with Carl Koch, based on an idea by Nina Martel-Dreyfus; *Cinematog* Alain Douarinou, Jean-Serge Bourgoin, Jean-Marie Maillols, Jean-Paul Alphen, and Jean Louis; *Music* Lalande, Grétry, Mozart, Bach, Rouget de l'Isle, Joseph Kosma; *Art dir* Georges Wahkévitch and Léon Barsacq; *Sound* Joseph de Bretagne; *Edit* Marguerite Houllé-Renoir; *Act* Pierre Renoir (Louis XVI), Lise Delamare (Marie-Antoinette), Elisa Ruis (Mademoiselle de Lamballe), Léon Larive (Picard), William Aguet (La Rochefoucauld), Andrex (Arnaud), Louis Jouvet (Roederer), Marie-Pierre Sordet-Dantès (the Dauphin), Irène Joachim (Madame de Saint-Laurent), Nadia Sirbiskaïa (Louison), Aimé Clariond (Monsieur de Saint-Laurent), Edmond Ardisson, Jean-Louis Allibert, Fernand Flamant, Julien Carette, and Gaston Modot.

The idea for this film can be traced back to the summer of 1936, when Renoir was making *Une partie de campagne* (#55). The Popular Front had taken power in June and initiated reforms aimed at improving the lot of the worker. Celebrations culminated on 14 July, when the idea of promoting the new left-wing government by identifying it as the legitimate successor of the French Revolution took root. In the exhilarating communal and democratic spirit of the times, and supported by the government, Jean Renoir and others launched a subscription drive in March 1937 asking citizens to contribute 2 francs toward the production of the film, to be deducted from the entry price. When unlike the subscription for the right-wing *L'Appel du silence* (#50) it fell far short of the necessary funds, its administration was refashioned by the CGT as a normal production company. With *Une partie de campagne, Les Bas-Fonds,* and *La Grande Illusion* completed, Renoir and his associates (multiple writers and technicians, dozens of leading actors, and a cast of about four thousand, assembled by the CGT) worked for four months to complete it (August–December 1937). Accounts of the atmosphere on the shoot are euphoric. Renoir talked of the exhilaration of participating in a task everyone considered useful to society.[95] Heavily promoted as "the film of national unity," "commissioned by the people for the people," it was released on 9 February 1938. Reviews were mixed, but even many of Renoir's friends and left-wing sympathizers were critical, some bitterly so. For Roger Leenhardt it was "a boring spectacle, not without moments of beauty . . . [but] a mediocre film." Henri Jeanson's vicious review spoke of the true and the false Renoir, seeing this as a product of the latter. For Marcel Achard, "the script is disastrous, the dialogue aimless and confused." Renoir complained wryly that everyone seemed desperate to prevent him from reading Jeanson's and Achard's reviews.[96]

There seem to have been two main problems. The first was the lack of epic grandeur when dealing with such a momentous topic. Most of the mythic revolutionary figures and events are missing—Robespierre, Danton, Marat, Charlotte Corday, the taking of the Bastille, the Declaration of Human Rights. This, of course, was deliberate. In line with the title, Renoir chose to avoid the grand historical sweep and focus narrowly on the 1792 march of the Marseillais battalion to Paris and the subsequent ousting of the monarchy. He wanted to show the lived experience and triumph of "the little people," "like you and me," to humanize and personalize history.[97] Time, he felt, had frozen the legendary figures and events into slogans and clichés, and he wanted to shatter traditional assumptions, simplifications, and preconceptions. But audiences found the result lacking in drama and passion: box-office numbers were not disastrous but were

95. In *Ce Soir,* 28 October 1937, reprinted in Renoir's *Écrits* with his other weekly articles for that paper.

96. For these reviews, see *Premier Plan,* nos. 22–23–24, 251–262, and Abel, *French Film Theory and Criticism,* 2:238–246.

97. Renoir, *Écrits,* 321–323.

barely a third of his immediately preceding and succeeding films. In a 1962 interview, Renoir acknowledged one possible explanation: "I try generally to struggle against the intellect in favor of the senses. [However, in] *La Marseillaise* . . . general ideas were the very essence of the subject. It was perhaps the only one of my films in which general ideas were central to the drama."[98] It was also the only one of his films for which he undertook extensive archival research, and this seems to have had a deadening effect. As Leenhardt noted, without Charles Spaak or Pierre Prévert, Renoir has fallen victim to his old enemies—diffuseness, fuzzy thinking, sloppiness.

The other flaw for which critics reproached Renoir reinforced the first: for a film promoting a political line, it was neither forceful nor persuasive. Certainly the situations and dialogue echoed the contemporary political situation and demonstrated (all too grossly, for some) that the Popular Front was the direct heir of the revolution. But the "enemy"—the monarchy, the aristocracy, and the clergy (who stood in, as Renoir stated explicitly, for the fascists of his day)—were represented all too sympathetically. Pierre Renoir as Louis XVI is an amiable and articulate fellow, as is Monsieur de Saint-Laurent, while the people are urged to reach out to the clergy (as the PCF was likewise urging in 1937). They too have their share of humanity, as the people have their share of nobility. Trying to defend this amiable inclusiveness, François Truffaut noted that "Jean Renoir argues for all sides with that objectivity, that generosity . . . for which he is renowned."[99] As Renoir himself was wont to say, "Every-one has their reasons" (everyone, that is, except Marie-Antoinette, who was of course a woman, and not French). This may be an admirable attitude, but it may also be ineffectual in a political crisis, and is certainly hard to reconcile with dramatic narrative. As various commentators have noted, then, this film is not a revolutionary film that might set Frenchman against Frenchman in the streets, but something closer to a blandly patriotic "national effusion."[100] The only section of the film that everyone agreed was enjoyable was the last half-hour—the court scenes in the Tuileries. Interestingly, these were also the scenes that Renoir had most enjoyed writing and filming. One consequence is that, in dramatic terms, the court (famous actors, incidentally, playing mythic historical figures) comes off rather better than the sentimentalized "little people."

98. For these *Cahiers du cinéma* interviews in English translation, see Renoir, *Renoir on Renoir*, 124–144, and *Premier Plan*, nos. 22–23–24, 22.

99. In Bazin, *Jean Renoir*.

100. Marcel Oms in "Renoir revu et rectifié" was particularly bitter. See *Premier Plan*, nos. 22–23–24, 48.

A further attempt by Renoir in 1967 to explain the film's commercial failure ran through numerous possibilities—it was not sufficiently reverential, it mixed genres, it had too many digressive storylines—but the most convincing conclusion was that it was out of synch with its times. When it was released, eighteen months had passed since its conception, and the world had changed decisively: the Popular Front government had opted out of confrontation in Spain, Radicals had become disillusioned with proworker reform and with the occupation of factories, the franc had been devalued and was threatening incomes, industrial production had stagnated, and unemployment was still high. The government called a halt to reforms, which outraged left-wing socialists and the PCF. The Popular Front alliance was falling apart, and the government resigned in June 1937. Its successors were nominally committed to the same aims, but belief in their ability to deliver had collapsed. As J.-P. Jeancolas says, "By the time [this film] was released the Popular Front was dead. . . . La Marseillaise is certainly a Popular Front film, but it's a posthumous film."[101]

74. *Prison sans barreaux* and *Prisons de femmes*

(1) Remade as *Prison without Bars* (1938); (2) (*Women's Prisons*)
France, 1938, (1) 98 min, (2) 94 min, b&w

(1) *Dir* Léonide Moguy; *Asst dir* Alexis Danan; *Prod* CIPRA; *Scr* Moguy, Hans Wilhelm, and Henri Jeanson, from the play by Thomas B. Forster; *Cinematog* Christian Matras; *Music* Will Grosz and Paul Bertrand; *Art dir* Georges Wakhévitch; *Edit* Boris Lewin; *Act* Annie Ducaux (Yvonne), Corinne Luchaire (Nelly), Roger Duchesne (Dr. Guy Maréchal), Ginette Leclerc (Renée), Gisèle Préville (Alice), Marthe Mellot (Madame Renard), and Maximilienne (Madame Appel).
(2) *Dir* Roger Richebé; *Asst dir* Aboulker; *Prod* Soc des Films Roger Richebé; *Scr* Francis Carco and René Jolivet; *Cinematog* Jean Isnard; *Music* Jean Lenoir; *Art dir* Roland Quignon; *Sound* Roger Rampillon; *Edit* Madame Bely; *Act* Francis Carco (Carco the novelist), Renée Saint-Cyr (Juliette), Viviane Romance (Régine), Marguerite Deval (Madame Gaby), Jean Worms (Max Régent), and Georges Flamant (Dédé).

These two 1938 films position themselves as humane liberal interventions into the debate surrounding the French legal system and its treatment of women. Both were very successful at the box office, though not necessarily for politically correct reasons. *Prison sans barreaux* was released first and has the more straight-

101. Jeancolas, *15 ans d'années trente*, 218–221.

forward story-line. The first half consists of a stark contrast between the rigorous punitive authoritarian administration of women's prisons consecrated by tradition and a new, more tolerant system based on trust and understanding, that is introduced here when, as a result of press campaigns, the state intervenes and appoints a younger, enlightened director, Yvonne. This contrast in directors and systems is deliberately played for effect, with the sinister disciplinarians of the old school dressed in black and resembling vultures, in scenes reminiscent of *Metropolis*, as they regiment the sullen, oppressed female inmates in the prison yard. The new director, however, sees the inmates as "guests" rather than criminals, to be cared for rather than punished, not embittered, hardened offenders but open to rehabilitation. In a powerful attack on the existing system, she declares that their "criminality" is largely due to suffering, poverty, and disrupted family life rather than innate evil. Her methods (inevitably) bear fruit, resulting in the (instantaneous and somewhat miraculous) transformation of young Nelly, innocently imprisoned after her stepfather attempted to rape her.

After this impressive first section of "film à thèse," the second half, which is less interesting, consists of melodramatic situations that result from the sexual rivalry between Yvonne and Nelly for the affections of the reformatory doctor. Yvonne, the director, is "forced to choose between being a woman or a saint," and not entirely voluntarily opts for sainthood: she will devote her life to the reformation of the reformatories (!) and the salvation of the young. Seen from this angle, the film could be classified among those numerous films of the late 1930s that agonize over the failures of the parents' generation and the threat that these failures constitute to the innocent young, and as one of the films that uses the prison as a metonym for contemporary France. If in narrative terms the story-line is straightforward, the lighting and acting verge at times on the expressionistic, and some wild punctuation effects are exploited.

The other film, Roger Richebé's *Prisons de femmes,* is far from straightforward. Again it is set in a prison for women and narrates the unjust imprisonment of a particular woman, Juliette, but the focus is primarily on her life after release—she marries a wealthy businessman, reluctantly keeping from him the fact of her earlier incarceration, which leads to blackmail and marital misunderstandings. More importantly, these facts are not presented chronologically but mediated through a diegetic narrator, the (real-life Goncourt) novelist Francis Carco, who researched the material for the film. This reflexive intrusion of an author figure who "manages" the narrative to ensure a just outcome requires a complicated multiple flashback plot in which the audience gradually comes to realize along with Juliette's husband the origins of her suspicious behavior. Carco thus plays "Carco the novelist," a part written for him by Carco the playwright-novelist who, like his diegetic namesake, has been campaigning for a more humane treatment of adolescents who he feels are too often locked away for petty crimes, when in most cases, those crimes are due primarily to the unscrupulous, drunken behavior of the parents. The social nature of criminality that has seen Juliette imprisoned is clarified in the flashbacks: her family treated her as a slave and sold her off to the highest bidder. When desperate to escape her situation she tries to steal from the till, her husband discovers her and in the struggle is stabbed. We are taken through the rigors of the prison system and her efforts after her release to rehabilitate herself. At one point, in a slightly surprising "pluperfect" tense, Carco *recounts* within his existing flashback narrative how he *recognized* Juliette as the businessman's wife because he *had come across her* in prison while researching his novel, which is to be called (of course) *Prisons de femmes*.

This second film is the more interesting technically as well as structurally, since the narrative provides ample opportunity to contrast the elegant lifestyle of the grande bourgeoisie to which her marriage has provided access both with prison life and with the louche night-club life of "the people": smoke-filled bars, music halls, and thugs on the lookout for a fast buck. Geneviève Guillaume-Grimaud provides a useful summary of the actuality behind these films (and others, notably the abrupt outburst at the end of Richebé's next film, *La Tradition de minuit*). She lists a series of journalistic reports in the preceding decade on reformatories (one by Léonide Moguy's assistant here, Alexis Danan) that revealed their role in the "moral contamination" of the young, who during their imprisonment become confirmed in their criminality. She also summarizes the Popular Front government's attempts to reform the system and right-wing condemnation of those attempts (such as Lucien Rebatet's scorn for "the maudlin yids" who had initiated the reforms).[102] Pierre Prévert and Marcel Carné had earlier prepared a scenario based on a young offenders' revolt in 1934 at the Belle-Île reformatory but were prevented by censorship pressures from realizing it, and Charles Spaak mentions the authorities' efforts to prevent *Prison sans barreaux* from being released as well. Richebé's account of the evolution of *Prisons de femmes* from a bundle of Carco's notes to a finished film, however, contains no hint of such censorship problems. Indeed, to facilitate his documentation, the director of prisons at the Justice Ministry appointed him temporary inspector of prisons, and vouched for the validity of the incident related in the film, an actual correlative of which he had himself encountered. Richebé was permitted to film his script in a disused prison at Montpellier.

The first of these films not only represented France in Venice and won an award but was filmed in an English version that came out soon afterward.

102. Guillaume-Grimaud, *Le Cinéma du Front Populaire*, 117–118.

75. *La Tragédie impériale*

(*An Imperial Tragedy*)
France, 1938, 116 min, b&w

Dir Marcel L'Herbier; *Asst dir* Robert-Paul Dagan; *Prod* Max Glass; *Scr* L'Herbier, Max Glass, and Alfred Neumann, from the novel by Neumann; *Cinematog* Michel Kelber and Philippe Agostini; *Music* Darius Milhaud; *Art dir* Guy de Gastyne and Eugène Lourié; *Sound* Pierre Calvet; *Edit* Raymond Leboursier; *Act* Harry Baur (Rasputin), Jean Worms (Tsar Nicholas II), Pierre Richard-Willm (Igor), Marcel Chantal (Tsarina Alexandra), Carine Nelson (Anya, Igor's fiancée), Jany Holt (Groussina, the madwoman), Jacques Baumer (Prokoff), Denis d'Inès (Bishop Gregorian), Martial Rèbe (Iliodore), Jean Claudio (Tsarevitch), Alexandre Rignault (Bloch), and Alexandre Mihalesco.

This is the second film directed by Marcel L'Herbier to figure in this filmography, but if box office success were the sole criterion, there would be many more. His amiable mystery films from the early 1930s were improbably popular, though not so popular as *L'Épervier* (1933), *Le Scandale* (1934), and *Le Bonheur* (1935, #37), while *L'Aventurier* (1934) and *Forfaiture* (1937) did nothing to harm his reputation. Nearly all of his twenty films in the decade exceeded 300,000 spectators in Paris alone, and several scored twice that many. So it is interesting to note that he himself saw this period as an unmitigated disaster. In the 1920s, he had been able to choose his own projects and (if at substantial cost) make them to his own high standards—"films involving experiment, ambition and liberty," which he considered his sole real claim to fame. But in the present decade, he experienced "ten years of constraint and misfortune involving exercises without honour . . . ten years of exile."[103] He further noted, "The cinema as I had known it, then lost it, then momentarily rediscovered it [for *Le Bonheur*] was no longer available to me. A sort of fatality kept it beyond my reach."[104] He attributed this "fatality" at times to the persistence with which he defended "authorship" in the cinema, which was anathema to producers. But a more convincing argument rests with the dramatic increase in production costs caused by the advent of sound, which threw him into the arms of profiteering producers who demanded populist subjects. His friends were dismayed at the way he resigned himself to these compromises, though the producers must have been delighted. Many of the films

103. Leprohon, *Présences contemporaines*, 40.
104. L'Herbier, *La Tête qui tourne*, 263–264.

he made were filmed theater. As Pierre Leprohon noted compassionately, "The cinema, art of movement, has become the prey of the theatrical fraternity. And Marcel L'Herbier has allowed himself to be manoeuvred into midwifing this catastrophe."[105]

L'Herbier made two systematic attempts to escape the trap, though both involved large-scale productions that his friends still dismissed as pompous and grandiose. The first was a series of maritime films often bordering on chauvinist propaganda (*La Route impériale, Veille d'armes, La Porte du large, Les Hommes nouveaux, La Citadelle du silence*), while the second was a series of historical reconstructions centering on mythic events and figures from the past. He labeled these latter productions "filmed chronicles" and aspired to introduce an element of documentary realism into the representation of the myths. He made three such films in the years 1938 and 1939, the other two being *Adrienne Lecouvreur* and *Entente cordiale*. These also were dismissed by Leprohon as the product of a "quasi-official director making films with as much care as ever but deprived of all audacity, of all originality, and manifesting a sadly limited artistry." Despite their popular success (or because of it), L'Herbier felt they were outside his natural field of interest and competence, and quoted approvingly the music critic Vuillermoz, who said, "[L'Herbier] could give us works of great fantasy, charm and finesse. But this virtuoso of the harp and the flute sees himself allocated by imperious orchestral conductors a trumpet solo or a turn on the bass drum."[106]

These derogatory remarks are not entirely fair. *La Tragédie impériale* is an at times delightful and even astounding evocation of the reign of Tsar Nicholas II focusing on the doings of Rasputin, the mad monk (1864–1916). It thus contributed to the ever-increasing number of Russian-themed films that had proliferated since the 1920s, and was the third of L'Herbier's to do so. The subject had been suggested by the producer, and L'Herbier agreed once Harry Baur accepted to play the role of "that monster of vice," Rasputin. The subject did in fact have a personal significance for L'Herbier since he was distantly related to Prince Youssoupoff, Rasputin's assassin, whose memoirs form the basis of the narrative, and L'Herbier had been in occasional communication with him about the incidents. Indeed, he originally considered talking the prince into playing his own role in the drama, but finally settled on Pierre Richard-Willm.

The fascination with Rasputin is largely due to the apparently incompatible values of spirituality and earthy sensuality that he embodies. A sort of peas-

105. Leprohon, *Présences contemporaines*, 39.
106. Ibid., 40–41.

ant saint, he brings these values to the Russian court, where his rusticity appears even more incongruous. One way of looking at his character is as a variant of that well-established type, the French village priest who is one with his flock to the extent that, like them, he smokes, curses, and drinks to excess. To the outrage of the formal church authorities, Rasputin preaches (and practices) enjoyment of the sensual life, engaging in orgiastic festivities and "curing" the women of the parish in a less than spiritual way. Miracles seem to occur spontaneously in his vicinity, and seeing him as an instrument of God to be exploited to the church's advantage, the bishops introduce him to court. This provides a pretext for ever greater sensual excess. Blamed for the people's unrest under the tsar, he is exiled to Siberia, where he is knifed by order of the church but recovers. In time of crisis, he is summoned back to court, where his undue influence and profligacy in time of war outrage the military, and notably Count Igor, who now has jealousy to add to his visceral distrust of Rasputin. There is a truly wonderful account of his assassination, closely based on Prince Youssoupoff's memoir, in which a gun aimed at him misfires twice; his food and wine is copiously poisoned, to no effect; assassins shoot him again and again, in the back, in the head, and believe him dead, only to see his eyes flicker open: he springs to his feet, attacks the prince, then staggers out into the snow, *singing*.[107] He has said he loves life as an animal does, and he clings to it no less tenaciously. This is a spectacularly entertaining representation of a "people's saint," a Russian Christ who "might have saved the monarchy if they'd only listened." Finally drowned beneath the ice of a frozen river, his last prediction is of the end of the Russian monarchy.

76. *Les Disparus de Saint-Agil*

(*The Disappearing Boys*)
France, 1938, 94 min, b&w

Dir Christian-Jaque; *Asst dir* Jean Darcy; *Prod* Dimeco; *Scr* Jean-Henri Blanchon and Jacques Prévert, from the novel by Pierre Véry; *Cinematog* Marcel Lucien; *Music* Henri Verdun; *Art dir* Pierre Schild; *Sound* Jacques Hawadier; *Edit* Claude Nicole; *Act* Erich von Stroheim (Walter), Michel Simon (Lemel), Armand Bernard (Mazeau), Robert Le Vigan (The Invisible Man), Aimé Clariond (director), Marcel Mouloudji (Philippe Macroy), Serge Grave (André Baume), Jean Claudio (Mathieu Sorgue), and René Génin (Donadieu).

107. See Le Boterf, *Harry Baur*, 145–150.

Les Disparus de Saint-Agil is a murder mystery concerning the unmasking of a gang of forgers based on a novel by Pierre Véry. As such, it is shot through with those elements of the bizarre and fantastic for which his books were notorious. The film can also be recognized as one of the youth films that were becoming more numerous in the late 1930s: it is set in a boy's boarding school, and must be one of the few films ever to have been made with an exclusively male cast. Finally, in the tradition of institutional films, it seeks to make that boarding school stand as a metonym for (at least the male elements of) the whole of French society, governed by fools and faced with the threat of impending war.

It was the first film directed by Christian-Jaque to generate critical interest. Trained like Claude Autant-Lara as a set decorator, Christian-Jaque had been directing feature films since 1932, and made no less than twelve in two years for Paramount. This was his twenty-seventh in six years, mostly lighthearted sentimental comedies, yet he was subsequently to be classified as one of the wartime "wave" of directors on the basis of a number of quality films that he shot between 1940 and 1945. Notable among those was *Sortilèges* in which Jacques Prévert was again involved. The exact role Prévert played in the preparation of *Disparus* is contested: some say just the dialogues, others that the adaptation was his alone, though he refused to sign it. While it is not a great film, seeming slow-paced and labored now, it has several points of continuing interest. There are elements of film noir, for instance, and it features a number of key actors, "monstres sacrés" who never fail to entertain, notably Michel Simon, Robert Le Vigan, and Erich von Stroheim.

The story involves a trio of lads, "The Three Musketeers" (Baume, Macroy and Sorgue), who defend themselves as best they can against the ludicrous school authorities by forming a secret society and planning their escape to America. One of their main forms of defense is fiction: Sorgue is writing a novel, the autobiography of their society's figurehead (a science-lab skeleton). They witness a mysterious intruder, "The Invisible Man," who appears and disappears as if by magic, and one by one they themselves disappear. In fact, the oldest has "disappeared" to investigate the disappearance of the others. He discovers that a gang of forgers with a secret engraving room in the school is based in a nearby mill, that the mysterious figure played by Le Vigan is a go-between contacting the school's art-master (Michel Simon), who acts as their engraver, and that the school's headmaster is chief of the gang. Clearly authorities are not favorably represented here. Where they are not criminal and corrupt, the teaching staff are weird to the point of grotesqueness. Their eccentric behavior even when innocent is accentuated by the lighting (much of the film takes place at night or in gloomy rooms fitfully lit by lamps and candles that cast sinister shadows) and by recurrent references to the occult—a former teacher and the current janitor are both believers in paranormal forces, which can indeed seem at first to have taken over the institution.

But the sense of threat hanging over the boarding school in this March 1938 film is also expressly related to the approaching war, which is evoked anxiously at several key moments. "Don't fight amongst yourselves," the brawling teachers are urged, "with the foreigners at the door." "Foreigners, I detest foreigners." "It's always with foreigners that we have wars." This anxiety focuses on Walter, the English teacher of German extraction, played by von Stroheim, who becomes a lightning-rod for the accumulated chauvinist distrust of his colleagues. Costume and lighting conspire early on to confirm him as the chief suspect, but he turns out, of course, to be innocent, the one reliable and sane ally of the lads. In this respect, the film constitutes an appeal for international understanding, an appeal not to penalize all Germans because of the bellicose behavior of the Nazi government—an appeal the more poignant as von Stroheim was of Jewish extraction (the "von" is his own invention) and had himself fled Germany precisely to avoid the effects of the German government's oppressive policies.

The other two "monstres sacrés," Robert Le Vigan and Michel Simon, have more scope to exploit the eccentricities for which they were notorious. Simon overacts wonderfully, the drunken grotesque who is in danger of betraying the gang in his moments of alcoholic abandonment. When the "invisible man" (Le Vigan) comes to warn him not to talk, they engage in the exchange for which the film is best remembered: the go-between belittles the art-master's profession, asserting that art serves no useful purpose. A box of matches is much better, since it can burn down a house or a forest. Art just *is*, it's too static; something more dynamic is needed. This picks up on the opposition between the static and dynamic, talk and action, fiction and reality, which sinews much of the film, with Le Vigan playing the (right-wing) anarchist that he in fact was, and which got him into serious trouble at war's end because of his vocal support for the Nazi occupiers. Simon reported being entertained during filming by hearing him shouting racist insults down the studio corridors: "When the blacks come, you'll see . . . with their big pricks . . . they'll bugger the lot of you." These nice correlations between actor and character, film and contemporary reality, were underlined when Simon had to take three days off shooting to take his parents back to Switzerland because they too were terrified that the Germans were about to invade France.[108]

108. See Loubier, *Michel Simon*, 166–168.

In the film itself, the sinister atmosphere is undercut in typical Pierre Véry fashion: when we finally reach the forgers' den, we find the burly but amiable forgers fussing over young Sorgue whom they have abducted, delighted to find themselves being written into his account of his adventures.

Short-listed for the Prix Louis Delluc, *Les Disparus de Saint-Agil* was awarded the inaugural Prix Jean Vigo, a prize created by the self-designated Academy of Film for "a courageous work," later to be specified as "the best French film on a social subject." Michel Simon was singled out by the same academy for his performance in this film and awarded the inaugural (and perhaps only) Prix Pierre Batcheff for best actor.

77. L'Étrange Monsieur Victor

(*That Strange Mr. Victor*)
France-Germany, 1938, 113 min, b&w

Dir Jean Grémillon; *Prod* ACE; *Scr* Albert Valentin, Charles Spaak, and Marcel Achard; *Cinematog* Werner Krien; *Music* Roland-Manuel; *Art dir* Willy Schiller; *Act* Raimu (Victor Agardanne), Madeleine Renaud (Madeleine Agardanne), Pierre Blanchar (Bastien Robineau), Viviane Romance (Adrienne Robineau), Marcelle Géniat (Victor's mother), Andrex (Robert), Georges Flamant (Amédée), Maupi (Rémi), Édouard Delmont, and Charles Blavette.

The enormous extent of German influence on the French cinema has already been discussed. German sound technology was widely used, German personnel (often fleeing Nazi threats) were omnipresent, and German production companies were responsible for a large proportion of "French" production. Much of this took place at the Tobis studio in Épinay, just outside Paris, but a lot also took place at the Neubabelsburg studios in Berlin. In the early 1930s, the films produced at this latter studio were all French versions of German originals, usually with a French "subdirector."[109] Forty French versions of this sort were shot in 1931 alone. Roy Armes estimates that in 1934, 20 percent of all French films were shot abroad, while another 20 percent were made in France by transients without French roots.[110] Raoul Ploquin was in charge of the quasi-French production in Germany, and earned UFA's respect such that he was later put in charge

109. See, for instance, *Le Chemin du paradis* (1930, #4).
110. Crisp, *Classic French Cinema*, 71–72.

of all French production in France under the German occupation (see #77). The fiercely chauvinist attack on this production system as "un-French" by the aggressive Henri Jeanson is well known, but there were many others, notably an anonymous and heavily ironic "defense" of it, which makes the point even more strongly.[111] Nevertheless it served Jean Grémillon well. He had access to the best French scriptwriters and the best French actors (Jean Gabin, Raimu, Pierre Brasseur, Mireille Balin, René Lefebvre, Pierre Blanchar, and Madeleine Renaud), since these and most others were at various times under contract to UFA. With *Gueule d'amour* and this film, he finally reestablished his reputation for making efficient and financially viable films.

The scenario that Charles Spaak and Albert Valentin produced for Grémillon was recognizably parallel to numerous others from this period in which the mercantile class, here embodied by Monsieur Victor himself, is represented with marked cynicism as two-faced, concealing a corrupt and criminal nature behind a public facade of respectability. Widespread since the Depression, the production of such scenarios only increased as war approached. The theme proved a mainstay of poetic realism but was most explicitly presented by Yves Mirande, ever sensitive to social and cultural trends, in the script he wrote for and codirected with Georges Lacombe, *Derrière la façade* (1939): as the police investigate the murder of an apartment block owner, each tenant proves to be hiding some guilty secret, none more so than those associated with finance, commerce, and government. Respectability, wealth, and power are never more than hypocritical fronts, and in this present film, a sign outside Monsieur Victor's emporium announcing "Maison de confiance" (A Trustworthy Firm/Confidentiality Guaranteed) is dwelt on at key moments with heavy irony. Monsieur Victor is therefore related to several dubious characters figuring in this filmography, most notably Batala from *Le Crime de Monsieur Lange* (#46), Gédéon from *Ces messieurs de la Santé* (#30), the amnesiac from *Carrefour* (#84), and even Ying Tchai from *Macao* (#101), but also protagonists from more lighthearted films such as *Fric-Frac, Circonstances atténuantes* (#96), and *Drôle de drame* (#66). Raimu was to embody another such during the war in *Le Bienfaiteur*.

On the face of it, a kindly and generous member of the Toulon community, Monsieur Victor, is also, we discover, a fence, a gangmaster, and (when one of his gang tries to blackmail him) a murderer. He allows Bastien, an innocent cobbler, to take the rap for his crime. The brief glimpse we get of Bastien's incarceration in the prison colony in Guiana recalls Grémillon's earlier film *La Petite Lise* (#6), though life there is better evoked by Léon Mathot's clumsy yet

---

111. *Les Dessous du cinéma allemande*, 9–10. See Crisp, *Classic French Cinema*, 178–179.

interesting film *Chéri-Bibi*, contemporary with this one, where the innocent man's odyssey from prison to prison ship, then from prison colony to remote work-camp, recalls Joseph Conrad's *Heart of Darkness*. Here, when the cobbler escapes and returns to Toulon, Monsieur Victor hides him and hypocritically pretends to help him. Part self-interest, this aid to the man he has wronged and whose son he has consequently turned into a vicious hooligan contributes to the complex psychological characterization with which Grémillon (and Raimu) endow Monsieur Victor, making the film something more than a mere schematic critique of the establishment. The psychological credibility of the situation provided by Victor's contradictions and indecisions is further enhanced by Madeleine Renaud's portrayal of Victor's wife. While being sheltered by Victor, the cobbler falls for her and she for him. Renaud and Blanchar were true actors, capable of living and bringing to life a wide variety of different characters. In this they were different from Raimu (and Michel Simon, Jules Berry, Jean Gabin, etc.) who had basically one emphatic persona that they imposed on any role they played. The latter group's acting style, acquired most often on the stage, tended to produce characters who were larger than life. This was the characteristic of those actors commonly termed "monstres sacrés." The contrast between Raimu's excessive volubility and wild gestures and the restrained realism of Blanchar and Renaud is nicely captured at one moment in the film: believing that Bastien (Blanchar) had joined the foreign legion because of a tragic love affair, Madeleine says in just the right, slightly melancholic tone: "For women like me, people don't join the foreign legion. Women like me, they marry."

The lived credibility of the diegesis constructed by these convincing actors and by the complexity attributed to Victor is enhanced by the somewhat astonishing fact that, despite being largely shot in a Berlin studio, the film leaves the spectator with a quite precise understanding of and feel for the port of Toulon in the 1930s. Location shots of the harbor, the hills behind the town, the dockside, and the narrow alleyways of the old town are integrated extremely well into the continuity, providing the documentary feel that Grémillon had always valued. One of his prime concerns was to situate his main characters socially within a network of credible relationships, within a working and living environment constructed from a great number of apparently incidental elements in the frame. Claudette Peyrusse in her book on filmmaking in and on Provence quite justifiably rapturizes about the way the exterior shots and glimpses of local sights and sounds evoke the atmosphere of the city and its environs.[112]

---

112. Peyrusse, *Le Cinéma méridional*, 146–147.

78. Quai des brumes

Port of Shadows
France, 1938, 91 min, b&w

Dir Marcel Carné; *Asst dir* Walter; *Prod* Grégor Rabinovitch; *Scr* Jacques Prévert, from the novel by Pierre MacOrlan; *Cinematog* Eugen Schüfftan; *Music* Maurice Jaubert; *Art dir* Alexandre Trauner; *Sound* Antoine Archaimbaud; *Edit* René Le Hénaff; *Act* Michèle Morgan (Nelly), Jean Gabin (Jean), Michel Simon (Zabel), Pierre Brasseur (Lucien), René Génin (ship's doctor), Aimos (Quart-Vittel), Édouard Delmont (Paname), Robert Le Vigan (suicidal painter), Marcel Pérès, and Roger Legris.

Quai des brumes is a key film for understanding the term "poetic realism" so often applied to French films of the late 1930s. It concentrates all the main tropes of narrative, character, and setting in an atmosphere that mythologizes them more effectively than does any other film. Carné was still only twenty-nine when he directed it. Immensely popular at the box office, it won numerous awards (see appendix) but was the subject of intense controversy about its ideological stance, particularly with respect to its screening outside France. It had its origins in a novel set in Montmartre; the rights were bought by Raoul Ploquin, UFA's French producer, but when UFA (and reputedly Joseph Goebbels himself) rejected the script as too decadent, these were sold on to Grégor Rabinovitch, a Russian Jew who himself had produced films for UFA before Hitler's ascension to power. Jacques Prévert, who had wanted a port setting such as Hamburg, now opted for Le Havre.[113]

The narrative can be summarized simply: Jean Gabin plays Jean, a deserter arriving in Le Havre, hoping to jump ship to Venezuela. In Le Havre, he meets Nelly and they experience a night of love, but Jean gets gunned down by a petty thug whom he has humiliated and the ship sails without him. The whole film is enveloped in night and fog, which implies an omnipresent evil soon manifest in suffering, malice, and murder—in fact, it evokes what Jean-Paul Sartre was currently characterizing as the Absurd—the formlessness and meaninglessness of existence. It is also a state of mind: when Jean hitches a ride with a truck driver, he talks gruffly of his time in Tonkin—shooting the enemy like clay pigeons at a fair, the horror, the fog—and when the truck driver protests that there is no fog

---

113. For often conflicting accounts of the film's origins, see, for instance, Carné, *La Vie à belles dents;* Chazal, *Marcel Carné;* Leprohon, *Présences contemporaines;* and Brunelin, *Jean Gabin.*

in Tonkin, Jean points to his head and says, "It's in there." While we never learn the details of his desertion, it is clear that it relates not just to the horrors he has witnessed but to his insubordination, his inability to endure those military hierarchies of power that constitute yet another aspect of the Absurd.

Much of the film takes place in Panama's Bar, a dilapidated shack in the dockside wasteland. There Jean finds refuge and meets the painter who paints "the things that are behind things," and who subsequently commits suicide. Again, no concrete explanation is given for his suicide, but he too has clearly been overwhelmed by the futility of existence—whatever he painted turned sinister, murderous; you always kill someone or something, so better it be yourself. Despite appearances, and partly because of the owner's name, Chez Paname is an oasis of kindness—Jean may never reach Venezuela but at least he has known Panama. As the drunk says, "There's no fog here," and it is here that he meets Nelly, another outcast, another "orphan," on the run from persecution by her guardian Zabel, a "respectable" small businessman through whose crapulous hypocrisy Prévert mocks both respectability and commerce (and, some have argued, Carné sneers at Jews). Chez Paname is where tenuous bonds can be established between the loners of this world—Jean, Nelly, the dog that he has saved from being run over and that he finally acknowledges as effectively "his."

But the forces of bastardry prove too much for these bonds. Pierre Brasseur does a wonderful job of portraying the cowardly braggart who finally guns Jean down on the wet cobbles of the dockside street, while Michel Simon is even more wonderful as the louche guardian who, like so many father-figures of the 1930s, has designs on the lovely body of his "daughter." Jean catches him at it and beats him to death with a brick. But then Zabel has done much worse to the mysterious Maurice, whose absence puzzles the thugs: in a scene forbidden by the censors, Zabel was to kill and behead Maurice because of his tentative relationship with Nelly; the wrapped head was to have been left in the cloakroom when he met the thugs, then forgotten, then retrieved and carried off under his arm.[114] Several such picturesque and brutal scenes were forbidden or toned down, either by the censors or by the nervous producer—notably the painter's suicide— and arguably the indirection that results has its advantages: the film is allusive rather than explicit, as Carné's next two films were.

Of such films Roger Munier said these are the "real films" where the damp paving stones remember the criminal actions, and the waves of the sea speak of violence and passion, where "reality provides its own counterpoint." Louis Da-

114. *Premier Plan*, no. 14, 16; Loubier, *Michel Simon*, 164.

quin agreed, seeing *Quai des brumes* as a "realistic film," "a real and sensitive reflection of the anguish which seized us by the throat confronted with the spectre of war" and social collapse.[115]

It is astonishing that this representation of a deserter from the French Army should ever have been permitted by the censors, at a time when an official letter had just been circulated forbidding the screening of all films that tended to shed a poor light on the army or lessen its prestige.[116] Indeed, all Carné was required by them to do was never to mention the actual word "deserter," and ensure that Jean folds his castoff uniform neatly when he changes into his civilian disguise. This did not stop right-wing critics like Lucien Rebatet from slamming the film for "slack flabby populism," or the Catholic Church from seeing it as profoundly demoralizing and forbidding members from viewing it (which hundreds of thousands of Catholics must have ignored).[117] More surprisingly, Jean Renoir called it "a fascist film"; and though he partially withdrew when confronted by Prévert, Henri Jeanson likened Carné to Vinneuil (Monsieur Vile Neuilly, as he called him[118])—a totalitarian agent of the Communist Party disguised as a filmmaker. In between the two political wings, most commentators agonized over the wisdom of representing France abroad in these terms. For Vuillermoz, the film was "detestable because it demonstrated to the whole world that we are a down-and-out people, consumed by the gangrene of vice . . . , a bunch of pitiful social derelicts pullulating in a climate of truly stupefying immorality." While recognizing the film's virtues, he asserted that "film is a mode of expression that cannot ignore its international responsibilities." Although not going so far, others nevertheless saw it as "unfortunate propaganda for France abroad, and demoralising to national morale."[119] Later it was to be centrally blamed for France's catastrophic defeat in 1940, and banned for the duration of the war.[120]

115. Munier, cited in Martin, *Le Langage cinématographique*, 74; Daquin, *Le Cinéma, notre métier*, 140.

116. 25 October 1937. See Crisp, *Genre, Myth and Convention*, 251.

117. For critics of this film, see Abel, *French Film Theory and Criticism*, 2:149, 248–254; Jeancolas, *15 ans d'années trente*, 270–273; Courtade, *Les Malédictions du cinéma français*, 166–168, 199–200; and Chazal, *Marcel Carné*. For an exhilarating account of its reception by the young, see Raymond Borde in *Cahiers de la cinémathèque*, no. 5.

118. Neuilly is a posh outer suburb of Paris.

119. Abel, *French Film Theory and Criticism*, 2:149ff.

120. In December 1940, along with ten other films, though it was screened semiprivately at times.

79. *La Femme du boulanger*

The Baker's Wife
France, 1938, 127 min, b&w

Dir and Scr Marcel Pagnol, from an anecdote in Jean Giono's *Jean le Bleu; Prod* Films Marcel Pagnol; *Cinematog* Roger Ledru; *Music* Vincent Scotto; *Sound* Marcel Lavoignat; *Edit* Suzanne de Troeye and Marguerite Houllé-Renoir; *Act* Raimu (Aimable Castanier), Ginette Leclerc (Aurélie Castanier), Fernand Charpin (the Marquis), Charles Moulin (Dominique, the shepherd), Robert Vattier (the curate), Robert Bassac (the teacher), Édouard Delmont, Charles Blavette, Maupi, and Maximilienne.

René Jeanne and Charles Ford considered this film "a miracle," and along with *Angèle* (#34), the best of Marcel Pagnol's Provençal films. Georges Sadoul was equally flattering, while D. Lacotte praised Raimu's "naturalness." More recently, Roy Armes has seen this as one of Raimu's most memorable performances, "well served by Pagnol's excellent dialogues."[121] There is a case for righting the balance. The film is not in the same class as *Regain* (#67), *Angèle*, or the postwar *Manon des sources*. After a number of colorful location films, Pagnol reverted to the painfully theatrical productions that he had earlier defended. Its main charm resides in the quaint Provençal accent of its endless conversations. Characters rush up to the camera, engage in stilted exchanges, then rush off. It was elaborated from a two-page anecdote in Jean Giono's novel, and would have benefited enormously from being edited down to an equivalently short film. The anecdote can be easily summarized: when the baker's wife abandons him for a sexy Italian shepherd, he despairs and ceases baking bread, so the villagers round her up and return her to her husband.

Despite its apparently innocuous surface, however, Pagnol's version of this anecdote has accumulated nationalist and misogynist connotations that recall its original social setting, and these have quite rightly aroused the ire of recent critics. Almost as reprehensible, the characterization is schematic and the acting nowhere near as credible as it seemed at the time. Ginette Leclerc as the baker's wife is fortunately not called upon to act, since she is typecast as a sensual slut. Pagnol had initially intended the role for Joan Crawford, who spoke no French, so the dialogue was kept to a minimum. When Raimu suggested that Pagnol ex-

---

121. Jeanne and Ford, *Histoire encyclopédique du cinéma*, 101; Sadoul, *Le Cinéma français*, 85; Lacotte, *Raimu*, 179–192; Armes, *French Cinema*, 96.

tend it, Pagnol replied ambiguously that Leclerc had "perhaps enough talent to know how to be silent, to listen and to look." Raimu's own performance consists largely of facial tics, twitches, and grimaces. The villagers are no better served, standing in for uncomplicated theoretical positions: there is the curate who says appropriately religious things, the teacher who defends appropriately rational positions, and the marquis who indulges in appropriately aristocratic behavior. Further schematic oppositions include "formal religion versus authentic religion (bread)," "the flesh versus the spirit," and "age versus youth." Finally, there is the mass of unindividuated but colorful locals played by Pagnol's regulars—notably Édouard Delmont, Charles Blavette, and Maupi (for whom the role of the baker was originally intended, since he fitted Giono's description).

As several commentators have noted, the relationship between the baker and his wife echoes that of many earlier gendered relationships between old men and younger women. Aurélie is "young enough," as the baker himself says, "to be my daughter," and the situation is exacerbated by the baker's total absence of interest in her sexually. The choices with which Aurélie is presented—between an unattractive old husband who is uninterested in sexual matters or impotent and a handsome young shepherd who is smoldering with sexuality—is therefore no contest, and her enforced return to the bakery at the end can scarcely be seen as a happy end. The Freudian significance of her relighting the baker's fire at this point has been noted by many, but only Claudette Peyrusse to my knowledge has noted the recurrence of the geo-sexual metaphor that underlay Pagnol's earlier film, *Angèle:* the baker is new to the village, coming down from the high country; his wife descends still further to the marshland for her sexual escapade; and the shepherd is finally banished down to the marquis's property in the (sea-level) Camargue, at which point the wife is led back up to the village.[122]

Charles Ford condemned the film as a scenario with great potential, poorly exploited;[123] while in their aggressive feminist attack on this decade's films, Noël Burch and Geneviève Sellier have rightly skewered it for its repulsive representation of woman. They categorize it as an extreme instance of the antifeminist reaction that greeted the advent of liberated and independent women on screen or in society. The baker's wife's adultery is paralleled throughout by the sexual adventures of the female cat, and at the end, in his wife's presence, the baker harangues the cat, who has likewise slunk back home, in vivid and derogatory terms intended for his wife. The implication is that women are no better

122. Peyrusse, *Le Cinéma méridional*, 148, 115–117, 122–125 (quotations).
123. Ford, *On tourne lundi*, 60–61.

than animals, and "that woman, always somewhat whorish, will nevertheless ultimately swap sensuality for security, preferring a wealthy but gormless husband to a handsome Italian who is broke. . . . To the relief of everyone the patriarchal order reigns once again in the bakery and in the village." The curate, mocked throughout, nevertheless turns out to have his uses, ensuring "submission to the law of the father and an end to liberty, to youth and to pleasure . . . —a form of auto-mutilation that the film represents as essential to the preservation of the social order."[124]

Burch and Sellier also note the significance of the shepherd's Italianness, which colors the baker's final rant at the cat with references to disgusting foreigners who serenade "our" women in languages "we" cannot understand. Peyrusse, who also sees the film as "a reactionary (quasi-)Christian tract," makes more of this foreignness, seeing the villagers as typical in overcoming their initial family quarrels, coming together to ostracize the outsider as a threat, and finally banishing him to outer darkness.[125] She lists numbers of such foreigners, categorized as vagrants or perverts, in films of the late 1930s where a comparable ostracism takes place.

It may well have been this fundamentally reactionary, sexist, and chauvinist ideology that was responsible for the film's receiving such praise from contemporary critics and proving such a box-office success. Interestingly, when released in New York, it proved an even greater success, running for two (Lacotte says six) years, and earning Raimu an Emmy.

80. *Tricoche et Cacolet*

(*Tricoche and Cacolet*)
France, 1938, 107 min, b&w

Dir Pierre Colombier; *Asst dir* Fred Ellis; *Prod* Films Modernes and Émile Natan; *Scr* René Pujol, from a play by Henri Meilhac and Ludovic Halévy; *Cinematog* Armand Thirard; *Music* Casimir Oberfeld; *Art dir* Jacques Colombier; *Sound* Émile Lagarde; *Edit* Pouzet; *Act* Fernandel (Tricoche), Frédéric Duvallès (Cacolet), Ginette Leclerc (Fanny Bombance), Elvire Popescu (Madame van der Pouf), Monique Montey (Georgette), Jean Weber (Duke Émile), Saturnin Fabre (Baron van der Pouf), Sylvio de Pedrelli (Oscar Pacha), Jean Gobet, and Alexandre Mihalesco.

---

124. Burch and Sellier, *La Drôle de guerre des sexes*, 4, 43–44.
125. Peyrusse, *Le Cinéma méridionale*, 122ff.

Retrospectively, Fernandel can seem to have dominated the comic farce of the 1930s, and this film captures one of the best and least well-known of those farcical performances. His film career coincided with the arrival of sound cinema. Coming from the comic songs and routines of caf'conc, music hall, and revue, he was recommended in 1930 to Marc Allégret by Sacha Guitry for a minor role in the film version of Guitry's feeble racist comedy *Le Blanc et le noir* (1931). In the following three years, Fernandel had bit parts in some thirteen films. All were comedies, most military vaudevilles. Gradually he gained a wider recognition, but the only memorable role that he took in those years was opposite Françoise Rosay in *Le Rosier de Madame Husson* (1932), where he played a naive lad totally innocent of all knowledge of sex. In the absence of any female virgins in the region, he is crowned with the "rose wreath" of virginity (*rosière*, from which a fake masculine has here been back-formed), which immediately acts as a provocation to all the local girls.

Subsequently a few more significant vaudeville roles saw him recognized as a popular talent in 1934 (six leading roles), and thereafter he was sole or joint star in all his films—another twenty-one, making a total of forty-four by the outbreak of war. Already figuring in the popularity charts in 1933, he came third in the *Cinématographie française* poll of 1936; top in 1937 after no less than six box-office hits, three of them military vaudevilles (*Ignace, Un de la légion,* and *Les Dégourdis de la 11e*); and third after Jean Gabin and Viviane Romance in 1938.[126] These prewar years constituted the grand period for Fernandel, as J.-P. Jeancolas notes, featuring a steady stream of popular comedies, "lively and spiced with songs, in which the stupidity of the scripts was less important than the actors' doing their well-known thing."[127]

His appeal was always to working-class audiences rather than to sophisticates, and to provincial rather than to urban audiences—originating in Marseilles, he was particularly popular in the Midi—so his films tended to be less successful in exclusive release in Paris but to explode on general release in the suburbs and provinces. Most of his films are "innocent entertainment" where he plays the gormless naïf, the provincial idiot; but the narrative usually has him coming out well in the end (typically as a result of some idiocy that ought to sink him), and consequently puncturing pretensions of one sort or another, notably romantic delusions and the self-promotion of braggarts. But quite often this comic deflation of respectable egos can, as in all vaudevilles, verge on satire. Military vaudevilles, of course, were notorious for representing the various

126. For these charts, see Crisp, *Genre, Myth and Convention,* 300–301.
127. Jeancolas, *15 ans d'années trente,* 62.

branches of the army in a dubious light, and his are no exception (though *Un de la légion*, mentioned above, is an atrocious schizophrenic film, beginning as a farce of mistaken identity and evolving into an improbable homage to the foreign legion, which can make a real man out of the least promising material), while *Le Rosier de Madame Husson* takes pleasure in mocking prudish moralism, and several others (for instance, *Le Schpountz, Jim la Houlette*) take the mickey out of literary and cinematic pretentions. In several of his comedies, he represents France in a farcical contest pitting him against earnest representatives of other European nations. One later film, *Ernest le rebelle* (1938), in which Fernandel is shanghaied from a cruise ship to work on a South American plantation where he and his fellow workers are ruthlessly exploited by the managers, can easily be read as an almost accidental satire of international capitalism.[128]

Tricoche et Cacolet itself transcribes to the cinema a successful vaudeville of the time, largely devoid of satire. It begins in the manner of that supremely popular film *Le Roi des resquilleurs* (#5), also directed by Pierre Colombier, with the two protagonists, Fernandel and Frédéric Duvallès, conning their way into a racetrack without paying, disguised as cops then as waiters. From then on, it resembles rather a boulevard comedy in which upper class twits (Oscar Pacha, Duke Émile, and the Baron van der Pouf!) attempt to do down or cuckold one another, or prostitute their own wives in the interests of a profitable business deal. The two protagonists turn out to be private detectives, employed by one or another of the above parties. Disguising themselves so as to infiltrate the boulevard set, they appear (separately or jointly) as not just cops and waiters but an Arab, a buyer of used dentures, a valet and maidservant, a fire-chief, a server of writs, a military officer in a bearskin, and the lawyer and mother of their client's mistress, the luscious Fanny Bombance. In the course of the plot, they extort through trickery and blackmail ever greater amounts of money from their clients and their victims, and appear more and more rapidly in disguise after disguise, until a somewhat arbitrary dénouement sees Tricoche (Fernandel) waltz off with Fanny.

The clash between, on the one hand, Saturnin Fabre and Elvire Popescu, habitués of the boulevard comedy, and, on the other, Fernandel and Duvallès, habitués of the transvestite vaudeville, is a constant delight, but the main reason for singling out this film to represent Fernandel's comic career is that the pace is so frenetic that he does not have time to fall back on those grotesque contortions of his long horse-face that elsewhere so often mar his performances. As André Sal-

128. For a good summary of his persona in these films, see Peyrusse, *Le Cinéma méridional*, 131–132.

lée says, his face "seems to have been taken over by his dentures," and his acting "is based on grimaces, tics and facile effects." As Claudette Peyrusse puts it, "his hippomorphic grin and accent" becomes ritualized into cliché, resulting in "facility, exaggeration and approximation." This makes it surprising that he should have remained so popular for so long.[129] He was still high on the charts after the war, and his role as Don Camillo took him to even greater heights. It was while acting in the fourth Don Camillo film, in 1970 (over 150 films in all), that he became aware of having contracted the cancer that killed him the following year. That he was not simply a comic actor dependent on face-stretching grimaces is apparent from the rare films where his Provençal compatriot, Marcel Pagnol, entrusted serious roles to him, notably *Angèle* (1933, #34), *Regain* (1937, #67), and *La Fille du puisatier* (1940).

81. *La Maison du Maltais*

(*The Man from Malta*)
France, 1938, 99 min, b&w

Dir Pierre Chenal; *Asst dir* Henri Calef; *Prod* Gladiator Films; *Scr* Jacques Companeez and Chenal, from a novel by Jean Vignaud; *Cinematog* Curt Courant; *Music* Jacques Ibert and Mahieddine; *Art dir* Georges Wakhévitch; *Sound* Émile Lagarde; *Edit* Boris Lewin; *Act* Marcel Dalio (Mattéo le Maltais), Pierre Renoir (Chervin), Louis Jouvet (Rossignol), Viviane Romance (Safia), Jany Holt (Greta), Florence Marly (Diana), Gina Manès (Olga), Fréhel (Rosina), Lorna Rode (the dancer), Aimos (Gégène), Sinoël, Gaston Modot, Martial Rèbe (Mattéo's father), Max Dalban, and Pierre Labry.

Like *Sarati le terrible* (#61), this film is based on a novel by the right-wing apologist for colonialism, Jean Vignaud. Unlike earlier Vignaud film versions, however, this one pays scant attention to the ideological orientation of the original novel, making it over into something much more liberal—arguably even an attack on right-wing anti-Semitism. In David Slavin's summary, the original novel focuses on a Maltese sponge-fisherman living in the Tunisian city of Sfax who marries a Bedouin girl and is ruined by this disregard of social convention. His son Mattéo, raised as a Muslim, also meets and marries a Bedouin girl, Saffiyah, but she runs off to Paris with Chervin, an unscrupulous pearl-dealer. Mattéo

---

129. Sallée, *Les Acteurs français*, 124; Peyrusse, *Le Cinéma méridional*, 61.

steals his father's hoard of pearls, follows Chervin to Paris, and uses his wealth to ruin the dealer. Avenged, he takes Saffiyah back to Sfax and sequesters her in his father's house.[130]

Offered the chance to film this book, Pierre Chenal decided it was better to make a film based on a lousy book than not make a film at all. Given the producer's ignorance of the novel, he figured he could twist it to his purposes.[131] Working with Jacques Companeez, he eliminated the Bedouin element and made Safia a European good-time girl in a nightclub. Mattéo, now a dreamer and poet, marries her, but while attempting to earn much-needed money through gun-running to support her and their forthcoming child, he is captured and "disappears." Safia, blamed by Mattéo's father, is thrown out of the house; in desperate straits, she is rescued by Chervin, now no longer an unscrupulous dealer but rather an honorable archaeologist with a respect for North African civilizations. Safia has Mattéo's daughter, but Chervin believes the child to be his. When Mattéo follows her to Paris, she is faced with a difficult choice between the sophisticated elegance of Parisian life, which has hardened her and led her to think of Mattéo as a possible blackmailer (in fact, Chenal created a lovely role as a blackmailing private detective for Louis Jouvet), and the impoverished Tunisian world of criminality and of prostitution but also of true feeling, of poetry, and of dreams. Her decision is preempted by Mattéo, who recognizes that he must withdraw from her life: in a noble gesture, he confronts Chervin, convinces him that the child is indeed Chervin's, and that Safia is devoted to her protector, then commits suicide.

This reworked narrative refuses all Arab stereotypes. Mattéo is no longer a jealous Arab exacting vengeance by means of his wealth but an impoverished dreamer who sacrifices what he values most in the name of love. Moreover, Chenal, himself a Belgian Jew, weighted the dice in casting Marcel Dalio, another Jew more accustomed to playing the sly, the cowardly, and the corrupt, as that noble poet. In the context of the late 1930s, the casting of a known Jew in a noble role could not help being a pointed political gesture. (In this respect the film prefigures Jean Renoir's use of Dalio the following year.) It is now fate, as embodied by the police, that prevents him from returning to Safia, and gratitude rather than vengeance that he feels toward the Frenchman who has offered her refuge. The film suggests that an idyll is possible across racial barriers between a half-cast Maltese/Bedouin and a French prostitute, and that the child born of that idyll is

---

130. See Slavin, *Colonial Cinema and Imperial France,* 25, 173, 191–198.

131. Matalon et al., eds., *Pierre Chenal,* 115–125.

destined to be brought up in a respectable bourgeois family where it will itself become a symbol of racial reconciliation.

Noël Burch and Geneviève Sellier provide a detailed analysis of the twin forms of exploitation outlined by the film—that of man by man and that of female by male.[132] Initially, Safia and her tubercular friend Greta are represented as exploited creatures within the "colonial economy of prostitution." Greta in particular feels exiled from the land of her birth and nostalgic for the countryside and streams of her childhood—an exile that is evoked here in terms familiar from *Pépé le Moko* (#56). Mattéo wins Safia, toughened by her experiences but basically good at heart, by his poetic innocence: his naive love for "his princess" is something she has never experienced before. But his success is his downfall. The hitherto happy-go-lucky dreamer who exchanged his stories against the necessities of life is now obliged to submit himself to "the economy of exploitation," becoming a docker and gun-runner. "To liberate an exploited woman, he has had to renounce his own utopian liberty."[133]

There is then a fundamental opposition of poetry and money running throughout the film, and the two forms of exploitation are both of course dictated by the commercial pole. Burch and Sellier go so far as to see (see *L'Opéra de quat'sous,* #7) the underworld society as a parody of the capitalist world and patriarchal authority—an authority to which Mattéo improbably accedes by knocking out the big boss and taking over. Another improbability arises when Mattéo and Safia "just happen" to meet once again in Paris, a coincidence that Chenal and Companeez spent much time attempting to mitigate, finally hitting on the idea of the daughter hearing Mattéo tell the pearl story. In the end, Mattéo rejects the corrupt material world of commercial exploitation by reassuming the garb he had worn as an Arab poet, and by his suicide metaphorically returns to the land and the house of his childhood.

Burch and Sellier see his death as the price he must pay for his double transgression—that of the colonized "subhuman" transgressing the barriers of race and class, and that of the gentle poet forced if he is to survive in the colonized world to play the role of macho brute. They also rightly insist on the startling succession of genres through which the film moves on its way to this pessimistic ending—the Oriental tale, the realist melodrama, the boulevard drama, and the gangster film—figuring the different worlds that the various protagonists inhabit.

132. Burch and Sellier, *La Drôle de guerre des sexes,* 63–67.
133. Slavin, *Colonial Cinema and Imperial France,* 193–194.

82. Entrée des artistes

(*Stage Door*)
France, 1938, 92 min, b&w

Dir Marc Allégret; *Asst dir* Jean Huet; *Prod* Régina; *Scr* Henri Jeanson and André Cayatte; *Cinematog* Christian Matras; *Music* Georges Auric; *Art dir* Jacques Krauss, based on maquettes by Alexandre Trauner; *Sound* Georges Leblond; *Edit* Yvonne Martin; *Act* Louis Jouvet (Professor Lambertin), Janine Darcey (Isabelle), Claude Dauphin (François), Odette Joyeux (Coecilia), André Brunot (Grenaison), Julien Carette (journalist), Mady Made (Denise), Marcel Dalio (judge), Robert Pizani (Jérôme), and Bernard Blier (Pescani).

In the final prewar season, two films surprised commentators by their box-office success—*Entrée des artistes* and *La Fin du jour* (#93). Both were relatively small-budget films, both dealt with life (and death) among the theatrical fraternity, and both had Louis Jouvet in the lead role. The former dealt with young artists, for whom Jouvet was mentor, the latter with retired actors in a rest home, where Jouvet plays an aging Don Juan. Jouvet had never had any affection for the cinema. For him, acting was synonymous with the theater, which he revered, and he accepted film roles merely to fund his theatrical productions. In 1922, he had founded the Théâtre des Champs-Élysées, which during the 1930s included many actors later famous for their film roles—Valentine Tessier, Michel Simon (briefly!), Pierre Renoir, Jean-Pierre Aumont, Robert Le Vigan, and Madeleine Ozeray. One aspect of Jouvet's managerial role was the selection and preparation of young actors—his was one of several dozen *cours d'art dramatique* (acting courses) that cumulatively in any one year were training some three thousand aspiring Parisian students. The scenario of *Entrée des artistes* is therefore constructed around his real-life role as teacher and mentor, and when Henri Jeanson outlined to him the general lines of his intended script, Jouvet agreed on condition that several of his actual students play their real-life roles alongside him, notably Odette Joyeux, Claude Dauphin, and Bernard Blier. At Jouvet's suggestion, Jeanson sat in on Jouvet's classes to gather appropriate material for his script. Unfortunately, Jeanson felt the need to graft onto this milieu and the basic initiation narrative a rather incongruous melodrama involving a love-triangle (Isabelle-François-Cécilia) beset by the usual clichés of narrative and character (not least an overwrought stable-boy) and the unconvincing suicide of Cécilia.

For most spectators of the time, much of the enjoyment of the film derived from its documentary aspect as it "revealed" what went on behind the scenes of the Conservatorium, where it was in fact partly shot. Not least it provided a transcription of the teaching of Jouvet, one of the foremost theatrical personalities of the day, as he initiated his students into the quasi-sacred ranks of the acting fraternity, though these precepts can easily nowadays seem somewhat pretentious. He tells the students they have chosen a career without comfort, and when they protest a lack of confidence says, "What does that matter as long as you have confidence in the character you play?" Pronouncing on the relationship between art and life, he says, in effect, that life transposed to the theater can provide access to Truth, which no servile copy of reality can ever provide. Subsequent events ensure that for the students, the interrelationship of life and art will be complex, as the roles they are called on to act intersect with and correspond uncomfortably to their current romantic situations. Inevitably, the theme of acting and sincerity comes to the fore: can inveterate actors ever be sincere? François has written to Cécilia orotund phrases that he now uses "sincerely" to woo Isabelle. When the latter discovers this, as such scripts invariably require she should, she comes to believe that this is what he says to all the girls. There aren't all that many ways to say it, he protests. Later during the students' exam performance, there is a scene in which François is to poison Cécilia; to everyone's horror, she proceeds to drop dead (by her own hand, in fact, but calculated to implicate François). Accused of murder, he protests his innocence. ("He acts innocence well.") On being acquitted, as he and Isabelle leave the courtroom, they speculate that their experiences could form the basis of an interesting play . . . or a film, perhaps. This recalls the earlier scene where he and Isabelle have just made love: they discuss how in the cinema this fact would be suggested . . . thus, and thus, and in the process, the camera both recapitulates the cinematic conventions and varies them.

All this reflexivity can seem a charming play on the concept of art, acting, and the theater, at least on first viewing. In his book on Jouvet, Jean-Marc Loubier acknowledges that it could also seem prodigiously tacky were it not for the fact that these are just adolescents.[134] Many viewers will not find this an adequate excuse.

The late 1930s was a moment when the cinema devoted a high degree of attention to adolescents. Several upbeat films like *Altitude 3200* (1938) and *La Vie est magnifique* (1939, aka *La Belle Jeunesse*) exalted youth for its ideals and its healthy outdoor activities. More often, however, the cinema agonized over the inadequacy of parents' and families' treatment of the young, which saw adolescents all too often resorting to crime or violence, if not as here to suicide. In the early 1930s, such themes had been relegated to historical melodramas where they were played affectingly, but later in the decade, the tone became more realistic and

134. Loubier, *Louis Jouvet*, 212–218.

more somber. Numerous films in these years are set in boys' or girls' boarding schools or at universities or even prisons. *Hélène* and *Le Coupable* (1936), *Les Disparus de Saint-Agil* (#76), *L'Enfer des anges* and *Prison sans barreaux* (1938, #74), and Georg-Wilhelm Pabst's *Jeunes Filles en détresse* (1939) are among the better known, but *Éducation de prince* (1938), *Ménilmontant* (1937), and Max Ophüls's *Sans lendemain* (1939, #97) all touch on the theme in different ways. The war years were to see an almost hysterical emphasis on this theme of adolescents wronged by parents and society. Here we note that Jouvet seeks to separate his students from their unappreciative families, dressing down Isabelle's uncle for expecting her to renounce the theater in favor of commerce, as he ought to have reprimanded his own father: "Parents are indeed guilty when they don't respect the [ideals of the] young."

For many the success of the film was due to Jeanson and to Jouvet rather than to the director, Marc Allégret. According to Pierre Leprohon, Allégret was a mere technician, and Jeanson communicated directly with Jouvet "over Allégret's head."[135] Yet one only has to look at Allégret's astonishing sequence of box-office successes during the 1930s to recognize that he too may have had something to do with the film's unexpected success. It was short-listed for the Louis Delluc Prize of 1938, which ultimately went to *Quai des brumes*.

83. *Monsieur Coccinelle*

(*Mister Ladybird*)
France, 1938, 100 min (now 86 min), b&w

Dir and Scr Bernard-Deschamps; *Asst dir* Pierre de Hérain; *Prod* Films Coccinelle; *Cinematog* Victor Armenise; *Music* Daniel Rogers; *Art dir* Boris Bilinsky; *Sound* Paul Boistelle; *Edit* Raymonde Delors; *Act* Pierre Larquey (Alfred Coccinelle), Jane Lory (Mélanie Coccinelle), Jeanne Prévost (Aunt Aurore), Yette Lucas (Hortense Dupont), René Bergeron (Dutac), Robert Pizani (The Great Illusio), and Marcel Pérès (Brutus Dupont).

This is another little-known but hilarious comedy that would, like *Quelle drôle de gosse* (#40), be worthy of inclusion for its entertainment value alone. It was scripted and directed by Bernard-Deschamps (real name Dominique Deschamps), who early in the century had entered Pathé's service as a scientist/technician, later helping Henri Chrétien develop the cinemascope lens. Bernard-De-

135. Leprohon, *Présences contemporaines*, 159–160.

schamps made about eight films around 1914, then a scattering of films over the next fifty years. Unusually prolific in the 1930s, he made four films, notably *Le Rosier de Madame Husson* with Fernandel and Françoise Rosay, which is best remembered for the outrage it caused among the religious authorities. From a Guy de Maupassant story, it deals with the sexual initiation of a gormless youth whose virginity is coincidentally being just then celebrated by the local moral establishment. *Monsieur Coccinelle* is the only one of these four that Bernard-Deschamps scripted himself, which perhaps accounts for the meticulous attention he devoted to its structure and pace. Most importantly, it is one of the few commercial narrative feature films of the decade to break entirely at times with all forms of realism.

Monsieur Coccinelle (Mister Labybird) lives in browbeaten suburban misery in Béton-sur-Seine (Concrete-on-Seine) and works as a lowly civil servant at the Bureau of Statistics. Glumly resigned to his lot, he fantasizes sporadically about the possibility of some revolutionary form of liberation, and dreams of becoming a dictator. "Like all wimps," as his wife sourly observes. At work, long lines of equally doomed wimps file robotically through his bureau like a scene from *Metropolis*. Contrasting with all this comic bleakness, his rich aunt preserves a naive faith that the love of her life, a fairground magician called the Great Illusio, will return to carry her off to the brighter world he had long ago promised her. But she dies, or seems to. Hope of an inheritance brings eager shopkeepers and funeral directors, and the reflected glory of a family drama brings to Monsieur Coccinelle respectful recognition from friends and neighbors as well as from toys and mannequins in shop windows. Of course, on the day of the funeral, to the dismay of the hopeful creditors, the aunt revives; there will be no inheritance, and an angry crowd marches on the Coccinelles' house for disturbing the social order. But the Great Illusio duly arrives and calms them with a rain of gold. In a fantasy ending, he drives off with the aunt, leaving the dismayed Monsieur Coccinelle to another day at the office, another henpecked night at Béton-sur-Seine.

The red tape jokes and the sardonic attitude toward the bleakly mercenary bourgeoisie are enjoyable but routine. What really surprises is the extension of Monsieur Coccinelle's fantasy into the technical sphere. Robotic acting, vivid dreams, and animated dolls are not all: on the night of the aunt's death, when Monsieur Coccinelle goes to retrieve from her room a singing-bird-in-a-box that the magician had given her, we have thunder and lightning, howling winds, and angry paintings on the wall resenting his intrusion. When the ladies of the quarter come to the wake, a fly irritates them and they hunt it as a pack. An extravagant soundtrack includes sounds off, synchronisms, and a comic commentary. By the standards of this decade's cinema, which had seemed rapidly and definitively to repress all the modernist technical practices of the silent era, such technical exuberance is hilariously eccentric. This may be why the film was not released normally but through the art-house world of Studio 28, though this injustice was to be rectified during the war, when a temporary shortage of films triggered a much more impressive re-release in the Gaumont Palace.

Two further matters are worth mentioning: the film's protagonist and production. Monsieur Coccinelle is played by Pierre Larquey, one of the most beloved character actors of the decade, whose cinema persona was normally that of a mild-mannered modest artisan, helper to the lead actor. No account of the decade would be complete without a reference to such second-role players whose faces became so well known by dint of their many appearances that they seem retrospectively to form the whole body of French citizenry of the interwar years. At a time when films might be shot in three weeks, and second-role actors would seldom be needed for more than two weeks, they could rack up an improbable number of films in a career. In this decade alone, even lead actors like Harry Baur, Fernandel, Albert Préjean, Henri Garat, Ginette Leclerc, Raimu, Françoise Rosay, and Jean Gabin made between thirty and forty-five films, while among second-role actors, Jean Tissier, Lucien Baroux, Saturnin Fabre, and Paulette Dubost appeared in over forty; Julien Carette, Marguerite Moreno, and Paul Azaïs in over fifty; Jeanne Fusier-Gir, Mady Berry, and Pauline Carton in over sixty; and Raymond Cordy, Aimos, and Sinoël in over eighty; but Larquey holds the all-time record of ninety-nine films in the decade, including eighteen in 1934 alone, though the present film may be the only one in the decade aside from *La Terre qui meurt* (#48) in which he took the lead role.

The production company formed by Bernard-Deschamps specifically to make *Monsieur Coccinelle* was called "Les Films Coccinelle." He had done the same for *Madame Husson*, registering a company called "Les Films Ormudz," which disappeared immediately afterward, and he was to do the same for his 1939 film *Tempête*, registering yet another company called "Belgatos." This practice of single-film production companies is best known in the case of Pierre Renoir's *La Marseillaise* (#73), but it was widespread during the decade. As a statistical indication, of the sixty-eight production companies whose name begins "Les Films . . . ," forty were created for a single film, while another ten produced only two films. Of the seventy-one entitled "Les Productions . . ." or "Société de Production . . . ," forty-one never produced another film, and eleven produced only one other. This fragmentation of the production arm was one of the chief factors in the structural fluidity and financial instability of the so-called film industry—though one that it shared with most other arms of French industry. It generated a lack of continuity in planning and in worker's contracts, a high financial risk of bankruptcy with every film (about a third of companies going bankrupt each year), an inability to renew filmmaking infrastructure, and a poor technical finish to most films. But it had what was generally considered at the time one great advantage—it eliminated any tendency toward generic conventionalization in the resultant products, as witness *Monsieur Coccinelle*.[136]

84. *Carrefour*

(*Crossroads*)
France-Britain, 1938, 84 min (version viewed 71 min), b&w

Dir Kurt Bernhardt; *Prod* British Unity Pictures; *Scr* Robert Liebmann, Bernhardt, and Andé-Paul Antoine, from an original story by Kafka; *Cinematog* Léonce-Henri Burel; *Music* Henry Herblay; *Art dir* Jean d'Eaubonne; *Sound* Marcel Courmes; *Edit* Lantz; *Act* Charles Vanel (Roger de Vétheuil/Jean Pelletier), Suzy Prim (Michèle Allain), Jules Berry (Lucien Sarrou), Tania Fédor (Madame de Vétheuil), Marcelle Géniat (Madame Pelletier), Jean Claudio (young Paul de Vétheuil), and Jean Tissier.

This is a splendid film—one of several fine 1930s films that are relatively unknown but that can still resonate with a modern audience. In the case of *Carrefour*, this is largely because of the sober acting style of Charles Vanel, several of whose films are included in this filmography. He appeared in some forty-four films during the decade, out of the nearly two hundred in which he acted between 1912 and 1984. Working with the Ermolieff troupe of Russian émigrés in the 1920s, he had absorbed the principles of Constantin Stanislawski's system—authenticity and credibility through interiority—whose dictum was that it does not matter whether you act well or badly; what matters is that you act truthfully. As Vanel himself said, "I always did my job as a carpenter does his—I'm no intellectual and I don't try to analyse my roles; it's their relationship to lived experience, to brute reality, that interests me."[137] Firmin Gémier had inculcated the same morale during Vanel's time in the theater around 1920: "Don't intellectualise, feel. Think what you are saying, not *about* what you are saying."[138]

In *Carrefour*, Vanel is (or thinks he is) Roger de Vétheuil, a successful and happily married middle-class businessman. When someone tries to blackmail him about secrets in his past, he sets the police on them. Gradually, though, evi-

136. See Crisp, *Classic French Cinema*, 26–42.
137. Quoted in Sallée, *Les Acteurs français*, 224.
138. Cartier, *Monsieur Vanel*, 104.

dence begins to accumulate that he is not in fact de Vétheuil but Jean Pelletier, a bad lad who supposedly died during World War I. This ambiguity concerning his identity is nicely sustained by the script, but finally de Vétheuil comes to accept that he must indeed be Pelletier, and had involuntarily exchanged names with de Vétheuil while suffering amnesia at war's end. Whichever he is, the film makes clear that as de Vétheuil he has lived as (or become) an honorable and useful member of society. Women recognize this: it is not clear whether his fiancée, now wife, had knowingly recognized the slippage of identity, but she is loyal and supportive; Pelletier's mother privately recognizes it but supports his belief in his new identity at the cost of losing her son a second time; while Pelletier's former mistress, a nightclub hostess, likewise recognizes him as Pelletier but finally sacrifices herself to preserve his current facade, believing it worth preserving.

This then is a most interesting variation on that favorite 1930s theme, the falsity of the respectable businessman. Usually behind a facade of respectability we discover corruption and hypocrisy. Here, behind the blockage of his amnesia, the respectable businessman Roger de Vétheuil comes to recognize his violent former self. This time, unlike Monsieur Victor in *L'Étrange Monsieur Victor* (#77), which had just screened a few months before, the businessman doesn't know he is or was a crook. The (somewhat Freudian) amnesia has allowed the vicious Jean Pelletier to become that good and honorable man whom he might always have been had he been born into different social circumstances. And Vanel's sober acting not only succeeds in carrying off this distinctly melodramatic plot but contrasts tellingly with the gesticulatory, sinister, slimy persona that Jules Berry as his blackmailer once again so effectively constructs. After seeming to confirm at the trial that de Vétheuil is who he thinks he is, Sarrou, the blackmailer, turns up at de Vétheuil's home to cash in on the current wealth of "his old mate," Jean Pelletier. While in the end, thanks to his former mistress, de Vétheuil triumphs over this blackmailer, the narrative has served to completely undermine his initial identity as what Noël Burch and Geneviève Sellier call "le Père tranquille," a paternal figure confident of his right to enjoy tranquilly the fruits of an honorable and dominant existence. Now he learns not just that he was Pelletier but that he still is Pelletier, still is (potentially) violent: his investigations into his own past lead him to attempt to murder his blackmailer in order to suppress the implication that he is a murderer. And the representation of the family that emerges from the film is also far from reassuring: the self-sacrifice of a nightclub hostess to save a wife and family is as interesting in this sphere as the necessary suppression of the criminal to save the industrialist in the other.

Kurt Bernhardt, the director of this fascinating film, was one of the many German Jews who found refuge in France from the Nazis. He had made films in

Germany with a French version in 1930 and 1933, then *L'Or dans la rue* in France in 1934 and *The Beloved Vagabond* with Maurice Chevalier in England, again with a French version, then returned to France for this film. It has a lot in common with other films made by the German contingent of filmmakers. The influence of the German scriptwriter, of Bernhardt and of Eugene Tuscherer, the producer, is evident in the sets and cinematography. The opening shots of rain-swept cobbled streets, in fog and at night, are wonderfully dramatic, though they turn out to be more purely aesthetic than diegetically relevant. Equally dramatic are the shadowy half-lit faces, the lattices and lattice shadows that pattern the image. All this is reminiscent of expressionist films, echoing the atmosphere of threat, suspicion, ambiguity, and doubt as Pelletier's uncertain memories of a criminal past are awakened. Various commentators have noted the tendency of this German contingent to privilege objects over actors, to have sets and lighting that comment on the characters and seem to determine the outcome of the narrative—indeed, to choose precisely those subjects that lend themselves to such treatment.[139]

After *Carrefour*, Bernhardt made one more film, *La Nuit de décembre*, before again having to flee the Nazis, this time to America where he made films under the name Curtis Bernhardt. Despite these potentially suspect origins, *La Nuit de décembre* was approved for release by the German authorities during the occupation and screened throughout 1941 into 1942, becoming one of the ten most successful films of the war years.

85. *Le Drame de Shanghaï*

(*Shanghai Story*)
France, 1938, 105 min (now 95 min), b&w

Dir Georg-Wilhelm Pabst; *Asst dir* Marc Sorkin; *Prod* Lucia Films/Gladiator Films; *Scr* Léo Lania, Alexandre Arnoux, and Henri Jeanson, from the novel *Shanghaï, Chambard et Cie* by Oscar-Paul Gilbert; *Cinematog* Curt Courant and Eugen Schüfftan; *Music* Ralph Erwin; *Art dir* André Andrejew; *Sound* Robert Teisseire; *Edit* Jean Oser; *Act* Christiane Mardayne (Kay Murphy), Elina Labourdette (Véra), Raymond Rouleau (Franchon, the reporter), Louis Jouvet (Ivan), Valéry Inkijinoff (Lee Pang), Suzanne Desprès, Foun-Sen, Mila Parély, Gabrielle Dorziat, Linh Nam (Tcheng), Dorville, and André Alerme.

139. See Crisp, *Classic French Cinema,* 171–172.

This is arguably Georg-Wilhelm Pabst's finest French film, and the only film of the decade to recognize the significance of contemporary social and political events in China—to attempt, that is, to do in the cinema what André Malraux's *La Condition humaine* had done in the literary sphere only three years before. As is usually the case with historical films, it weaves together two contrasting but interlinked stories—one public (about the attempt to construct a new China) and one private (about a Russian émigré family caught up in these struggles), which aims to personalize and humanize the public story.

The former focuses on Tcheng, an idealistic young revolutionary whose aim is to unite the workers of Shanghai in a nationwide movement to liberate their country from foreigners and from profiteers. Opposing him is the Black Snake/Black Dragon, a sinister coalition of militias consisting of drug- and arms-traffickers run by Lee Pang, which exploits the current situation for private gain. The mass scenes of rallies, demonstrations, and marches form an extended and exhilarating spectacle (which incidentally would at the time have echoed similar French events in the recent past of the Popular Front). The role that foreigners had had in the oppression of the Chinese people is played down, however, no doubt for strategic and commercial reasons. Aside from a group of U.S. sailors who serve a limited narrative purpose, the United States, United Kingdom, and France only appear briefly in this public story when they rescue their nationals from the conflagration at the end.

The main foreign focus is on a Russian mother and daughter, Kay and Véra, with whose plight the audience is invited to identify. Véra returns from seven years of schooling in Hong Kong to a weird and unsettling Shanghai: her mother fails to meet her at the station because she has been detained by Lee Pang's manager in the nightclub where, in order to support her daughter's studies, she has become a lead singer and good-time girl, the "Queen of Shanghai." Véra finally discovers to her horror the extent to which her mother is in the grip of the Black Dragon, but also that Ivan, her father, believed dead, has turned up again and is a prime ally of the Black Dragon. The two narratives, political and personal, are therefore variously interconnected, not least by a French journalist, Franchon, who has a relationship with Kay and is reporting on the political crisis. Sympathetic to the revolutionaries, he saves Tcheng from assassination by poison then rescues Véra herself at the end. It is possible that the presence of such a dashing character holding the strands of the narrative together was central to Pabst's desire to make the film. In a 1933 interview, he had indicated that, as a filmmaker, he felt a close affinity with political journalists, whose pen equated to the filmmaker's camera. "These two professions have in common the anxiety they arouse [in the establishment], though the journalist is the more effective of the two because less dependent on capital. If I hadn't been a film director I would have been a political journalist."[140] To some extent, then, Franchon can be considered a projection of Pabst's persona in the film, and his role echoes that of many late 1930s protagonists, who see no hope of redemption for the older generation but are still willing to strive for the salvation of the young.

The representation of China in the two stories is radically different. In the private story, it functions in a way that had become conventional in the course of the decade: the Orient is a place of eroticism and corruption, of malice, violence, and despair, where Europeans meet their dark Other and are destroyed by that encounter. It is thus a pretext for "uncovering" a woman's double identity as mother and as prostitute, notably when Kay rather self-mockingly shucks off her persona as queen of the Shanghai nightlife and dons a "respectable" outfit to meet her daughter. The same contrast, however, occurs in the case of her husband Ivan, who is sardonically derogatory of his earlier "innocent" self as revealed in family photographs, though his darker self involves not sexuality, as in the case of the woman, but the more typically masculine Other of violence and power. Seeing no way to escape him, Kay shoots him (in the back), and his last words are, "Why didn't you do that fifteen years ago?"

In the political story, China is seen in more inspirational terms. Tcheng's theme is that in the face of Japan's invasion (and subsequent occupation) of Shanghai, a unified and more enlightened China must be constructed. As his group marches through the city streets, workers down tools and swell their number until they form a mighty throng, an endless serpent of the oppressed to oppose the Black Serpent of profiteers. When the two serpents meet, Tcheng appeals to the Black Serpent's militia to join them: "Don't fire on your brothers!" The echo of Sergei Eisenstein's *Potemkin* is unmistakable. Tcheng's sister has been working for the Black Dragon, and the two are now reunited. The optimism of this Asian political story and the pessimism of the European family tragedy is beautifully captured in the final triumphal procession, as Kay is assassinated by a knife in the back but carried along dead by the rejoicing throng. This scene lovingly encapsulates the trope "Public Gaiety, Private Grief," and foreshadows closely the ending of *Les Enfants du paradis*.

It is not hard to see how this film fits into Pabst's filmography, with its cosmopolitanism and promotion of a left-wing cause. The cosmopolitanism derives from his experience: born to Austrian parents in Bohemia, now the Slovak Republic, near the Hungarian border, he was an actor in Switzerland, Germany,

140. Amengual, *Georg-Wilhelm Pabst*, 93–94; interview in *Je suis partout*, no. 462, 19 January 1933.

and France before directing films in Germany, France, the United States, then France again. The location shots for this film were taken in Saigon. Pabst had traveled widely (including to Shanghai) and considered himself a citizen of the world. His pacifism and internationalism derived from this, and he was happy to acknowledge left-wing sympathies—"proud to be called Red Pabst," he repeatedly refused Joseph Goebbels's insistent invitations to return to Germany. "There is scarcely a film of Pabst's where the great contemporary crises are not foregrounded . . . ; his work traces the history of the great social and political problems that marked the age."[141] An exile who worked regularly with other exiles, his film here thematizes that exile.[142] This makes it all the harder to understand why, the following year, he should have changed tack and opted to return to Hitler's Germany, where he made three films within the wartime Nazi production system. His friends professed astonishment: he had tickets for America but did not use them. He may have returned to Germany to liquidate family property or because his son had been conscripted into the Wehrmacht, or perhaps because his previous venture into filmmaking in America had left a bitter taste. His own silence on the matter after the war suggests that he considered the decision a mistake, for which he could blame no one but himself.

86. *La Route enchantée*

(*The Enchanted Road*)
France, 1938, 84 min, b&w

Dir Pierre Caron; *Prod* Films Saca; *Scr and Music* Charles Trénet; *Cinematog* Georges Benoit; *Art dir* Jean Douarinou; *Sound* Joseph de Bretagne; *Edit* André Gug; *Act* Charles Trénet (Jacques Minervois), Marguerite Moréno (Countess), Jacqueline Pacaud (Geneviève), Catherine Fonteney (Madame Minervois), Jeanne Fusier-Gir (Gwendoline), Maximilienne (governess), Julien Carette (Cosaque), Aimos (Marche-Toujours), Marcel Vallée (Monsieur Minervois), and Serge Grave (Jean Minervois).

Also *Je chante* (*I Sing*), released 30 November 1938: *Scr and Dir* Christian Stengel and René Wheeler; *Music* Charles Trénet; *Act* Charles Trénet, Julien Carette, Félix Oudart, Jean Tissier, Janine Darcy, and Margo Lion.

141. André Michel, 1963, quoted in Amengual, *Georg-Wilhelm Pabst*, 154.
142. See Karsten Witte, quoted in Rentschler, *The Films of G. W. Pabst*, 167–174.

Charles Trénet was the popular-music revelation of the late 1930s. A film from 1932 (*Bariole*) incorporates some of his lyrics, but his first hit songs date from the mid-1930s, and the two prewar films in which he featured on the basis of these hits were both filmed in 1938 (and, incidentally, released in the same week—of 30 November—to catch the Christmas season). He was as distinct in his singing style as Tino Rossi, but whereas Rossi can best be described as a suave crooner, Trénet was altogether more lighthearted, whimsical, and dynamic. He aimed at catchy word-play and fantasy, and the films in which he figured exploited this harebrained zany image. *Je chante* is an awful film, which would be totally forgettable were it not for his presence and his songs, while *La Route enchantée,* using a script he himself wrote, is distinctly better though still no cinematographic triumph. The implication of both (as in *La Crise est finie,* #33) is that no problem, public or private, need be taken too seriously—a catchy tune will sweep them all away. This is the mythologization of verve and vitality, the infectious goodwill of the "fou chantant"—the singing fool, a man of the people who at the drop of a hat bursts spontaneously into song.

Retrospectively, Trénet can be seen as one of a marginal group of filmmakers and actors who, consciously or not, were trying to introduce into the French cinema something of the whimsy and wacky hilarity of the Anglo-Saxon comic tradition. The Prévert brothers had attempted this with *L'Affaire est dans le sac* (#21) and *Drôle de drame* (#66), and would do the same again with *Adieu Léonard* in 1943. Trénet would appear as lead in this latter film, not chosen by the Préverts but imposed by Pathé (and reportedly their association was a little fraught). Like all those films (except *Drôle de drame,* where Marcel Carné's discipline helped), it is not only the script and editing in Trénet's two films that lack dynamism but also the acting. Trénet's attempts involve bounding onto the set, overacting with grotesque gestures and bulging eyes, then bursting into song while managing to smile fixedly. Deliberately or not, he cultivated the appearance of Harpo Marx, with effusive blonde curly hair and an inane innocence, but the comedy is nowhere near as rapid-paced nor as inventive as in the Marx brothers' films. Nevertheless, for those who enjoy his songs, it is worth enduring the slack narratives and incompetent acting to watch him perform them.

Je chante is, appropriately enough, orchestrated around the popular success of a new young singer. He is the nephew of a count who runs a girls' boarding school, which allows for a generous display of nubile flesh and a rather unmotivated romance. The gambling peccadillos of his uncle have caused a financial crisis for the school, which is finally resolved when Trénet and his editor turn the boarding school into a music school. Based on, but not featuring, his hit song "Je chante," this film does however feature "Les Oiseaux de Paris," "Ah dis, Ah dis, Ah dis, Ah Bonjour," and "La Vie qui va." Aside from the title song, his second film, *La Route enchantée,* features "Vous êtes jolie," "Il pleut dans ma chambre," and the ever popular "Boum." This time the story is set in a boys' school, where Jacques Minervois's father teaches. Jacques (Trénet, of course) and his brother, Jean, fantasize about a (yellow brick?) road that leads through idyllic countryside to a fairytale castle where all their dreams will come true. But to get there they must thwart the evil designs of the wicked witch (their mother). The rest of the narrative has Jacques realizing this dream and, after a few perfunctory narrative problems, finding romance. If the romance is never pushed far in these films, it may be because of the well-known fact of Trénet's homosexuality.

Julien Carette, whose comic persona and unforgettable voice had enlivened many 1930s films, not least *L'Affaire est dans le sac,* and were to do so for the next twenty-five years (133 altogether, in 35 years) appeared in both these films as Trénet's "accomplice," and was to figure again alongside Trénet in *Adieu Léonard.* It has been said of Carette that "his face, his peculiar drawl, his gift of the gab and his populist manner confer on even the most banal of dialogues an irony which the spectator immediately appreciates."[143] Certainly he endowed many secondary roles with an improbable density and humanity, and was memorable in the roles Renoir gave him during these years, notably as the poacher in *La Règle du jeu* (#95), but even he could not save these films from banality. Only Trénet's songs justify watching them—those songs that "revolutionized the music hall, marked a generation, survived the war and the decades to remain as fresh as ever, and which even today convince us to accept the directorial inadequacies of Pierre Caron."[144]

87. *Le Joueur d'échecs*

(The Chess Player)
France, 1938, 90 min, b&w

Dir Jean Dréville; *Prod* Société des Films Véga; *Scr* Albert Guyot, with André Doderet, Roger Vitrac, and Bernard Zimmer, from the novel by Henri Dupuy-Mazuel; *Cinematog* René Gaveau; *Music* Jean Lenoir; *Art dir* Lucien Aguettand; *Sound* Robert Ivonnet; *Edit* Raymond Leboursier; *Act* Conrad Veidt (Baron Kempelen), Françoise Rosay (Catherine II), Micheline Francey (Sonia), Paul Cambo (Boleslav, the Polish resistance leader), Bernard Lancret (Serge Oblonsky, his Russian friend), Gaston Modot (Nikolaieff, the Russian commander), and Edmonde Guy (Wanda).

143. Mazeau and Thouart, *Les Grands Seconds Rôles,* 248.
144. Borde et al., *Deuxième cinécure,* 73.

This is a fine film from a director who was not to become well known until the war years, and who is still little known outside of France. Critic and editor of film magazines in the late 1920s, Jean Dréville came to film-directing via photography, cinematography, and documentary. He had directed eleven sound films before *Le Joueur d'échecs*, many of them filmed versions of Roger Ferdinand's plays. A friend and admirer of Marcel L'Herbier, Dréville had in 1927 organized a short documentary around the making of L'Herbier's famous silent film *L'Argent* and was assistant on *Le Bonheur* (1934, #37), later taking over the direction of *La Brigade sauvage* (1939) when L'Herbier fell ill. In 1937, two of Dréville's films (*Troïka sur la piste blanche* and *Nuits blanches de St. Pétersburg*, based on Tolstoy's *Kreutzer Sonata*) had already exploited the French fascination with everything Russian, but none of his previous films foreshadowed the ambition of *Le Joueur d'échecs*.

Based on a novel that Raymond Bernard had already filmed in a silent version, it exploits to the full that favorite 1930s metaphor of "the mechanical man." The notion that industrial capitalism constituted a form of enslavement that deprived human beings of their humanity and their autonomy, turning them into robots, had already been exploited by expressionist films such as *Metropolis*.[145] *Tumultes* takes it up briefly, as does René Clair's *À nous la liberté* (#12). The pianolas triggered in *Pépé le Moko* (#56) and in Max Ophüls's *Liebelei* suggest humans subject to a relentless destiny, while mechanical toys perform a similar task in Jean Renoir's *La Nuit du carrefour*, in Jean Vigo's *L'Atalante* (#32), and in *Éducation de prince*. *Le Joueur d'échecs* complicates this metaphor in a variety of ways. The film opens in an automated forge where Baron von Kempelen is at work constructing automata. His quarters are crowded with shrouded figures that can be set in motion by chain-pulls. The baron is the protector at Catherine's court of the Polish patriots/revolutionaries struggling for freedom from Russian rule, and various of the automata are constructed to represent the main protagonists, with interesting implications for the historical inevitability of the political outcome. There are fascinating shots in which characters dance with their automated doubles.

In supporting the Poles, the baron is carrying out the posthumous wish of a countess, but apart from this executive role, he, like his automata, has abandoned all humanity. Pitied by others for living exclusively amid characters lacking all human warmth, he protests that this is the essence of their virtue—life's "vitality" is nothing but a weakness. He is working on an automated army, the army of the future, which will eliminate life with ruthless efficiency, but his prime ambition is to create a mechanized chess-player that will be able to defeat all human opponents because it will not be subject to their irrational impulses.

145. This section is largely borrowed from Crisp, *Genre, Myth and Convention*, 27–29.

When the leading Polish revolutionary is wounded and must hide, the baron trains him to live inside this automated chess-player. Unfortunately, the chess-piece ends up as a gift to Catherine, who has penetrated the ruse and plays with the baron's fears for the Polish patriot inside. Parallel to this drama, we witness a hallucinatory scene in which the Russian army commander, searching the baron's quarters, casually "slaughters" various automata, hangs from a gallows the one that is the double of the baron himself, and sets the automated army in motion just as he has set his own army in motion against the Poles. When in Catherine's presence the chess-player is finally "executed," it is the baron himself who staggers forth from it, having sacrificed himself to save the Polish leader. A final series of images shows the baron's body lying disarticulated in the snow, like a broken automaton. The Russian commander is also dead, surrounded by the lethal automated army that he has set in motion.

The automata are therefore used throughout the narrative to keep in play the themes of doubles; of pawns, puppets, and puppet-master; of the ruthless inhumanity of modern warfare; and of fascism—indeed of politics and of narrative itself as complicated chess games, not to mention the themes of history, destiny, and what it means to be human. This then is the decade's summative statement on the possible uses of mechanized humans in fictional narrative, and provides an essential context to any thorough appreciation of Renoir's great film La Règle du jeu (#95), which came out the following year.

In a fairly conventional if heavily symbolic subplot, the Poles' spirit of independence is embodied in an attractive woman, Sonia, who is fought over by two friendly rivals, one Russian and one Polish (Serge and Boleslas). The first half of the film leads up to the rebellion, which goes badly for the Poles, and the second half deals with Boleslas's concealment in the automaton, which also begins to go seriously wrong. Inevitably, the private catastrophe occurs amid public celebration, as Catherine persecutes the leading Poles during Carnival celebrations. It is clear, however, where the film's heart is, since an intercut scene shows Boleslas and Sonia escaping across snowy wastes to freedom in a sleigh.

Perhaps the clearest memory one will take away from the film is the spectacular art direction. The sets, especially those involving the automata in their workshop, are enormously impressive. They were designed by Lucien Aguettand, who worked for Pathé-Natan. He had been trained in Germany, which he considered "the solidest form of training I ever had. You met in Berlin people from all countries—Hungarians, French, English, but few Americans. German production was international. There was still a lot of evidence of expressionism, right up to Hitler's time, indeed—a violent lighting set-up that you find in France with cinematographers like Kruger, Hubert, Hayer. They were in a sense realistic, but a German form of realism." Like nearly all French art directors, he detested first-degree realism, a "servile copy of appearances," and reserved his approval for the poetic interpretation of reality. Dréville himself had been trained in this tradition.[146] This film is one of their most impressive achievements, and it is not hard to see why it was awarded the international jury prize at the Venice Festival in 1938.

88. Remontons les Champs-Élysées

(*Retracing the Champs-Élysées*)
France, 1938, 100 min, b&w

Dir and Scr Sacha Guitry and Robert Bibal; *Asst dir* Jeanne Étiévant; *Prod* Serge Sandberg (Cinéas); *Cinematog* Jean Bachelet; *Music* Adolphe Borchard; *Art dir* René Renoux; *Sound* Joseph de Bretagne; *Edit* Myriam; *Act* Sacha Guitry (the lecturer, Louis XV, Ludovic, Jean-Louis, and Napoléon III), Lucien Baroux (Marquis de Chauvelin), Lisette Lanvin (Louisette), Josseline Gaël (Léone), Jacqueline Delubac (Flora), Jeanne Boitel (Madame de Pompadour), Germaine Dermox (Marie de Medici), Émile Drain (Napoléon Ier), René Fauchois (Marat), Raymond Galle (Louis XIII), Robert Pizani (Wagner, Offenbach, and Olivier Métra), Jacques Erwin (young Louis XIV and the Duke de Montpensier), and Jane Marken.

Also *Les Perles de la couronne* (*The Pearls in the Crown*), France, 1937, codirected by Christian-Jaque.

As well as filming five of his own stage-plays between 1935 and 1939, Sacha Guitry wrote eight original scenarios specifically for the cinema (see #68). All thirteen were box-office successes, especially *Le Roman d'un tricheur* (1936, #53), which was his most innovative, being largely dependent on silent film techniques with a voiceover commentary by the Guitry persona, whom we see from time to time writing this "monologue" in a café. Such was its success that Guitry was motivated to adapt the technique to historical material. What resulted were his two most popular films of the decade, *Les Perles de la couronne* (1937) and *Remontons les Champs-Élysées* (1938). They are important mainly for what they say about the ideological interests and needs of the audience of the day, but also because their popularity generated two of Guitry's greatest postwar successes, which exploited the same techniques—*Si Versailles m'était conté* (1953) and *Si Paris nous était conté* (1956).

146. For these quotations, and more on this training, see Crisp, *Classic French Cinema*, chs. 4, 7.

Essentially, these films all take the form of episodic history lessons in which certain moments and events in French (and occasionally European) history are organized around the story of a well-known object or place. The principal satisfaction that this technique offered Guitry was that it allowed him to pontificate—to instruct his compatriots somewhat patronizingly in their national history by way of a voiceover from the master himself. He appears at the beginning of each of these two films as himself: *Perles* opens with his telling Jacqueline Delubac (his wife and lead actress) that he has found this brilliant topic for a film, while *Champs-Élysées* opens with his ringing the school-bell and informing the class that he will for an hour provide them with a novel form of history— the history of the Champs-Élysées. Thereafter in both films, his nasal, drawling voiceover holds together a series of historical sketches, which can now seem atrociously slow-paced and appallingly acted, in the most stagey of operatic traditions, underlining redundantly every point. This clumsiness of presentation is not helped by the painfully strained humor of the commentary.

Of the two, *Perles* is the more innovative, if only because the history of the English royal pearls links three European countries—England, France, and Italy —through alliances and conflicts, and this is exploited to produce three separate introductory episodes and three endings, one in each of the three languages. Three "investigators," chosen to represent national stereotypes (a French writer, the Pope's chamberlain, and the warden of the Tower of London, called respectively Jean, Giovanni, and John), hear and respond to one another, each in his own language, across national frontiers and across the centuries. To maintain this multilingual fantasy while ensuring the film's comprehensibility to a French audience was a remarkable feat, perhaps only before attempted by Julien Duvivier in *Allô Berlin, ici Paris* (1932).

Remontons les Champs-Élysées lacks this degree of innovative flair: any connection to the title is tenuous at best, and soon abandoned. Like *Perles*, however, it offers the audience a rather charming pleasure, namely the challenge of recognizing the various lead actors in different guises in the successive historical episodes. Thus in *Perles*, Jacqueline Delubac appears as the writer's wife, as Mary Stuart, and as Josephine, to Guitry's writer, Francis I, Paul, Viscount Barras, and Napoleon III, while in *Champs-Élysées*, Guitry is the lecturer, Louis XV, Ludovic, Jean-Louis, and Napoleon III). Both films suffer from similar failings, however, as the master of ceremonies relentlessly takes his class/audience through four hundred years of history, from the Medicis in the sixteenth century through assorted monarchs, conquerors, and artistic geniuses to (in the latter film) the birth and life of the greatest of them all, namely himself. Exalting the director/actor as supreme genius, he implies that France's history is his own family history: France is him, so "Vive la France!" While this chauvinism and egotism can be rather wearing to a foreigner, it was clearly most welcome to Parisian audiences of the day. Indeed, as J.-P. Jeancolas recognized, both films were in their way radically prophetic: "[The unbearable Sacha] was one of those who foresaw what the 1960s would call the 'modernity' of the cinema. . . . It's the demiurge-like subjectivity of the author which grounds the fiction . . . , the quality—the insolence—of the author which provides that of the films."[147]

Because of the major role played in *Perles* by representatives of England, some had seen Guitry as momentarily joining the Anglophile brigade, at a time when France urgently needed the support of the "entente cordiale." But a glance at *Champs-Élysées* is enough to correct this error: in it, he manifests a profound distrust of the English, and indeed of all foreigners, characterizing the Germans by the tramp of fascist jackboots. In fact, as noted earlier, this film makes clear the extent to which he despised not only all other nations but 90 percent of his own compatriots. But what is hardest of all to endure is the simplistic view of history. Constructed of crude right-wing simplifications and heavily dependent on cliché and on anecdote, this history never resists the temptation to name-drop or to reproduce (often fictitious) myths of incident, posture, and dress. The most trivial and boring events related to the monarchy are presumed to have an inherent interest; only the aristocratic are considered able to experience the higher and finer emotions; revolutionaries are decried as greedy slavering sadists; and "the people" are seen as intrinsically unreliable because they are motivated exclusively by unthinking envy. In effect, this film constituted an "anti-*Marseillaise*," correcting the view of the French Revolution purveyed by that earlier film (February 1938, #73). It proposes history from above, according to a profoundly conservative ideology that exalts powerful and artistic men and indulgently patronizes pretty, simpering aristocratic women. "Destiny" gives a sense of rightness and inevitability to this order of things, presided over by a procession of ruling generations with remarkably similar faces. As Noël Burch and Geneviève Sellier say, when discussing directors who critiqued the status quo, "Guitry, however, was at the very heart of this system of [patriarchal] values, and was to remain there all his life."[148] No doubt this is what aroused the ire of Henri Jeanson, and of Renoir, who went so far as to say, "I think [Guitry's] films are awful. They are sufficient justification for all revolutions."[149] Needless to say, that was far from their intention.

147. Jeancolas, *15 ans d'années trente*, 265.
148. Burch and Sellier, *La Drôle de guerre des sexes*, 181.
149. Quoted in Guillaume-Grimaud, *Le Cinéma du front populaire*, 89.

89. *Hôtel du Nord*

(*Hôtel du Nord*)
France, 1938, 95 min, b&w

Dir Marcel Carné; *Asst dir* Claude Walter and Pierre Blondy; *Prod* SEDIF (Lucacev-itch); *Scr* Jean Aurenche, then Henri Jeanson, from the novel by Eugène Dabit; *Cinematog* Armand Thirard; *Music* Maurice Jaubert; *Art dir* Alexandre Trauner; *Sound* Marcel Courmes; *Edit* René Le Hénaff; *Act* Jean-Pierre Aumont (Pierre), Louis Jouvet (Monsieur Edmond/Paolo/Robert), Annabella (Renée), Paulette Dubost (Ginette), Arletty (Raymonde), Jane Marken (Madame Lecouvreur), Ray-mone (Jeanne), Génia Vaury (the nurse), Andrex (Kenel), André Brunot (Mon-sieur Lecouvreur), François Périer (Adrien), Bernard Blier (Prosper), Henri Bosc (Nazarède), René Bergeron, Jacques Louvigny, and Armand Lurville.

This is a film quite unlike those made before and after by Marcel Carné. Given an opportunity to build a film around Annabella, one of the most popular actresses of the day and recent winner of the Coupe Volpi at Venice, he thought of the novel by Eugène Dabit that he had enthused about as a critic five years be-fore. At that time, promoting what he foresaw as "street cinema," he had recom-mended it as "an evocation of the characteristic atmosphere of a popular quarter of Paris, where in a setting of factories, garages, footbridges and carts . . . the whole picturesque restless world of the St Martin canal comes to life." Such a nar-rative would allow a filmmaker "to describe the simple life of the little people of Paris."[150] But the novel was in fact little more than a succession of incidents ob-served by Dabit in his parents' hotel, and Carné felt that some sort of psycho-drama was required to bring them all together. Jacques Prévert was away in the Soviet Union, so he called on Jean Aurenche, who fashioned it around a pair of suicidal young lovers. Then Carné turned to Henri Jeanson, who marginalized those lovers and refashioned the narrative around his friends Arletty and Louis Jouvet as the tart and her pimp. He was probably right in this: the weakest parts of the film nowadays seem those maudlin sentimental scenes involving the wimp-ish young lovers' failed suicide pact. Jean-Pierre Aumont himself acknowledged that "Our feeble gormless roles could scarcely inspire Jeanson."[151] Moreover, Carné reported that Jeanson had no time for either of the two young actors.[152]

150. Marcel Carné, "Quand le cinéma descendra-t-il dans la rue?" *Ciné-Magazine*, no. 13, November 1933.
151. Aumont, *Le Soleil et l'ombre*, 62.
152. See Carné, *La Vie à belles dents*, 121–137.

Carné was never very successful at casting young heroines or at representing passionate relationships, a weakness sometimes attributed to his homosexuality. This may also explain in this film the notably sympathetic treatment of Adrien, the young homosexual who waves to a soldier with whom he clearly has a relationship.

The story can be briefly summarized: when Pierre and Renée's double suicide in the hotel fails, Pierre is imprisoned and Renée employed by the hotel proprietors. She talks Monsieur Edmond, Raymonde's pimp, into taking her away from all this to a new life "là-bas," but in Marseilles has second thoughts and returns to Pierre, soon to be released from prison. In stolid despair, Monsieur Edmond allows himself to be killed by the gangster whom he had shopped to the police, and who had been hunting him. All these people, together with the blood-donor lock-keeper and his wife and her lover make of the Hôtel du Nord one of those tight-knit little communities so beloved of 1930s cinema. The absence of Prévert, however, his poetry and dark atmosphere of fatality, and the absence of Jean Gabin, together with the authorial presence of Jeanson, better at witty dialogue than at atmosphere, all contribute—with the jaunty theme-tune of Jaubert and the fundamental likableness of so many characters—to producing a lighter, less threatening film, resembling not *Quai des brumes* (#78) or *Le Jour se lève* (#94) but more communitarian films such as *Le Crime de Monsieur Lange* (#46), *La Belle Équipe* (#51), and *La Fin du jour* (#93). This sense of community is further developed through the opening first communion celebrations that bring them all together around a table, and the closing 14 July celebrations with their chain dance and formalized embraces (but which, in the standard 1930s trope of public gaiety/private grief, serve to cover the murder/suicide of Monsieur Edmond). At a broader level, the film reminds the viewer of the *international* communion of the oppressed through the presence of the young refugee from the Spanish Civil War whom the proprietors have adopted. "He's not really foreign, he's an orphan"—like so many other characters in the films of this decade, like Renée herself—and that trumps all other factors. In Carné's next film, of course, this orphanhood, this quest for a sense of belonging, was to be extended to the whole of France, since the strategically named François and Françoise are both orphans.

What all these disenfranchised individuals are seeking in the hotel is the healing sense of community they have never known, and which the hotel/France/the world seems unable to provide. Existence is meaningless, is absurd—a place where love is doomed, a prison where most are trapped in squalor and poverty, loneliness, and alienation. All the lodgers are transient, outside of society, or unfulfilled, and will seek to escape their reality in one way or another. For the immigrant child, France itself has represented such an escape, but the

French in turn seek it elsewhere—the young couple in a suicide pact and the ex-gangster Paolo in a new identity as Monsieur Edmond, who in turn glimpses the possibility of a more hopeful future in a new land with the aptly named Renée (reborn). This also is a trait that we know all too well from earlier 1930s films. Hope is "out there": all dream of parting but are cheated of it at the last moment—the lock-keeper, Madame Raymonde, and now Monsieur Edmond with Renée, who realizes her error and leaves him. In the recurrent motto of the film, "On ne part plus" (We're not going, after all). All hope evaporated, Monsieur Edmond allows the ship to sail for Port Said without him and accepts at the end what the young couple had believed at the beginning—that the only attainable form of escape, of freedom, is to be found in death.

Given these dire thematics, the relatively jocular atmosphere is hard to comprehend. This is not really a poetic realist film since it does not have the intensity, the metaphoric and therefore metaphysical density of a true poetic realist film. The gangsters are not weird or sinister but parodic, and the memorable moments are humorous: Jouvet's persnickety performance as a photographer and Arletty's nasal Parisian twang, especially when she says, "Atmosphère, atmosphère, est-ce que j'ai une gueule d'atmosphère?" Critics were quick to identify this "incoherence" in the film, part maudlin sentimental drama, part good-humored evocation of the little people of Paris.[153] Dabit's friends felt the dramatic script had betrayed the author's tachiste original, substituting destiny for Dabit's affectionate evocation of his parents' lodgers, while right-wing critics like Lucien Rebatet condemned it as "slack flabby populism" and attacked it for suggesting that France was exclusively peopled by losers. Even Georges Sadoul, normally sympathetic to Carné and Jeanson, thought it something less than a masterpiece. The public, however, welcomed it: arriving as it did just before Christmas 1938, it joined six other films within as many weeks that also achieved over half a million entries in Paris alone—*Katia, Gibraltar, Remontons les Champs-Élysées* (#88), *Trois Valses* (#90), *La Bête humaine* (#91), and *J'étais une aventurière*. The French cinema had reached a high point of popularity and quality in this final Christmas before the conflict. *Hôtel du Nord* was banned in 1940 by the French government, then by the Vichy État, but what outraged Arletty most was that when it was released by the Germans, the scene where she appeared naked, except for a strategic sponge, had disappeared (perhaps turned into a souvenir by an enterprising officer?).

153. For a selection of critical commentaries, including those listed here, see Abel, *French Film Theory and Criticism*, vol. 2, and Guillaume-Grimaud, *Le Cinéma du Front Populaire*, 82.

90. *Trois Valses*

(Three Waltzes)
France, 1938, 104 min, b&w

Dir Ludwig Berger; *Asst dir* Gilles Grangier and Martin Michel; *Prod* Sofror; *Scr* Léopold Marchand, from the operetta by Albert Willemetz; *Cinematog* Eugen Schufftann; *Music* Oscar Straus, based on waltz motifs of Johann Strauss; *Art dir* Jean d'Eaubonne; *Sound* Joseph de Bretagne; *Edit* Bernard Séjourné; *Act* Yvonne Printemps (Fanny, Yvette, and Irène Grandpré), Pierre Fresnay (Octave, Philippe, and Gérard de Chalencey), Henri Guisol (young Brunner), Louis-Jacques Boucot (old Brunner), Jean Périer (the president), Robert Vattier (the director), Guillaume de Sax (the marshal), France Ellys (the marquise), Jane Marken (Céleste), Jeanne Helbling (the Empress Eugénie), and E. A. Licho (the producer).

Trois Valses, an operetta directed by Ludwig Berger and featuring two of the top stars of the day, is now practically unknown. Histories of the cinema seldom mention it, unless dismissively, yet released at Christmas 1938, it attracted an audience of nearly 900,000 in Paris alone, and its re-release, interrupted by the outbreak of war, resumed in 1941. This audience far exceeded that of *Hôtel du Nord* (#89), *Entrée des artistes* (#82), *La Fin du jour* (#93), and even the probable box office of *Le Jour se lève* (#94), remarkable though all those were. Its only probable equal would have been *La Bête humaine* (#91), had that film been able to complete its release. This alone would justify its inclusion here. Certainly its acting does not.

Berger was a German director of Jewish origins who had directed Maurice Chevalier in a very successful Hollywood production *Playboy of Paris,* released in France as *Le Petit Café,* which ranked highly in the 1930–1931 season, and then respectable French versions of two of his UFA productions, which would have done his reputation no harm, notably *La Guerre des valses,* in which Fernand Gravey played Johann Strauss. Clearly Berger's talent lay in bringing musicals to the screen, and when he returned to Paris from a spell in the Netherlands (like many others, he had left Germany on Hitler's rise to power), he opted to bring to the screen this successful 1937 musical with Yvonne Printemps and Pierre Fresnay as leads. Printemps had married Sacha Guitry in 1919 and specialized in operetta. When in 1932 under Guitry's direction she and Fresnay played opposite each other, their mutual attraction was obvious: as a consequence, in 1934, Guitry's second wife became Fresnay's third, and they remained devoted to each other through several decades until retirement in 1959–1960 and their deaths in 1975 and

1977. They worked together, managing the Michodière theater. Printemps continued to focus on operetta, making only seven further films, possibly because her excessively theatrical style of acting, which involved facial grimaces, much simpering and flashing of eyes, was less appropriate in camera close-up. It is certainly possible to feel that in *Trois Valses*, her teeth and eyes upstage the rest of the cast by their overacting. Fresnay adopts an altogether more restrained style, which comes across as more natural. In Printemps's defense, one might argue that her character is that of a theatrical actress, so she is merely carrying over her persona into "real life."

Like so many 1930s productions, then, this film is reflexive, dealing with the relationship between acting and being, between the theater and reality. It does this in three sections and across three generations. The two stars play first (1869) a military man who falls for a famous actress, Fanny, who withdraws from the relationship when she realizes that it might ruin his career; second (1900), their respective son and daughter, a marquis and an operetta singer, Yvette, who fall in love but prove to have incompatible temperaments and social backgrounds; and third (1939), their respective grandchildren, he an insurance salesman seeking to insure the film production in which she, Irène, is acting. In the course of these three "acts," situations and dialogues echo, repeat, and reverse one another such that they constitute three variations on a single well-loved set of oppositions—the respectability, propriety, and convention of the establishment versus the more free-living theatrical world of gaiety, wit, and charm. In addition to this pattern of variation and repetition, there is a certain charming circularity to the plot engendered by the fact that the film in which Irène is acting in the last episode is the biography of her grandmother from the first episode. In this last episode, the couple are finally brought together by her impresario who acts as deus ex machina to get the young insurance salesman cast opposite her in the role of his grandfather, with inevitable romantic consequences. The cinema and the twentieth century are represented as a more democratic environment in which a love that has been thwarted for generations can at last be realized. In an epilogue, we discover that she has bought his family mansion, complete with portraits of their predecessors, as a wedding present for him.

While the opening of the film is a little clumsy, it soon emerges as an elaborate production involving expensive sets and costumes, all glitter and swirl as Oscar Straus's arrangement of Johann Strauss's waltzes determine the atmosphere of the various acts. The success of *Trois Valses* would only have confirmed the suspicion the French film establishment was forming in these prewar years that lavish prestigious productions with an export potential constituted the future of the nation's cinema. Even Lucien Rebatet had a good word for this film, despite Berger's Jewish background: "I regret that this film was not directed by a Frenchman; but . . . henceforth we must distinguish Monsieur Berger from the rabble of his horrible fellow-Jews who are undesirable in all respects. And the case of *Trois Valses* will not prevent us deploring once more that Jewish domination of the French cinema which opens the way for 100 Israelite grubs for every one Berger."[154]

With the outbreak of war, Berger left for England where, for Alexander Korda, he codirected with Michael Powell *The Thief of Baghdad*. If his *Trois Valses* has been largely forgotten, it may be partly because it seems (and seemed at the time, which may have been part of its charm) quaintly dated, a relic of an earlier, less neurotic age.

91. *La Bête humaine*

(*The Beast in Man*); remade as *Human Desire* (1954)
France, 1938, 100 min, b&w

Dir and Scr Jean Renoir, from the novel by Émile Zola; *Prod* Paris Film Productions; *Cinematog* Curt Courant, Claude Renoir, and Jacques Natteau; *Music* Joseph Kosma; *Art dir* Eugène Lourié; *Sound* Robert Teisseire; *Edit* Marguerite Houllé-Renoir and Suzanne de Troeye; *Act* Jean Gabin (Jacques Lantier), Simone Simon (Séverine), Fernand Ledoux (Roubaud), Julien Carette (Pecqueux), Blanchette Brunoy (Flore), Jenny Hélia, Colette Régis, Jacques Berlioz (Grandmorin), Gérard Landry (Dauvergne), and Jean Renoir (Cabuche).

Jean Renoir only rarely participated in the initial construction of the scenarios of his 1930s films (*Toni*, #38; *La Marseillaise*, #73; *La Règle du jeu*, #95). More often he adapted, frequently jointly, an established play (*On purge bébé; Chotard et Cie; Boudu sauvé des eaux*, #20; *Les Bas-Fonds*) or a novel (*La Nuit du carrefour*, #84; *Madame Bovary;* and now Émile Zola's *La Bête humaine*). In fact, the present film was proposed to Renoir by the Hakim brothers, possibly at the urging of Jean Gabin, and Renoir promptly went off to (re)read it.[155] It is interesting to speculate why the producers and Gabin thought it a promising proposition, and why Renoir agreed to direct it. The central element in the novel is Jacques Lantier's inheritance, from degenerate alcoholic forebears, of an irresistible compulsion

---

154. *L'Action française, 23* December 1938, quoted in Jeancolas, *15 ans d'années trente*, 125.
155. Renoir's own accounts of these matters differ on several points.

to kill, notably when sexually aroused. This hereditary "flaw" dominates his life to the point where he has resigned himself to avoiding liaisons with women. We witness the compulsion at work early on in the film, when he becomes aroused by his relationship with Flore. In this case, it is fortuitously defused by the thundering passage of a train, but later in a passionate encounter with Séverine, no such distraction intervenes, and he murders her.

Renoir must have found this genetic motivation unconvincing to judge from his reflections on the hero's atavistic compulsions: "I thought: all that is not particularly attractive, but if a man as attractive as Gabin said it, in an exterior setting, with lots of horizon behind him and perhaps a little wind, it could attain a certain grandeur."[156] It is easier to see why the producers and Gabin would have been seduced by the idea in the current political climate: the doom-laden narrative was in line with the pessimistic scenarios that had proven so successful in a number of recent films, arguably because of the approaching war and a widespread disillusion with the Popular Front government. Furthermore, the character of Lantier offered an analogue of that persona of a tragic working-class hero which had been accreting around Gabin for several years. For Renoir, the class theme would have been equally attractive. Speaking on its release in December, he reasserted his left-wing credentials by decrying the depressing material greed of the bourgeoisie, and described Zola as a great revolutionary for "situating his finest characters in the working class, and giving them all those preoccupations which in classical literature seemed reserved for individuals of the middle and upper classes."[157] Later, he noted, "To be tragic in a classical sense, while wearing a cloth cap and mechanic's overalls, and speaking everyday speech—that was a tour de force on Gabin's part."[158]

Renoir would certainly have found the camaraderie of the railway workers to his taste at this time: the bond between Lantier and his stoker, played by Julien Carette, is genuinely affecting, as is their integration into the wider world of railway workers, united by ties of professional pride in the dignity of their work. The time and attention that all concerned devoted to endowing Gabin's and Carette's roles with credibility—several weeks of apprenticeship in the cabin of a train and constant monitoring by their tutors during filming—gave the long opening sequence on the Paris–Le Havre run and its later ana-

156. In an interview with Bazin and Astruc in 1951, quoted in Leprohon, *Présences contemporaines*, 120.

157. Interview for *Ce Soir*, 4 November 1938, collected in Renoir, *Écrits*, 343.

158. *Cinémonde*, 7 December 1938. Pierre Duvillars described this aspect of the Gabin myth most forcefully in *Cinéma, mythologie du XXe siècle*, 72–76.

logues an undoubted documentary feel. Again for credibility's sake, the rather gothic sequence of violent events structuring the novel had to be played down. If listed coldly, these can easily seem grotesque: Grandmorin the godfather's sexual use of Séverine as a young girl; her husband Roubaud's recognition of that abuse and decision to murder Grandmorin, not least because, as he now tells her, she may well be Grandmorin's own daughter; Roubaud's forcing her to participate in the murder; Lantier's near strangling of Flore and accidental witnessing of the other murder; Séverine's consequent liaison with Lantier and her urging him to murder her husband; the failed attempt with the iron bar, then a second attempt with a revolver, when he instead strangles Séverine; then his dramatic suicide leaping from the careering train, in despair at being unable to control his madness. Pedophilia, possible incest, uncontrollable outbursts of mad rage, multiple murders (actual or intended), and a despairing suicide. Not surprisingly the Office Familial of the Catholic Church categorized the film as "atrocious and perverse. Not to be viewed." The Ligue de Moralité agreed.[159]

This is the sort of excess of social squalor and violence that was known as "naturalism," and Renoir attempted in the film to tone it down, preferring, as he later said, Zola's poetic to his naturalist side.[160] One stratagem is to have the murders committed just out of sight, and more generally, to shift motivation wherever possible in the direction of the psychological. It is no doubt also with this end in view that he introduced the Railway Workers' Ball, borrowing from one of the stock tropes of the decade (public gaiety/private tragedy) to set its bland music and vacuous song against the somber yet sensational activities happening in the yard outside.

Critical acclaim was general—unqualified on the left but recognized even on the right where Lucien Rebatet, who had repeatedly ridiculed Renoir's attachment to the Popular Front, acknowledged that he had captured what the editor of *Cinémonde* called "la poésie du rail": "It seems likely that Monsieur Jean Renoir decided to compose his *La Bête humaine* out of a love of trains, stations, speed and steam. This is by far the finest part of the work." Rebatet thus neatly characterizes Renoir as "playing trains," while attributing his partial success to the futurist dynamics that were so much a part of right-wing heritage.

159. See *Premier Plan*, nos. 22–23–24, 263–273, for quotations in this entry unless otherwise noted.

160. Renoir, *Renoir on Renoir*, 96.

92. *Métropolitain*

(*Underground*)
France, 1939, 82 min, b&w

Dir Maurice Cam; *Asst dir* Maurice Schutz; *Prod* S. B. Films; *Scr* Michel Herbert and Max Maret; *Cinematog* Nicholas Hayer; *Music* Marcel Lattès; *Art dir* Robert Dumesnil; *Sound* Jean Dubuis; *Edit* Lantz; *Act* Albert Préjean (Pierre), André Brulé (Zoltini, the magician), Ginette Leclerc (Viviane), and Anne Laurens (Suzanne).

The "métropolitain" of the title is, of course, the urban transit system in Paris, and the film begins with the protagonist, Pierre, witnessing a staged murder from an elevated section while passing an apartment window, then failing to witness a real murder at the end. The characters and atmosphere might lead one to classify this as a poetic realist film, were it not that it lacks gravitas—primarily because the lead male role is played not by Jean Gabin but by the relentlessly lightweight Albert Préjean, but also because the character he plays is allowed a (somewhat ironical) happy ending. In fact, the narrative has a remarkable resemblance to the *Contes Moraux* (Moral Tales) of Éric Rohmer thirty years later: the protagonist knows very well who is his destined partner in life but is momentarily led astray into a "narrative digression" with a more sensual creature. The problems that Pierre encounters during the digression are such as to confirm his early choice, namely his wife, Suzanne, and the final sequences see him return to her. She is a switchboard operator, and their working hours allow for little time together. This has resulted in his being seduced into a nocturnal world of nightclubs and sensuality by Viviane, the assistant to Zoltini, a magician who attacks Pierre in a fit of jealous rage. Pierre murders him (or believes he has murdered him). Finally, informed by an amiable tramp (and what 1930s tramp was not amiable?) that Zoltini is not dead after all, he is able to return to his happily married life, now intensely aware of the dangers of sensuality.

Much of the interest of the film, then, is in the digression, which features Ginette Leclerc yet again as a *garce* who is assistant to Zoltini, a slick-talking con-artist given to sleight of hand and sleight of mind. He resembles the character played by Jules Berry in *Le Jour se lève* (#94), which was released four months later, and the situation is recognizably similar. When Pierre witnesses Viviane apparently being killed by Zoltini, he summons the police and rushes back to the relevant apartment, only to be fed a cock-and-bull story by the magician about their poverty which so moves him that he parts with 200 francs. When he subsequently discovers that they were simply rehearsing an act with a retractable dagger, he is outraged, and "rescues" her from the villainous magician, who subsequently, thinking she has betrayed him, really does murder Viviane—in front of the same window, and just as Pierre is passing in the metro with his newly reconciled wife. There is a nice irony in his initially believing he saw her murdered when she wasn't, then failing to see her murdered when she is. (An equally nice irony might have been for him to witness the real murder at the end but turn to his wife and say, "They're only rehearsing an act."). Instead, Pierre turns blithely to his new wife and says, "Life's really great, isn't it?"

The *garce* was a version of the destructive female particularly common in the mid-1930s. Dark and fleshy, a vortex of sensuality, unpredictable and apparently uncontrollable, she was sultry, sulky, tempestuous, and treacherous but irresistibly fascinating. Often played by Leclerc or by Viviane Romance, this femme fatale was usually connected in some way to an underworld of crime and fast money. But the message is not so much that there are two kinds of women— quiet modest wives and raunchy lascivious vamps—but that female sexuality is double: inherently destructive (especially of male friendships, which equate in these films with a harmonious community), it can only be rendered tolerable to a civilized society by subduing it or constraining it within the bonds of domesticity, when it ceases to be destructive and becomes maternally productive. Intensity and immediacy are the characteristics of the vamp: she wants to live *now*, and when Pierre offers Viviane his modest life, she rejects it out of hand. She wants more than he could ever give; she wants the world. The producer's offer of a ticket to America is more to her liking, though it will be the death of her.

One of the more interesting aspects of this film is the almost documentary glimpses it allows us of certain aspects of Parisian life in the 1930s, and most particularly the life of the worker. Numerous critics have bewailed the absence of this concrete lived social reality from the films of the decade, even those that mythologize the worker, and François Garçon spells out certain ways in which *Métropolitain*, like the sparse scattering of better-known poetic realist films by Jean Renoir and Marcel Carné, foregrounds the cloth-cap worker and his daily routines.[161] The film opens with fascinating location shots of the day's beginning, the city streets being cleaned, the first metros, and later the timber yards on the docks where Pierre works as a crane-operator. Both his work and that of his wife, Suzanne, as a hotel switchboard operator have a credibility rare in the films of the day. Garçon stresses the recurrence of workers facing unemployment in such films. Both Pierre and Suzanne are threatened with dismissal here—her

---

161. Garçon, *De Blum à Pétain*, 69–75.

for failing to wake a hotel guest on time so that he misses his plane (it crashes) and Pierre for being late and implicitly disrespectful to the boss. Garçon points out that similar situations involving abrupt firings had occurred in Renoir's trade union film, *La Vie est à nous* (#49, twice), as they would in *Fric-Frac* (#96), *Sur le plancher des vaches*, and *Menaces* (#98) (all 1939), not to mention *La Règle du jeu* (#95). He underlines the defenselessness of the proletariat of the day, who could be let go at the whim of a boss: "These films reveal just how little consideration is given to the worker. . . . They show the instability of the relationship between employer and employee in small businesses, where no regulations existed to limit the boss's arbitrary decisions."[162] And in 1936, 50 percent of all workers were employed in such small businesses. The social conflict arising from this situation was such that it became one of the principal planks of social reconciliation under Vichy: the Charte du Travail (Work Charter) of 1941 laid out detailed procedures for mediation in case of workplace disagreements, though if the number of arbitrary layoffs that continued to recur in wartime films is any indication, the charter seems not to have been very effective.

93. La Fin du jour

(*Twilight*)
France, 1939, 102 min, b&w

Dir Julien Duvivier; *Asst dir* Pierre Duvivier; *Prod* Régina; *Scr* Charles Spaak; *Cinematog* Christian Matras; *Music* Maurice Jaubert; *Art dir* Jacques Krauss; *Sound* Tony Leenhardt and Antoine Archaimbaud; *Edit* Marthe Poncin; *Act* Louis Jouvet (Saint-Clair), Madeleine Ozeray (Jeannette), Victor Francen (Marny), Michel Simon (Cabrissade), Gabrielle Dorziat (Madame Chabert), Gaston Modot, François Périer, Arthur Devère, Charles Granval, and Sylvie.

Of the two surprise successes in the 1938–1939 season related to the theatrical life, *Entrée des artistes* (#82) and *La Fin du jour,* this latter is far the better film. The ensemble cast of established actors is significantly more competent than the adolescents of *Entrée des artistes,* whose concerns it is hard to take seriously, and Charles Spaak's script is structured more effectively than the crude melodrama of Henri Jeanson, who was renowned for witty dialogue rather than structure, while Julien Duvivier's control of his team leads to better pacing and more interesting technical effects.

162. Ibid.

The script originated in an idea that came to Spaak as he and Duvivier were driving past a home for aging actors. He remarked that there was a film to be made there. Duvivier agreed, and they worked out a narrative for which Spaak wrote the dialogue.[163] Michel Simon, Louis Jouvet, and Raimu were foreshadowed for the lead roles, but when Raimu opted out (due to inadequate salary), Victor Francen was offered the vacant role, which does in fact seem a continuation of his preceding roles as glum cuckold. Much of the interest of the film is in the interactions among these three "monstres sacrés." Jouvet plays Saint-Clair, an aging Don Juan desperate in old age to perpetuate his reputation as a lady-killer, and Francen plays Marny, whose wife had left him for Saint-Clair then died in mysterious circumstances, while Simon plays Cabrissade, who struggles to conceal behind inflated accounts of his theatrical career the fact that he has been a perpetual understudy.

Where Jeanson sat in on Jouvet's classes to develop the script for *Entrée des artistes*, Spaak was no less attentive to Jouvet's personality and biography in developing that of *La Fin du jour*. Central to the story is the sequence in which Saint-Clair steals the affections of the young waitress, Jeannette, as he had stolen the affections of Marny's wife. Deserted by Saint-Clair, Jeannette contemplates suicide and is encouraged in this by Saint-Clair himself who sees it as a useful contribution to his reputation as a Don Juan. This would have seemed a nice touch to the contemporary audience, aware that Madeleine Ozeray, who plays Jeannette, although twenty-four years younger than Jouvet, had been his partner for the last twelve years. Indeed, Jeannette's failed suicide recalls an incident the previous year when, to Ozeray's disgust, Jouvet had a brief liaison with one of his young acting students, who, abandoned by Jouvet, had attempted suicide. Gossip aside, however, this representation of the theatrical life is far from the romantic myth of Art that Jouvet was allowed to perpetuate in *Entrée des artistes*. Certainly the myth is voiced here—"la vie, quel théâtre" (life, what a spectacle)—but only to be undercut by the egotism inherent in it. Saint-Clair, confronted with the excessive egotism of which he has been guilty in pushing Jeannette to attempt suicide, is unable to cope. His eyes glaze over, and he will be confined to a home for the bewildered. Cabrissade is scarcely better. Childish, preferring an invented past to his real lack of professional success, he too is forced to confront his inadequacy, which leads to his death. Marny, if glumly noble, is no less self-obsessed, unable to accept the fact that his wife found him inadequate and committed suicide when rejected by Saint-Clair.

163. Marion, ed., *Le Cinéma par ceux qui le font*, 109.

As J.-P. Jeancolas says, the film "tramples underfoot the romantic myth. . . . The characters destroy one another with a malice constructed patiently out of all the bitterness, humiliation and vileness of their drab careers."[164] Michel Simon felt that Duvivier had been, if anything, too kind to the characters, managing to render them sympathetic when everything about them was odious. In their history of the cinema, René Jeanne and Charles Ford describe the film as "a bitter, painful and melancholy tableau of the life led [by actors] deprived of the spotlight. Memories, jealousy, petty squabbles, every pathetic form of baseness . . . permitted Louis Jouvet, Michel Simon, Victor Francen and Gabrielle Dorziat to show what great actors they are."[165] Indeed, Spaak's script, though decidedly cynical about the myth of theatrical transcendence, depended on great actors to dismantle it. This ambivalence is nicely captured in the final scene when Marny is called on to read the eulogy over Cabrissade's grave. Typically, it has been written by Cabrissade himself, but half way through it, Marny is permitted the all too conventional gesture of tearing it up and speaking "from the heart, simply and sincerely," about Cabrissade as "un brave homme." This is at once very moving and hopelessly inappropriate, given what we have witnessed.

Duvivier had a great affection for technique as the mark of a truly cinematic work. Competent artisan, as everyone acknowledged, he was never just an "invisible hand" behind his films. He enjoyed assembling a talented team and pushing them to extremes. This sometimes resulted in the excesses of a Gothicism bordering on expressionism, as in *Le Golem, Golgotha*, or his final prewar film, *La Charrette fantôme*. It always, however, provided material of visual and aural interest related to the central theme of his films. Here the soundtrack is repeatedly foregrounded, not just through diegetic piano and song but especially through extra-diegetic effects and Maurice Jaubert's martial music during the revolt of the rest-home inmates. Visually, that same scene is notable for its furtive candlelit assembly, but throughout the film, the sets are dramatically lit in the careful style developed in quality French films from 1936 to 1939. Christian Matras, Duvivier's cinematographer, had been trained by Curt Courant in the expressionist traditions that fed directly, if less extravagantly, into poetic realism. As I have written elsewhere, "Whilst a few French cinematographers concentrated on the stark contrasts of expressionism, most proclaim an aesthetic that marries this expressionist pooling and shafting of light with the molding effects of panchromatic film to produce a representation of reality which, though monochrome, has a

164. Jeancolas, *15 ans d'années trente*, 274–275.
165. Jeanne and Ford, *Histoire encyclopédique du cinéma*, 4:75.

wealth of those clues to distance and the relationship between people and objects which we obtain in real life."[166] One aspect of cinematography that can still surprise, however, is the aggressively assertive focus pull that forcibly shifts our attention from one character to another, thereby foregrounding technique arguably to the detriment of narrative credibility.

La Fin du jour was awarded the Coupe de la Biennale de Venice in 1939. After eleven weeks in the prestigious Madeleine cinema, it had just received the benediction of a week in the vast (3,500-seat) Rex when war broke out. Subsequently it ran through March 1940 and was revived several times during the war.

94. *Le Jour se lève*

Daybreak; remade as *The Long Night* (1947)
France, 1939, 93 min, b&w

Dir Marcel Carné; *Asst dir* Pierre Blondy and Jean Fazy; *Prod* Sigma; *Scr* Jacques Viot and Jacques Prévert; *Cinematog* Curt Courant; *Music* Maurice Jaubert; *Art dir* Alexandre Trauner; *Sound* Armand Petitjean; *Edit* René Le Hénaff; *Act* Jean Gabin (François), Jules Berry (Monsieur Valentin), Jacqueline Laurent (Françoise), Arletty (Clara), Mady Berry (concierge), Arthur Devère (Gerbois), Bernard Blier (Gaston), René Génin (concierge), and Marcel Pérès (Paulo).

No doubt it was the structure of the narrative that appealed to Marcel Carné when his neighbor Jacques Viot proposed it—contained between two gunshots, the tale moves from a murder to a suicide. Told mainly in flashback, it consists of two parallel stories, the past one leading up to the crime, the present one to the suicide. Contrasting technical practices characterize the stories very differently, as a hopeful past leading to a nightmarish present. The film concludes with the protagonist's death at dawn, so the apparent innocence of the title (which, perhaps coincidentally, picks up on the hopeful final fragment of dialogue in Carné's previous film) is in fact heavily ironic.

Most commentators, both then and now, underline the class elements. This was the culmination of Jean Gabin's prewar mythic persona as a no-nonsense man of the people, set apart because, "hounded by a malevolent destiny; his stoic and solitary endurance of it, the glimpse of a possible salvation in the form of a woman, the disillusion caused by her impurity/betrayal, the outburst of anger which places him in thrall to a fatality he thought he had outdistanced (as per-

---

166. Crisp, *Classic French Cinema*, 381.

sonified by the cops, the law) and his final submission to that destiny."[167] Critics discussing this myth usually see Gabin's persona not as a criminal but as a victim of brutalizing social forces beyond his control. *Le Jour se lève* in particular is (as in *Métropolitain*, #92) one of the few 1930s films where we witness the protagonist at his daily work. Here François is a sand-blaster—a debilitating job requiring weird science-fiction suiting to survive unscathed—and it is hard to avoid mention of industrial alienation and class conflict, with François seen as "a worker who gets his revenge on a society founded on lies. . . . A social tragedy," says Francis Courtade, "a drama of alienation, a working-class film of the highest order, the strongest and best-made film the Popular Front ever inspired . . . reflecting the hopes and anguish of a class betrayed, beaten, and finally destroyed."[168] Reviewing it on its release, Georges Altman saw it as "one of the rare films to depict the human condition—factories, workers, poverty. . . . The prison-house of labor, life without feeling, lost love, leaden clouds, the stifling air of the city, a certain contemporary anguish."[169]

For such critics who see the film as capturing that mounting wave of death, alienation, solitude, despair, exile, and suicide that signaled the end of all hopes placed in the Popular Front and a premonition of the disastrous war to come, *Le Crime de Monsieur Lange* (#46) provides a useful contrast. Likewise based on a flashback leading up to a murder, which is likewise the murder of a sly treacherous character played by Jules Berry and likewise scripted by Jacques Prévert, it ends by contrast with the liberation of the workers and a successful flight to freedom by the assassin, absolved of all guilt by an impromptu jury. The two films are justifiably seen as marking the rise and fall of Popular Front idealism.[170]

Noël Burch and Geneviève Sellier have a quite different approach to this film: while not denying any of these social concerns, they shift the focus from class (after all, the notion of class conflict is diminished because the exploiting class is invisible, unless one includes Valentin and the nasty comments from the petty bourgeois crowd[171]) to gender relations, seeing the film as the archetypal instance of the Incestuous Father and the Oedipal rivalry between father and son.[172]

---

167. André Bazin, 1947, quoted in Chevallier and Egly, eds., *Regards neufs sur le cinéma*, 162.

168. Courtade, *Les Malédictions du cinéma français*, 166–167.

169. In *La Lumière*, 16 June 1939, quoted in Abel, *French Film Theory and Criticism*, 2:266–269.

170. Most clearly by Jeancolas, *15 ans d'années trente*, 276–277.

171. Prédal, *La Société française à travers le cinéma*, 217–219.

172. Burch and Sellier, *La Drôle de guerre des sexes*, 68–73.

In this reading, Jules Berry embodies the Evil Father—unworthy, autocratic, and libidinous—with patriarchal claim to exclusive possession of the young female. Françoise's previous lover, Valentin at one point actually convinces François of his claim to be the girl's father. One of the many useful points made by Burch and Sellier is that François, in attempting to wrest Françoise from her "evil father," is not proposing an alternative set of values to his but is rather assuming them in his own right. From his point of view (and the film constantly underlines his subjectivity with bars of light and visors isolating his eyes), women are seen in simplistic terms as dual—there are those one sleeps with (Clara) and the virginal flower-women that one can idolize (Françoise, whom he first sees in the sand-blasting factory carrying a bouquet of flowers, which spontaneously wither in the industrial atmosphere).

The other useful point they make is that the film itself offers an alternative view of both these women, complicating the men's simplistic, patriarchal opposition, in which Clara is *also* a calmly independent, generous, and mature woman worthy of love, and Françoise's "flower-like" innocence is illusory—she has been Valentin's mistress and is *also* a sensual creature not unwilling to sleep with François. In this view, the tragedy arises largely from his patriarchally conditioned refusal to recognize either Clara's virtues or the possibility of happiness with a nonvirginal Françoise. So his murder of Valentin becomes an (unsuccessful) attempt to silence the Voice of the Father in himself, and the wilting flowers acquire a more complex metaphorical significance, not just as an industrial statement but pointing to Françoise's prior deflowering and perhaps even to the broader social catastrophes triggered by his patriarchal attitudes.

Again, in addition to these class and gender readings, any global reading of the film must acknowledge that it is no accident the young protagonists are named François and Françoise nor is it an accident that they are both orphans. Not belonging—alienation—is an inherent element of the national condition of the age. (Carné, accused of making films that were too depressing, with love affairs that were doomed, protested that his lovers always experienced at least a moment of happiness, and "un moment de bonheur, c'est déjà beaucoup.") Finally, a full analysis must pay due attention to the ways in which various technical practices—the music by that great French film-musician Maurice Jaubert, who had worked with René Clair, Jean Vigo, and Duvivier, and who was to lose his life the following year in the invasion; the sets by Alexandre Trauner, whose account of his work is an invaluable guide to the ideology behind poetic realism;[173] and the editing, which marks a point of departure in Carné's

173. Trauner, *Décors de cinéma.*

films from that very poetic realism in the direction of a more psychological realism—conspire to support and complicate the rich texture of ideas outlined above.

The release of *Le Jour se lève* was unfortunately timed, being interrupted after thirteen weeks by the declaration of war, the temporary closure of all cinemas, and subsequent audience restrictions. Moreover, condemned by the Catholic Church for pessimism, despair, and lack of faith, declared "an abortion" by its original conceiver Viot, it was banned as undesirable during the phony war—a ban later confirmed by the Vichy government for the Zone Libre. The German authorities were happy, however, to allow its release in the Zone Occupé, which included Paris, where it was a great success, still in release late in 1942. Oddly enough, Maurice Bardèche, in the postwar re-edition of his and Robert Brasillach's *Histoire du cinéma*, was permitted to remark that Carné's talent was undeniable but "remained, in these small-minded years, too long associated with a sort of Jewish esthetics which even the most indulgent were beginning to find wanting. Pimps, whores and their sordid affaires constituted a distinctly odd subject-matter for the French cinema of those years, analogous to that of the German cinema before 1933, and for the same reasons."[174] Hitler had put an end to all that nonsense, and not before time.

95. *La Règle du jeu*

The Rules of the Game
France, 1939, 113 min (reduced to 85 min, then reconstructed in 1965 to current length of 105 min), b&w

Dir Jean Renoir; *Asst dir* André Zwobada and Henri Cartier-Bresson; *Scr* Renoir with Carl Koch; *Prod* NEF; *Cinematog* Jean Bachelet; *Music* Roger Desormières and Joseph Kosma; *Art dir* Eugène Lourié and Max Douy; *Sound* Joseph de Bretagne; *Edit* Marguerite Houllé-Renoir and Marthe Huguet; *Act* Nora Gregor (Christine, Marquise de la Chesnay), Marcel Dalio (Marquis de la Chesnay), Roland Toutain (Jurieu), Jean Renoir (Octave), Gaston Modot (Schumacher), Julien Carette (Marceau), Mila Parély (Geneviève de Marrast), Odette Talazac (Charlotte), Paulette Dubost (Lisette), Pierre Magnier, Pierre Nay, Richard Francœur, André Zwobada, and Henri Cartier-Bresson.

174. See Prédal, *La Société française à travers le cinéma*, 218–219, and *Avant-Scène Cinéma*, no. 53, November 1965.

This is one of the most nearly perfect films ever made. It is impossible to do justice to it in the available space. Unlike most of Jean Renoir's films, it was largely his own conception (and incidentally production), though he acknowledges being inspired by eighteenth- and nineteenth-century satirists such as Beaumarchais, Marivaux, and de Musset—especially the last's *Les Caprices de Marianne,* which provided the basic situation of a woman hesitating between several men, to the exclusion of the one man who really loves her and who dies when mistaken for one of the other suitors. It is also notably close to Yves Mirande's boulevard comedy *Sept hommes . . . une femme* (1936), which situates its action in a chateau owned by a widowed countess who tests the suitability of seven suitors representing different social and moral positions. A crucial montage hunting scene in that film leads to the widow being discovered in a half-embrace with one of her suitors, and ends with a round of boisterous bedtime rituals in a tiled corridor of the chateau. Both that film and Sacha Guitry's *Désiré* (1937, #68) establish a systematic pattern of parallel conversations and situations upstairs and downstairs, recognizably similar to this, while in *Désiré,* the cook's husband is a policeman who plays a role analogous to that here of Schumacher the gamekeeper.

Renoir's great achievement is to weld together this disparate material and to modulate from the original comedy of manners through the cold brutality of the hunt scene and the riotous farce of the consequent hunt *inside* the chateau to the tragedy of its "accidental" conclusion. It seems clear from contemporary reviews that it was at least partly this disjunction of tone and mood that disconcerted opening night audiences. Georges Sadoul and others reported whistles, boos, outbursts of rage, seats destroyed, and newspapers being set alight in the aisles. Probably emanating from a right-wing cabal, these disruptions resulted in multiple cuts to the film.[175] Renoir himself attributed the reaction to an audience accustomed to romantic narratives being confronted with a classical, distanced style. All commentators exaggerate the extent of the film's failure, however, in the interests of artistic myth-making. The film had, after all, just completed a moderately successful first-release run when the declaration of war cut short that exclusive release. It was bidding fair to exceed the annual average box-office return, and was due to be screened in the Rex, the Gaumont Palace, 157 suburban cinemas, and 52 provincial towns. Nevertheless, there is little doubt that it would have fallen far short of the phenomenal success of his two recent triumphs, *La Grande Illusion* (#60) and *La Bête humaine* (#91).

175. See, for this and many other reasons, Curchod and Faulkner's account of the evolution of the text in *La Règle du jeu,* ed. O. Curchod and C. Faulkner (Paris: Nathan, 1999), esp. 19–20.

Another possible source of initial disaffection is the lack of any name actor in the cast—no Jean Gabin, but Marcel Dalio, Roland Toutain, Julien Carette, Gaston Modot, and Paulette Dubost, who were accustomed to playing secondary roles, and Nora Gregor, an unknown in France, having appeared only in German-language films. Exacerbating this lack of focus is the lack of a central character with whom the spectator could identify. This absence was, however, probably deliberate, since Renoir's aim was the analysis of a group, a class, a whole society, rather than a personalized "adventure." As he often repeated, the failure of the Popular Front and the imminent war were sufficiently unsettling to inspire him to target the national and international bourgeoisie whom he considered responsible. Sadoul, speaking as always as a communist, saw *La Règle du jeu* as a continuation of Renoir's socialist class analysis, doing for the approaching war what Beaumarchais's *Mariage de Figaro* had done for the French Revolution—namely portray a refined civilization blindly unaware of its decadence, a civilization that, as de Boïeldieu and von Rauffenstein had already foreshadowed, was doomed to extinction.

Much of the delight in viewing and reviewing the film is in coming to appreciate the way a relatively small number of simple metaphors are mobilized to construct a complex satire of that society. The rules of the social game are maintained by "gamekeepers" such as Schumacher, whose job is to keep animality in check. Poachers are outsiders who do not know or who refuse to recognize these rules. The tragedy of the film is generated by an ill-advised intrusion by poachers above and below stairs (Jurieu and Marceau) into a society of which they ignore the conventions and traditions. The gamekeepers (the marquis and Schumacher) are likened in the extreme to "machine men" who regulate the routine functioning of society, by force if necessary. The marquis's delight in his collection of mechanical people is as appropriate as his confused pride and self-consciousness at his latest acquisition, a mechanical organ. That the consequent hunting(s) of the poachers/animals by the gamekeepers/mechanical men leads to the killing of Jurieu rather than Marceau is only superficially therefore an accident.

Yet this already powerful system of metaphors becomes more complex even as it is being elaborated. If the two poachers are not averse to a little animality, neither is the marquis, who is conducting an affair with Geneviève. If the same two poachers are prime examples of outsiders, their "not belonging" is shared to some extent by everyone in the cast: Christine herself is an Austrian, as is Schumacher, out of place in French society; and Christine's dalliance with Saint-Aubin, Jurieu, and Octave links her with the poachers. The casting of Dalio, a Jew, more normally allotted the role of sleazy half-cast, as the Marquis de la Chesnaye, arbiter of French traditions, was a masterstroke. Defended by his cook as the representative of authentic taste, he needs to be defended precisely because of the cultural baggage of outsiderness that he brings with him, and of which others are not slow to remind us. Hence his recognition of what might seem an improbable compatibility between the marquis and Marceau the poacher. When Christine looks through field glasses to see a squirrel, she sees instead her husband.

Renoir updates and personalizes all this material by having the intruder be an aviator, just as he himself had been in World War I, when as a nonaristocrat he joined the aristocratic cavalry. He further personalizes it, of course, by casting himself as Octave, point of contact between outsiders and insiders, upstairs and down, prey to all the divisions embodied in these metaphors: an artist and dreamer who struggles to divest himself of his animal-skin, and who emerges onto the balcony at the height of the chaotic festivities to conduct an imaginary orchestra—this film—only to let his hands drop in despair. Friend, confidant, and finally suitor to Christine, he also dallies with Lisette—an Eve, crunching her innumerable apples. Renoir/Octave is a sensualist (like his father), and this film can be seen as a transitional film between the class-obsessed films he had been making for the last five years and the pantheistic, woman-obsessed films he was to make after the war.

As well as being the most formally exquisite film he ever made, *La Règle du jeu* is technically impressive: the montage hunt has always been widely admired, but despite that flurry of brief shots, the film's average shot length is a slow 18.4 seconds because of the numerous long takes elsewhere. Making the case for a metaphysical realism, André Bazin singled out this film in particular for the way in which extreme depth of field allows Renoir to film a number of different nodes of action at varying distances from the camera, all in focus. Renoir himself notes the delight that he and Dalio took in one such scene, where their antics behind the foreground action totally undercut the difficult explanations that Christine is trying to give of her relationship with Jurieu. He and Jean Bachelet, the director of photography, had ordered special fast lenses which still allowed great depth of field so that they could keep their backgrounds in focus all the time. It is for feats such as this that Bazin singled Renoir out as the great realist filmmaker of the prewar period, predecessor of Orson Welles and William Wyler through his attempts to capture the intricate ambiguities and complexities of existence, while for this film's outspoken attack on contemporary social structures, Jacques-Bernard Brunius identified it as the true heir of Luis Buñuel's *L'Âge d'or*.[176]

176. Brunius, *En marge du cinéma français*, 176–177.

96. Circonstances atténuantes

(*Mitigating Circumstances*)
France, 1939, 87 min, b&w

Dir Jean Boyer; *Asst dir* Christian Chamborant; *Prod* Société Française de Production et d'Édition; *Scr* Boyer, Yves Mirande, and Jean-Pierre Feydeau, from the novel *À l'héritage, ou Les Vacances singulières* by Marcel Arnac; *Cinematog* Victor Armenise; *Music* Georges van Parys; *Art dir* Jacques Colombier; *Sound* Antoine Archaimbaud; *Edit* Maurice Serein; *Act* Michel Simon (Monsieur le Sentencier), Arletty (Marie Qu'a d'Ça), Marie José (Madame Cinq de Canne), Liliane Lesaffre (Madame Bouic), Suzanne Dantès (Madame le Sentencier), Mila Parély, Dorville (Le Bouic), Andrex (Môme de Dieu), Robert Ozanne (Cinq de Canne), Georges Lannes (Coup de Châsse), Michel François, Émile Saint-Ober, and Robert Arnoux.

Also *Fric-Frac*
Break and Enter
France, 1939, 100 min, b&w

Dir Claude Autant-Lara; *Scr* Michel Duran, from the play by Édouard Bourdet and Fernand Trignol; *Prod* Maurice Lehmann; *Act* Arletty, Michel Simon, and Fernandel.

Circonstances atténuantes and *Fric-Frac* can be discussed together for various reasons: they were the two outstanding comic successes of the final prewar season, and both were adapted from successful literary works, while Michel Simon and Arletty are central to the cast of each. Moreover, both involve an encounter between "respectable" bourgeois figures and the underworld, which results in mildly satirical representations of the middle classes and of the legal system that privileges them. This satirical attitude toward the middle classes had, as we have seen, a solid tradition, both in the cinema and elsewhere, which the Great Depression had only served to confirm. *Boudu* (1932, #20) is an instance of it, as is *Dédé* (1934), in which a lawyer becomes humanized by contact with shop-girls and criminals, while the respectable businessman's wife fantasizes about an affair with Dédé and ends up doing an erotic Arabian dance to escape arrest.

In *Circonstances atténuantes,* it is that old narrative ploy, his car breaking down, that brings a notoriously rigorous judge, appropriately named Monsieur le Sentencier (but improbably played by Michel Simon) into uncomfortably close contact with a working-class community and its inevitable criminal activities, which center on the Bons Vivants bar. At first revolted, the judge soon begins to loosen up and to appreciate the simple joys of working-class humanity (notably as represented by Arletty). His wife finds analogous reasons to enjoy the encounter. The judge's knowledge of the law earns him a reputation with the amiable gang, and he finds himself appointed its leader, in which position he derives considerable satisfaction from infringing those legal regulations that he had previously worked to uphold. Admittedly, he cheats a little, organizing robberies involving his own petty cash, a motorbike that he has surreptitiously paid for, and the tacky furniture from his own home that he has always hated, but it is all in the interest of maintaining his reputation as a master criminal with his new mates in the gang.

In a somewhat similar way, *Fric-Frac* develops an encounter between the moral rectitude of middle-class convention and the working class in its criminal guise when a jeweler's assistant, destined for a life of stultifying rectitude in his employer's workshop and his employer's daughter's bed, accidentally discovers the warmth, affection, humanity, humor, and community of the working class (again in the form of Arletty, but with Michel Simon now more at home as one of the marginals). When he is caught up and caught out in their less than legal activities, his new-found friends stick by him. They may be thieves, but many respectable people would not have done as much, he notes. The message of both films is that respectability is a facade: they are all thieves, but the working-class gang doesn't try to hide it. They are open and honest about it rather than hypocritical. If the jeweler's assistant emerges from the "underworld" at the end to marry the jeweler's daughter after all, it is with a totally different slant on the world, not least because she too (like Monsieur le Sentencier's wife) has experienced the vivifying effects of the marginal.

It was normal, then, for the revitalization of the middle classes to involve at least a metaphorical experience of criminality, and for the agent to be a worker, a marginal, or a social outcast. In all such films, there is a tendency to regard working-class criminality as incidental—little more than a metaphor for their marginalized status—but these films can also be seen as a soft/comic version of the propaganda, insistently present in the late 1930s, in favor of a more humane social justice system that would take into account the social background and upbringing of the "criminals." As the judge says to his wife,

> "Ah, *the people*—we don't really understand them."
> "That didn't stop you from passing judgment on them. In your time you've passed judgment on a goodly number of them without understanding them."
> "Indeed, if we understood people better we'd create a more humane justice system."
> "I can't believe I'm hearing the word 'humane' in your mouth!"

Of course, this campaign to humanize the justice system had been treated much more seriously in such dramas as *Prisons de femmes* and *Prison sans barreaux* (#74).

In both of the present films, the working-class/criminal milieu is characterized primarily by its manner of speech, and notably by its slang. This is particularly true of *Fric-Frac*, the argotic (slang-based) play for which even French theatrical audiences had been provided with a lexicon when it triumphed in 1936. Slang serves to authenticate the milieu as lacking in pretentiousness, yet full of vitality and creativity—a milieu into which the stuffy bourgeois need to be plunged if they are to experience rehumanization. But in *Circonstances atténuantes*, the reverse also happens—perhaps to disarm moral censors, the amiable criminals are rather unconvincingly converted by the judge's final homily to a more moral way of life, and last seen engaged in depressingly honorable activities, to which the film tries to give a positive spin by surrounding them with jocularly eccentric forms of punctuation.

The productivity of comic actors in these tense prewar years is impressive: Michel Simon starred in both these films and appeared in another sixteen (not all comedies) from 1937 to 1939, while Fernandel, who in the film version of *Fric-Frac* replaced the actor Victor Boucher as the jeweler's assistant, appeared in fifteen films in the same period, thirteen of them comedies. One explanation is that many of these were based on plays that could be filmed often with minimal adaptation (critics were severe on *Fric-Frac* and others for this), and even *Circonstances atténuantes*, based on a novel, was allocated only twelve days for filming.

97. Sans lendemain

(*No Tomorrow*)
France, 1939, 82 min, b&w

Dir Max Ophüls; *Asst dir* Henri Aisner; *Scr* Hans Wilhelm, André-Paul Antoine, and Hans Jacobi; *Prod* Ciné-Alliance and Inter-Artistes Films (Grégor Rabinovitch and Oscar Dancigers); *Music* Allan Gray; *Art dir* Eugène Lourié; *Cinematog* Eugen Schüfftan; *Sound* Pierre Calvet; *Edit* Bernard Séjourné and Jean Sacha; *Act* Edwige Feuillère (Babs/Evelyne Morin), Michel François (Pierre, her son), Georges Rigaud (Dr. Georges Brandon), Paul Azaïs (Henri), Daniel Lecourtois (Armand), Georges Lannes (Paul Mazuraud), Gabriello (Mario, owner of La Sirène), Pauline Carton (maid), and Jeanne Marken and Mady Berry (concierges).

Max Ophüls was the ultimate cosmopolitan director, making films in his native Germany, then in Italy, Holland (in English), and later the United States. But in 1919, when the League of Nations assumed control of the Sarre and offered its citizens a choice, he had opted for French citizenship, and though he normally spoke German, his output is essentially French. Most critics focus on *Liebelei* (1933), remade in French as *Une histoire d'amour,* and on his four astonishing postwar films, *La Ronde, Le Plaisir, Madame de . . .* and *Lola Montès,* barely mentioning what came between. But *Liebelei* flopped badly in its French version (as indeed did all of his 1930s French-language films except the last two) and is basically a banal costume drama concerning an officer who is a bit of a lad with the girls, and who is called to account just when he has found his true love. Like the bulk of Ophüls's films, it is set in the Vienna of the Austro-Hungarian Empire.

Only two of his films from this decade are worth saving, a fantasy called *La Tendre Ennemie* (1935) in which the ghosts of three men involved in a girl's past offer a delightfully distanced commentary on and intervention in her current sentimental affairs, and the present film, *Sans lendemain,* about an upright woman fallen on hard times who becomes a good-time girl to feed her son. A past love reappears, and she has to conceal the facts of her sordid present life just as before she had had to conceal from him the facts of her previous unhappy life. The tenor of most of Ophüls's films is this sense of regret for what was and melancholy at what might have been. Edwige Feuillère, who here plays the lead, spoke of "that perfume of gentle despair that emanates from this melancholy material," and Pierre Leprohon notes the general sense of the end of an affair, the end of an era, the end of an empire.[177] Both of these films share a focus on women, and Paul Willemen has noted how Ophüls always managed to pull his narratives in that direction, even if the original material had to be rather violently refashioned to achieve it.[178]

Sans lendemain was commissioned by the same firm that had just triumphed with *Quai des brumes* (#78), and it is possible they saw this subject as a fitting sequel. It is certainly as near as Ophüls ever came to making a poetic realist film. His own account of it tends to underline this:

> *Sans lendemain* was born of my impressions of Paris—sensations and events experienced during numerous nights amongst people of a sort sure to shock bourgeois sensibilities—scenes which in all countries have been suppressed by the censors. I have never seen a single uncensored copy of this film. I was always attracted precisely to what I was not allowed to show, always fascinated by pimps and

177. Leprohon, *Présences contemporaines,* 165–168.
178. Willemin, ed., *Max Ophüls,* 70.

prostitutes, that universe where so many unknown soldiers have fallen in love's battles, and which constitutes the shameful but all too real underpinning of bourgeois morality. I often dreamed of making a film about that milieu, to a script by a modern Maupassant. Here and there in *Sans lendemain* some trace of this dream can be glimpsed—at least I hope so.[179]

The similarity in tone to *Quai des brumes* and poetic realism more generally is unmistakable—dockside squalor half concealed by drifting fog, a bleak world hastening to its end, and a resigned sort of fatalism. For Claude Beylie, these exquisitely constructed sets, often replicating real locations, were a French version of the German expressionism out of which poetic realism arose.[180] There is certainly a stark contrast between squalor and purity: the film insists on whiteness several times, notably when Evelyne escapes her drear environment for a sleigh-ride in the snow. This opposition is further underlined by the split persona of Babs/Evelyne, the respectable mother trapped in a prostitute's existence and now offered the prospect of regaining respectability. Yet as so often in the 1930s, the narrative implies that women are inherently duplicitous, at once Evelyne and Babs, mother and whore. Now a high-class tart, she re-meets her past love and has to struggle to construct a respectable present so as not to disillusion him. But we gradually come to understand that the reason she deserted him without explanation all those years ago was that even then she had a shady past—her husband was, as she had learned too late, a criminal and a brute—which she had striven to conceal from her love. The result is a psychodrama in which this (and by implication any) woman's life is revealed as a series of deceits, and any current facade of respectability is represented as merely the latest in a series of hastily contrived paperings-over of an association with criminality and illicit sexuality. Like all women, she is two-faced, and she has to pay for it with the loss of the man she loves, the loss of the son she adores, and ultimately the loss of her own life.

Although she treats *Sans lendemain* rather cursorily (as do most commentators on Ophüls's films), Susan White has oriented her study of Ophüls specifically around his female characters' self-presentation as erotic objects, and their consequent assignment as objects of exchange between men—a sad form of sexual economy in which they end up losing everything that matters to them.[181] But if Evelyne, like Kay in Georg-Wilhelm Pabst's *Drame de Shanghaï* (#85) before her,

179. Quoted in Beylie, *Max Ophüls*, 58–59.
180. Ibid., 58–62.
181. White, *The Cinema of Max Ophüls*, 54.

is beset by an inexorable fatality, she, again like Kay, manages to "save" her off-spring. There is no escape for the older generation, but the younger generation—here a son, there a daughter—can be fantasized as escaping to a better life in a better land, "over there" in Canada.

First screened in March 1940 during the phony war, the film's release was interrupted by the German invasion. When permission was granted for re-re-lease in March 1941 (surprisingly, given Ophüls's Jewishness and prudent flight to America), the film experienced another twenty-three weeks of exclusive re-lease and was still screening at year's end.

98. Menaces

(*Threats*); original title *Cinq jours d'angoisse* (*Five Days of Anguish*)
France, 1940, 88 min (now 77 min), b&w

Dir Edmond T. Gréville; *Asst dir* Robert Rips; *Prod* Société de Production Cinq Jours d'Angoisse; *Scr* Gréville with Curt Alexander and Pierre Lestringuez; *Cinematog* Otto Heller; *Music* Guy Lafarge and Maurice Bellecour; *Art dir* Jaquelux; *Sound* Tony Leenhardt; *Edit* Tennisen; *Act* Mireille Balin (Denise), Erich von Stroheim (Professor Hoffmann), Ginette Leclerc (Ginette), Jean Galland (Louis), Vanda Gréville (the American), Henri Bosc (Carbonero), John Loder (Dick Stone), Maurice Maillot (Mouret), and Madeleine Lambert (hotel owner).

This film is the best cinematic evidence that we have of the contemporary state of mind of France, or at least "a certain France," at the outbreak of war. As the initial title suggests, it seems to have been intended as a series of personal dramas interacting with the public drama of the Munich Crisis during five days of September 1938. The film's ending would thus have coincided with general relief at its apparently pacific resolution. It was set in a hotel (the Hôtel du Panthéon), which like so many hotels, schools, prisons, and apartment complexes of the 1930s cinema, was intended as a microcosm of French society. Right from the beginning, therefore, the film included elements of political documentary.

But just as it was nearing completion, the negative was destroyed in the notorious fire at the Saint Cloud studios, and Gréville set to work reshooting it. This time, however, the narrative was allowed to continue through the period of refilming (July–September 1939), with characters reacting from day to day to the lead-up to the declaration of war. Consequently, the film is littered with newspaper headlines and radio broadcasts chronicling Hitler's increasingly belligerent ambitions. This second version was to have ended with the invasion of Czechoslovakia and Poland. Indeed, it was in this form that it was first screened in January 1940.[182] It was at best modestly successful. In June of that year, when German armies invaded France and a German administration took over the French cinema, many films were banned or destroyed. *Menaces* was supposed to be one of the latter. As a (somewhat self-important) introductory title proclaims, the film was "banned and burnt by the German authorities, saved by a miracle and up-dated in 1944 following the Liberation of Paris." This updating involved significant additions and modifications to the final sequences, which now include a voiceover noting "the cruel anguish of the occupation years and the requisitioning of the film's hotel by the Germans," together with news of the Normandy invasion and documentary clips of General Leclerc's tanks arriving in Paris. At this point, the personal narratives are rounded off when some of the hotel's occupants are reunited, while the death of another (Doctor Hoffmann, played by Erich von Stroheim) is solemnly remembered at his graveside. The film now ends with the flags of all Allied nations superimposed over cheering crowds. Edmond Gréville subsequently had second thoughts about this (third) ending, and some copies have the second ending restored.

The film is therefore a fascinating political document, but inevitably somewhat chaotic in structure and tone. At different moments it was heading toward a relieved, or an anguished, or an exhilarating ending. Documentary inserts of fighter planes, mobilization, and tanks heading for the front vie with pseudo-documentary and (often clumsily acted) fictional scenes, such that any sense of coherence and continuity is lost. The sole relic of traditional narrative structure (a French woman is longing for a visit from her English fiancé, but is moved by compassion to accompany an anguished man to his unit, so she misses her fiancé's visit with obvious consequences) rings disastrously false. But the Englishness of the fiancé is true to a theme that seems to have been present from the first: the need for international understanding and cooperation in the face of Nazi aggression. Gréville had himself lived in England from 1936 to 1938, and reiterated calls for the renewal of the World War I French-English alliance that had been voiced numerous times in these final prewar years, notably by Marcel L'Herbier in *Entente cordiale*. The Hôtel du Panthéon where much of the film takes place provides refuge for innumerable foreigners fleeing fascism—a Hungarian, a Czech, a Russian, a Dutchman, and an Austrian, not to mention an American played by Gréville's Slav wife—who form a community of outsiders. At one stage, they constitute an informal court to try a newcomer (a Spaniard—so much for Franco) who turns out to be a bully and a thief, and to preserve the reputation of immigrant peoples, he is promptly condemned and evicted from the community.

182. See Jeancolas, *15 ans d'années trente*, 167, 290–291, for details.

The film explicitly signals the community as bonded together in a cosmopolitan *family*, caring for one another's interests in the face of the mounting international crisis. Indeed, the diffuseness of the narrative structure is due not solely to repeated improvisations during filming but also to the focus on an interactive community where no one individual dominates. Nevertheless. it is true that Dr. Hoffmann (von Stroheim, who was himself, of course, just such a refugee) and Denise (Mireille Balin) are followed more insistently than other characters. Dr. Hoffmann's face is an image no spectator of the film is ever likely to forget: a veteran of World War I, he bears "the only decoration I ever received," a terrible scar which he customarily conceals with a half-mask that divides his face vertically into black and white halves. "Mine is the true face of mankind," he notes, "divided between life and death, between peace and war." Singled out early on for his humanity toward both man and beast, he is nevertheless fired from his hospital job as a foreigner three days before his French citizenship is due to take effect. Foreseeing the catastrophe about to befall this community, Paris, and the world as a whole, he resigns himself to death. His suicide note reads, "I cannot live in a world where freedom is doomed. Peace founded on promises is an illusion. If you would remain free, be strong."

If you have any investment in this period and place, see this film: it is one of the clumsiest films that is ever likely to move you to tears.

99. *Battement de cœur*

Remade as *Heartbeat* (1946)
France, 1940, 92 min, b&w

Dir Henri Decoin; *Asst dir* Fred Pasquali; *Prod* Ciné Alliance Grégor Rabinovitch; *Scr* Jean Willème and Max Colpet; *Cinematog* Robert le Febvre; *Music* Paul Misraki; *Art dir* Jean Perrier and Léon Barsacq; *Sound* William Sivel; *Edit* René le Hénaff; *Act* Danielle Darrieux (Arlette), Claude Dauphin (Pierre de Rougemont), André Luguet (the ambassador), Saturnin Fabre (Aristide), Jean Tissier (Roland), Julien Carette (Yves), Charles Dechamps (Baron Dvorak), and Junie Astor.

This is a well-made romantic comedy that has slipped from sight, but which was probably viewed by more spectators than any other French film of the decade. Certainly it would rank with *Le Roi des resquilleurs* (#5) and *La Grande Illusion* (#60), totaling over a million viewers in Paris alone. Its success was partly due to timing: it was released in February 1940 during the phony war, and ran until the invasion in June, then resumed its exclusive release in January 1941, which in turn lasted until October. In general release, it was screened in seventy-seven cinemas in Paris. These were, of course, grim times, and a lighthearted romp that revived memories of the Henri Decoin–Danielle Darrieux films of prewar days was well placed to succeed with the public. Indeed, it was still in exclusive release when their next film, *Premier Rendez-vous*—the last of their collaboration and the first produced by UFA's French production company, Continental—was released in August 1941.

The story exploits two contrasting locations—on the one hand, a school for thieves; on the other, high-class diplomatic circles. Darrieux plays Arlette, an orphaned and reluctant student in the former who "graduates" to a happily romantic marriage in the latter. The implicit class differences here pick up, though in the comic mode, on the usually more somber theme of impoverished and abandoned youngsters that was already apparent in earlier melodramas and social realist films (and indeed in the Decoin-Darrieux's *Abus de confiance*, 1938, #69), and that was to become a central preoccupation of wartime cinema. The school for thieves likewise picks up on earlier thematics involving a "natural" link between the working-class poor and criminality. Saturnin Fabre plays the eccentric and autocratic professor instructing his students in the art of picking pockets and of lying convincingly, while Arlette is forced to lodge there because, without parents, home, or papers, she has just run away from a corrective services establishment. The first professional exercise of her newly acquired skills is stealing a tie-pin from a wealthy man who turns out to be an ambassador; catching her at it, he employs her to steal a watch from a diplomat whom he suspects of conducting an affair with his wife, whose photo should be in the watch. Because Pierre, the diplomat, is played by Claude Dauphin, Arlette will inevitably fall in love with him and vice versa. The class difference in their background is constantly foregrounded as a problem, but is initially overcome by a Pygmalion-like process during which Arlette is coached to pretend to be a baron's niece, and the problem is definitively "solved" when the baron is prevailed upon to adopt her for real.

Like *Abus de confiance*, this film is evidence of Decoin's self-conscious effort to explore unconventional technical practices. Here it is the systematic refusal of punctuation that astonishes. Not even the major divisions of the narrative are distinguished by punctuation, which is only used for the titles and for the final images. Extra-diegetic music is also notable by its absence, except once where it reinforces a bit of fake piano playing and in two subjective moments when the soundtrack reminds Arlette of the ball where she danced the night away with Pierre. And as in *Abus de confiance*, there is a surprising moment of reflexivity when Arlette, having just stolen the tie-pin, watches a movie in which a thief is condemned to prison for theft. "Au suivant" (Who's next in the dock?), says the trial judge. This "Godardian" playfulness in Decoin's films has never been adequately recognized.

Battement de cœur was produced by Grégor Rabinovitch, a German Jew who had worked for UFA and had then effectively transferred to France his production activities. This moment, on the verge of war, is an appropriate point to expand on this matter. While German Jews were by no means the only refugees flowing through France in these years, ingrained French anti-Semitism was quick to characterize the large numbers entering the cinema as a problem that needed "solving." Those who had fled to France early in the decade had been greeted by the industry with suspicion, though their money was welcomed. Their dominance in the French cinema during the following seven years has already been noted. The film criticism of Lucien Rebatet, Maurice Bardèche, and Robert Brasillach has several times been cited in this filmography as evidence of right-wing anxiety about this dominance. Their paranoia about an insidious Jewish plot was no doubt exacerbated by the fact that the Popular Front president, Léon Blum, was also of Jewish extraction.

During the occupation, Vichy introduced anti-Semitic laws with unseemly rapidity, and except for a few fortunate and brave individuals, most Jews either went underground or left France as Nazi troops approached. The extent of the deprivation that this imposed on the French cinema can be measured from the statistics, not necessarily entirely reliable, provided both by those demanding the "cleansing" of the cinema and those bewailing its destitution. If Lucien Rebatet, writing under the pseudonym François Vinneuil, was the most notorious of these because he was also the most outspoken, Marcel L'Herbier's memoirs published thirty years later are almost as uncomfortable to read. Rebatet in *Les tribus du cinéma* notes that in five films of 1938 and 1939 that he analyzes, most of the personnel were Jewish—only ten out of sixty were Christian, and of those, only five were French. He lists 82 Jewish producers behind the 1938 output of 110 "so-called French films," compared to twelve "Frenchmen." Certainly Natan of Pathé-Natan was Jewish, as were Osso, Braunberger, Haïk, and the Hakim brothers, as well as Niebenzahl, Lucacevitch, and Rabinovitch. But Rebatet's lists do not stop at producers: probably exaggerating, he claims that 80 percent of all personnel in the cinema were Jewish, 10 percent were "émigrés without papers," and only 10 percent were "French."[183] The first of Vichy's Commissaires Généraux aux Questions Juives estimated that 85 percent of all film personnel were Jewish, and prided himself on having eliminated three thousand public servants and the same number from the media. François Garçon acknowledges that the wartime anti-Semitic legislation resulted in the banning of 46 percent of all directors who had filmed two or more films between 1936 and 1940, notably

183. Rebatet, *Les Juifs en France*, 4:64–65, but see also 40–41, 56–61, 86–87, 123–124.

Raymond Bernard, Pierre Chenal, René Pujol, Pierre Colombier, Kurt Bernhardt, Max Ophüls, Jean Epstein, and Henri Diamant-Berger, as well as Siodmak. This wholesale purging left an opportunity for new faces, and Claude Autant-Lara, one of those thus provided with an opening, estimated at 50 percent the loss of directors and 80 percent that of producers.

100. *Remorques*

Stormy Waters
France, 1941, 90 min, b&w

Dir Jean Grémillon; *Asst dir* Louis Daquin; *Prod* MAIC; *Scr* Charles Spaak, then André Cayatte and Roger Vercel, then Jacques Prévert, then Georges Gombot, from the novel by Roger Vercel; *Cinematog* Armand Thirard; *Music* Roland-Manuel; *Art dir* Alexandre Trauner; *Sound* Joseph de Bretagne; *Edit* Yvonne Martin; *Act* Jean Gabin (André Laurent), Michèle Morgan (Catherine), Madeleine Renaud (Yvonne Laurent), Fernand Ledoux (Kerlo), Charles Blavette (Gabriel Tanguy), Jean Marchat (captain of the Mirva), Marcel Duhamel (Poubennec), Jean Dasté (radio operator), Nane Germon (Renée Tanguy), Anne Laurens (Marie Poubennec), Henri Poupon (Dr. Maulette), Raymone, Sinoël, Alain Cuny, and Lucien Coëdel.

This is another film so rich that it cannot be done justice within the available space. For Noël Burch and Geneviève Sellier, it rivals *La Règle du jeu* (#95) as the great precursor of modern French cinema. It capitalized on Jean Gabin's developing screen persona, and on the Gabin–Michèle Morgan couple established the year before in *Quai des brumes* (#78). Indeed, in setting, in character and in atmosphere, it can be seen as a sort of sequel to that film, not least because Catherine (Morgan) who appears to Captain André Laurent (Gabin) out of a storm is mentioned as having met her husband, the vicious freighter captain, in Le Havre two years before, where she and Gabin parted company in *Quai des brumes*.

Gabin is once again that solid block of a man, unable to articulate his feelings, at home with men rather than with women, especially his crew with whom he shares a solidarity and commitment to their common work. As his crew say, "he is a [real] man"—upright, dependable, loyal, unswerving. At least, to this point. It will be the role of women to call into question this moral code, this version of masculinity. The principal drive of the narrative is to suggest that the world and human relationships are altogether more complex than André has ever imagined. During the first half of the film, he several times reprimands or abruptly corrects crew members who step out of line, notably in matters involving sexual irregularities. Once, however, he himself becomes "inexplicably" entangled with Catherine, willing to give up everything to leave with her, his attitude changes—he takes Tanguy, a crew member, aside and apologizes for his earlier reprimand, recognizing that judgments are never so clear-cut as he had formerly believed.

Morgan, playing Catherine, is here again the mysterious woman who emerges from storm and sea, fascinating, irresistible, apparently demanding nothing but irrevocably disrupting everything. Remarking on this figure when the film was released in 1941, and Morgan long since departed (like Gabin) for the United States, Roger Régent asked rhetorically, "Who could now replace in our cinematic mythology this unforgettable face, gaze and voice?"[184] From the first moments of the narrative, at the crewman's wedding, the inherent rivalry between sailor's wife and sea, between land-based marital link and maritime profession, is foregrounded. Catherine emerging from the sea embodies the fascination and mystery of the latter element of this opposition. The wife cannot compete, or, as the film puts it, she develops a "weakness of the heart" that will be the death of her. Catherine, distraught at the involuntary destruction she has caused by her very presence, leaves in the final storm as she arrived in the initial storm. The links between husband and wife have snapped, as did the towline between tugboat and freighter. Catherine and the sea are more potent than worldly bonds, as witness the Freudian loss of the just-married bridegroom's fingers in the storm.

This mass of suggestive images might seem a heavy metaphorical burden for the narrative to bear, but a particular delight of the film is the way they all arise "naturally" in the course of the tugboat crew's work. The same cannot be said for Catherine's "secret name" (Aimée), for the shattering of André's diploma by the storm, or for the starfish that André and Catherine gather during their idyll, and which she subsequently asks crewmen Kerlo to pass on to André in memory of her: these metaphors, however poetic, are clumsily foregrounded. Kerlo himself is an interesting figure. A philosophic crew-member and ingrained pessimist, grimly resigned to the way the world works, he has learned to distance himself from colleagues and work—he has "tried everything" (implicitly, to give meaning to life), and "there is nothing to be done." Spokesman for this absurd fatality that dogs their lives, he is an appropriate messenger to bear the grim news to André of the death of his wife. But interestingly, both of the principal female characters—wife and mistress—are as articulate as Kerlo about the fatal-

184. Régent, *Cinéma de France*, 36.

ity working itself out through their lives. Perhaps the most moving moments in the film are when Catherine, in mid-idyll, is nevertheless clearheaded enough to voice undesirable truths to André.

As Burch and Sellier note, a second major theme arising from the narrative is the excessive importance accorded to male friendship, solidarity, and work, and the barrier that this creates between the sexes within a patriarchal society: it has displaced and become a substitute for "the sacred."[185] Yet Jean Grémillon does justice to that poetic realist theme of work in his poetic yet quasi-documentary representation of the tugboat's operations, raising it moreover to a transcendental level by the ironically antidocumentary strategy of imposing on it a lyrical musical accompaniment. In the initial and final storm scenes, the working of the machinery, the shouts of the crew, and the blasts of the storm are accompanied not just by an orchestral score but by a choral incantation that ultimately emerges as a quasi-biblical chant. The soundtrack as a whole at these points has been likened to an oratorio, an "eolian symphony." For Pierre Leprohon, "By the use of these rarely employed techniques the film attains a magical, even supernatural character. Music is here the mysterious voice of the unknowable, the secret song of the soul of the protagonists and of the world. It expresses the tempest within their souls."[186] Expanding on this, Burch and Sellier note that for Georges Bataille the great founding principle of western civilization is the rigorous separation between, on the one hand, the realm of the sacred, which is gratuitous, and on the other, the profane and pragmatic, that of work. "This separation is a sort of ontological necessity, but feminist thought has long seen (it) as one of the mutilating effects of patriarchal society. . . . Roland Manuel's score 'contaminates' work by the intrusion of the sacred. . . . All Grémillon's subsequent films will explore this contradiction."[187]

There can be no doubt that *Remorques* forms an appropriate climax to the great tradition of prewar poetic realist films. But released during the occupation, when that great tradition (and not least its Jewish producers) were seen as bearing the blame for the collapse and defeat of France in 1940, it is a little surprising that the film should have been distributed at all, let alone by the German firm Tobis. Like most of Grémillon's films, it appealed to Paris intellectual circles more than the general public, and was not widely appreciated in the provinces.

185. See Burch and Sellier, *La Drôle de guerre des sexes*, 80–84.
186. Leprohon, *Présences contemporaines*, 145–146.
187. Burch and Sellier, *La Drôle de guerre des sexes*, 84.

101. *Macao, ou L'Enfer du jeu*

(*Macao, or The Gambling Hell*)
France, 1942, 93 min, b&w

Dir Jean Delannoy; *Prod* Demo Films; *Scr* Pierre-Gilles Weber and Roger Vitrac, from the novel by Maurice Dekobra; *Cinematog* Nicholas Hayer; *Music* Georges Auric; *Art dir* Serge Pimenoff; *Sound* Marcel Ormancey; *Edit* Maurice Menot; *Act* Erich von Stroheim (Hubert Krall), Mireille Balin (Mireille), Roland Toutain (Pierre Milley), Louise Carletti (Jasmine), Sessue Hayakawa (Ying Tchai), Henri Guisol (tour guide), Georges Lannes (captain), and Jim Gérald.

The principle reason for still watching *Macao* is that it is a well-told, enthralling tale analogous in several ways to Georg-Wilhelm Pabst's *Le Drame de Shanghaï* (#85).[188] There are certain major themes worthy of comment on the periphery (nation, race, gender), but the initial focus is on a generic narrative (orientalism, exoticism, adventure) typical of a Maurice Dekobra novel, acted out by competent actors (Erich von Stroheim, Mireille Balin), but here embodying unusually complex characters. Often treated dismissively by biographers of Jean Delannoy, *Macao* is notably better than the 1940s films that made his reputation (*Pontcarral*, *L'Éternel Retour*, and *La Symphonie pastorale*). The first screening of *Macao* was delayed for some years: completed too late to be released during the phony war, it could not be screened under the occupation because any film with von Stroheim was anathema to the Germans. Roger Régent recalled being favorably impressed by it at one of Delannoy's home screenings, but for public release, all sequences featuring von Stroheim had to be reshot with Pierre Renoir.[189] The result (called simply *L'Enfer du jeu*) was perhaps understandably judged by Régent to be uneven and incoherent, mutilated and disfigured by comparison with the original, which was reinstated at war's end and is the version now available.

The film relates several interconnected narratives: Krall (von Stroheim) is an arms merchant contracted to supply guns from Macao to Chinese armies in Canton, but funding problems constantly thwart the transaction. He saves a vagrant actress (Balin) from probable execution and takes her with him to Macao to buy arms from Ying Tchai (Sessue Hayakawa). Ying Tchai's daughter, Jasmine, is returning from finishing school, but on the boat has fallen in love with a French reporter, Pierre (Roland Toutain), who, as it happens, is preparing to

---

188. See Martin, *The Golden Age of French Cinema*, 75–77.
189. Régent, *Cinéma de France*, 102–104.

write on gaming and gun-running in Macao. Such coincidences connect the various strands of the narrative. For instance, Ying Tchai, unaware of his daughter's affections, has Pierre (who is winning tactlessly large sums in the casino) mugged and thrown in the harbor, where he is picked up fortuitously by Krall, whom it turns out he knows well. Ying Tchai is somewhat taken aback when Pierre reapppears on the arm of his daughter as his future son-in-law, and even more so when Pierre announces that he is determined to have the casino boss locked up, not realizing that Ying Tchai, his prospective father-in-law, is himself that casino boss. Jasmine is also somewhat disconcerted when she learns that her father is not the upright banker she imagined but rather a casino owner, gang boss, and racketeer. In a climactic military conflict, Krall's boat is destroyed, along with Krall and Mireille. Ying Tchai, believing his daughter also aboard, suicides in despair.

The warring factions/nations are not at all clearly established within the narrative, which contributes to the atmosphere of chaos and confusion that reigns at the beginning. A long steady tracking shot past war-torn streets and shanties being demolished by shells and bombs takes in a tattered poster advertising holidays in Japan and ends up on Mireille casually exhibiting her leg as she mends a stocking in the midst of the carnage. Another virtuoso tracking shot follows her past an execution squad as she is taken to the commanding officer, and contributes an improbable degree of credibility to the war scenes framing the main narrative. Far from being a simple adventure story, the narrative attracts a variety of other generic elements—romance, comedy, and eroticism. Toutain is here reprising his role as Rouletabille, the daredevil reporter from Marcel L'Herbier's early 1930s films, which figured prominently among at least twenty positive representations of reporters to occur in the course of the decade. Here, comic scenes include several involving Krall's bulky steward, or again the local tour guide who continues to tout his tours in the midst of the machine-gun fire. In particular, the chase scene (Pierre rightly blames the tour guide for ratting on him and therefore causing his watery adventure, and chases him through densely crowded streets where the guide conceals himself in novel ways) is brilliantly choreographed, and allows Toutain to demonstrate his trademark acrobatic skills. Again, there are genuinely moving moments as the relationship between Krall and Mireille develops, notably when he enjoys playing the proper gentleman who refuses to take advantage of Mireille in her distress, though she obviously expects and half hopes to be taken advantage of. Subsequently, they acknowledge their common outcast status as "soldiers of fortune," or rather of misfortune as it turns out. And von Stroheim's trademark eroticism comes into play as he enters Mireille's cabin in her absence and delicately fingers her various undergarments.

Indeed, one of the most important things to note about this film is the density that is attributes to characters who might be expected in such a generic narrative to constitute cardboard cutouts. Even Hayakawa playing his well-oiled Oriental despot is allowed considerable complexity. The moment when, a respectable banker, he opens what looks like his safe and walks through into the El Dorado next door, his gambling-den-cum-nightclub complete with adoring go-go dancers, then through another door to monitor the activities of his gang of racketeers who have Macao's social services tied up, not only recapitulates that favorite theme, "the dark side of capitalism," but is rather like witnessing a stroll through the different aspects of Ying Tchai's personality. And of course his despotic role is subsequently undermined by the progressive disintegration he undergoes under threat of his daughter's death. But all of the characters have past histories evoked, usually obliquely—Jasmine's parentage, Krall's mistresses, Mireille's career. Such references constitute a useful reminder in this, one of the last films made during the 1930s, that a transformation was taking place in France from a primarily social cinema to a primarily psychological cinema, from class and nation to individual, and that Delannoy was to be one of the principal agents of that transformation. This move, as I have outlined elsewhere, involved a more inward, intimate form of acting rather than the extrovert theatrical "emplois" (character types); more realistic sets rather than the poetically stylized designs of Lazare Meerson and Alexandre Trauner; and the adoption of psychological editing practices focusing on shot/reverse-shot interpersonal exchanges.[190] Cumulatively, these practices were to become the principle mechanisms of spectator identification within the diegesis. Psychological editing in particular, where successive shots correspond to successive glances, was to be four times more common in 1945 than it had been in 1935. Designed to generate, then answer, the spectator's questions concerning narrative causes and character motivation, it was a powerful means of integrating the viewer into the action, and thus incidentally of naturalizing the ideology of individualism.

190. See Crisp, *Classic French Cinema*, ch. 7.

Within France

Grand Prix du Cinéma Français (GPCF)

Awarded by the Société d'Encouragement à l'Art et à l'Industrie under the patronage of Louis Lumière. Effectively taken over by the state in 1937, it became known in 1939 as the Grand Prix National du Cinéma Français (GPNCF). By then some felt it had become a prize less about quality than virtue. Usually presented in January for films released in the preceding year, it was in 1939 (wisely) awarded in July. The changing terms of reference as to what constituted an eligible French film (e.g., "all collaborators must be French") often eliminated likely contenders (*Les Bas-Fonds, Mayerling, Jenny, Le Crime de Monsieur Lange*, etc.) and would retrospectively have eliminated *Maria Chapdelaine* and *La Kermesse héroïque*.[1]

1934   *Maria Chapdelaine* (Julien Duvivier), over *Itto* and *Zouzou*

1935   *La Kermesse héroïque* (Jacques Feyder)

1936   *L'Appel du silence* (Léon Poirier), after three rounds, over *Un amour de Beethoven, Les Hommes nouveaux, Hélène*, and *Courrier-Sud*

1937   *Légions d'honneur* (Maurice Gleize), in the first round, over *Ces dames aux chapeaux verts, J'accuse*, and *L'Affaire du courrier de Lyon*

1938   *Alerte en Méditerranée* (Léo Joannon), after two rounds, over *Entrée des artistes, Trois de St-Cyr, Fort-Dolorès*, and *Les Filles du Rhône*

1939   *Quai des brumes* (Marcel Carné), over *Feu de paille* and *La Fin du jour*, tied for second

In 1937, a special additional prize was awarded on the occasion of the Paris Exhibition. Called Le Prix de l'Exhibition, it went to *La Mort du cygne* (Jean Benoit-Lévy and Marie Epstein), with the jury's congratulations to *Abus de confiance* (Henri Decoin), *Les Hommes sans nom* (Jean Vallée), *Les Perles de la couronne* (Sacha Guitry), and *Gribouille* (Marc Allégret).

In 1939, another special award called the Grand Prix National du Film Documentaire was awarded to *Sommes-nous défendus?* (Jean Loubignac).

1. Most of the information in this section comes from *La Cinématographie française*, but see also Claude Aveline's article in Abel, *French Film Theory and Criticism*, 2:262–266.

Prix Louis Delluc

Awarded each December by young "independent" critics, as a reaction against the conformity of the official GPNCF, it was to be awarded to the best film "made in the true French spirit" (i.e., made in French but regardless of the nationality of cast and crew). The jury of twenty-three (or twenty-four) initially included Marcel Achard, Georges Altman, Maurice Bessy, Pierre Bost, Georges Charensol, Nino Frank, Paul Gilson, Henri Jeanson, and Roger Régent (but not François Vinneuil, who abstained because he saw its creation as a left-wing strategy)—all then under forty years of age.

1937   *Les Bas-Fonds* (Jean Renoir), in the first round (12 votes), over *Sous les yeux d'Occident, La Belle Équipe, Le Roman d'un tricheur, César, Jenny* (10 votes), and *Le Crime de Monsieur Lange.*

1938   *Le Puritain* (Jeff Musso)

1939   *Quai des brumes* (Marcel Carné), over *Les Disparus de Saint-Agil, La Femme du boulanger, La Bête humaine, Conflit, Hôtel du Nord,* and *Entrée des artistes*

In February 1939, a group of 150 cinéastes calling themselves L'Académie du Film designated a new range of awards, most of which did not outlast the war:

> Prix Méliès (for overall quality)
> > *La Bête humaine* (Jean Renoir) and *Quai des brumes* (Marcel Carné), tied
> Prix Jean Vigo (for a courageous work)
> > *Les Disparus de Saint-Agil* (Christian Jaque)
> Prix Janie Marèse (for best actress)
> > Arletty in *Hôtel du Nord*
> Prix Pierre Batcheff (for best actor, "a totally original performance")
> > Michel Simon in *Les Disparus de Saint-Agil*

Festival de Cannes

This festival was designed as a counterweight to the Venice Festival, to provide a "non-political" film festival grouping "the free world," as opposed to the "authoritarian" festival of Venice. After much hesitation, Cannes was chosen over Biarritz and other coastal resorts, and the festival was due to take place in September 1939. French entries due to be screened at it were *La Piste du nord, La Charrette fantôme, L'Homme du Niger,* and the documentary *La France est une empire.* The outbreak of war led to its being deferred until January 1940, then again until conditions allowed, which turned out to be September 1946.

1931   Marcel Vandal, producer

1932   Raymond Bernard, director

1935   Sacha Guitry, writer, director, and actor (mainly for his theatrical work)

1937   René Clair and Jean Renoir, directors

1938   Raimu and Maurice Chevalier (actors), Julien Duvivier and Léon Mathot (directors)

1939   Louis Lumière; also Gael Fain, head of the Crédit d'État, an economist who had written on the cinema, and Charles Bauche, a relatively little-known producer

Foreign Recognition

Venice Film Festival

The film element of the Venice Biennale began in 1932 as a small-scale event held in August, featuring twenty-nine films chosen informally. Confronted with its unexpected success, the organizers made it a regular event accompanying each Biennale. Despite its name, it was from 1934 an annual event.

1932   French entries: *Au nom de la loi*, *Azaïs*, *À nous la liberté*, *La Bande à Bouboule*, *David Golder*, *Hôtel des étudiants*, and *Un coup de téléphone*. Also the documentary *Le Chant de la mine et du fer*. No prizes were offered until 1935, but this year a vote was taken among spectators, and *À nous la liberté* was voted most amusing film of the festival.

1934   Four entries are mentioned: *Le Paquebot Tenacity, Jeunesse, Le Scandale*, and *Le Grand Jeu*. In July, these and five others were nominated. The others were *La Porteuse de pain*, *Bouboule 1er, roi nègre*, *La Croisière jaune*, *Amok*, and *L'Atalante*. No prizes were awarded.

1935   French entries: *Itto* (Best Colonial Film), *Crime et châtiment* (Coupe Volpi to Pierre Blanchar for his role as Raskolnikoff), *Maria Chapdelaine*, and *Un voyage imprévu* (honorable mentions); also *Marie des angoisses*. *Maria Chapdelaine* was not in competition for a prize because it had already won the GPCF; *Pension Mimosas*, *Les Nuits moscovites*, and *Remous* were excluded because their producers were not French nationals.

1936   French entries: *Anne-Marie*, *L'Appel du silence*, *Le Grand Refrain*, *Mayerling*, *La Tendre Ennemie*, and *Veille d'armes*. *Le Roman d'un tricheur* was subsequently added to this list. *La Kermesse héroïque*, eliminated by the French government as not fully French, was reinstated at the request of the jury, and *Le Grand Refrain* was dropped to make way for it. The Coupe Volpi went to Annabella for her role as Jeanne de Corlaix in *Veille d'armes*. The Coupe Alfieri went to Jacques Feyder for best director for *La Kermesse héroïque*. Also Lazare Meerson received Best Art Direction.

1937   French entries: *La Grande Illusion, Hélène, Les Perles de la couronne*, and *Un carnet de bal*; subsequently, *Le Messager* was added. Coupe Mussolini for best foreign film: *Un carnet de bal* (Duvivier). Coupe du jury international for best overall artistic production: *La Grande Illusion* (Renoir). Coupe de la Direction Générale de la Cinématographie for the best scenario: *Les Perles de la couronne* (Guitry).

1938   French entries: *Abus de confiance, L'Affaire Lafarge, Altitude 3200, L'Innocent, Le Joueur d'échecs, La Mort du cygne, Paix sur le Rhin, Quai des brumes*, and *Ramuntcho. Prison sans barreaux* was subsequently added, and both Raymond Chirat and Francis Courtade report that it won a prize in this year. *Quai des brumes*, which lost the prize for best film to *Lion de St. Marc*, was awarded a prize for the best *mise en scène*, while *Le Joueur d'échecs* received the International Jury Prize.

1939   French entries: *La Bête humaine, Derrière la façade, La Fin du jour, Le Grand Élan, Jeunes Filles en détresse*, and *Le Jour se lève*. War intervened, and no awards were announced, but reports suggest that *La Fin du jour* received exceptional applause.

United States

Reports in French film journals suggest that between 1930 and 1935, very few French films had any impact in the United States. Those few that are reported as attracting critical praise are *Sous les toits de Paris, À nous la liberté, Le Million*, and *La Maternelle*; while in a 1933 survey, *Poil de carotte* was pronounced best foreign film.

1935   The New York Film Daily referendum, seeking to find the ten top foreign films of the past year, identified five French films among them: *Crime et châtiment* (best foreign film), *La Maternelle, La Bandera, Maria Chapdelaine*, and *Le Dernier Milliardaire*.

1936   *La Kermesse héroïque* screened for fifteen weeks in New York, and was subsequently named best film of the year, defeating all U.S. films—the first time ever that a foreign film had been so named.

1937   The National Board of Review's list of the best foreign films listed *Les Bas-Fonds* (2), *Mayerling* (4), and *Golgotha* (6). In the New York list of ten best films of the year, *Mayerling* was the top foreign film. Also, the U.S. Academy of Arts and Sciences designated Charles Boyer as best actor but for his role in an American film (*Marie Walewska*). *Mayerling* and *La Bandera* experienced successful runs in New York.

1938   The National Board of Review's list of ten best foreign films included four French films—*La Grande Illusion* (best foreign film), *La Mort du cygne* (2), *Un carnet de bal* (3), and *La Guerre des gosses* (4; a 1936 production). *La Grande Illusion* screened for ten weeks and *Roman d'un tricheur* for nine.

1939   The National Board of Review designated *Quai des brumes* as joint best film of the year, together with *Confessions of a Nazi Spy*. In the same year, *Regain*, originally banned in the United States as immoral but subsequently released uncut, was awarded first prize by a jury of the American press, while *La Bandera* (again) and *Double Crime sur la Ligne Maginot* screened successfully in New York.

Another measure of success is the production of English-language remakes of French films. The following 1930s French films reputedly or certainly experienced such remakes within a year or two of release in France: *La Chienne* (1931); *Adémaï aviateur* (1934); *Les Yeux noirs* (1935); *Pépé le Moko* (1936, remade in 1938 as *Algiers*); *Prison sans barreaux, Carrefour,* and *Café de Paris* (1938); *La Bataille silencieuse* and *Alerte en Méditerranée* (1938, remade in 1939); and *J'étais une aventurière* (1939, remade in 1940).

Elsewhere

In 1936, *La Kermesse héroïque* was voted Grand Prix du Cinéma International in Japan. In May 1937, four French films were voted by Japanese viewers into the list of the top ten foreign films of the year—*Pension Mimosas* (2), *Maria Chapdelaine* (4), *La Bandera* (5), and *Crime et châtiment* (6). In 1938, Sweden designated five French films among the top ten: *Le Roman d'un tricheur, Les Perles de la couronne, Les Bas-Fonds, La Grande Illusion,* and *Prison sans barreaux*. *Le Bonheur* received an honorable mention at the Moscow Film Festival.

Books

Abel, R. *French Cinema: The First Wave, 1915–1929*. Princeton, N.J.: Princeton University Press, 1984.

———. *French Film Theory and Criticism: A History-Anthology 1909–1939*. 2 vols. Princeton, N.J.: Princeton University Press, 1988.

Agel, H. *Jean Grémillon*. Paris: Seghers, 1969.

Agel, H., and G. Agel. *Précis d'initiation au cinéma*. Paris: L'École, 1957.

Agel, H., et al. *Sept and de cinéma français*. Paris: Éditions du Cerf, 1953.

Altman, G. *Ça c'est du cinéma*. Paris: Les Revues, 1931.

Amengual, B. *Les Français et leur cinéma 1930–1939*. Créteil, France: Losfeld, 1973.

———. *Georg-Wilhelm Pabst*. Paris: Seghers, 1966.

———. *René Clair*. Paris: Seghers, 1963.

Andrew, J. D. *Mists of Regret: Culture and Sensibility in Classic French Cinema*. Princeton, N.J.: Princeton University Press, 1995.

Andrew J. D., and S. Ungar. *Popular Front Paris and the Politics of Culture*. Cambridge, Mass.: Harvard University Press.

Arcy-Hennery, R. *Destin du cinéma français*. Paris: Société Française d'Éditions Littéraires et Techniques, 1935.

Arlaud, R. *Cinéma bouffe*. Paris: Jacques Melot, 1945.

Arletty. *La Défense*. Paris: La Table Ronde 1971.

Armes, R. *French Cinema*. London: Secker and Warburg, 1985.

Arnoux, A. *Du muet au parlant: Souvenirs d'un témoin*. Paris: La Nouvelle Édition, 1946.

Atwell, L. *G-W Pabst*. Boston: Twayne, 1977.

Aumont, J.-P. *Le Soleil et l'ombre* (expanded version of *Souvenirs provisoires*). Paris: Robert Laffont, 1976.

Auric, G. *Quand j'étais là*. Paris: Grasset, 1979.

Autant-Lara, C. *La Rage au cœur*. Paris: Henri Veyrier, 1984.

Bächlin, P. *Histoire économique du cinéma*. Paris: La Nouvelle Édition, 1947.

Bachy, V. *Jacques Feyder, artisan du cinéma*. Louvain, Belgium: Librairie Universitaire, 1968.

Bardèche M., and R. Brasillach. *Histoire du cinéma*. Rev. edn. Paris: André Martel, 1954.

Barrault, J.-L. *Memories for Tomorrow*. London: Thames and Hudson, 1974.

Barrot, O., and R. Chirat. *Noir et blanc: 250 acteurs du cinéma français 1930–1960*. Paris: Flammarion, 2000.

Barsacq, L. *Le Décor de film*. Paris: Seghers, 1970.

Bazin, A. *Jean Renoir*. Paris: Champs Libre, 1971.

Benoit-Lévy, J. *Les Grandes Missions du cinéma*. Montréal: Parizeau, 1945.

Bergfelder, T., S. Harris, and S. Street. *Film Architecture and the Transnational Imagination*. Amsterdam: Amsterdam University Press, 2007.

Bessy, M. *Les Passagers du souvenir*. Paris: Albin Michel, 1977.

Beylie, C. *Marcel Pagnol*. Paris: Seghers, 1974.

———. *Max Ophüls*. Paris: Seghers, 1963.

Billard, P. *L'Âge classique du cinéma français*. Paris: Flammarion, 1995.

Blanc, J.-J. *Marcel Pagnol inconnu*. Paris: Robert Laffont, 1998.

Bonnefille, E. *Julien Duvivier, le mal aimant du cinéma français*. Vol. 1. Paris: L'Harmattan, 2002.

Borde, R., et al. *Deuxième cinécure: Les Français et leur cinéma 1930–1939*. Toulouse, France: Éric Losfeld, 1973.

Bordwell, D. *The Films of Carl-Theodor Dreyer*. Los Angeles: California University Press, 1981.

Bourgeois, J. *René Clair*. Geneva and Paris: Roulet, 1949.

Braunberger, P. *Cinémamémoires*. Paris: Centre Georges Pompidou, 1987.

Brunelin, A. *Jean Gabin*. Paris: Robert Laffont, 1987.

Brunius, J. *En marge du cinéma français*. Paris: Arcanes, 1954.

Burch, N., and G. Sellier. *La Drôle de guerre des sexes du cinéma français 1930–1956*. Paris: Nathan, 1996.

Cadars, P. *Les Séducteurs du cinéma français (1928–58)*. Paris: Henri Veyrier, 1982.

Carné, M. *La Vie à belles dents*. Paris: Jean-Pierre Ollivier, 1975.

Cartier, J. *Monsieur Vanel*. Paris: Robert Laffont, 1989.

Catelain, J. *Marcel L'Herbier*. Paris: Jacques Vautrain, 1950.

Charensol, G. *40 ans de cinéma*. Paris: Sagittaire, 1935.

———. *Panorama du cinéma*. Paris: Jacques Melot, 1947.

Charensol, G., and R. Régent. *Un maître de cinéma: René Clair*. Paris: La Table Ronde, 1952.

Chauvet, L. *Le Porte-plume et la caméra*. Paris: Flammarion, 1950.

Chauville, C. *Le Cinéma français (1935–1939) à travers la critique* (Mémoire de maîtrise). Besançon, France: Université de Franche-Comté, 1993.

Chazal, R. *Marcel Carné*. Paris: Seghers, 1965.

Chenal, P. *Souvenirs du cinéaste*. Paris: Dujarric, 1987.

Chevallier, J., and M. Egly, eds. *Regards neufs sur le cinéma*. Paris: Seuil, 1963.

Chirat, R. *Catalogue des films français de long métrage*, vol 1, *Films sonores de fiction 1929–1939*. Brussels: Cinémathèque Royale de Belgique, 1981.

———. *Le Cinéma français des années 30*. Paris: Hatier, 1983.

Choisel, F. *Sacha Guitry intime*. Paris: Scorpion, 1957.

Clair, R. *Cinéma d'hier, cinéma d'aujourd'hui*. Paris: Gallimard, 1970.

————. *Réflexion faite.* Paris: Gallimard, 1950.

Cocteau, J. *Entretiens autour du cinématographe.* Paris: André Bonne, 1951.

Courtade, F. *Les Malédictions du cinéma français.* Paris: Alain Moreau, 1978.

Crisp, C. *The Classic French Cinema, 1930–1960.* Bloomington: Indiana University Press, 1993.

————. *Genre, Myth and Convention in the French Cinema, 1929–1939.* Bloomington: Indiana University Press, 2002.

Dale, R. C. *The Films of René Clair.* 2 vols. Metuchen, N.J.: Scarecrow Press, 1986.

Dalio, M. *Mes années folles.* Paris: J.-C. Lattès, 1976.

Daniel, J. *Guerre et cinéma.* Paris: Armand Colin, 1972.

Daquin, L. *Le Cinéma, notre métier.* Paris: Les Éditeurs Français Réunis, 1960.

Desrichard, Y. *Julien Duvivier.* Paris: La Bibliothèque du Film, 2001.

Les Dessous du cinéma allemand. Paris: Courrier du Centre, 1934.

Dreyer, C. T. *Réflexions sur mon métier.* Paris: Cahiers du Cinéma, 1964.

Durgnat, R. *Luis Buñuel.* London: Studio Vista, 1967.

Duvillars, P. *Cinéma, mythologie du XXe siècle.* Paris: Éditions de l'Ermite, 1950.

Epstein, J. *Écrits sur le cinéma.* 2 vols. Paris: Seghers, 1974–1975.

Estève, M., ed. *Jean Vigo.* Paris: Minard, 1966.

Fabre, S. *Douche écossaise.* Paris: Fournier Valdès, 1948.

Ferro, M. *Cinéma et histoire.* Paris: Gallimard, 1977.

Fescourt, H. *La Foi et les montagnes.* Paris: Paul Montel, 1959.

Feyder, J., and F. Rosay. *Le Cinéma, notre métier.* Geneva: Pierre Cailler, 1946.

Flitterman-Lewis, S. *To Desire Differently: Feminism and French Cinema.* Urbana-Champaign: Illinois University Press, 1990.

Ford, C. *Le Cinéma au service de la foi.* Paris: Plon, 1953.

————. *Jacques Feyder.* Paris: Seghers, 1973.

————. *On tourne lundi.* Paris: Jean Vigneau, 1947.

————. *Pierre Fresnay.* Paris: France-Empire, 1981.

Frank, N. *Petit Cinéma sentimental.* Paris: La Nouvelle Édition, 1950.

Garçon, F. *De Blum à Pétain: Cinéma et société française 1936–1944.* Paris: Cerf, 1984.

Gilson, R. *Jean Cocteau.* Paris: Seghers, 1964.

Gorel, M. *Le Monde truqué.* Paris: Nilsson, 1931.

Guérin, W. *Max Ophüls.* Paris: Cahiers du Cinéma, 1988.

Guillaume-Grimaud, G. *Le Cinéma du Front Populaire.* Paris: Lherminier, 1986.

Guillot, G. *Les Prévert.* Paris: Seghers, 1966.

Guitry, S. *Le Cinéma et moi.* Paris: Ramsay, 1977.

Harcourt, P. *Six European Directors.* Harmondsworth, Eng.: Penguin, 1974.

Hayward, S., and G. Vincendeau. *French Film: Texts and Contexts.* London: Routledge and Kegan Paul, 1989.

Houssiau, B. *Marc Allégret, découvreur de stars.* Morges, Switzerland: Cabédita, 1994.

Icart, R. *La Révolution du parlant.* Perpignan, France: Institut Jean Vigo, 1988.

Jacques Feyder, ou le cinéma concret. Brussels: Comité National Jacques Feyder, 1949.

Jeancolas, J.-P. *15 ans d'années trente: Le Cinéma des Français 1929–1944.* Paris: Stock, 1983.

Jeanne, R., and C. Ford. *Histoire encyclopédique du cinéma 1895–1945,* vol. 4, *1929–1939.* Paris: Robert Laffont, 1948.

Jeanson, H. *70 ans d'adolescence.* Paris: Stock, 1971.

Keim, J. *Un nouvel art: Le cinéma sonore.* Paris: Albin Michel, 1947.

Kemp, R. *Edwige Feuillère.* Paris: Calmann-Lévy, 1951.

Kyrou, A. *Luis Buñuel.* Paris: Seghers, 1970.

———. *Le Surréalisme au cinéma.* Paris: Terrain Vague, 1963.

Lacotte, D. *Raimu.* Paris: Ramsay, 1988.

Lagny, M., et al. *Générique des années 30.* Paris: Presses Universitaires de Vincennes, 1986.

Landry, B. *Marcel Carné.* Paris: Jacques Vaulrain, 1957.

Lapierre, M., ed. *Anthologie du cinéma.* Paris: La Nouvelle Édition, 1946.

Le Boterf, H. *Harry Baur.* Paris: Pygmalion, 1995.

Leenhardt, R. *Chroniques de cinéma.* Paris: Cahiers du Cinéma, 1986.

Lefebvre, R. *Le Film de ma vie 1939–1973.* Paris: France-Empire, 1973.

Léglise, P. *Histoire de la politique du cinéma français,* vol. 1, *Le Cinéma et la troisième république.* Paris: R. Pichon et R. Durand-Auzias, 1970.

Leprohon, P. *L'Exotisme et le cinéma.* Paris: J. Susse, 1945.

———. *50 ans de cinéma français.* Paris: Cerf, 1954.

———. *Jean Epstein.* Paris: Seghers, 1964.

———. *Les 1001 métiers du cinéma.* Paris: Jacques Melot, 1947.

———. *Présences contemporaines.* Paris: Nouvelles Éditions Debresse, 1957.

L'Herbier, M., ed. *Intelligence du cinématographe.* Paris: Correa, 1946.

———. *La Tête qui tourne.* Paris: Pierre Belfond, 1979.

Lorcey, J. *Marcel Achard.* Paris: France-Empire, 1977.

Loubier, J.-M. *Louis Jouvet.* Paris: Ramsay, 1986.

———. *Michel Simon, roman d'un jouisseur.* Paris: Ramsay, 1986.

Marion, D., ed. *Le Cinéma par ceux qui le font.* Paris: Arthème Fayard, 1949.

Martin, G. *The Golden Age of French Cinema 1929–1939.* London: Columbus Books, 1987.

Martin, M. *Le Langage cinématographique.* Paris: Éditions du Cerf, 1955.

Mast, G. *A Short History of the Movies.* Indianapolis: Bobbs-Merrill, 1976.

Matalon, P., C. Guignet, and J. Pinturault, eds., *Pierre Chenal: Souvenirs d'un cinéaste.* Paris: Dujarric, 1985.

Mauriac, C. *Amour du cinéma.* Paris: Albin Michel, 1954.

Mazeau, J. *Les Grands Acteurs français.* Paris: PUF, 1982.

Mazeau, J., and D. Thouart. *Les Grands Seconds Rôles du cinéma français.* Paris: PAC, 1984.

Milne, T. *The Cinema of Carl Dreyer.* New York: A. S. Barnes, 1971.

Mitry, J. *Histoire du cinéma: Art et industrie,* vol. 4, *Les Années 30.* Paris: Jean-Pierre Delange, 1980.

Moussinac, L. *L'Âge ingrat du cinéma*. Paris: Sagittaire, 1946.

Noë, Y. *L'Épicerie des rêves*. Paris: Baudinière, 1933.

O'Brien, C. *Cinema's Conversion to Sound*. Bloomington: Indiana University Press, 2005.

Olivier, P. *Raimu*. Paris: Fournier-Valdès, 1947.

Ophüls, M. *Souvenirs*. Paris: Cinémathèque Française, 2002.

Où va le cinéma français? (Report of the Renaitour Enquiry). Paris: Baudinière, 1937.

Pagnol, M. *Confidences*. Paris: Julliard, 1981.

Pérez, M. *Les Films de Marcel Carné*. Paris: Ramsay, 1986.

Peyrusse, C. *Le Cinéma méridional 1929–1944*. Toulouse, France: Eché, 1986.

Pinel, V. *Filmographie des longs métrages sonores du cinéma français*. Paris: La Cinémathèque Française, 1985.

Porcile, F. *Maurice Jaubert, musicien populaire ou maudit*. Paris: Éditeurs Français Réunis, 1971.

———. *La Musique à l'écran*. Paris: Cerf, 1969.

Pornon, C. *Le Rêve et le fantastique*. Paris: La Nef de Paris, 1959.

Prédal, R. *La Société française à travers le cinéma 1914–1945*. Paris: Armand Colin, 1972.

Quéval, J. *Marcel Carné*. Paris: Cerf, 1952.

Rachline, M. *Jacques Prévert: Drôle de vie*. Paris: Ramsay, 1981.

Rebatet, L. *Les Juifs en France*, vol. 4, *Les Tribus du cinéma et du théâtre*. Paris: Nouvelles Éditions Françaises, 1941.

Régent, R. *Cinéma de France*. Paris: Bellefaye, 1948.

———. *Raimu*. Paris: Chavane, 1957.

Renoir, J. *Écrits 1926–1971*. Paris: Belfond, 1974.

———. *Ma Vie et mes films*. Paris: Flammarion, 1974.

———. *Renoir on Renoir*. New York: Cambridge University Press, 1989.

Rentschler, E. *The Films of G. W. Pabst*. New Brunswick, N.J.: Rutgers University Press, 1990.

Reynolds, J. *André Citroën: The Man and the Motorcars*. Stroud, England: Sutton, 1996.

Richebé, R. *Au-delà de l'écran: 70 ans de la vie d'un cinéaste*. Monaco: Pastorelly, 1977.

Rim, C. *Le Grenier d'Harlequin*. Paris: Denoël, 1981.

———. *Mémoires d'une vieille vague*. Paris: Gallimard, 1961.

Rivers, F. *50 ans chez les fous*. Paris: G. Girard, 1945.

Rosay, F. *La Traversée d'une vie*. Paris: Robert Laffont, 1974.

Sadoul, G. *Le Cinéma*. Paris: La Bibliothèque Française, 1948.

———. *Le Cinéma français 1890–1962*. Paris: Flammarion, 1962.

———. *Les Merveilles du cinéma*. Paris: Les Éditeurs Français Réunis, 1957.

Salès-Gomès, P. *Jean Vigo*. Paris: Seuil, 1957.

Sallée, A. *Les Acteurs français depuis Sarah Bernhardt*. Paris: Bordas, 1988.

Sellier, G. *Jean Grémillon: Le Cinéma est à vous*. Paris: Méridien-Klincksieck, 1989.

Sesonske, A. *Jean Renoir: The French Years, 1924–1939*. Cambridge, Mass.: Harvard University Press, 1980.

Slavin, D. *Colonial Cinema and Imperial France, 1919–1939.* Baltimore: Johns Hopkins University Press, 2001.

Spaak, J. *Charles Spaak, mon mari.* Paris: France-Empire, 1977.

Toulet, *René Clair; ou, Le Cinéma à la lettre.* Paris: Association Française de Recherche et d'Histoire, 2000.

Trauner, A. *Décors de cinéma.* Paris: Jad-Flammarion, 1988.

Tual, D. *Au cœur du temps.* Paris: Carrère, 1987.

Vignaux, V. *Jean-Benoit-Lévy, ou le corps comme utopie.* Paris: AFRHC, 2007.

Vincendeau, G., and K. Reader. *La Vie est à nous: French Cinema and the Popular Front.* London: British Film Institute, 1986.

Wahkévitch, G. *L'Envers des décors.* Paris: Robert Laffont, 1977.

Weil-Lorac, R. *50 ans de cinéma actif.* Paris: Dujarric, 1977.

White, S. *The Cinema of Max Ophüls: Magisterial Vision and the Figure of Woman.* New York: Columbia University Press, 1995.

Willemen P., ed. *Max Ophüls.* London: British Film Institute, 1978.

Periodicals

Film Magazines and Journals

Avant-Scène cinéma (A-S-C, see below)
Cahiers de la cinémathèque
Cahiers du cinéma
Choisir
Ciné-Journal
Cinéma 61
Cinéma-Bibliothèque
Ciné-Magazine
La Cinématographie française
Ciné-Miroir
Cinémonde
La Collection du film
Le Courrier cinématographique
Enfin film
Le Film chez soi
Le Film complet
Films et romans
Le Film vécu
Les Grandes artistes de l'écran
Les Grands films
Je suis partout
Leur Vie romanesque
Mon Film, mon ciné
La Nouvelle Revue française

L'Omnium cinématographique
Positif
Pour vous
Premier Plan, No. 5 (Jean Grémillon). Lyon: SERDOC, 1960.
Premier Plan, No. 14 (Jacques Prévert). Lyon: SERDOC, 1960.
Premier Plan, No. 19 (Jean Vigo). Lyon: SERDOC, 1961.
Premier Plan, Nos. 22–23–24 (Jean Renoir). Lyon: SERDOC, 1962.
La Revue du cinéma (series I)
Romans-cinéma
Screen
Stars et films
Studies in French Cinema
Vedettes françaises
Visages et contes du cinéma.

Non-Cinematic Press

L'Action française
Candide
Comœdia
Esprit
Figaro
Gringoire
L'Humanité
L'Intransigeant
L'Œuvre
Paris-Soir
Regards

Published Film Scripts

L'Âge d'or. A-S-C (*Avant-Scène cinéma*) Nos. 27–28.
À nous la liberté (with *Entr'acte*). A-S-C 1968. Trans. R. Jacques and N. Hayden. London: Lorrimer, 1970.
La Bandera. A-S-C.
La Grande Illusion. A-S-C No. 44.
Jenny. Paris: Gallimard, 1988 (with *Quai des brumes*).
Le Jour se lève. A-S-C 1965. Trans. D. Brooke and N. Hayden. London: Lorrimer, 1970.
La Kermesse héroïque. A-S-C No. 26.
Lac aux dames. A-S-C.
L'Opéra de quat'sous. A-S-C.
Pépé le Moko. A-S-C No. 269.
Quai des brumes. Paris: Gallimard, 1988 (with *Jenny*).

La Règle du jeu. Ed. O. Curchod and C. Faulkner. Paris: Nathan, 1999. A-S-C 1965. Trans. J. McGrath and M. Teitelbaum. London: Lorrimer, 1970.

Sous les toits de Paris. A-S-C.

Toni. A-S-C Nos. 251–252.

Une partie de campagne. A-S-C No. 21.

Un grand amour de Beethoven. A-S-C.

Vampyr. A-S-C.

Zéro de conduite. A-S-C No. 21.

Note: Page numbers followed by *t* indicate a table. Page numbers in **bold** refer to the main entry for a film.

Circonstances atténuantes (Boyer), 2, 230, **281–283**

La Citadelle du silence (L'Herbier), 225

Citroën, André, 98–99

city/country opposition, 112–113, 135–136, 151–153, 203–205; as geo-sexual metaphor, 236; nightclub settings in, 214–215

Clair, René, 2, 7, 112, 162, 299; À nous la liberté, 27, 42, **48–51**, 79, 81, 256, 299; avant-garde style of, 11, 54; Un Chapeau de paille d'Italie, 20, 40, 190; Le Dernier Milliardaire, 81, 86, 131, 300; early sound experiments of, 17, 20–22, 21, 40–42, 50–51, 79; editing techniques of, 50; Entr'acte, 23; film collaborators of, 41–42; leftist class politics of, 20, 22, 33, 49–50, 79–80; Le Million, 20, 28, **40–42**, 79, 190; on Pagnol's theatrical films, 43; Quatorze juillet, 20, 41, **79–81**; sentimental criminals of, 126; Le Silence est d'or, 81; silent films of, 5, 20, 119; Sous les toits de Paris, **19–22**, 41, 49, 79, 121

class oppositions, 109–111; antiestablishment figures of, 47, 71–76, 216–217; in boulevard comedies, 114–116, 206–208, 239; Clair's portrayals of, 20, 22, 33, 49–50, 79–80; on criminality and prison life, 125–126, 223; gambling and fantasies of wealth in, 116–117; in Gay's The Beggar's Opera, 34–36; hypocritical respectability and, 230–231; in naturalist street films of poverty, 95–98, 268; in Pagnol's films, 168–169; prankster figures of, 86; in Renoir's films, 184–185, 267–268; social satire on, 87–88, 176–177, 184–185, 281–283; socially engaged films on, 90–92, 122–123, 178–180, 279–280; Spaak's portrayal of, 197, 230; surrealist portrayals of, 23–24; of workers and bosses, 109–111, 123, 145–148, 154–155, 159–161, 267–268, 271. See also capitalism; leftist politics; working class lives

Cocteau, Jean, 10–11, 23; Orphée, 54; Le Sang d'un poète, **52–54**; Le Testament d' Orphée, 54

Coeur de Lilas (Litvak), 93–94, 139

Colette, 149

Colombier, Pière, 291; Ces messeiurs de la Santé, **101–103**, 230; Le Roi, 176; Le Roi des resquilleurs, **28–30**, 84, 197, 239, 288; Le Roi du cirage, 30; Théodore et Cie, 30, **84–86**; Tricoche et Cacolet, 2, 30, **237–240**

colonialism: Feyder's films on, 104–106; misogyny in, 60, 62; native actors and, 198; portrayals of otherness of, 55–57, 61–62, 104, 135–137, 241–242, 294–296; racist civilizing mission of, 57, 60–61, 104–105, 133–134, 135–137, 157–158, 174–175; sexualized exoticism of, 198–200; traditional patriarchal view of, 187–189, 240

color films, 151–153

comedies, 2; American screwball style in, 127, 200–201, 254–255; boulevard style of, 86, 113–116, 176, 206, 239; by Clair, 20; Fernandel's work in, 238–240; military vaudevilles, 63–65, 84–85, 176, 238; popular styles of, 84–86; populist worker themes in, 109–111; Prévert's anarchic style of, 73–76; Renoir's tramp figures, 47, 71–73; romantic style of, 82–83, 288–289; the singing fool in, 254–255; social satires, 87–88, 176–177, 184–185, 281–283; technical approaches to, 245–248

communism/the Communist Party, 1, 3, 123; propaganda films of, 154–157; surrealism and, 23–24, 161. See also leftist politics; Popular Front

Compartiment de dames seules, 114

Le Comte Obligado (Mathot), 30

La Condition humaine (Malraux), 251

Le Congrès s'amuse (Charell and Boyer), 26–27

Conrad, Joseph, 149–150, 231

conservative films. See right-wing films

Construire un feu (Autant-Laura), 152

Contes Moraux (Rohmer), 269

Copeau, Jacques, 149–150

Le Coq du regiment (Cammage), 63

Corniglion-Molinier, Édouard, 218

316   Index

167, **258–260**, 297, 300–301; *Remontons les Champs-Élysées*, 167, **258–260**, 263; *Le Roman d'un tricheur*, 2, **164–167**, 258, 301; *Si Paris nous était conté*, 258; *Si Versailles m'était conté*, 258; theatrical films of, 10, 165–167, 207–208

L'Habit vert, 114, 176
hand-painted color films, 152
Harvey, Lilian, 25–26
Hayakawa, Sessue, 294, 296
Heart of Darkness (Conrad), 231
Hélène, 245
L'Herbier, Marcel, 11, 39, 140, 196, 290; *L'Argent*, 256; *Le Bonheur*, **118–121**, 224, 256, 301; *La Brigade sauvage*, 256; historical chronicle films of, 225–226; *L'Inhumaine*, 119; maritime films of, 225; mystery films of, 224; silent films of, 5, 119; *La Tragédie impériale*, 130, **224–226**; transition to sound by, 119
Hercule, 146, 176
Une histoire d'amour (Ophüls), 256, 284
historical films: of Guitry, 258–260; of L'Herbier, 225–226; of Pabst, 251–253
Hollywood. *See* American film industry
Holt, Jany, 215
L'Homme à l'abatre (Dumas), 181
L'Homme à l'Hispano (Epstein), **81–84**
L'Homme de nulle part (Chenal), 9, **177–180**, 180
L'Homme du Niger, 198
Les Hommes nouveaux (L'Herbier), 198, 225
honors and awards, 9–10, 12, 297–301; *Abus de confiance*, 129, 210; *La Bandera* (Duvivier), 300–301; *Les Bas-Fonds* (Renoir), 164, 298, 300–301; *Le Bonheur* (L'Herbier), 301; *Un carnet de bal* (Duvivier), **192**, 300–301; *Crime et châtiment* (Chenal), **131**; *Croix de bois* (Bernard), 60; *Le Dernier Milliardaire* (Clair), 300; *Les Disparus de Saint-Agil* (Christian-Jacque), **229**; *Double Crime sur la Ligne Maginot* (Nord), 301; *La Fin du jour* (Duvivier), **274**; *Golgotha* (Duvivier), 300; *La Grande Illusion* (Renoir), **183**, 300–301; of Groupe Octobre, 75; *La*

Guerre des gosses, 301; *Le Joueur d'échecs* (Dréville), **258**; *La Kermesse héroïque* (Feyder), **141**, 299–301; *L'Appel du silence* (Poirier), 159; *Maria Chapdelaine* (Duvivier), 297, 300–301; *La Maternelle* (Benoit-Lévy and Epstein), 300; *Mayerling* (Litvak), 297, 300; *La Mort du cygne* (Benoit-Lévy), 297, 301; *Pension Mimosas* (Feyder), 301; *Les Perles de la couronne* (Guitry), 300–301; *Prison sans barreaux* (Moguy), **223**, 300–301; *Quai des brumes* (Carné), 297, 298, 300–301; *Regain* (Pagnol), 301; *Le Roman d'un tricheur* (Guitry), 301
L'Hôtel du Libre Échange (Allégret), **113–116**, 148–149
Hôtel du Nord (Carné), 32, 126, **261–263**, 264, 298
Houllé-Renoir, Marguerite, 46, 172
Hugon, André: *Sarati le terrible*, **187–189**, 240

Ibert, Jacques, 56
Ignace, 238
Il a été perdu une mariée, 153
Il est charmant (Mercanton), 26
L'Illustre Maurin, 125
Ils étaient 5 permissionnaires, 64–65
immigration, 123
Impasse des Deux Anges (Tourneur), 125
incest themes, 94–95, 117–118, 187, 207
individualism, 296
L'Inhumaine (L'Herbier), 119
Itto (Benoit-Lévy), 299

J'accuse (Gance), 57
Jaubert, Maurice, 81, 89, 108, 202, 262, 273, 276–277
Je chante (Stengel and Wheeler), **253–255**
Jean de la Lune (Achard), 84, 119
Jeanson, Henri, 156, 230, 243, 260–263, 271–272
Jenny (Carné), 118, **162–164**, 202, 297
J'étais une aventurière, 263, 301
Jeunes filles à marier (Vallée), 152
Jeunes filles en détresse (Pabst), 245
Jeunesse, 95, 97

Rebatet, Lucien, 59–60, 139, 186, 223, 266, 268, 290

Récif de corail, 173

reflexive tropes, 18, 62, 119–120, 136, 222–223, 265, 289

Regain (Pagnol), 9, 112, 152, **203–205**, 235, 240, 301

La Règle du jeu (Renoir), 9, 83, 115–116, 120, 202, 205–206, 255, 266, 271, **277–280**, 291

Remontons les Champs-Élysées (Guitry), 167, **258–260**, 263

Remorques (Grémillon), 74, 134, 163, 173, **291–293**

Renard, Jules, 68

Renaud, Madeleine, 230–231

Renoir, Auguste, 170

Renoir, Jean, 2, 9, 54, 124, 234, 299; banned films of, 126; *Les Bas-Fonds*, 130, 161, 180, 216, 266, 297, 298, 300–301; *La Bête humaine*, 9, 134, 173, 263, 264, **266–268**, 278, 298; *Boudu sauvé des eaux*, **71–73**, 123, 147, 266, 281; *La Chienne*, **45–48**, 71, 147, 301; *Chotard et Cie*, 266; *Le Crime de Monsieur Lange*, 9, 28, 41, 70, 73–74, 123, **145–148**, 155, 161, 210, 216, 230, 262, 275, 297; funding challenges of, 123–124; *La Grande Illusion*, 28, 31, 140, **183–186**, 214, 278, 288, 300–301; leftist politics of, 73, 146–147, 171, 218–219, 267–268; literary sources of, 266–267; long takes and deep focus of, 47, 72–73, 147–148, 172, 186, 280; *Madame Bovary*, 266; *La Marseillaise*, 157, **218–221**, 259, 266; *Nana*, 46; *La Nuit du carrefour*, 71, 147, 256, 266; *Une partie de campagne*, 70, 121, **169–172**, 214; *La Petite Marchande d'allumettes*, 123–124; *On purge bébé*, 46, 114, 266; *La Règle du jeu*, 9, 83, 115–116, 120, 202, 205–206, 255, 266, 271, **277–280**, 291; silent films of, 46; socially-engaged realism of, 47, 121–123, 171, 279–280; *Tire au flanc*, 63; *Toni*, 9, 112, **121–124**, 266; *La Vie est à nous*, 73, 123, **153–156**, 216, 271. *See also* Groupe Octobre

Renoir, Marguerite, 46, 172

Renoir, Pierre, 82, 128, 149, 220, 243, 294

Un rêve blond (Martin), 26

revenues from French films, 4*t*, 5, 8–9, 28

Richard, Marthe, 180–183

Richard-Willm, Pierre, 198

Richebé, Roger: *Prisons de femmes*, **221–223**, 283; *La Tradition de minuit*, 223

right-wing films: anti-Semitism in, 240–242; censorship and, 25, 48; city/country opposition in, 152–153, 203–205, 236–237; on colonialism, 187–189, 240; funding of, 219; nationalism of, 60, 234; popularity of, 157–159; simplifications of history in, 259–260; traditional patriarchy in, 187–189, 204, 235–237, 260; virile cinema of, 133–134. *See also* fascism

Rive gauche (Korda), 26

Rivers, Fernand: *Fauteuil 47*, 118

Robison, Arthur, 93

Le Roi (Colombier), 114, 176

Le Roi des resquilleurs (Colombier), **28–30**, 84, 197, 239, 288

Le Roi du cirage (Colombier), 30

Roland-Manuel, 31

Romains, Jules, 176

Roman d'un spahi, 138

Le Roman d'un tricheur (Guitry), 2, **164–167**, 258, 301

Romance, Viviane, 181, 212, 270

romantic comedies, 82–83, 288–289

La Ronde (Ophüls), 284

Rosay, Françoise, 104, 116, 118, 164, 191, 201, 238, 247

Le Rosier de Madame Husson (Bernard-Deschamps), 238–239, 246, 247

Rossi, Tino, 211–213, 254

La Route enchantée (Caron), **253–255**

La Route impériale (L'Herbier), 158, 225

La Rue sans joie, 95

La Rue sans nom (Chenal), **95–98**, 178, 180

Russian filmmakers, 93–94, 129–130, 150, 154, 207

Saint-Cyr, Renée, 181

Salonique, nid d'espions (Pabst), **180**

Sandberg, Serge, 207

Le Sang d'un poète (Cocteau), **52–54**

COLIN CRISP is a leading scholar in French film history and author of *The Classic French Cinema, 1930–1960* (IUP, 1993), and *Genre, Myth, and Convention in the French Cinema, 1929–1939* (IUP, 2002). In this new series of filmographies, he aims to introduce the wider public to the range and richness of the films produced by the French cinema between 1929 and 1975, covering such crucial social, technological, and cultural factors as the introduction of sound, color, and scope; the depression; the war years and the occupation; the so-called quality cinema of the 1950s; and the startling advent on the international scene around 1960 of the New Wave. This period includes some of the greatest films of all time, such as *La Règle du jeu, Lola Montès, L'Année dernière à Marienbad,* and *Pierrot le fou,* not to mention such popular favorites as *La Grande Illusion, Les Enfants du paradis, Jeux interdits,* and *Les 400 coups*—all the greatest films by the most celebrated directors—Renoir, René Clair, Carné, Cocteau, Pagnol, Truffaut, Godard, Rohmer, Chabrol, Resnais, and dozens of others.

CPSIA information can be obtained at www.ICGtesting.com
Printed in the USA
LVOW06s2123040116

469073LV00002B/119/P